E-Government in Canada

Governance Series

Governance is the process of effective coordination whereby an organization or a system guides itself when resources, power and information are widely distributed. Studying governance means probing the pattern of rights and obligations that underpins organizations and social systems; understanding how they coordinate their parallel activities and maintain their coherence; exploring the sources of dysfunction; and suggesting ways to redesign organizations whose governance is in need of repair.

The Series welcome a range of contributions – from conceptual and theoretical reflections, ethnographic and case studies, and proceedings of conferences and symposia, to works of a very practical nature – that deal with problems or issues on the governance front. The Series publishes works both in French and in English.

The Governance Series is part of the publications division of the Program on Governance and Public Management at the School of Political Studies. Nine volumes have previously been published within this series. The Program on Governance and Public Management also publishes electronic journals: the quarterly www.optimumonline.ca and the biannual www.revuegouvernance.ca

Editorial Committee

Caroline Andrew
Linda Cardinal
Monica Gattinger
Luc Juillet
Daniel Lane
Gilles Paquet (Director)

E-Government in Canada

Transformation for the Digital Age

Jeffrey Roy

University of Ottawa Press

The University of Ottawa Press gratefully acknowledges the support extended to its publishing programme by the Canada Council for the Arts and the University of Ottawa.

We also acknowledge with gratitude the support of the Government of Canada through its Book Publishing Industry Development Program for our publishing activities.

National Library of Canada Cataloguing in Publication

Roy, Jeffrey
E-government in Canada : transformation for the digital age / Jeffrey Roy.

(Governance series, ISSN 1487-3052)
Includes bibliographical references and index.
ISBN-13: 978-0-7766-0617-0
ISBN-10: 0-7766-0617-4

1. Internet in public administration--Canada. 2. Electronic government information--Canada. 3. Public administration--Canada. 4. Organizational change--Canada. I. Title. II. Series: Governance series (Ottawa, Ont.)

JL86.A8R69 2006   351.71'0285'4678   C2005-907821-9

All rights reserved. No parts of this publication may be reproduced or transmitted in any form or by any means, electronic or mechanical, including photocoping, recording, or any information storage and retrieval system, without permission in writing from the publisher.

Cover design: Sharon Katz
Interior design and typesetting: Brad Horning
Copy-editing: Dallas Harrison
Proof-reading: Sylvie Nantais-Bourdeau
Indexing: Nancy Mucklow

Published by the University of Ottawa Press, 2006
542 King Edward Avenue, Ottawa, Ontario K1N 6N5
press@uottawa.ca / www.uopress.uottawa.ca

Printed and bound in Canada

Reprinted in 2008.

Contents

Introduction ix

Part One: Four Main Dimensions of Change
Chapter 1: Service 5
Chapter 2: Security 29
Chapter 3: Transparency 49
Chapter 4: Trust 77

Part Two: The Canadian Experience
Chapter 5: Government of Canada 111
Chapter 6: The Provinces 139
Chapter 7: Local and Intergovernmental Perspectives 167

Part Three: Looking Ahead
Chapter 8: Organization and Accountability 201
Chapter 9: Participation and Engagement 229
Chapter 10: Beyond Canada's Borders 255

Conclusion 283

Notes 295

References 331

Index 351

Acknowledgements

This book examines the emergence of e-government in Canada over the past decade. My own learning path during this time frame extends across doctoral studies at Carleton University, teaching and research duties at the University of Ottawa, and a recent sabbatical at the University of Victoria. I have benefited from a rich assortment of affiliations and friendships across this country's finest academic venues devoted to public sector management and governance.

Indeed, much of this book was written on a beautiful Pacific island. My sabbatical at the University of Victoria was made possible by the Director of the School of Public Administration, Evert Lindquist (as well as Jim McDavid who served as acting director in 2004). I am grateful for their support and that of the school's highly competent administrative and academic staff. The research assistance of In-In Pujiyono was particularly helpful. Discussions with faculty enriched my time in Victoria, and the opportunity to collaborate with John Langford on research that parallelled this book proved both intellectually beneficial and thoroughly enjoyable. IPAC's Patrice Dutil would join us in a shared effort that has since provided a platform for a stimulating and still-unfolding research agenda.

Much of my interest and activities in the realm of e-government began within the confines of the Centre on Governance at the University of Ottawa. Drawing on the best of the School of Management, the Faculty of Social Sciences, and elsewhere, the centre served as a dynamic and entrepreneurial setting for both scholarly exchange and outreach activity. With regard to specific e-government projects, the efforts of Barbara Ann Allen and Chris Wilson would prove particularly instrumental, as would the intellect and friendship of Luc Juillet. Funding provided by the Social Sciences and Humanities Research Council proved essential to our efforts.

I must also acknowledge and thank all of those officials and managers from government, industry, and elsewhere who took the time to partake in interviews. With few exceptions, names are withheld in the book due to the promise of confidentiality: it is clear that what progress has been made in furthering the e-government agenda in Canada is owed to the creativity and determination of a great many individuals striving to realize positive change. Many others provided strategic counsel and collaborative support, including Fawn Annan, Stuart Culbertson, John Eger, Patricia Fletcher, Mila Gasco, Don Lenihan, Don Norris, Greg Lane, Bob Parkins, Dan Remenyi, and Teddy. The editing expertise of Dallas Harrison and the production oversight of Marie Clausén have also been invaluable. Feedback provided by anonymous reviewers has proven extremely useful, although any errors in the final product remain the responsibility of the author alone.

Finally, I must acknowledge and thank two special individuals. Amanda Coe's efforts within the Government of Canada to help forge a more encompassing e-government agenda than online service, as well as her subsequent research at Harvard University's National Center for Digital Government, have been enlightening in terms of both academic debate and government policy. Gilles Paquet's intellectual leadership in forging critical reflections and new insights on matters of governance is unmatched: the same is true of his teaching and mentoring capacities. Professionally and personally, the presence of Amanda and Gilles in my life has been and remains a blessing.

Introduction

The purpose of this book is to examine the prospects for Canada's public sector in this emergent era shaped increasingly by digital technologies, human and organizational connectivity, and institutional change. The book progresses through a conceptual presentation of e-government's main drivers (Part One), an assessment of e-government's first decade in Canada (Part Two), and finally a discussion of the major challenges and choices that lie ahead (Part Three).

Electronic government (e-government) has emerged over the past decade parallel to the rapid, mainstream expansion of the Internet in many regions of the world. In one sense, this development is hardly new since information technologies and electronic systems have been engrained in public sector operations since the advent of the mainframe computer. There is indeed much debate within the literature on e-government as to whether digital technologies and the Internet are new tools to be deployed mainly within current public sector structures and traditions or whether they are inherently transformational in driving the need for more holistic changes to our systems of democratic governance (Perri 6 2002).

The former view is often espoused by public sector traditionalists who view the present model of democratic governance as fundamentally sound and argue that either failure to understand the workings of the system or deviant behaviour by those in it can be addressed without abandoning the current model. Another school of thought echoing this view is rooted, however, in the nexus between information technologies (IT) and organizational structures. There is much historical evidence that new technologies have been adopted by those already in possession of power and status organizationally and that the resultant changes merely reinforce and indeed often strengthen existing tendencies (Kraemer and King 2003). In other words, if an organization is loose, flexible, and participative, new technologies will facilitate such dynamics; if it is centralized and top-down in its managerial approach, IT can prove useful in such an environment as well.

Lately, however, a more digitally transformative view has been gathering steam, a view premised on more radical organizational, socio-economic, and political adaptations to new governance realities, more digitally networked, participative, and empowering. Perri 6 (2004) views electronic governance (or e-governance) in precisely such a manner, underscoring the need to go beyond a technocratic focus on electronic government (i.e., applying IT to existing systems and processes) in order to encompass what he terms the central importance of 'political judgment.' Here he refers to the broadest possible set of individual, organizational, and institutional dynamics exerting influence on decision making, accountability, and performance both within the public sector and in terms of how it functions independently of and interdependently with other sectors. Yet even Perri 6 underscores that public sector reform will only come about as those inside government make use of new potentials while abiding by and perhaps gradually reshaping the constraints brought about by the origins and applications of contemporary institutions.

In reality, there is little question that both views (tradition and transformation) have merit and exert influence on government today. Political leaders and managers must work incrementally — often shaped and constrained by tradition — in adapting public sector organizations to new technological realities. In doing so, however, they must have some appreciation of those broader forces gathering outside government and asserting new pressures: at some point, bolder responses and innovations are required, and they will be either embraced by design or imposed as tradition gives way to experimentation and reform. This interface between the internal and the external environments, between current practices and processes and new potentials, represents an increasingly important imperative for all levels of public sector activity.

To be more precise about the scope of e-government adopted for this study, it is useful to turn to one definition adopted by many governments of late: "The continuous innovation in the delivery of services, citizen participation, and governance through the transformation of external and internal relationships by the use of information technology, especially the Internet." This broad starting point explains why many commentators have suggested dropping the *e* from the e-government label entirely: as digital connectivity becomes more ubiquitous, the rationale for doing so is that it is now simply a matter of ensuring the relevance, adaptiveness, and performance of a public sector in a modern context. Such semantics aside, this book adopts the term 'e-government' since the major reforms and tensions examined have resulted in whole or in part from the widening presence of IT infrastructures, new and more portable communications devices, and the Internet itself.

The invocation of 'relationships' is also a strength of the definition provided above since it underscores the fluidity of governance (a more generic term denoting processes or mechanisms of coordination that need not be limited to and should not be confused with government) both inside the public sector and outside it. Internally, relationships are changing rapidly both structurally (among government departments and agencies) and interpersonally (among different groups of public servants) as integrated service delivery models and the need for more seamless governance become intertwined with the technological potential afforded by a digital networking of information and managerial systems across government.

Much of this networking is taking place to better reach out to constituencies outside government. Whether through the opportunities of customer service and citizen engagement or in reaction to the threats of cybercriminals and terrorists, the public sector cannot afford insularity. Nor can governments act alone: the transformation of external relationships extends to partnerships with industry (to create and maintain a digital infrastructure) as well as an array of stakeholders across civil society engaged in shared governance systems of one sort or another. As with the World Wide Web, these new governance patterns can and must also extend beyond national borders, a particularly acute challenge for governments in the Western world accustomed to domestic democracy organized within the confines of a country.

Four Main Challenges

The conceptual examination of e-government that is the basis of Part One is built upon Fountain's view that e-government involves organizational and institutional dynamics rooted in three fields of study: political science, organizational theory, and interactions of technology and organizational structure (Fountain 2001, 2004). To make sense of the various issues and dynamics at play, four separate yet interrelated story lines of e-government are introduced: service, security, transparency, and trust.

The first and second of these story lines, service and security, represent how e-government has evolved within the public sector over the past decade. Initially, e-government was often synonymous with online service delivery as the public sector sought to replicate the e-commerce model within its own confines. Security was quickly viewed as a critical enabler of Internet-based delivery—although in the aftermath of September 11th, 2001, it would expand into a more encompassing government agenda of anti-terrorism and public safety. Although service and security agendas are related to such external events and the shifting public (and political) mood, the reorganization efforts—and the deployment of new digital technologies—reflect changes to the organizational architecture of the public sector. Transparency and trust, in contrast, denote how e-government has evolved in a manner tied to perceptions, trends, and expectations outside the formal confines of government. More democratic than operational, the Internet has fuelled widening calls for a restructuring of democracy itself.

Service and Security

The first two of these dimensions are primarily focused on changes to the internal decision-making architecture of government, in response to pressures and opportunities associated with the Internet. Indeed, delivering services online became the hallmark of e-government during the 1990s: as more and more citizens conduct their personal and professional affairs online, these 'customers' of government look to do the same in dealing with the state, whether it is paying their taxes or renewing permits and licences of one sort or another (Curtin et al. 2003). As governments developed an online presence, it became clear that online reiteration by government departments and agencies would not be the most effective way of developing more transactional and interactive capacities in an efficient and effective manner (Fletcher 2004; Kearns 2004). Thus, the notions of life events and service streams were developed, clustering and organizing service offerings in a more citizen-centric manner (ICCS 2003; Coe 2004; Goldsmith and Eggers 2004).

Many initial strategies proved to be overly optimistic due to forecasts predicated on massive transaction cost savings from Internet communication (relative to paper and telephone) or strong, short-term growth in demand for online services (relative to other channels) (Roy 2003). Functionality also remains limited, particularly with respect to the processing of financial payments. This is a limitation due in large measure to the concerns about security (Holden 2004; Radl and Chen 2005).

The ability to interact effectively with customers online requires a safe and reliable architecture, particularly for handling personal information—such as credit card numbers—that often underpins financial transactions. Yet fostering government-wide capacities for receiving, storing, and sharing secure information is a complex undertaking, and the benefits of more efficient and integrated care through networked information systems are entirely dependent on secure and interconnected governance architectures (Joshi et al. 2002; Bellamy et al. 2005).

Security issues have clearly risen to the top of political agendas as of late, and governments have become conscious that more citizen-centric manners may not always be consistent with a philosophy of friendly customer service, for security can mean surveillance as well as service (Lyon 2004; Torrisi and Mezzanotte 2004). It may entail extracting and sharing information not only in response to requests by citizens but also as a way to better forecast potential actions and choices. The trade-offs between privacy, freedom, and convenience have therefore become more politicized, particularly in a post-9/11 context that has seen the security dimension of e-government expand from a technical precursor for better service to a more overarching paradigm of public sector actions, particularly those tied to anti-terrorism (De Rosa 2003; Hart-Teeter 2003, 2004; O'Harrow 2004; Strickland and Hunt 2005).

These first two dimensions, service and security, are primarily about how governments are reorganizing themselves internally to adapt to new opportunities and threats in the external environment. In contrast, transparency and trust speak to changes rooted less in the internal structures of government and more in the evolving democratic environment within which governments operate—as the Internet has facilitated the creation of new channels of political mobilization and interaction between citizens and their governments.

There is a clash of cultures between the expectations of an increasingly open and online society and the traditions of hierarchy and control that permeate public sector structures. As a result, there is some cleavage between current practices inside government and the more open and participative nature of processes emerging across society — particularly online (Nelson 1998; Prins 2001; Coleman 2003). Governments themselves have not been immune or ignorant to these pressures for reform, responding increasingly with calls for more public participation and citizen engagement (Oates 2003; Oliver and Sanders 2004; Coleman and Norris 2005). At issue in doing so is the central notion of trust as a basis for democratic legitimacy — an increasingly tenuous and contentious concept due to shifting social expectations and governance patterns across the citizenry.

Transparency and Trust
According to some well-informed observers, we live in the "age of transparency" (Tapscott and Ticoll 2003). For organizations in all sectors, openness must be embraced as routine and ongoing since secrecy invites suspicion, resulting in questions, exposures, and increased costs and complexities down the line (Mitchinson and Ratner 2004). As e-government creates optimistic expectations for improved transparency, and as information is more readily made available and more widely shared by public sector authorities themselves, the Internet has greatly facilitated potential efforts by neutral observers and vested interests to find and share information, expose secrets and shortcomings, and mobilize public opinion accordingly (Wilson and Welch 2004).

Although there has never been one standardized definition of what it means for the public sector to be 'transparent,' a useful starting point is to equate transparency with some degree of openness to those with either a right or an expectation of being able to examine and understand the activities of government. Some level of openness is a prerequisite for effective mechanisms of accountability (Paquet and Roy 2000; Good 2003). The emergence of e-government has sparked an unparalleled sense of optimism that greater levels of government transparency are both attainable and beneficial to society as a whole, "to the extent that increased transparency, accountability and predictability (of rules and procedures) are made priorities, e-government can be a weapon against corruption" (Pacific Council on International Policy 2002, 10).

More than a mere technical apparatus for providing information, the Internet has become an associational infrastructure, enabling knowledge and power to be more widely distributed and contested (Paquet 1997; Courchene 2005). One specific result is a lessening of tolerance for secrecy as individuals and new forms of associational movements mobilize around specific issues and interests (Evans 2002; Dwyer 2004).

Here lies the basis of a major foundational shift under way for democratic governance. A world of information scarcity is one that bolsters bureaucratic power and organizational secrecy (Fountain 2001; Kamarck 2004). A democracy of limited information and knowledge means an uneducated citizenry deferring to the authority of the ruling elite: pressures for more openness are limited and easily repressed. In a world of digital communications and growing networks of social and political interests (both online and offline), governments face rising pressure to adapt to a much more fluid and dynamic informational environment—one that is far less conducive to secrecy (Juillet and Paquet 2002; Tapscott and Ticoll 2003).

The emergence of web logs (blogs or weblogs) is a case in point. As weblogs are catching on, they are capturing more attention: *Time* magazine declared 2004 the year of the blog.[1] The growth of blogs is in many ways akin to the open source software movement. Aided by expanding broadband, individuals are able to network more freely, join groups of like-minded members, and express themselves in innovative and uninhibited ways. Not surprisingly, blogging is viewed by many as a grassroots orientation, often with the aim of circumventing mainstream traditional power structures in both industry and government.[2]

One of the first serious efforts to examine the democratic potential of blogging came from a leading UK think tank, the Hansard Society. This group created a citizens' jury to analyze the perceptions of potential bloggers and the potential for their usage and integration in more formal democratic processes (part of the impetus for studying the politics of blogging in the UK came from several Members of Parliament who recently created their own blogs). The results of the study are decidedly mixed. Many participants thought that blogs seem to be devoted more to specialized constituencies than to mainstream appeal. Perhaps the most important observation, however, is that "a higher frequency of broadcasting was taking place rather than two-way dialogue" (Hansard 2004). In other words, blogs are more about publishing and communicating than about listening and debating.

Such challenges in making better use of blogging are indicative of a widening scope of new forms of participation and mobilization that are creating stronger pressures for governments to adapt not only their internal governance systems (most often within the executive branch) but also the institutions of democracy that shape the roles and relationships among politicians, public servants, and the public. Yet, despite such pressures, governments may also resist change, as "the culture of secrecy is deeply engrained" (Reid 2004, 82; Roberts 2005). The degree to which this resistance is durable, as well as its impact on public perceptions and ultimately on the performance of government itself, are interwoven with the notion of trust.

Trust is a multifaceted concept. In the present context, it connotes the credibility of government as it seeks, retains, and deploys legitimacy in pursuing policies and actions tied to the public interest (O'Hara 2004). Many of the determinants of trust predate the e-government challenge, reflecting long-standing political and philosophical questions and the role and structure of the state. Kearns (2004) underscores trust as an essential element of e-government's capacity to generate value for citizens, despite little attention being paid by governments to matters beyond more narrow and specific invocations of trust tied to security and privacy.

Democratic legitimacy — defined here as recognition and consent granted by the citizenry to their political institutions — is a central and fluid concern in the e-government era. Driving this fluidity is a widening body of evidence pointing to declining public confidence in government, heightened suspicion of and cynicism toward traditional authoritative bodies, and a shifting of socio-political and civic activity to organizations and venues outside the traditional state apparatus (Lenihan 2002).

In light of such trends, many proponents of e-democracy seek new opportunities for more direct and continual forms of public participation.[3] While calls for such expanded forms of engagement predate the Internet, online connectivity is a powerful enabler given the potential to both distribute information and power more widely and facilitate a broader conversation with stakeholders and the public (Clarke 2004). Other observers underscore the importance of aligning both digital and social technologies in order to generate useful innovations in governance (Paquet 2004).

Indeed, any systemic introduction of more digital forms of democracy would constitute a major revolution in all aspects of the public sector apparatus, both technologically and organizationally (Pavlichev and Garson 2004). As with the emergence of blogs or weblogs, many difficulties in structuring such a conversation and, indeed, many questions surrounding whether online exchanges can facilitate meaningful venues for democratic decision-making remain (Allen et al. 2001; Slaton and Arthur 2001). For instance, experiments in Denmark revealed some potential for government-sponsored online forums to yield more civil and interactive dialogues than the more spontaneous, self-expressive culture of grassroots versions, although serious questions persist about whether these online channels expanded political participation beyond those segments of the population already politically engaged (Jensen 2003).

Gronlund (2003) underscores tensions between the bottom-up and participatory nature of political engagement outside formal government mechanisms and the more top-down processes of service and implementation within them. If such tensions are not resolved through a holistic effort to adapt governance to a more participative era, a compelling case can be made that digital technologies will be used by those in power to reinforce their authority or, at the least, resist efforts that may erode it (Kraemer and King 2003). Such tensions may also be prevalent in intergovernmental relations, particularly federalist environments, where the efforts of national bodies to implement national e-government strategies may conflict with the traditional advantages of proximity, familiarity, and informality that are typically invoked by proponents of devolution and a stronger role for local governments.

A further cause of democratic reform friction is the source of changes and initiatives to reach out to the public. While the service and security apparatuses of e-government have been managed largely from within the executive branch, whether these bodies have the mandate to engage the citizenry is often more contentious, given the potential to circumvent the role of elected politicians. The importance of this point is illuminated by evidence pointing to politicians as a key source of resistance to wider e-democratic experimentation (Mahrer 2005). Thus, e-democracy is not only about government-citizen relations but also about how politics is organized between those in power and those elected to nonetheless represent the public and hold the governing executive to account.

In sum, taking democracy online can be about either a simple application of online channels to existing electoral and political processes or the adaptation of these processes to more interconnected and participative forms of governance based less on representation and deference and more on empowerment and engagement. Both the pace and the scope of change greatly depend on the underlying characteristics of a given system (i.e., its point of departure prior to reform) as well as the dynamics of reform within the public sector and outside it. In general, however, the three sources of design tensions are apparent in shaping the emergence of e-democracy. We therefore turn to a more specific examination of e-democratic initiatives and contexts within the Canadian public sector at federal and provincial levels.

More needs to be done to both understand and assess the interdependence of these four dimensions of e-government: service delivery, security, transparency, and trust. In particular, more must be done to foster a more meaningful interface between inward-oriented reforms of administration and management and outward-leaning processes for more participative governance forums.

While the Internet is certainly not the only factor driving such reforms, there is no question that its widening presence matters. It is insufficient for any government to focus on internal governance reforms, even those making use of digital technologies, without paying close attention to the shifting expectations of a citizenry increasingly more informed and interconnected. For e-government to co-evolve with democratic reform in a positive manner, the technical design work of deploying technology internally must become more fully integrated with efforts to design, or redesign, our systems of democratic governance. Demographic change will make this tie ever more essential, as the new generations of those who have lived with online commercial, familial, and civic engagements will see no valid reason to exempt the political sphere.

There is a need to think more holistically about e-government as not only a set of digital capacities inside government but also a new and more participative ethos of how government should work in a digital society. Much more discussion is required about the shifting roles and interrelations between politicians, public servants, and the public in this new era. Although the widening scope of the Internet implies expanded opportunity for more efficient and convenient 'customer service,' it also offers the prospect of expanded and more productive dialogues across governments and their stakeholders. Structuring these dialogues with both online and offline forums and tying them to government-wide decision-making processes will be a central component of public sector management in the years ahead.

The Canadian Experience

Canada is a useful jurisdiction in which to study e-government for several reasons. First, as one of the world's leading countries in terms of broadband coverage across households and industries, a number of basic infrastructure conditions are in place to warrant interest and investment in online mechanisms. Second, the Government of Canada and many provincial and municipal governments have been aggressively pursuing e-government (although their definition of this term and the relative space accorded to democratic reform require careful examination). And third, the fact that Canada is a federation translates into at least the prospect for varying levels of interest and engagement across different levels of government.[4]

Federally, the emergence of e-government began in the mid-1990s with the Connecting Canadians agenda spearheaded by then Minister of Industry John Manley. While the primary focus was external, in terms of connecting Canadian citizens, companies, and communities to the Internet, recognition soon spread to the potential for internal government modernization — and reforms to the service delivery mechanisms linking government and its stakeholders. Since that time, the Government of Canada has received international acclaim for its efforts, although other research has demonstrated the limitations and challenges that have shaped what remains a work in progress.

In some respects, this book arrives on the scene at the end of e-government's first phase in Canada. Indeed, at the federal level, e-government has retracted as a major theme of reform, in part since the flagship Government Online (GOL) initiative has come to an end (having achieved its objectives, according to the federal government, though of course the truth is more complex). In its place has emerged the next stage of service transformation, denoted by Service Canada's formal launching in September 2005. Envisioned as the federal government's primary vehicle for citizen-centric service delivery in a multichannel world, Service Canada may be regarded as the beginning of the second phase, building upon the foundational efforts of GOL and venturing forward in new and more ambitious directions.

Organizationally, Service Canada's transformation effort is a tall order with many layers of complexity. First, after much delay and trepidation, the government must declare its intentions for Service Canada itself: will it be a new department or special agency with a status akin to that of the Canada Revenue Agency (CRA), or will it be a subunit of one of its founding departments? Second, new and more horizontal governance arrangements must be worked out between this new entity and its two parent departments, Human Resources and Skills Development Canada (HRSDC) and Social Development Canada (SDC). And third, Service Canada is intertwined with the restructuring of Public Works and Government Services Canada (PWGSC), which houses procurement authorities and the subagency responsible for managing a government-wide digital infrastructure. Procurement is central to new service delivery capacities since it directly shapes the private sector's role and relationships with government and plans to foster a shared services initiative within and across all government departments that includes an IT dimension.

At its inception, Service Canada will be designated as the common infrastructure secretariat for HRSDC and SDC, working in concert with authorities in PWGSC and Treasury Board, where a strategic review of the chief information officer (CIO) function is under way. But it must also coordinate with and perhaps even incorporate the management functions of the federal government portal and secure channel (the gateway to online service delivery) and call centres (the inroad to government services via telephone) that now reside within PWGSC. Once these issues are resolved (estimates range from one to three years of initial reform and planning), Service Canada can extend its scope to the rest of the roughly dozen federal departments for which it has been designated as the eventual service vehicle for these units.

Finally, there is a commitment to further extend the interjurisdictional integration of program information and service offerings across other government levels.

In parallel to this friendly and service-oriented prism of citizen-centric governance has emerged a reframed and widened lens of digital security as a central tenant in the war on terror in a post 9/11 environment. Even prior to such events, the security of the Canadian government's digital infrastructure (viewed at the time as primarily a facilitator of service) was a widening concern.

Along with these technical difficulties one must add the considerable challenges of organizational and managerial coordination across government. The auditor general again concluded that horizontal coordination has been inadequate: "gaps and deficiencies point to a requirement to strengthen the management framework of issues that cross agency boundaries, such as information systems, watch lists, and personnel screening" (Auditor General of Canada 2004, 39). The Senate Standing Committee of National Security and Defence conducted its own review of security readiness and emergency preparedness, noting similar concerns and quoting a senior official's assessment of what is required—namely, "an unprecedented level of cooperation inside and outside of government" (Standing Senate Committee 2004, 14). The response to such pressure came in 2004 via Canada's first ever National Security Policy: the American Department of Homeland Security served as a reference point for what would become the Department of Public Safety and Emergency Preparedness Canada (PSEPC).

In short, the federal government is embarking on one of the largest organizational transformations in its history, yet most people are unaware of it. Overshadowed by minority politics, scandals, and commissions of inquiry, health care, and other more visible policy issues, not only is the public generally ill-informed and unengaged, but so too are most federal politicians. Public sector reform and service transformation efforts are not top-of-mind voter issues, and the political context of the past few years shaped by the Sponsorship Scandal and the Gomery Inquiry has done much to reinforce a cautious, risk-averse, and electorally fixated mindset, the tone for which is set by the Prime Minister's Office.

Prior to assuming power (and immediately inheriting the auditor general's report on the sponsorship inquiry), Paul Martin intended nothing short of revolutionizing parliamentary democracy and Canada's public sector (not just at the federal level but also in concert with provinces and a more empowered municipal level). Once his government was reduced to minority status, he refocused his ambitions accordingly: managing high-profile policy issues, reacting to the Gomery fallout, and preparing the ground for an anticipated election early in 2006. Such political conditions are hardly conducive to administrative transformation, particularly when what little oxygen remains for internal governance reform is consumed by the creation of a bolstered infrastructure for public safety and security that is viewed as both a domestic necessity and a continental imperative.

Such is the context within which GOL has given way to Service Canada. At the same time, this caution and penchant for incremental change explain why, within the dimensions of transparency and trust, the federal government's appetite for reform has been further stunted. While e-democracy experimentation widens around the world (many examples of which will be reviewed throughout this book), and as evidence mounts that the federal government is suffering from a loss of credibility and legitimacy in the eyes of the electorate, reforms in Ottawa have become limited to tinkering with parliamentary procedures. Despite an innovative and promising effort at online consultation by the Parliamentary Subcommittee on the Status of Persons with Disabilities, its recommendations for expanding digital resources and capacities have not found a receptive audience in the federal executive branch.

Perhaps such reasons explain the strange occurrence of a rookie Liberal minister and defector from her former party, Belinda Stronach, who has so quickly inherited the title of minister responsible for democratic reform. Politics aside, Stronach's interest in this area is said to be tied to a sincere and much-needed passion for re-engaging youth in political life, but whether the minister overseeing Service Canada should in fact be the interface for democratic engagement is an interesting question. This dual role is indicative of how the federal government—mainly via the public service—prefers to interpret and measure trust: 'customer satisfaction' surveys and focus groups are the preferred mechanisms for reassurance that Canadians do indeed appreciate their government.[5]

And there can be little question that, by any reasonable measure, the Canadian public service functions admirably well, often being taken for granted. But the twofold question presenting itself is the following: first, is there adequate political leadership to drive forward the service and security governance reforms required to both maintain and improve performance capacities; and, second, are democratic processes, and relations between citizens and stakeholders and their governments, being sufficiently adapted and refurbished to ensure stronger legitimacy and widened participation in the future?

In terms of transparency, the absence of openness by the federal government is hardly encouraging. John Reid, Canada's outgoing information commissioner, makes this point forcefully in reflecting on his tenure: "the clear lesson of these seven years is that governments continue to distrust and resist the Access to Information Act.... Vigilance (by all stakeholders) must be maintained against the very real pressures from governments to take back from citizens the power to control what, and when, information will be disclosed."[6]

Reid's views are largely supported by a US-based scholar, Alasdair Roberts, who has studied access-to-information laws and resulting government practices around the world. His findings in Canada point to systemic efforts by the government to stymie and limit disclosure, particularly with respect to matters of political sensitivity (Roberts 2005). His research also demonstrates that new technologies—far from contributing to greater openness—are being deployed by public authorities to impose greater controls and heightened surveillance over the flow of information in and from governments.

Defenders of secrecy (or, rather, proponents of limited openness) point to times when public interest dictates that information be withheld. National security is most obvious: sensitive information pertaining to perceived threats and planning by governments to intercept such threats must be carefully guarded. Perhaps more contentiously, matters of performance that expose government weakness are also off limits. Security and law enforcement agencies, then, routinely tell us what they are doing right, but they cannot say, for our own good, what they may be doing wrong. Others will say, however, or at least make every effort to try. As a result, paranoia is reinforced. It is no exaggeration to postulate that, with each of the four explosions that rocked London on the frightening morning just after the city's stunning Olympic coup, governments there and here became just a bit more insular and guarded, not only for the moment itself but in future proceedings as well.

Some view such trends as the beginnings of an Orwellian-inspired Big Brother state. This may be a provocative image perhaps, but it misses the mark (at least in mature democracies). Thanks in large part to the Internet, there is simply too much networking and scrutiny going on in the world to permit such overt control and too much respect for rights and freedoms by our politicians and citizens alike (even as some would take exception to such a claim). A more pressing danger, however, is the emergence of a national and global governing technocracy that is out of step with the sort of intelligent, participative, and responsive governance mechanisms required — not only within the public sector but also across society as a whole. In place of open deliberation and collective learning, we get information control, spin, and after-the-fact reporting.

Given the relative importance of the federal government in terms of national leadership, budgetary resources (annual spending of nearly $200 billion), and IT spending in particular (upward of $5 billion annually[7]), a book on e-government in Canada must invariably focus much of its attention accordingly. It is also important to both acknowledge and address the fact that the first decade of e-government has been marked by a resurgence of national (or, in the Canadian case, federal) government and identity after a previous decade characterized by a dispersion of the national sphere (a dispersion that has not entirely subsided as well).

Part of this reversal may be attributed to cyberspace and global connectivity and the fact that countries that are large geographically can become quite small demographically (and comparatively on a broader, globalized grid). The events of 9/11 also matter here, as national borders and domestic boundaries have become as important as commercial flows (and the nexus between the two recasts political and digital ties between countries, particularly those in close proximity such as Canada and its neighbour to the south).

These trends create some tension between public sector reform over the past twenty years or so (a period in which new public management has emerged by and large in a bottom-up manner, influenced by subnational activity and innovation that would later shape federal or national efforts) and e-government's tendency in many jurisdictions to be dominated by larger, national public sector bodies with more resources and technological needs (and conversely more challenges rooted in size and scope in engineering reforms quickly and effectively) than smaller, more localized government.

On the one hand, governments at the provincial level have mirrored to varying degrees the service delivery focus of their federal counterpart, in terms of online portals, integrated services, and citizen-centric mindsets. In many cases, moreover, provincial models may be influencing the current choices and transitions occurring in Ottawa, as the lessons from examples such as Service New Brunswick are in many ways microcosms of the larger, more complex changes unfolding federally. Provinces have also begun to enter into the realm of democratic reform, experimenting with more varied approaches to citizen engagement and electronic democracy.

Although the federal government has also pursued these avenues, what emerges is an interesting contrast between these two levels, with more variance and degrees of experimentation and reform found across the different provinces. British Columbia's recent experience with a constituent assembly and electoral reform (which failed by a narrow margin in a May 2005 referendum that nonetheless saw some fifty-seven percent of the population vote in favour of change) and Ontario's newly established Democratic Renewal Secretariat are cases in point, examined in more detail in Chapter 6.

At the municipal level, one finds a conundrum of sorts between the advantages and the disadvantages of being small. Much of the new public management reform models of the previous decades was rooted in the advantages of more local, nimble, and flexible public sector bodies adapting and innovating to new realities. To some degree, this perspective has carried forward into the domain of e-government, where municipalities have been able to envision reforms and alternative models of both delivering services and making decisions more quickly than at other levels; in other areas, municipalities appear to be deeply constrained by limited resources and weakening democracy.

By the same token, the structures of Canadian federalism, and the distribution of fiscal resources in particular, create a context in which federal and provincial governments remain much more visible and aggressive in investing in their own technological capacities than in supporting local capacities — notwithstanding the rhetoric of the 'new deal for cities and communities' that has emerged in Ottawa over the past few years. Thus, a major challenge of e-government in a federal environment lies in the fact that the vision and technological promise of more seamless forms of governance need not apply exclusively to any one government; rather, they would apply to the public sector as a whole. The same pressures of horizontal integration and interoperability across departments within an agency (prerequisites to more coordinated and integrated offerings online) are also extending themselves to interjurisdictional arrangements, particularly as governments themselves point to such collective action as a guiding principle of e-government and good governance generally.[8]

Although the federally-led Government Online (GOL) initiative has long been envisioned as a platform to intergovernmental collaboration, providing citizen-centric service delivery across all levels of government, the structures for doing so remain in their infancy. Similarly, in terms of domestic security and emergency preparedness, where the stakes are arguably higher, the situation is similar, as a recent Senate committee reported major intergovernmental blockages that are particularly harmful to local governments and front-line delivery agents most in need of informational and tangible resources in order to respond to crises of various sorts.

Whether the public endorses a primarily competitive view of federalism and intergovernmental relations or a more collaborative view is a critical variable in shaping e-government's future. Some observers suggest that the federal government may well be the beneficiary of a more digital future as citizens maintain their national attachment — facilitated in part by online connectivity — while lessening their traditionally strongest ties to provincial governments since these latter identities may erode in visibility and relevance over time.

If so, provinces may be less willing to seek more integrative governance solutions that erode their presence. Although the current CIO Council (comprised of voluntary participants among senior public managers from federal and provincial governments) could evolve into a collective entity of some importance in addressing such matters, it is currently not empowered in such fashion. Municipalities also cannot be forgotten, and this intergovernmental dimension is central to the evolution of a more digital public sector for the country as a whole.

Looking Ahead

Part Three presents an examination at both the probable and the optimal trajectories of public sector reform in the years ahead. The first chapter of this section is devoted to the need for new accountability arrangements encompassing shifting roles, responsibilities, and interrelationships among public servants, elected officials, and the citizenry. The implications of this changing accountability environment for procurement and public-private sector collaboration are also examined, as is the government's role as a producer, handler, and broker of information, which is considered in terms of the link between transparency and accountability both inside government and across all sectors.

Service Canada and other federal reforms pertaining to the machinery of service transformation are a major focus of this chapter. A case is made for a more autonomous and empowered Service Canada entity, underpinned by more visible and direct managerial accountability for public servants and a new architecture for shared political accountability to oversee and guide its operations. To counter the widening danger of a more centralized and bureaucratic apparatus to guide government-wide transformations in both service and security realms (a danger further accentuated by a stubbornly narrow interpretation of the doctrine of ministerial accountability), it is imperative that the conditions for a more networked model of public sector management be understood.

The Swedish variant of such a model is termed 'contractual' governance, where agencies and bodies enjoy widespread freedom and autonomy to manage their own affairs and, when appropriate in order to pursue shared outcomes, partner with one another accordingly. Importantly, senior public servants in Sweden exert managerial freedom and flexibility without direct interference from politicians who prefer to focus their energies on policy decisions and operational outcomes. In return, these government managers are held directly and visibly accountable for their decisions.

Although use of the term 'contractual' denotes competition and legalistic and contractual controls in a North American setting, the opposite is also true: the freedom to enter into such agreements translates into a more collaborative culture underpinned, within the public sector, by a supportive and facilitative set of central agencies there to assist as opposed to control these more horizontal governance relationships.

Such changes denote reforms within the executive branch (i.e., cabinet ministers and the public service), but there is also a pressing need for reforms to better engage the legislative branch through modified and improved relations between it and the executive. The central role of information – the basis of external communications and the public's ability to both exert a more direct oversight role and undertake new forms of policy engagement – demands a rethinking of the information architecture of the public sector.

In place of strict partisanship and what has arguably become a central agency-led set of mechanisms focused largely on information control (i.e., political spin and communications), there is a need for a more politically shared and thus neutral body. Such a body would oversee the informational capacities of not only the government (as defined by the executive branch and ruling party) but also the public sector as a whole, including both the legislature (and its various parties) and the citizenry at large now viewed as a more constant participant in governance than the traditions of representational democracy have dictated in the past.

Indeed, many of these informational changes discussed imply a new set of roles and capacities for the legislature. The next chapter in Part Three examines the need for a more participative democratic ethos to redefine citizenship as a basis for political engagement in a digital age. More than an issue for the national polity, the extent to which any expansion of citizen participation can and should be facilitated locally, provincially, or federally – or across all levels – is an important issue in shaping a more participative form of governance.

A basis for a new 'federated architecture' of democratic engagement is discussed, one that recognizes that public engagement takes place at all levels of government. In an online world, there are both ongoing advantages stemming from proximity in terms of localized forums for dialogue consultation and new opportunities for provincial and federal governments to make use of this localized learning via intergovernmental partnering rather than replicating and overshadowing local democracy with their own apparatus and resources. In other words, federalism must be viewed as a tripartite framework of both service and policy responsibilities on the one hand and citizen engagement opportunities on the other hand. The design challenge for the public sector as a whole is to coordinate these different levels in a strategic manner – recognizing the value of complementing new opportunities for dialogue in cyberspace with a traditional reliance on geographic place.

Along with this potential one must also be cognizant of the very real danger – embedded in status quo arrangements – for intergovernmental competition primarily between federal and provincial governments both seeking to assert their 'brands' and reach through cyberspace while doing little more to address municipal governance issues than increasing financial transfers in a manner that promotes dependency more than stronger capacities for self-governance.

The last chapter of this part shifts the focus from the domestic apparatus for governance and public sector management to the transnational environment beyond Canada's borders. Security concerns now predominantly shape relations between Canada and the United States (as well as those between the United States and Mexico). Moreover, the pursuit of this common security agenda is increasingly informational and digital, and a level of interoperability between authorities must be achieved in order to facilitate a collective sense of confidence in one another and a basis for joint action.

Yet, such a path is not without difficulties. From the Canadian perspective, historical concerns about US dependency (and dominance) remain a major political issue, and as a result 'interoperability' is a term often interchanged with 'integration' in political debates. Some observers argue that in accordance with this focus the post-9/11 context is viewed as more about bilateral commerce than about domestic safety (Kruger et al. 2004).

One can expect the United States and Canada to continue down a cooperative path, with the US model of homeland security continuing to serve as an important reference point for Canadian–American relations. For the Canadian government, such a path risks relying on deception or, at best, something less than full candour in publicly asserting independence while privately pursuing interdependence with US authorities wherever practically possible.[9] Moreover, this incremental approach to continental interoperability aligns itself rather well with the already secretive nature of domestic security within each country. The danger of such a path lies in both the expanded realm of secrecy across many aspects of public sector operations pertaining to security that will grow to include a wider set of transborder provisions and the resulting governance apparatus that will become insular and unaccountable, provoking either dangerous overextensions of authority or unintended consequences from mismanagement or error.

The Canadian government is not without some understanding of these pressures, widening calls for more openness and accountability in security matters. Accordingly, a new joint parliamentary committee is being established to provide — for the first time in Canadian history — a mechanism of direct political review over the security community. Yet it is less clear if this new body will serve as a vehicle for expanding public awareness and involvement in security matters and thus a basis for strengthened accountability. New tensions may also arise in devising workable relationships and a division of duties between the new parliamentary committee and other review bodies in place, particularly as all of these actors adjust and adapt to the ongoing and potential changes to the security apparatus.

The expanding canvas of interoperability and connectivity extends beyond the continental plane and underpins the intensification of efforts to craft some workable basis of global governance for an increasingly interconnected and interdependent world. Although the issues and range of stakeholders are more diffuse, in some ways the US-centric characterization of debates remains evident as the technical requirements of the Internet, the security fixation on anti-terrorism and more traditional forms of illegitimate activity such as organized crime, and the politics of institutional reform all converge around and become more intertwined with the emergence of e-governance.

These emerging challenges also create new pressures for policy and process coordination within the federal government (and, to a lesser degree, across government levels). Increasingly, matters such as trade, foreign policy, public safety, health, and defence all become more interdependent both within domestic government boundaries and across the transnational environment with other countries and within international institutions.

The main lessons drawn from Part Three are twofold: first, to underscore the lack of sufficient progress in Canada at present in terms of overall public sector adaptation to e-government's four dimensions of change; and, second, to sketch out a basis for more meaningful reforms that nonetheless require both widened and ongoing dialogue in order to develop a crystallized blueprint for moving forward. Indeed, the endpoint of such a blueprint is itself less important than the process requirements and parameters of a more participative and adaptive polity capable of meeting the challenges of the digital age.

The conclusion to this book summarizes some of the main themes emerging from the preceding analysis and provides a final discussion that serves as a basis for further dialogue and adaptation. A definitive blueprint of the digitally transformed public sector is not what is sought, for such a blueprint must itself be the product of a discursive, participative, and negotiated process. Nonetheless, there are some critical contours of future reform that can serve as guideposts along such a path.

Part One
Four Main Dimensions of Change

The purpose of Part One is to both introduce and dissect the four main dimensions of change (service, security, transparency, and trust) that have arisen during the first decade of the e-government era. Collectively, they encompass a basis for digital transformation, although whether or not such transformation occurs depends very much on how each dimension is recognized and responded to in any given jurisdiction. Thus, while interdependent in many respects, each dimension also comprises a partially distinct sphere of issues and challenges that have arisen due either directly or indirectly to the advent of the Internet.

Service: For most public sector managers, the initial impetus for thinking about online dimensions of government operations came during the 1990s, when the mainstream advent of the Internet began to translate into dramatic declines in the cost of both communicating and processing information. Partially aligned with the re-engineering movement of the preceding decade, public sector organizations sought new ways to control costs and improve organizational efficiencies: new and better approaches to managing information technology and the emergence of online channels of service delivery promised significant financial savings.

While e-government has improved efficiency at times, such savings have often been overshadowed by both escalating costs and widening purposes as the strategic scope of e-government has extended beyond the realm of financial savings. Three different images of e-government, in terms of the underlying objectives, have been well summarized by Remmen (2004) as (1) efficiency: cost reductions; (2) public service: better quality, easier access (i.e., 24/7), new services; and (3) democracy: participation and interactive dialogue. This chapter explores the nature of e-government's evolution within and between the first two of these images: efficiency and public service reform. It seeks to explain why the initial hype and hope for efficiency have been quickly overtaken by a more ambitious and complex set of challenges tied to public service performance in terms of both providing information and access to services and programs online and better integrating such offerings in manners based less on the needs and preferences of the citizen (or customer) than on organizational structure.

Security: The emergence of security as a multifaceted governance challenge is a critical variable in government efforts to adapt to the increasingly digital and interdependent realities of today's world. Although there are many dimensions and meanings of 'security,' I invoke the term here in two interrelated uses. First, cybersecurity and online reliability represent important foundational platforms necessary to underpin the sustained expansion of e-commerce, e-government, and all forms of online activity. Second, security strategies devised to both respond to and proactively thwart criminal and terrorist threats are based upon information management capacities and a widening digital infrastructure in order to plan, coordinate, and conduct action.

September 11th, 2001, marks a critical turning point. Prior to this date, security could arguably have been presented as primarily an extension of e-commerce and e-government in terms of technologically-enabled service delivery. Indeed, security remains central to such activity, and as such companies and governments devote considerable attention to encryption, information management systems, and related elements that underpin online transactions. The overarching aim is to bolster confidence among Internet users while spoiling the intentions of would-be commercial criminals and/or thrill-seeking hackers. The details of such efforts often remained shielded from widespread political and consumer debate. What mattered more were beneficial outcomes for consumers and citizens in terms of improvements in convenience and/or cost. Service delivery is now accompanied by surveillance, data-mining, and integrated anti-terrorism and public safety strategies. Such activities constitute an important dimension of e-government as a nexus of technology, politics, and organization that has triggered a bolstered and more assertive presence by national governments.

Transparency: According to two prominent observers of Internet-induced change, we live in the "age of transparency" (Tapscott and Ticoll 2003). Organizational openness is in, and it must be viewed as routine and ongoing, whereas secrecy invites suspicion, resulting in questions, exposure, and increased costs and complexities down the line. Although this particular invocation offered by Tapscott and Ticoll refers primarily to the actions of private corporations that face greater investor and public scrutiny (ultimately rendering traditional efforts to curb and manage disclosure futile, they argue), governments are not immune to such pressures. Moreover, e-government has created optimistic expectations for improved transparency, as information is more readily made available and more widely shared by public sector authorities themselves. At the same time, the Internet also facilitates efforts by neutral observers and vested interests to find and share information, expose secrets and shortcomings, and mobilize public opinion.

Yet transparency is more complex and consequential than simply increasing the supply of information. Many questions stem from concerns about both the quality and the availability of such information and whether or not governments are genuinely committed to being more open in terms of objectives, processes, and results. Preliminary efforts to examine such questions point to a cultural clash between traditional operating procedures and processes consistent with Westminster origins and the widening pressures—both online and offline—for more accessibility into, and awareness of, most facets of what government is doing and how it is doing it.

Trust: Trust is interwoven with processes of both administrative modernization and institutional innovation. Moreover, trust directly shapes government's capacity to adapt to a more participatory and multistakeholder environment that challenges conventional notions of authority and traditional methods of organization. E-government's ultimate destiny will be determined by the confidence and support of the citizenry and all stakeholders.

In a world characterized by more information and knowledge availability and new opportunities for power sharing as a result, there are many ties between transparency and trust. Over the past decade, it has been unclear whether the emergence of e-government has done much to stem the tide of eroding public confidence in democratic governance generally—despite much optimism surrounding electronic or digital democratic experimentation designed to update such processes in order to make them more relevant and appealing to an increasingly informed and online citizenry. Within the public sector, there are similar contradictions between the potential for information and communication technologies (ICTs) to either empower staff or reinforce hierarchical control. Governments must view trust not only through the service prism of customer relationship management but also through citizenship and democracy and the resulting pressures for institutional reform. Reconciling these internal and external pressures is the holistic challenge of digital transformation that requires relational trust among all stakeholders.

Chapter 1
Service

The rapid expansion of Internet access and online connectivity in the 1990s gave birth to the e-government movement as the public sector sought ways to capitalize on the vaunted potential of a new, more pervasive and interactive digital infrastructure. With e-commerce as a model, online service delivery became the hallmark of e-government as efficiency, responsiveness, and simplicity became the guiding principles of public sector action. These principles have since underscored the need for 'enterprise-wide perspectives' in order to align technology, share information, and coordinate organizational action in order to realize the sorts of integrated outcomes being promised by 'one-stop' portals and political rhetoric alike. Although much progress has been made, the considerable amount of risk and complexity involved in creating a new set of governance mechanisms that nonetheless coexist with traditional structures and channels has resulted in a more modest gravitation of public services online than initially conceived.

In dissecting this complexity and the main challenges that have arisen, this chapter unfolds as follows. Section 1.1 provides a brief introduction to the emergence of e-commerce and e-government in terms of their present scope. Section 1.2 describes the citizen-centric governance mentality at the heart of online and multichannel service delivery strategies. Section 1.3 then examines the term 'federated architecture' as a shifting balancing act between decentralized autonomy on the one hand and central coordination and government-wide capacities on the other. Section 1.4 outlines the major relational scenarios involving new partnerships, both externally with industry and internally via shared services entities within the public sector. And, finally, section 1.5 concludes the chapter with a summary of the key issues and some lessons learned.

1.1 Introduction

Remarkably new by any historical measure, the rapid emergence of the Internet as a mainstream tool in all sectors has altered the mindsets and strategies of all organizations thinking about delivering products or services in this new environment. With respect to e-commerce, expansion in the private sector is linked to an online population that has now surpassed half a billion people worldwide. Yet, despite progress in most regions of the world, this group remains relatively concentrated in the developed world, within the most advanced economies of Asia, Europe, and North America (Geiselhart 2004).

This concentration stems, in part, from the catalytic role played by the private sector. Across most industries, the Internet has served three main purposes in shaping market behaviour and organizational dynamics: a source of product and process innovation, an efficiency tool, and an alternative channel of client service. The widening scope of digital technologies means that few, if any, industries are exempt from some degree of transformation (Andal-Ancion et al. 2003) and electronic commerce levels, though a modest proportion of overall economic activity continues to grow in a manner that would have been unthinkable only a decade ago.

In terms of the Canadian online marketplace, for example, consumers spent more than $3 billion shopping over the Internet in 2003—a twenty-five percent increase in spending from 2002 levels that comprises the collective purchases made by more than 3 million Canadian households.[1] South of the border, retail sales online are expected to reach nearly $120 billion by 2008, according to Jupiter Research. Beyond these direct lines of sale, organizations and industries are deploying new technologies to restructure their corporate boundaries and extended networks of outsourcing partners, suppliers, and other stakeholders. An April 2005 cover of *Business Week* in the United States claimed that "IBM wants to run your business," a portrayal of the efforts of this bellwether company to reinvent itself yet again for a more flexible, digital, and virtual age.[2]

For governments, such Internet-induced trends are relevant. Much of e-government reflects private sector activity that has both encouraged and pressured public sector organizations to act in a similar manner. Fiscal constraints imposed by a quasi-competitive system of global investors and domestic politics, as well as a strategic desire to generate cost savings and reallocate spending to new and politically attractive priorities, make the nexus between technology management and efficiency a central concern in government today (McIver and

Elmagarmid 2002; Pavlichev and Garson 2004). Thus, both corporations and governments share many common challenges, both in deploying new technologies and adapting to emerging online realities (Cairncross 2002; Gasco 2003).

At the same time, a careful examination of government reveals important differences across the private and public sectors. Efficiency, for example, is a much more politically contested principle in government. Stakeholders such as unions and political parties may oppose worker mobility and job cuts—moves generally applauded in the market sector. Equally important, while private corporations may aggressively cater to select client groups, governments carry broader public interest responsibilities involving all citizens that, in turn, shape both the feasibility and the perceived appropriateness of e-government as a service strategy.

The modest and uneven results of online service delivery by governments, even in those countries leading in Internet use, are indicative of both the organizational complexities and the diverse clienteles shaping e-government (Hart-Teeter 2003; Eggers 2005). As such, the emergence of more digital and online mechanisms for service delivery must be situated within a broader movement of citizen-centric governance within which online channels are more likely to coexist with, rather than replace, other forms of communication and transaction. This movement is central to understanding e-government's evolution from a primarily cost-savings technique toward a broader vehicle for both organizational and managerial renewal.

1.2 Citizen-Centric Governance

The face of e-government is literally the website, and an enriched site is said to be a portal that offers the potential of online functionality and purpose. Pages on a website provide information in a digital format, while a portal provides entry into a broader set of possibilities to complete transactions, learn about what government can offer, and even participate in its decision-making processes.

These varying levels of both information and interaction are dependent on both technological and organizational capacities. A static website is conducive to a basic support function, linear in purpose, mainly that of another channel to provide information to potential users. More recently, websites that supplant traditional, paper-based processes have become commonplace. More advanced forms of websites and portals foster innovation and creative alternative mechanisms of service delivery that would not otherwise be feasible.

During the 1990s, as countries and other jurisdictions began to develop a web presence, it became intuitive that an online reiteration of government departments and agencies would not be the most effective way of developing more transactional and interactive capacities. The notions of life events and service streams were developed to reflect an online perspective of government operations based less on organizational charts and more on citizen usage and outcomes, with Singapore credited by some observers as the first nation to organize its public sector online in such a manner (McIver and Elmagarmid 2002). Integrated service offerings that hide, simplify, or transcend the traditional machinery of government have thus become a centrepiece of the e-government project, in reference to one of four variations of what it means to integrate services.

1. All relevant agencies offer the same service in a common manner, sharing data definitions and at best sharing data, but no technological integration between the services is offered.
2. Services are collected together under a common theme or event. The services are not inherently integrated, or even have a common look and feel, but are grouped in ways that aid discovery and promote comprehensive completion of necessary services.
3. Services are delivered by a single provider as an agent of other government agencies. Singular services are offered by the agent, and the integration is hidden from the 'customer.'
4. Services are technologically integrated into a pseudosupply chain application. This requires the most sophisticated integration work and is not often implemented. (Turner 2004, 130)

Whereas the first two levels represent the realm of e-government as a service delivery strategy as it took shape in the late 1990s, most governments today (in developed countries with the Internet widely available) are grappling with the latter two challenges, which by and large represent the focus of the discussion and analysis presented in this book. New organizational and technological models for delivering services both online and by complementing more traditional channels are taking hold and beginning to generate encouraging results (Marche and McNiven 2003).

A notable example in the United States is New York City's NYCServ Epayment Project, indicative of the parameters of a service delivery architecture predicated on more citizen-centric services via a range of separate yet integrated channels:

> The NYCServ application streamlines and integrates three key business processes for the city of New York—processing payments, conducting adjudication hearings, and tracking towed vehicles. It has four separate revenue channels: walk-in payment centers, Internet, interactive voice response (IVR) and kiosks. The system processes 1.9 million receipts for a total of over $6 billion in 2003. Citizens can make payments with a single transaction for parking tickets, tow releases, environmental violations, property taxes, business taxes, health and consumer affairs violations and license/permits, water bills and several other items.
>
> The NYCServe application integrates the legacy systems of six city agencies. Most of NYCServ is custom-built using Java 2 Enterprise Edition (J2EE)... . It was developed by an integrated team of approximately 20 per cent Finance Department staff and 80 per cent IBM staff.... NYCServ has opened three new public revenue channels: Internet, IVR and kiosks. These new channels accounted for over 750,000 transactions, or 30 per cent of all payments processed through NYCServ in 2003... . This shift in payment source has significantly reduced the workload of customer service representatives and cashiers in payment centers.[3]

Although gains in efficiency have resulted, any net benefit calculation is a more complicated undertaking since financial savings incurred over time must be weighed against the upfront investment costs of new technological systems and the corresponding training and organizational development requirements (OECD 2001). Despite hopes for widespread cost savings (mainly from reduced online transaction costs relative to other channels), many of the initial models put forth proved to be excessively optimistic due to inflated forecasting in terms of upfront investments, maintenance and transition costs, and demand for online services (Roy 2003).[4] It is also noteworthy that, despite a perception of online transactions proving to be inexpensive compared with other forms of communication, many governments have recovered some of these upfront costs by imposing a 'convenience fee' for users of such channels. While there was some fear among New York City officials that such a fee would be accepted, such fears quickly dissipated in light of rapid uptake by citizens and businesses alike, with the system routinely processing tax payment of several million dollars (ibid.).

The use of such convenience fees by many governments to finance online delivery strategies is an example of the complexities involved in determining net costs and benefits from such systems, since gains in efficiency are not in such instances being transferred to citizens (in their role as customers). Conversely, many individuals and organizations are all too prepared to sacrifice a small financial sum for the savings in time and transportation over other service channels such as sending traditional mail or visiting a government office.

While such examples point to the legitimate and irreversible arrival of online services and multichannel integration schemes, after a decade or so of e-government developments, the general performance of electronic service delivery has been uneven and sporadic due to a range of other demand and supply considerations. What is clear in countries with widespread Internet availability is that there has been a huge uptake in government-sponsored websites for various forms of information (Fletcher 2004). Beyond these one-way information flows, transactions completed online are growing only modestly and unevenly, often a result of limited offerings by governments (due to a variety of governance factors reviewed below). Paradoxically, in those jurisdictions where Internet use is the highest (predominantly in North America and Europe), a relatively sophisticated and well-performing public sector (even without an online dimension) means that many people remain relatively content with their traditional processes of interacting with governments when necessary.

Such a notion of 'necessity' is important since, unlike the marketplace, in which more often than not there is an element of choice involved in conducting a purchase or transaction, many users of government services do so only rarely and are under an obligation of one sort or another. Often the most sophisticated users of online channels, including the most affluent and educated, are generally the least likely to interact frequently and directly with public sector authorities (a notable distinction between the banking sector and government).

The demand for electronic services is therefore segmented in a complex fashion and intertwined with the notion of a digital divide — namely, the division of those citizens with regular and reliable online access and those without it. In terms of the former, a group approaching 1 billion strong worldwide by the end of 2005, there is growing interest in and support for online processes across all realms of professional and private pursuits, but the latter group — itself a complex mosaic of subgroups of individuals — also comprises a critical clientele of public sector programs, information, and services preferring or needing alternative channels of interaction.

To illustrate, consider a recent profile of online users in the United States, where eighty-eight percent of online Americans (now more than half of the population) say that the Internet plays a role in their daily routines (one-third of this group characterizing it as a major role) — whether it is communicating with friends and family, finding information, banking, job searching, or conducting general interest learning and recreation, nearly two-thirds of those online indicate that their daily routine would be disrupted without the Internet.[5]

Governments are thus faced with the predicament of already having a significant segment of the citizenry expecting to conduct, or at least being open to conducting, their public services online. At the same time, many Internet users may be indifferent to online channels or prefer other means of interacting, such as face-to-face encounters or telephone call centres, while a significant number of citizens remain without reliable Internet access at home or work.[6]

The following chart illustrates the level of Internet use and speed in the home across Canada in a manner that underscores both the undeniable expansion of an online infrastructure and the potential for a digital divide that is a critical variable in the multichannel realities of public sector service delivery efforts.

The service delivery focus of governments must account for an increasingly important but still partial amount of online activity by the

Speed of household connection by region in Canada (2003)[16]

	Proportion of total households using regularly from home	High speed from home	Low speed from home
Atlantic Canada	47%	56%	44%
Quebec	45%	59%	41%
Ontario	60%	62%	38%
Manitoba and Saskatchewan	52%	70%	30%
Alberta	58%	74%	26%
British Columbia	62%	77%	23%
Total	**54%**	**65%**	**35%**

citizenry. Thus required is the existence of a multichannel governance framework within which traditional program and service delivery processes coexist with newly emerging online strategies—the shared objective being better customer relationship management or citizenship governance (within the service realm, little distinction is made between customer and citizen). Nevertheless, the online mechanisms represent an important new dimension to public sector governance in terms of both technological and organizational coordination.

1.3 Federated Architectures

On the supply side of online service delivery, the transition is potentially more challenging due in large measure to the slowness with which governments have developed an organizational infrastructure to enable more service transactions to be conducted online. Although many examples exist where online channels are in operation, such as business registrations and tax filing, the vast majority of government programs continue to involve the need for human interaction, the submission of signed forms, and other more traditional actions that take place offline.

A difficult transition for governments lies in achieving the sorts of internal mechanisms for integration and coordination required across the public sector in order to enable a more integrative approach to web-enabled service delivery. These necessary changes are primarily about fostering more horizontal governance to cut across traditionally separate vertical entities, perhaps the single most crucial organizational challenge to realizing citizen-centric portals and service delivery mechanisms (Fountain 2001; Allen et al. 2005). These pressures for more horizontal ties stem directly from the sort of alternative, more citizen-centric, forms of organizing represented by a portal no longer organized around the government department but the purpose of the service stream.

For instance, businesses are often required to submit information on their operations to several government departments (and often levels of government) for various programs, including registrations, regulation compliance, and various forms of assistance. A truly client-centric approach to customer service and information management by one government would mean that, once such information is provided by the company online, it should be readily available to all units of government requiring it for some purpose or another. The company would then not be required to repeat the information-processing routine with multiple agencies and departments, creating a potential gain in efficiency for government and industry as well as a more satisfied 'client' of the public sector.[8]

Achieving this horizontal collaboration therefore requires political will and a set of organizational mechanisms to facilitate information sharing and joint action (Batini et al. 2002). There are both structural and cultural impediments to such mechanisms, reflecting traditional resource allocation processes and separate accountability systems based on vertical hierarchy and, in the case of parliamentary models, ministerial accountability (Allen et al. 2005). Typically, ministers are rewarded and/or punished on the basis of performance within their fiefdoms of jurisdiction, which normally involve a single department or set of agencies thus accountable in a hierarchical fashion to that minister. In such a world, budgets are allocated on the basis of interministerial competitions for resources, with central agencies expected to sort out disagreements and, when required, impose a degree of coordination on initiatives that require an interdepartmental set of actions.

The danger is that, in the absence of strong actions to overcome the boundaries engrained within traditional organizational structures, predicated for the most part on separate, silo-like functions, the rhetoric of portals as a basis for integrative services, one-stop encounters, and more seamless governance remains just rhetoric. In an online world, integrative mechanisms become reduced to a mere set of web links that direct citizens and organizations from one branch of government to another.

The resulting challenge of horizontal coordination is intertwined with the principle of interoperability, a central characteristic of governance reforms tied to the enabling of government-wide systems for information sharing and collective action across organizational boundaries (Ostroff 1999). Although at one time viewed predominantly as a technical challenge, where the absence of interoperability would be reflected in the disconnection between various hardware components and software programs in separate departments not being able to work with one another (often because each department designed its information system to work for its own unique purpose, with little incentive to be concerned about cross-governmental approaches), this principle cannot be viewed as an important element of organizational design in the digital age.

The contentious nature of achieving this principle and its potential for organizational complexity are rooted in decisions as to whether interoperability can be facilitated by collaboration between government units or ordained through more centralized mechanisms mandated with the task of ensuring that government-wide capacities are in place, with respect to both technology and all aspects of intra-organizational governance such as resource allocation systems and results-based management.

It is in this respect that the emergence of e-government as an organizational strategy carries the potential to contradict previous reforms tied to service improvement. While e-government represents a vehicle for improved service delivery that can be seen as the most recent step in a more evolutionary process of public sector reforms and (ideally) improvements designed to improve service delivery capacities and ultimately overall performance, the pressures for government-wide action and responses are also partially a reversal from the flavour of reforms in the public sector for the past twenty years.

Most notably, a recent impetus, predating the current focus on digital reforms and online capacities, can be seen in the movement over the past two decades known as new public management (NPM), which gave rise to an initial focus on delivering programs and services in a manner less based within traditional hierarchies and rules and more predicated on efficiency and results. The scope and purpose of the NPM are much debated, and there are many important differences between both how and why this philosophy was initially conceived and the present service improvement strategies now undertaken by many governments (Savoie 2003; Eggers 2005). For example, some observers interpret NPM as essentially an endorsement of market solutions over state intervention: accordingly, many NPM-inspired prescriptions involved various forms of competition between either government units or public sector providers and private sector entities, or they simply opted for the private sector over government by contracting out or outsourcing functions from the public sector to companies operating in the marketplace.

At the same time, NPM also influenced lines of authority and managerial practices within government operations. In particular, centralized command and control processes were shunned in favour of more decentralized forms of decision-making through wider degrees of operational freedom accorded to both individual departmental units and quasi-autonomous agencies better positioned, it was argued, to address the needs of their particular clienteles and develop innovations and solutions accordingly. NPM was therefore a predominantly decentralizing philosophy of public sector governance—both within individual governments and across levels of government within particular jurisdictions.

The United Kingdom, for example, moved aggressively in establishing executive agencies, essentially units of central government revised from their former departmental status to include more managerial autonomy from central agencies and a stronger focus on individual and business line performance (i.e., results for the business unit but not necessarily tied to government-wide agendas to any significant degree). Former heads of departments (secretaries in the United Kingdom or deputy ministers in Canada) became chief executives in charge of these more nimble organizations, with incentives and reporting requirements emphasizing performance over process.

It was perhaps New Zealand that went the furthest down this path by establishing performance contracts for senior officials, negotiating objectives between the minister and the head of a department, and replacing traditional job tenure with five-year contracts with renewal (and partial elements of compensation) determined on the basis of achievement.

With respect to information and communication technologies, prior to the widespread recognition of e-government and online service delivery as a major priority, such products and processes were by and large viewed as support functions to facilitate decision-making and information-processing within governments more generally. In other words, viewed as more technical and tedious than strategic, 'informatics' and 'information systems' became relegated to back office considerations for senior government managers and politicians alike.

The result of this positioning made ICTs prime candidates for outsourcing, and it has been during the past two decades that the emergence of widespread government outsourcing to the private sector has occurred within the realm of ICTs. In the United States, the United Kingdom, Australia, and New Zealand in particular, the scope, duration, and value of such arrangements continued to grow, although, importantly, the deals were mainly construed along individual departmental boundaries and authorities (in line with the NPM emphasis).[9]

While this trend continues to some extent, there is an important countervailing current in terms of e-government—namely, the centrality of more integrated and more horizontal capacities on a government-wide basis. Achieving this type of action across previously separate and autonomous organizational units requires some degree of central coordination—not only in terms of managing government ICTs on a more holistic basis but also in elevating such issues to a more senior and strategic rank in terms of organizational priorities.

Governments are not alone in facing such pressures, of course, since it remains an important paradox of governance in the digital age that new forms of information and communication technologies can be both centralizing and decentralizing—a new reality of governing and managing in any large organizational setting. "An implication is that corporate structures are becoming more heterogeneous at exactly the same time as power at the centre—over standards, systems and the like—is growing stronger. The company (organization) is becoming simultaneously more centralized and more diffuse and open. Internet technologies will enable the organization of the future to choose the appropriate structure in more flexible ways.... Corporate leaders will constantly have to manage the tension between centralization and decentralization" (Cairncross 2002, 174). Achieving such a balance between decentralized innovation and flexibility on the one hand and centralized leadership and coordination on the other has become the hallmark of the chief information officer's (CIO) position within large organizations, and governments are no exception. Often positioned within a central agency of government (with some form of management and expenditure oversight authority for government as a whole), the CIO has become the de facto head of e-government strategy in many jurisdictions. The CIO's work has increased in importance due to the widening need for alignment between technology, information, and strategy:

> **What is a CIO?** Chief Information Officers are senior managers responsible for all aspects of their companies' information technology and systems. They direct the use of IT to support the company's goals. With knowledge of both technology and business process and a cross-functional perspective, they are usually the managers most capable of aligning the organization's technology deployment strategy with its business strategy.... CIOs have taken a leadership role in re-engineering their organizations' business processes and the underpinning IT infrastructures to achieve more productive, efficient and valuable use of information within the enterprise. Many are also taking a leadership role in knowledge management and the valuation of intellectual capital.[10]

Over the past several years, with respect to putting in place an architecture for e-government and online service delivery, two main challenges have plagued CIOs in the public sector environment: the systemic barriers to more horizontal coordination tied to both technical and organizational interoperability on a government-wide scale, and an inconsistent level of political support from elected officials.[11] For many CIOs in the public sector realm, this latter frustration stems in part from an ongoing sense of inferiority in terms of strategic importance compared with their counterparts in industry.

This sentiment is conveyed to elected officials in the United States by one such CIO, who nonetheless points to a significant increase in the scope of his duties:

> The role of the CIO in public sector is evolving through various stages. In the first stage, the role was ill-defined and the CIO was thought of as a technician and then as an adjunct to the Chief Financial Officer (CFO). As a result of the Clinger-Cohen legislation, the work of the Federal CIO Council, the growth of the Internet, E-Commerce, and the success in addressing the Year 2K problem, the CIO is progressing towards a business partner and a peer with senior management. CIOs were able to demonstrate their value and the value of technology to their organizations while addressing the serious issues involved with Year 2K. In the private sector, many CIOs have evolved into a Chief Technology Officer working side-by-side with the CEO, as evidenced by the many .com organizations. The public sector CIO has not yet reached this level of influence.[12]

This influence gap has undoubtedly closed to some degree in the past few years due in large part to the growing profile of e-government as a public sector priority around the world (some evidence of this profile is reviewed below). Nonetheless, in the United States, despite the technological prowess of the country as a whole, Congress has been quick to scale back digital initiatives tied to e-government as a performance improvement strategy for the public sector, with the notable exception of homeland security, which has enjoyed large infusions of new resources, including an important emphasis on stronger ICT capacities and cybersecurity (Henrich and Link 2003; Strickland and Hunt 2005; Roy 2005c).

The issue of resource availability (one of the three main challenges of integrated service delivery highlighted at the outset of this chapter, along with cross-organizational cultural barriers and partnerships) is directly tied to influence and the extent to which financial investments in digital technologies and the necessarily related organizational changes are viewed as priorities worthy of attention by elected officials balancing priorities ranging from health care to homeland security, education, social services, and many others. Indeed, the sorts of enterprise-wide issues facing the most senior CIOs in governments do not take away from the existence of separate departmental equivalent CIOs with responsibilities for the technological betterment of their particular units. It is for this reason that e-government's service delivery dimensions are a multilevel reality, extending across both individual services provided by separate agencies and more integrated systems on a government-wide basis.

As complexity rises, the necessary degrees of engagement and support required by senior managers and elected officials rise as well, tied to a technological architecture that must also be increasingly political and strategic in terms of both project management processes and the broader alignment of such processes with objectives, resources, and results on a government-wide scale. The absence of such 'buy-in' from the top has been one of the most common causes of mismanagement in terms of underperformance and cost overruns with respect to putting in place the information systems and digital tools necessary to achieve the sorts of transformations hoped for (Langford and Roy 2005).

Culbertson (2004) summarizes the resulting scenarios for the sort of CIO function required in the public sector due to the advent of e-government as a spectrum of options ranging from 'cheerleader' and 'collaborator' on one end to 'controller' and 'commander' on the other. The former end of this spectrum implies a weak central authority in terms of formalized powers but one engaged in the pursuit of negotiated means with departments and agencies to achieve collective aims. Conversely, the latter options reflect a more centralized model of controlling resources and decision-making aimed at achieving interoperability and government-wide readiness and capacities.

The resulting need for a 'federated architecture' is often invoked as a compromising balance along such a continuum, with the precise location of any government reflective of its organizational history, its current political and managerial objectives (particularly within an identified set of e-government commitments), as well as the geographic and demographic environments shaping the size and complexity of the overall government architecture. While there is no definitive recipe for an optimal model, early e-government experiences underscore a broad shift toward stronger CIO models in most public sector jurisdictions due to the rising strategic importance of digital technologies for management and governance (Culbertson 2004).[13]

1.4 Partnering and Shared Services

One of the early studies on integrated service delivery strategies in Canada puts forth the following three challenges and three success factors (ICCS 2003). In terms of challenges, differences in organizational cultures, partnerships, and resources are identified; for critical success factors, leadership, governance, accountability, and partnerships are underlined as most important. Given the level of interorganizational and intra-organizational linkages at play in achieving service transformations, it is appropriate that partnerships be identified in both sets. Partnerships, particularly those tied to information technology and new capacities for more online and integrated forms of service delivery, are becoming increasingly commonplace in many jurisdictions.

The current agendas of governments around the world call for efforts to better communicate and provide information online and ultimately to transact with citizens and stakeholders in a similar manner. In this more citizen-centric environment, governments must restructure and retool the public service accordingly.

This transition often requires purchasing goods, services, and solutions from external specialists in the private sector and, at times, collaborating with private or civic sector organizations to better design decision-making and service delivery processes. To deliver services online effectively and efficiently, a technically secure and client-friendly infrastructure is necessary, and the need to create and/or upgrade infrastructure requirements for e-government often intensifies the pressure to look outside government for ideas, systems, and solutions.

The degree to which an appropriate set of competencies should be fostered in-house, within public departments and agencies, as opposed to being leveraged externally through an external agent, is complex and often contentious. Considerations ranging from performance objectives, costs, risks, ideologies, and labour relations can all exert influence. The following continuum is a useful portrait of the resulting trend away from static forms of contracting and toward more partnering:[14]

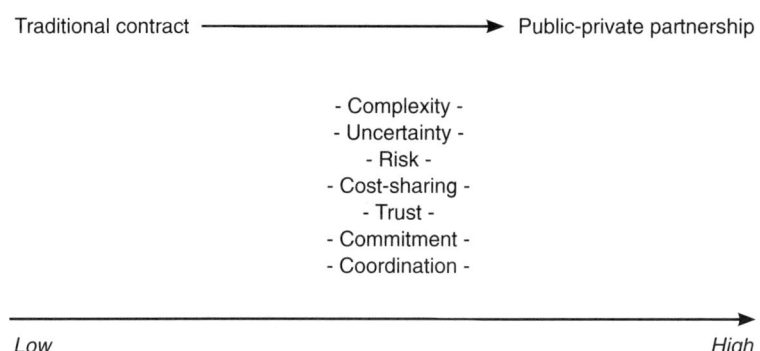

Partnering, then, means moving away from a traditional focus on contracting and toward arrangements that are both more complex and collaborative. This shift is not easy since the traditional focus of government procurement is to ensure fairness and transparency in both determining the public interest and providing accessibility for all potential suppliers: purchasing, not partnering, is the aim. The differences may be subtle in terms of words, but the consequences of this contrast are far reaching: "Partners respond to a need in a changing world by sharing control in the context of an assertive relationship to offer a future that facilitates innovation.... Contractors respond to a request in a ... world of deliverables" (Jelich et al. 2000, 52).

Similar confusion clouds differences and similarities between partnering and outsourcing. Outsourcing implies a transfer of assets from one organization to an external provider — a specialist — often through largely contractual measures. Yet to outsource implies that a function is not at the core of the organizational mission: a bank, for instance, transfers the management of its payroll services to a specialized company with stronger abilities in this service area. The problem with respect to e-government is that digital technology becomes a strategic rather than supportive lever in the broader transformation of organizations to improve performance (Corbett and Roy 2003).

As a result, both industry and government have altered their perspectives on outsourcing in manners that intensify the need for partnering (and perhaps render the boundary between these two approaches a bit more fluid than in the past). For governments, now engaged in efforts to become more client-centric through service transformation strategies that revolve around the use of multiple channels of communication and delivery (e.g., Internet, telephone, in person, etc.), a holistic outsourcing approach for technology becomes unrealistic.

With the role of technology central to the organization's ability to perform, it becomes imperative to retain at least a minimal set of competencies and some degree of in-house control. Still, it remains unrealistic for governments to be able to claim sufficient expertise and resources to completely internalize all capacities — and, as such, an important role for the private sector remains. While the outsourcing of specified support functions may continue in some respects, the growing integration of technology and organizational governance more generally creates greater pressures for collaboration, where both sectors contribute to the co-management of the changes and transformations required (Corbett and Roy 2003).

The evolution of the private sector is revealing in this regard. IBM views itself increasingly as a consulting company and a provider of solutions (disengaging itself from many of its previous production functions), EDS speaks of co-sourcing, and Accenture Consulting points to 'business process outsourcing,' an approach that embeds some level of functional outsourcing within the confines of a more ambitious and jointly managed set of organizational mechanisms to achieve a common set of objectives in a collaborative manner.

The ongoing example of the San Diego County government is a good illustration of the manner in which e-government has shifted the parameters of relational governance from a more simplistic 'outsourcing transfer' to the current emphasis on collaboration and interdependence. In 1999, the county government embarked upon what was then the most comprehensive experiment in public sector outsourcing, a move deemed essential in light of the degradation of the internal systems that had taken place: "The county has about 3 million residents, 18,000 employees and $4 billion in revenues per year. Before outsourcing, the county's IT infrastructure was outdated, and the projected cost of upgrades would cost some $100 million. The county's 50-odd departments each had their own IT staff, systems didn't integrate and there was no good communication mechanism. The county thought that outsourcing might be a solution, but a few months earlier, Connecticut had pulled the plug on an outsourcing project, and four or five municipal governments had unsuccessfully tried to outsource" (Hanson 2005, 1). Over the past six years, this closely watched partnership has resulted in a major overhaul of county government capacities for information management and service delivery, and all observers and stakeholders agree that the county is further along today than it would be without its reliance on the private sector.[15] Although significant hurdles were encountered over the course of this agreement, the determination and flexibility of both parties in finding room for common success sustained the relationship.

Notwithstanding this outsourcing initiative, the San Diego government continued to develop a stronger CIO-type presence within the public sector in order to manage both the external relationship with vendors and the internal set of organizational and technical changes required to adapt to the new systems being developed by industry. In other words, the outsourcing instigated a bolstered strategic focus on technology within government, and as San Diego looks beyond the current agreement, which comes to an end in 2006, it is now in a much stronger position to define the sort of management priorities, internal investments, and external partnerships that will shape the next phase of e-government evolution.

For these reasons, the necessity of significantly reforming IT procurement and project management systems (interlinked dimensions of the process of acquiring, deploying, and maintaining new technological systems) is widely viewed across OECD countries as a key issue for e-government, the 'hidden threat' that must be overcome in order to realize any potential and tangible benefits from e-government reforms (OECD 2001). Accordingly, governments have been experimenting with alternative procurement models based less on process controls—notably upfront costs—and more sensitive to outcomes, innovative solutions for achieving them, and shared results between the public and private sectors engaged in the service transformation effort (Langford and Roy 2005). Central to this more collaborative approach is the ability to increase levels of trust between both sectors as well as an increasingly sophisticated set of capacities within government in order to formulate and execute an expanding assortment of partnership arrangements with industry.

Insourcing via Shared Services

Within government, an equally prevalent methodology for upgrading digital systems involves the formation of a 'shared services' entity to provide overall functionality for separate departments and agencies. Such an approach is, in essence, a variant of outsourcing perhaps better defined as insourcing, as the specialized entity remains a public sector body, one with a set of responsibilities transferred from previously separate units. In return, this new entity works with individual departments as 'clients,' defining service-level agreements in much the same manner as a public-private partnership.

For some observers, there is a fine line between shared services and consolidation, and indeed a case can be made that the latter is a large component of the former. The difference driving the shared services movement today in many large organizations (public and private) is the emphasis on both specialized solutions and shared benefits that can be developed through an entity with horizontal coverage for all operational units. Moreover, some organizations distinguish between most administrative services (e.g., payroll, travel, human resources, and the purchasing of static goods) and information technology, placing the latter realm in a separate body.[16]

The arguments against shared services may be politically neutralized from more contentious outsourcing transfers to the private sector, but they are organizationally similar: separate departments and agencies lose operational freedom and managerial autonomy to focus on their own mission and achieve results in the matter most appropriate to their own mandate. Moreover, from the perspective of the shared services provider, there is a risk that such an organization may evolve into a larger, more centralized, and perhaps monopolistic entity unresponsive to or at least less effective than a set of smaller, devolved units within individual departments. For this reason, some advocates of shared services models suggest that the newly-created entity be required to compete for business with other providers, notably those in the private sector.[17]

A variant of this latter approach involves the shared-services provider itself turning to outsourcing arrangements to provide adequate capacities to the rest of government. In fact, whether through a shared-services entity or a CIO-type body, such an approach is becoming more common in the pursuit of e-government, as an internal set of mechanisms and resources is established to foster stronger government-wide capacities. This internal unit turns to partnering arrangements with the private sector in order to fulfill its mission. This type of approach is a notable reversal of past trends in jurisdictions such as the United Kingdom and New Zealand, where this decision to outsource would have devolved to the level of the subunit.

In short, governance patterns are becoming more complex within the public sector through a widening set of horizontal pressures that must coexist with the more traditional vertical structures of traditional government entities. These horizontal pressures can, in turn, involve relationships between different units of government internally, much as they can also comprise a complementing set of relationships with private industry. In such a world, the procurement and partnering functions are being both more strategic and more diffuse across the organizational infrastructure, creating new complexities in terms of ensuring accountability mechanisms that balance performance outcomes and traditional controls. These new governance design challenges are a prominent theme for the duration of this book.

1.5 Conclusion

Despite the differences in styles of industry-government relations characterizing many jurisdictions, there is a substantial degree of convergence around the main objectives and organizational strategies encompassing the move toward e-government globally (although the one important qualifying distinction lies between developed and developing nations, although even here many aims are similar, the underlying settings of technological sophistication, online availability, and the maturity of democratic government vary across these two groups in important ways[18]).

In terms of the most advanced jurisdictions, there have been numerous initiatives undertaken by private sector groups such as Accenture Consulting and international organizations such as the United Nations that rank countries according to various criteria of readiness and performance. Depending on the variables used, the order of countries varies from one report to another, but the cluster of top performers typically includes Canada, the United States, the United Kingdom, Scandinavia, Australia, Singapore, and Japan.

For instance, emphasizing service delivery and customer-centric capacities through online-induced change, an annual review and ranking study produced by Accenture Consulting has changed little over its five issues, with Canada, Singapore, and the United States claiming the top three positions for the third consecutive year in 2004 (followed by Australia, Denmark, Finland, Sweden, France, Netherlands, the United Kingdom, Belgium, and Ireland[19]). The United Nations 2003 "Global Readiness Index on E-Government" offers a different ordering of the top-ten performers based on broader criteria of both public sector infrastructure and broader environmental characteristics of the human and technological settings within which e-government resides (United States, Sweden, Australia, Denmark, United Kingdom, Canada, Norway, Switzerland, Germany, Finland).[20]

The utility of these sorts of ranking schemes may be viewed from two distinct vantage points. On the one hand, they underscore the globalizing context of e-government and the similarities for most countries in terms of adapting to a digital age. Forums such as the OECD have provided valuable learning venues for intergovernmental benchmarking and learning while raising the profile of a broad framework of challenges and priorities that tends to be reasonably portable across member jurisdictions.[21] In part as a response to such portability, companies such as Microsoft have begun to develop initiatives aimed at sharing what previously might have been tacit forms of knowledge with respect to technological solutions among public sector organizations around the world (at least those governments that remain Microsoft clients[22]).

By the same token, while demonstrating the most sophisticated jurisdictions in a relatively general sense, such surveys do little to address the more intricate variations of e-government when one begins to examine more specifically the nexus of organizational and political issues that tends to be quite different from one jurisdiction to the next. The UN "Global Readiness Index" referred to above reports that "there appears to be no one model of e-government development," and the authors of this survey acknowledge the absence of measures of the quality of those products or services provided by governments.

Nonetheless, such forums are useful in providing a lens on the sort of issues and challenges emerging along the e-government path. Their findings—coupled with the material reviewed in this chapter—lead to the following key trends in terms of the public sector's adaptability to the emergence of online and integrated forms of service delivery as one of the defining dimensions of e-government.

- First, e-government is viewed as a growing priority for most governments around the world, with integration of service delivery models serving as the most visible and tangible catalyst for crafting an online dimension to public sector operations.
- This heightened focus on service improvement through online channels is tied to a broader movement toward more citizen-centric governance where processes for information sharing and service transactions are organized less by traditionally separate units and more according to maximum value and convenience for the citizen.
- The corresponding pressures within governments are for more horizontal governance mechanisms to achieve interoperability and collaboration as the basis for government-wide service transformations.
- These transformations rely increasingly on external forms of collaboration with the private sector in particular as technical providers of the digital infrastructure and co-designers of the strategic solutions required to align this infrastructure with other dimensions of governance such as leadership, accountability, and resources.
- The calculus for such strategies in terms of cost and benefit flows has required a shift from myopic and overly optimistic cost reductions in the short-term toward a broader and more long-term approach to multichannel service delivery in line with a citizenry that varies considerably in terms of Internet availability and use.

In one sense, e-government has proven to be a powerful catalyst for a service improvement movement that predates the Internet's mainstream expansion of the past decade. The emphasis on better customer service and managerial improvements tied to gains, both in efficiency and effectiveness has been a familiar theme of public sector reforms for some time. What is new, however, is the heightened sophistication of new technologies that corresponds to a shift in their role from primarily backroom support functions to a strategic source of value creation.

Creating this value is not a straightforward proposition since it can mean significantly overhauling the organizational systems and processes in place. In particular, much of the potential for value lies in fostering government-wide capacities for information sharing and integrative decision-making and processing, a change from the emphasis on departmental autonomy that characterizes both the traditional models of bureaucracy and the more recent tendencies of new public management.

At the same time, delivering services online and in a more integrated fashion may be the most tangible and visible component of e-government as it has evolved across most OECD jurisdictions, but it is hardly the only one. The nexus of technology and public administration extends well beyond the service delivery components of government in terms of what is happening both within the public sector and outside it. Within government, security is a growing imperative that may be viewed as both a requirement of online service delivery and a parallel set of policy and program initiatives that also rely increasingly on digital networks and connectivity. This topic is the focus of the next chapter.

Chapter 2
Security

From one vantage point, the challenge of security as a dimension of e-government and the public sector's digital transformation closely follows that of service. Indeed, one is an enabler of the other since perhaps the largest barrier to a widening acceptance of online channels is the perception of security shortcomings. Because of concerns about technical flaws, privacy, and malicious acts, many segments of the public are apprehensive about providing personal information on the Internet and, by extension, completing transactions or purchases that require payment. The security of the technical architecture underpinning the online service delivery apparatus is therefore paramount. Since September 2001, however, security has been recast in an expansive array of mechanisms and programs aimed at countering terrorism and ensuring public safety. Surveillance, new identification schemes such as biometrics, data-mining and information-sharing are the parameters of this new security prism that relies on many of the technological and organizational attributes of digital and interoperable governance systems as those being created for integrated service delivery. Yet a new political calculus has also emerged, with a rethinking of the balance between privacy of information versus proactive action and intensifying pressures to extend an interoperable digital infrastructure beyond national borders.

Section 2.1 reviews the main challenges and parameters of cybersecurity, an underlying precondition of service delivery. Section 2.2 then examines the central issues of managing privacy and identity in a more virtual world, particularly as perception of risk varies in accordance to circumstance. Section 2.3 considers identity in the expansion of public safety and anti-terrorism, while section 2.4 addresses the transnational dimension of the governance of security. Finally, section 2.5 summarizes the main lessons from this chapter.

2.1 Securing Cyberspace

Since the advent of mainstream Internet use, also the beginnings of the e-government era, security has evolved through three cumulative stages of focus: the technical, the organizational and social, and now the political.

The technical architecture of security mainly has to do with safeguarding online communications and transactions from both inadvertent and intentional threats to reliable operations. Although the potential value of a network multiplies in accordance with an increase in the number of nodes (the former is proportional to the square of the latter, according to Metcalfe's Law), the corollary is that the potential for security breaches also rises in similar proportions (Nugent and Raisinghani 2002).

Such breaches may be viewed from a range of vantage points, including computer infections and cybercrimes: some estimates claim that PC viruses alone translated into roughly $55 billion in damages in 2003, whereas the same estimates from 2002 and 2001 were $20 billion and $13 billion respectively.[1] Although much of this activity involves specific and unrelated problems and threats, there is also the increasing potential for digital interdependence to heighten the stakes for organizations, sectors, and economies as a whole. One analysis of a computer virus known as the Sapphire/Slammer SQL worm revealed a 'virtual worm' that required a mere ten minutes to spread itself worldwide, doubling in size every 8.5 seconds while scanning over 55 million Internet protocol addresses per minute before infecting what is regarded as a low estimate of at least 75,000 victims.[2]

In addition to this malicious targeting of online infrastructures, there are growing assortments of cybercrime where online communication and interaction provide a platform for more specific criminal acts. Indeed, cybercrime estimates on a global basis now surpass $50 billion annually in North America alone, although precise figures are hard to compile and verify since most such occurrences remain unreported — as low as ten percent by one estimate, resulting in a conviction rate of just two percent (Hale 2002). One recent study reported that the FBI now estimates that total costs associated with cybercrimes worldwide exceeded $400 billion (US) in 2004 (McAfee 2005).

In the past, the intricacies behind such issues suffered from a narrow constituency of experts and interested parties — technical specialists doing work in the shadows of mainstream organizational activities. Within governments, such a backroom view of security fit well generally with a similar placement for most aspects of information systems and informatics — a necessary but not particularly strategic part of managerial and governance systems of the organization.

As Internet use has grown, however, so has the realization that, to be effective, many aspects of security must become engrained in both the organizational and the social systems of society. Many instances of security breaches have had less to do with technical design flaws and more to do with behavioural patterns of buyers and surfers engaged in cyberactivities of one sort or another with little understanding of the risks that may be lurking online (Heeks 1999; Hart-Teeter 2003). To underscore this point, one survey undertaken by a UK security organization, PentaSafe, found that two-thirds of commuters at London's Victoria Station were willing to reveal their computer password in return for a ballpoint pen (O'Hara 2004). These sorts of issues not only shape current Internet use but also act as an important barrier to extending the growth of e-commerce, e-government, and online activity generally since the perception of risk and uncertainty in venturing into previously uncharted spaces and channels remains prevalent for those who remain undecided about whether or not a move to cyberspace is necessary or desirable (Bennett and Raab 2003; Bots 2003; Clifford 2004).

For organizations, particularly large entities anxious to reap the benefits of greater connectivity both within and outside their corporate confines, addressing the potential for exposure to security gaps and shortcomings becomes a challenge far beyond ensuring a technically sound infrastructure internally. As a result, the technical dimensions of security must become elevated to a more managerial and strategic plane to design the set of policies and processes able to safeguard the enterprise as much as possible and prepare responses for a range of potential issues. Key findings of Deloitte Touche Tohmatsu's 2003 "Global Security Survey" are illustrative: "There is a lack of clarity on the impact of multiple governance initiatives on information security."[3]

At the same time, the interconnectedness of the Internet transcends any one particular organization, creating a host of shared externalities for all organizations in every sector. Security thus becomes a challenge of managing interdependencies in an increasingly open environment to ensure safety and resilience for both online activities and society as a whole. Security therefore becomes political in several respects—internally, in terms of how government itself functions as a set of interconnected organizations working with a variety of external stakeholder groups, as well as externally, in terms of the role of government in ensuring safety and security more collectively across all sectors within a jurisdiction (and, as discussed more fully below, across jurisdictions).

Such issues are central to the evolution of e-government: first, in terms of the service delivery architecture discussed in the preceding chapter; second, with respect to how governments address the emerging threats of terrorism that increasingly involve online dimensions by both the perpetrators of such activity and the types of proactive and reactive measures that can be deployed by public sector authorities; and third, insofar as governments are operating more generally in an environment where the convergence of pressures for technical interoperability and political and operational interdependency means that no entity or jurisdiction alone can address these issues (Su et al. 2005).

With respect to the nexus between organizational readiness and the surrounding political setting, one of the most complex and contentious issues shaping it is that of personal privacy and identity management. These issues not only arose early on within service transformation efforts but have also been heightened as of late by their applicability to, and centrality within, government-led policy and process changes to improve domestic security and public safety.

2.2 Privacy

Within the framework of new opportunities and risks associated with digital technologies and Internet connectivity, no issue has received more attention than that of privacy, which is tied to ongoing concerns about the handling of personal information. At a basic level, many individuals continue to shun online shopping for fear of releasing confidential details such as credit card information into a virtual gateway with a perceived host of potential, unintended consequences as to how such data can be shared and used. Such unease is largely a marginal element of the broader template of security-related privacy concerns emerging under the rubric of digital governance and e-government. This is so since it reflects a natural evolution of new products and technological processes, with a rather typical trend of early adapters leading the way before mainstream use follows.

The significant growth rates of both Internet use and online services suggest that, while some segments of the population may continue to shy away from online channels (or face barriers associated with the digital divide), clients and citizens in all sectors will be proportionally more likely to move in such directions over time. Banking online offers some support for this view: in 2003, online banking transactions in Canada rose 30.7 percent to 192.1 million transactions (compared with 26.6 million in 1999), whereas telephone banking transactions fell by just under five percent to 87.7 million (both channels trail volumes at electronic banking machines that nonetheless fell 6.2 percent in 2003 to 1.131 billion transactions).[4]

Despite glitches and incidents of varying degrees, Canadians and other nationalities around the world continue to flock toward more online and wireless forms of banking for its value creation of both cost savings and convenience (as well as other factors such as real-time monitoring capacities and a greater ability for self-management). Notwithstanding this growing acceptance of secure online transactions in the financial world, privacy-related concerns remain paramount to the sector's growth prospects via digital channels.

Perhaps more than fears about malicious acts, concerns about privacy and personal information weigh even more heavily on government efforts to deliver services online. This characterization reflects the interaction of technical, organizational, and sociopolitical variables shaping debates about information management and security (themes explored more fully in subsequent chapters). Moreover, government services often differ qualitatively from those of the commercial sphere, with more obligatory relationships resulting in the collection of highly sensitive information across a wide range of entities and functions that collectively comprise 'the public sector.'

There may well be sound reasoning for governments taking a more cautious and gradual approach than their private sector counterparts, much of it security related. The political risks of security breaches in the state settings are often perceived to be far more serious than proportionally similar risks in the private sector context, a comparison most often attributed to the significantly greater personal and sensitive information held by the public sector (Joshi et al. 2002; Holden 2004). This relationship is complex and dependent to a significant degree on the level of trust accorded to the public sector by the citizenry, both directly and in comparison to other organizations such as private firms.

In jurisdictions where trust is politically high, technical solutions are more readily supported, and the organizational changes required for more innovative and integrated forms of service delivery become much more feasible (Kernaghan 2005). The converse is true as well, where lower levels of confidence and trust translate into both organizational resistance and technical cautiousness. For such reasons, it is impossible to separate service delivery capacities of e-government from broader institutional reforms shaping the setting of democratic governance within which such processes occur.[5]

Nonetheless, even within a standardized set of social and political conditions, all governments must address both the perceptions and the realities of privacy within a broader spectrum of information and identity management that is at the core of both better client-centric responsiveness externally and the corresponding need for new forms of coordination internally. There are two interrelated components in doing so: putting in place an infrastructure of reliable interoperability, and ensuring mechanisms for accurate identity and authentication.

In terms of a reliable and interoperable infrastructure internally, a fundamental requirement for more citizen-centric governance is the ability — facilitated by a secure architecture — to both store and share personal information in a virtual manner across previously separate organizational units, separated either by policy function or by geographic boundary. In theory, it becomes possible for an individual or a company to expect (or endorse) that information provided through one public sector gateway (e.g., a service renewal or transaction completion) be readily available across the public sector for any other uses that may arise, be they related or unrelated to the initial encounter.

Perhaps nowhere is there more potential for tangible value creation than in the area of health care, where a workable system of electronically secure and shared individual health records could enable faster and more integrated forms of care for the patient on a scale that could profoundly transform the structure and performance of the health care system (Gath 2004). Indeed, the holy grail of e-health has become the electronic health record, which could provide the basis for revolutionary improvements in information management, patient responsiveness, and service delivery capacities: "An Electronic Health Record (EHR) provides each individual in Canada with a secure and private lifetime record of their key health history and care within the health system. The record is available electronically to authorized health care providers and the individual anywhere, anytime in support of high quality care. The Electronic Health Record Solution is a combination of people, organizational entities, business processes, systems, technology and standards that interact and exchange clinical data to provide high quality and effective healthcare."[6]

In areas such as health care, however, offsetting concerns about technical flaws and security glitches — leading to inappropriate access to personal information — are prevalent and of great sensitivity politically. Accordingly, the public authorities leading the development of this new architecture (the Canada Health Infoway, a nongovernmental foundation accountable to and funded by both federal and provincial governments) have developed a modest road map for any EHR solution in Canada, envisioning a prototype in limited form that could be introduced by 2010. Despite this caution, in public sector areas dependent on large administrative operations (notably health, education, and justice), the introduction of external online mechanisms and new forms of internal digital interoperability is rapidly creating the potential to transform systems, even as the realization of such potential remains dependent on complex and multidimensional reforms (Scholl 2005).

As information management and privacy issues continue to grow in their reliance on a digital infrastructure, three dimensions of computer security can be underscored as central: *confidentiality*, which requires that information be disclosed only to authorized parties at the authorized time and in the appropriate manner; *integrity*, which includes both the trustworthiness of the content and the origin of the information; and *availability*, which refers to the ability to access and use information or resources as desired (adapted from Radl and Chen 2005). Such a model (known as CIA) also demonstrates the interlayering of technical and organizational governance issues through a range of organizational determinants, including the size of the organization, the technology used, staffing and awareness, management commitment, technical competence, and support (ibid.).

2.3 Identity

The issues of identity and authentication are central to this model. Although once again not entirely novel, they are far-reaching in their potential to reshape both the expectations of the citizenry and the performance of government in a digital era. The potential is personified by the integrated offerings of a financial services company grouping together all products and service types available online to one particular client (who, in turn, can access the entire portfolio via a secure online portal — provided that he or she has an appropriate identification number and password).

Governments also maintain multiple points of contact and interactive dealings with single individuals or organizations, and as such they are increasingly keen to explore a similarly integrated approach on a holistic or even partial scale of service and transaction types. While the potential for 'value' creation is real (Kearns 2004), so are the risks associated with an 'identity' tied to more and more information flows that, in turn, must be stored and shared (Joshi et al. 2002; Loukidelis 2004). In a networked world, each mechanism for identity verification leads to another possible breach that can then be used to penetrate a variety of gateways into interconnected systems:

> As more identifiers are linked to one identity, the threat to privacy and data integrity increases, and the security of the data decreases. Absent substantial controls on how this information can be used, shared and stored, there are wildly varying management practises for the same data.... Any party looking to subvert data will seek data or systems at the lowest level of protection and then use the data for authorization to subvert the security surrounding high value users (Digital Government Civic Scenario Workshop Report 2004, 6).

Within such openness and connectedness, a growing problem is that of identity theft: a single identifier (or a small number of them, such as social insurance number, bank card number, and credit card number) is accessed and deployed by someone other than the authentic owner of such information for purposes of acting in that person's name in some manner. Identity theft is a problem that appears to be growing in some proportion to the growth of Internet use generally,[7] making it a particularly serious issue for the evolution of online and integrated services in the public sector (carrying both technical and political ramifications). The correlation between identity theft and more unintended mishaps of information mismanagement on the one hand, and growing Internet use on the other, underscores why such issues are rising in prominence. While these issues are hardly new, since concerns about privacy have permeated discussions about electronic information systems for decades (Burnham 1980; Science Council of Canada 1984; Bennett and Raab 2003), the stakes are rising, not only to the individuals involved in sharing the personal information electronically but also to the economy as a whole insofar as online channels for consuming and transacting are viewed as safe and reliable (OECD 2004). In short, fostering trust is both a private imperative and a matter of public interest if the virtual world is to continually expand in use.

Government efforts to address this public interest matter crystallized internationally in 1998 with the OECD Ministerial Conference on Electronic Commerce (held in Ottawa, Canada). Ministers adopted a "Declaration on Protection of Privacy on Global Networks" that not only reiterated an earlier set of OECD principles from 1981 (in many respects still relevant as a foundation) but also sought to expand these principles into cyberspace through a collective set of measures involving legal protection, industry self-regulation, and public education. In short, "the theme of trust and confidence, and the relevance of privacy protection, was ubiquitous in this conference" (Bennett and Raab 2003, 50).

While this particular forum adopted electronic commerce as its main focus, such matters apply at least in equal measure to emerging government efforts to deliver services online: in fact, this area represents a key commonality and source of collaboration between government and industry in not only devising new regulatory regimes but also developing tools and mechanisms to augment security in online channels of service delivery. Within the broad OECD-led framework, this relative balance between industry and government—in terms of the appropriate level of government enforcement and industry self-regulation—varies considerably across jurisdictions, shaped in large part by the views of the population in terms of their comfort level in sharing information online with private sector and public sector organizations.

Striking a balance between new forms of legal protection (e.g., privacy legislation codifying acceptable conditions for the use of personal information) and self-governance (e.g., public education) involves both the extension and the enforcement of new legal rules on the one hand (typically codified as individual rights and organizational responsibilities in terms of information collecting and use) and a more collective effort to foster a culture of risk management and behavioural adaptiveness on the other hand. Both avenues can lead to a strengthening of trust: in the former case, consumers come to rely on the legal protections accorded to them, while in the latter case overall awareness shapes individual ability and facilitates smarter choices about when and how to share such information in a reasonable manner (Galindo 2002; De Rosa 2003).

Evidence to date suggests that, in the realm of electronic service delivery in both industry and government, a reliance on both sets of measures is necessary due, in large part, to a segmentation of any population into three distinct camps: those highly suspicious about an erosion of personal privacy in a more digital world, those who are indifferent, and those—the largest proportion of more pragmatic individuals—whose views are likely to shift according to experience and circumstance (Bellamy et al. 2005). It is precisely because of the fluidity of this latter group that perceptions of risk have become so central to discussions about information management and privacy in an expanded realm of security measures since September 2001 aimed at preventing terrorism and ensuring public safety.

The parameters of the debate have thus shifted politically but also technologically as digital tools are viewed less as means toward convenience and efficiency (laudable aims but ones flexibly interpreted by many) and more as a matter of potential life and death. As a result, governments have enjoyed notable increases in support to expand their use of digital technologies in ways that prioritize collective safety over individual privacy in a manner that in many countries would have been highly resisted prior to September 2001 (De Rosa 2003; O'Harrow 2004; Roy 2005c).

Thus, many governments have begun exploring bolstered forms of identity management through more technologically sophisticated devices for authentication such as national identification cards and biometrically enabled passports.[8] The former approach, for example, has been adopted by the British government, which plans to introduce such a card by 2008.[9] Hong Kong is currently implementing a new national 'smart card' that would serve as an identity link to all public and private transactions conducted electronically. Italy has adopted a similar path (Torrisi and Mezzanotte 2004). Many other jurisdictions — including Canada and the United States — are currently exploring modified passports that would make use of biometric devices to improve authentication and identity management capacities (Meyers 2003). Radio frequency identification devices (RFID) are viewed as an area of particular interest in developing a more secure infrastructure for commercial transactions, transportation, human mobility and verification schemes (Hodges and McFarlane 2004).

Defenders of such measures point out that terrorist and criminal elements are making effective use of new technologies to conduct their own plans (e.g., the 9/11 hijackers used the Internet to communicate and jointly plan their attacks), and it is therefore both normal and desirable that governments counter in kind. Moreover, for the vast majority of citizens who are law-abiding and well-intentioned, there is a presumed comfort level in having 'nothing to hide'; it is this sentiment — coupled with fear from insecurity — that has reshaped public opinion over the past few years, creating a basis for an expansion of surveillance activity by public sector authorities. Yet some observers worry that this individual willingness to relax privacy in the name of public safety ignores the wider implications of a more digital information architecture based less on individualized human behaviour and more on patterns and profiles emerging from electronic data flows:

> A classic error is repeated endlessly in numerous contexts, and it reveals the depth of the misunderstanding that surrounds surveillance today. The claim is frequently made that if we have done nothing wrong, we have nothing to hide and thus nothing to fear... . The problem is that this is not how things work, especially in the context of surveillance as social sorting, as an aspect of complex assemblage of governance practises. Against the personal claims of individual innocence, surveillance practises are profoundly social, in the sense that persons are clustered into categories, whether potential consumer groups or potential lawbreakers. It is one's often unwitting membership of or association with certain groups that makes all the difference. (Lyon 2004, 140)

Prior to September 2001, such concerns were but a small and limited outgrowth of the widening interest in 'customer relationship management' and personal marketing techniques that often depend on this type of individual clustering and response. More recently, such issues have garnered more interest and attention in light of the expanded security imperative now pursued by governments, and nowhere is this more true than in the United States.

2.4 Safety and Surveillance

Since autumn of 2001, the mindsets of governments in most countries — notably the United States — have been dramatically reframed. The American fixation on homeland security denotes an important new face of e-government in terms of resources and priorities.[10] The United States is not alone: around the world, many governments have been quick to establish new anti-terrorism and homeland security measures that are premised on new or expanded capacities for coordinated information sharing, planning, and responding on a government-wide scale (Henrich and Link 2003; Kim and Lee 2004).

A sophisticated and reliable digital infrastructure is a necessary precursor to such government-wide action — and, as such, interoperability has become a guiding principle in such efforts. Although often viewed in a technical or digital manner (i.e., computers, networks, and databases being able to communicate with one another), in any organizational environment the human and managerial layers to such connectedness are as complex, if not more so (Allen et al. 2001, 2005; Scholl 2005). Moreover, in a public sector environment, with a host of managerial and political boundaries separating units both within and between governments, such complexity is further heightened. Finally, in terms of a holistic or systemic view of security within a jurisdiction such as a country, interoperability across sectors (notably the private sector) also becomes an important element (Dutta and McCrohan 2002). Accordingly, the US strategy for cybersecurity relies heavily on public-private sector cooperation, a priority significantly bolstered over the past few years within the realm of overall homeland security efforts.[11]

Central to cybersecurity efforts but also much of the homeland security apparatus are information flows and identities. With respect to information, the challenge is not generating more of it but rather making sense of it (and creating knowledge as a result[12]). Accordingly, an important tool in homeland security is data-mining, which — much like the term implies — involves digital and virtual trolling through massive amounts of information gathered in raw form and then analyzed for meaningful patterns or events (Chen 2002; Sirmakessis 2004). Cybersecurity and information management systems are thus crucial not only to gathering and processing information but also to safeguarding it against accidental or malicious threats. Even prior to 9/11, concern was growing about the accelerating costs of technical breakdowns from viruses, hackers, and the like. More recently, the problem is viewed as fundamental to national security and public safety as the potential for electronic threats against critical infrastructure components that include information holdings, defence operations, and energy and environmental management systems that all rely increasingly on computer systems and connectivity (Denning 2003).

For public authorities attempting to proactively expand and deploy a digital infrastructure for information management purposes tied to homeland security, there are three overriding factors, each one comprising a partially distinct set of risks, uncertainties, and controversies. The first factor is the significant financial investments now flowing into security efforts — and an expanded digital infrastructure for information analysis, communications, and research and development — and new screening and surveillance systems. Some industry estimates point to homeland security spending levels in the United States to surpass $180 billion by 2008, a figure that includes all levels of government and the private sector (and an amount that nearly equals the total annual budget of the Government of Canada).[13]

Clearly, future spending levels are subject to numerous uncertainties, not the least of which is the occurrence and scale of any future terrorist attacks. Recent and current spending levels have generally received little political opposition in the shadow of 9/11. However, such massive injections of public funds face growing questions about the extent to which managerial, accountability, and oversight capacities are up to the challenge of deploying these resources in a responsible and effective fashion. Therefore, the second and related factor is the size and complexity of the organizational deployment. Difficulties that plague the US Department of Homeland Security are a case in point: the department has been unable to fulfill its role in effectively consolidating and coordinating the formation and use of terrorist watch lists from its various subunits, a deficiency ascribed by department officials to an absence of resources and sufficiently developed infrastructure for doing so.[14]

The third factor — undoubtedly the most politically contentious — is the appropriate scope of security objectives and means to be undertaken by democratically accountable governments. Tensions in the United States between a traditional mindset of limited government and the post-9/11 jump in support for an expansion of state activity are thus central in shaping political debate, particularly in the spring of 2005 as the Patriot Act has undergone a congressional review under the guise of a sunset clause in the initial legislation. Although the spirit of the act appears to remain largely accepted, specific provisions — notably those pertaining to wiretapping, surveillance, and the so-called library clause — have generated scrutiny.[15]

A key issue in such an environment is an absence of sufficient openness by public authorities (Reid 2004). US government watchers claim that, over the past four years in particular, the culture of secrecy has been significantly reinforced at the expense of transparency and public accountability.[16] A related concern is that secrecy is becoming the norm in security matters, due in part to covert activity and in part to the extraordinary level of complexity that permeates an increasingly ubiquitous and invisible infrastructure extending across the realms of both government and commercial activities: "Law enforcement and intelligence services don't need to design their own surveillance systems from scratch. They only have to reach out to the companies that already track us so well, while promising better service, security, efficiency, and perhaps most of all, convenience. It takes less and less effort each year to know what each of us is about.... More than ever before, the details of our lives are no longer our own. They belong to the companies that collect them and the government agencies that demand them in the name of keeping us safe" (O'Harrow 2005, 300).[17]

Such concerns tie together the focus on capacities to gather and make use of information and the concept of individual identity.

They are interdependent because, to learn anything specific about an individual or group of individuals, there must be reliable identifiers. The existence and reliability of such identifiers thus become critical enablers of the functioning of the system as a whole.

For these reasons, the notion of identity is a central tenet of domestic security efforts as well as the digitization of such efforts (Heymann 2002). The most notable example of this trend is the envisioned deployment of biometric tools on passports and travel visas (and in some countries on newly introduced national identification cards[18]). Importantly, biometric devices not only allow national authorities to screen, control, and track visitors entering a particular country but also enable these authorities to monitor the movements of their own citizens abroad. This latter function, however, is predicated on the extension of interoperability on a transnational scale—at the least to ensure that countries partaking of such a network (thereby committing politically) share a basic degree of common infrastructure to make use of these new devices.[19]

This need for a more explicit form of collaboration and connectedness across countries underscores the fluid nature of identity and privacy for individuals as well as challenges to traditional notions of sovereignty and power for nations (Bennett and Raab 2003; Hayden 2005). Whereas recent decades have witnessed attempts to expand an ideology of individual freedom, mobility, and commerce beyond national borders, the present environment also features steps by national governments to curtail human and commercial mobility. Security and mobility thus become co-evolving agendas that carry at least the potential for tension and conflict, notably in the efforts of any one country to configure its border in terms of its own interests as well as its interrelated interests with other countries, particularly those in close geographic proximity (Salter 2004).

2.5 Sovereignty versus Interoperability

The security imperative presents a conundrum for governments in an increasingly global and digital age of interdependence. The increasing mobility of financial, cognitive, and human resources, both within and between countries, means that no government can possibly act sufficiently in isolation to achieve an optimal level of security, particularly online. The expanding technological canvas of shared networks and electronic linkages that serves as the necessary backbone for more collaboration also exposes governments to more pressures and threats than ever before. As the head of e-government strategy for the United States pointed out in 2003, "The Internet connects over 171,000,000 computers and continues to expand at a rapid pace... . Many attacks are fully automated and spread with blinding speed across the entire Internet community."[20]

A central challenge in terms of the role of technology is that within large organizational structures a central perspective on technical and organizational design (such as a CIO) is in place to either centrally impose or coordinate in a more facilitative but still directed manner. For a multinational corporation, for example, strategic design issues focus on coordination and leadership from above while facilitating some necessary and desirable degree of decentralized action and autonomy across a range of functional and geographic units from below. For systems of transnational governance, such architectures do not currently exist, particularly at the centre (global). Such systems are being crafted in a near-chaotic environment of power structures and relational processes with little agreement as to what the underlying purposes, objectives, and directions are or should be. As a result, digital connectivity and cyberactivity could facilitate closer collaboration and harmonization of purpose with respect to security — or they may well heighten dissent and instability.

The former avenue would essentially mean a concerted effort to achieve some form of meaningful interoperability on a global scale (or something near it) to counter terrorist and criminal interests not rooted in national jurisdictions (as well as underpin the expansion of more legitimate forms of market and civic activities). There are clearly resource and capacity issues here that significantly compound the already complex governance challenges facing authorities in each national jurisdiction (both within national government systems and across different levels of government). In sum, the vision and promise of more seamless e-government processes must extend beyond national borders — however fraught with obstacles this path may be.

In Europe, the existing architecture of the European Union means that a continental dimension of interoperability is more established than elsewhere, underpinned by an assortment of political mechanisms — although even here tensions between national sovereignty and continental authority remain prevalent not only in the politically visible and contentious realms such as the proposed constitution but also in more agreed-upon policy areas such as security (Shearman and Sussex 2004). For example, the separate Council of Europe emerged as a leading voice against cybercrime by adopting in 2001 its Cybercrime Convention (covering four main areas of activity: computer hacking, fraud, forbidden content, and copyright infringement). Since that time, the European Union itself has developed a robust online presence — albeit one less focused on transaction services (largely the domain of national and subnational governments) and more centred on providing information, promoting awareness and citizenship, and mobilizing interest in the democratic institutions of the European Union (notably the Parliament), as well as key issues of the day (e.g., the proposed European constitution).[21]

In North America, the aggressive and intense pursuit of homeland security in the United States has triggered an expanded focus on border management and related issues that underscore the growing interconnectedness of authorities in both Canada and the United States. For example, a new Canadian passport is rumoured to be under development, featuring biometric forms of personal identification with standards, specifications, and policies forged at a North American level. Such movements suggest that over time e-government could evolve from a solely domestic project to one intertwined with continental governance (for the purposes of this book, an examination of this potential extension is deferred until Part Three, reflecting the primary focus on existing e-government efforts that situate themselves within domestic polities; however, the Canadian domestic security apparatus is a key topic of Chapter 5, a discussion that includes consideration of how continental agendas and Canada-US relations are shaping Canadian action).

2.6 Conclusion

With respect to the technological and organizational dimensions of more digitally-enabled governance systems, there is much common ground across service transformation strategies and those of domestic security and public safety. The CIA model (confidentiality, integrity, availability) of computer security underpins both initiatives, much as both are threatened by an increasingly sophisticated set of malicious actions outside government, as well as the more mundane but equally consequential potential for error. Similarly, the level of organizational readiness required to achieve more citizen-centric governance processes includes changes and challenges that extend across both dimensions of e-government—namely, fostering more horizontal or government-wide capacities (interoperability) to share information and undertake more integrated forms of action (to provide either better service or increased protection and enforcement).

In terms of differences, one distinguishing feature is the style of change that has been adopted across service- and security-related transformation. While the former was by and large predicated on attempting to facilitate collaboration to achieve value for all stakeholders (inside and outside government), the latter has been much more centrally imposed through vertical integration and strong political visibility. This characterization of security undoubtedly stems from the crisis-driven mentality of such operations over the past few years versus the more opportunity-identification approach of integrated services predating the terrorist attacks of 2001.

Nonetheless, how governments choose to proceed with respect to e-government will depend significantly on how these differences are both recognized and managed. Does the overriding security imperative simply marginalize service integration in terms of resources and attention (and technology spending in particular)? Will there be separate CIO structures within the public service for service and security—despite their commonalities in terms of a focus on enterprise-wide architectural issues? Finally, will the styles and cultures of governments be able to accommodate effectively the different objectives and meanings to citizen-centric processes represented by service and security?

This last question points to a final distinguishing feature between these first two e-government dimensions: the relative degree of openness and transparency accorded to each one. Service transformation initiatives have largely been undertaken with a strong recognition of the need to both engage key stakeholders (e.g., industry partners and the public as the customer in particular) and foster a new and more collaborative mentality both within and outside government.

In contrast, homeland security begins from a dramatically different point of departure where the organizational and political ethos is information containment and secrecy. Indeed, it is arguable that this emphasis is more in keeping with Westminster traditions of parliamentary governance that limit openness and access to information. The recently heightened, terrorist-driven set of security measures creates the potential for a cultural clash both politically and organizationally for government—between the Internet persona of openness and transparency that translates into greater degrees of information sharing and a lessened tolerance of secrecy and the traditional and contemporary practices of more shielded security processes. These interrelated elements of e-government—transparency, complexity, and accountability—are the major themes of Chapter 3.

Chapter 3
Transparency

These first two dimensions, service and security, are primarily concerned with how governments are reorganizing themselves internally to adapt to new opportunities and threats in the external environment. In contrast, transparency and trust speak to changes rooted less in the internal structures of government and more in the evolving democratic environment within which governments operate — as the Internet has facilitated the creation of new channels of political mobilization and interaction between citizens and their governments. A fundamental challenge resulting is a clash of cultures between the expectations of an increasingly open and online society and the traditions of hierarchy and control that permeate public sector structures. Trends such as open source software and blogging are indicative of a widening scope of new forms of participation and mobilization that are creating stronger pressures for governments to adapt not only their internal governance but also the institutions of democracy that shape the roles and relationships among politicians, public servants, and the public. Yet, despite such pressures, governments may also resist change since "the culture of secrecy is deeply engrained" (Reid 2004, 82). The durability of such resistance — and ultimately the adaptability of government itself — are interwoven with the notion of trust discussed in Chapter 4.

This chapter begins with a consideration of the importance of transparency to democratic governance. Section 3.2 examines the open source software movement as both an element of e-government and a reflection of broader changes to the governance culture extending across the marketplace and society as a whole. Section 3.3 then explores the evolving nature of freedom of information in the public sector and how various governments are either experimenting with new capacities for openness and information-sharing or resisting with efforts to contain and control information flows. The nexus between secrecy and complexity is the focus of section 3.4, which asks whether or not the foundational principles of democratic organization accurately and transparently depict the governance requirements of today's realities such as those examined in the preceding chapters. Section 3.5 concludes this chapter with a gateway into the subsequent discussion of trust.

3.1 Why Transparency Matters

Although there has never been a single standardized definition of what it means for the public sector to be transparent, a useful starting point is to equate transparency with some degree of openness to those with either a right or an expectation of being able to examine and understand the activities of government. Accordingly, there is a close relationship between transparency and accountability since one is arguably a prerequisite for the other.

Yet, with regard to transparency as openness, a number of questions present themselves in terms of the degree of openness that is both desirable and feasible within the modern-day operations of large and sophisticated organizations. There are questions about the relative importance of process considerations versus performance outcomes as well as critical sequential questions about when any such openness should occur (i.e., before decisions are made and policies are formulated or after in reporting on results). Thus, although the objective of transparency as a staple of democratic governance is a given, there is much fluidity concerning its applicability and use as a guiding principle of political and managerial processes.

The emergence of e-government as an overriding agenda for the public sector in nearly all parts of the world has sparked an unparalleled sense of optimism that greater levels of government transparency are both attainable in and beneficial to society as a whole. This point is particularly relevant to the developing world, castigated for its absence of openness, which in turn limits accountability and breeds corruption. Reversing this mix through e-government is now firmly on the agendas of less developed countries and the institutions and agencies seeking to assist them in undertaking the requisite reforms for bettering governance: "To the extent that increased transparency, accountability and predictability (of rules and procedures) are made priorities, e-government can be a weapon against corruption" (Pacific Council on International Policy 2002, 10).[1]

Yet the mere existence of an online government apparatus in a jurisdiction plagued by corruption would do little if unaccompanied by a cohesive and far-reaching set of reforms, including — but not necessarily limited to — the sorts of information provided by the government and when, whether the citizenry and other stakeholders have access to the information (online or elsewhere), and the rules and processes governing their activities in making use of such information to influence government action and behaviour. Transparency, therefore, involves much more than the delivery of information online, and this point applies in equal measure to both developing and developed countries and the jurisdictions within them (Zinnbauer 2004).

The Internet matters, however, insofar as it presents itself as a new form of cognitive and associational infrastructure and the shaping of behavioural patterns within it, both individually and organizationally. From this perspective, individuals are empowered by the Internet with more information and knowledge than previously attainable, and the result is an altering set of viewpoints on authority and power (Courchene 2005). One specific shift is a lessening of tolerance for secrecy as individuals and new forms of associational movements mobilize around specific issues and interests. The rise of 'transparency networks' is one such example of this mobilization and the potentially destabilizing impacts for organizations that were previously able to contain information flows: "The information flow is also evasive—rendering information monopolies and opaque environments ineffective and transparent. Corporations, governments and industries have spent decades erecting barriers to information flow into and out of their various organizations (Stiglitz 2001).... The advent of the transparency network renders such control and management techniques ineffective" (Dwyer 2004, 119). Importantly, such networks are seen to operate, at least initially, outside the contours of democratic institutions, and the extent to which their role is welcome and utilized within these institutions depends on a major set of cultural and structural reforms that can lead to a more "inclusive government" (ibid.). The point to underline here is that information availability and changing patterns of social and political mobilization outside government will invariably create pressures for altering processes within it—and it is arguably this interface between the internal and external environments that represents the core of both the traditional importance and the changing shape of transparency in the public sector.

Here lies the basis of a major foundational shift under way for democratic governance. A world of information scarcity is one that bolsters bureaucratic power and organizational secrecy, much as a democracy of scarce information and limited and highly varying levels of knowledge and education among the citizenry tends to reinforce these characteristics of what becomes an indirect, technocratic form of ruling elite. Pressures for more openness are limited and easily repressed. In a world of digital communications and widening networks of social and political interests (both online and offline), governments face rising pressures to adapt to a much more fluid and dynamic informational environment—one that is far less conducive to secrecy (Roy 2005).

Nonetheless, change from within faces many hurdles. The reliance on secrecy in Westminster models of governance, for instance, begins at the apex of power, where the cabinet meets in the closed confines of a forum designed to contain information and shield intrusion as much as possible. The purpose of this secrecy has not remained constant, however. Originally, secrecy was viewed as a means to ensure a relatively free and open form of deliberation among ministers (albeit within limited and closed confines) in order to generate consensus on actions and policies that, in turn, would be presented to Parliament for further debate and, ideally, legislative passage (often in modified form). Indeed, matters of confidence aside, there was often an expectation within the government that parliamentary discussions would likely lead to a revisiting and reformation of specific ideas (Barber 1991). A decision would likely not result until this subsequent discursive level had been applied. At the same time, the public's role was highly removed from these arenas since the legislature acted as an indirect proxy for both their presence and their views.

In more recent times, cabinet secrecy has become less about open deliberation between ministers and more about leveraging such secrecy to define policies and communicate decisions not just to Parliament but also to the public via more direct means (facilitated by digital communications such as radio, television, and now the Internet). As Parliament's discursive role has become increasingly circumvented, the scope of secrecy has both intensified in the centre of power (i.e., the Prime Minister's Office and supporting central agencies) and expanded to encompass much of the executive branch of government—notably the public service. As a result, cabinet secrecy has become much more pervasive and defensive in purpose, while the costs of maintaining such protections increase.

Over the past half century, two somewhat diverging trends have shaped information flows and degrees of openness between the executive and legislative branches in such settings.[2] On the one hand, transparency has been continuously limited by the dominance of the executive branch in terms of both political control and the growing levels of complexity within a sprawling public sector reporting directly to central agencies and ministers. Accordingly, less and less useful information has flowed to Parliament in a timely manner, rendering this latter institution less effective in exercising its oversight and challenge functions.[3]

On the other hand, and partly as a result of this trend, a number of alternative mechanisms have been deployed—in particular an array of parliamentary officers (e.g., auditors and commissioners)—to report on specific issues of public concern directly to the public (thereby generating some additional level of transparency that would not otherwise have been present). In a manner indicative of a trend that is accelerated by the Internet's expansionist abilities with respect to informational flows, these officers of Parliament often appear to be much less interested in working with or reporting to Parliament itself and are more focused on engaging the public, either directly or indirectly, particularly through the media.[4]

Thus, for an auditor general or a privacy commissioner—while it may be both expected and welcomed that the findings will reach parliamentary chambers—the more central communicative outlet for his or her operations is the media in order to directly report findings to the public (facilitated increasingly by online channels of dissemination). Importantly, this type of communication is a specific form of transparency characterized in two important ways: it is both inherently adversarial and responsive (after the fact).

The result is that the citizenry invariably knows more about what governments are doing—after they have already done it. The focus of such coverage and reporting is on the most controversial, contentious, and corrupt dimensions of public sector operations, fuelling an inherently confrontational culture within which information is primarily a weapon of blame and gain to be assigned by a political contest taking place partly within Parliaments themselves but increasingly among the citizenry.

Although this more informational and visible style of politics takes place across an expanding and in some respects more transparent arena, the citizenry by and large remains relegated to the role of spectator—

with the exception of voting when called upon to do so. In such a manner, it is arguable that frustration, unease, and apathy are likely to be accelerated in two ways: first, by the information generated and shared via adversarial political and media forums; second, by a sense of powerlessness in being able to directly influence government action that is most often reported in terms of corruption, mismanagement, or contention.

It is this sense of powerlessness that represents the greatest source of friction between the perceptions, expectations, and to some degree changing realities of an online, digital world and the traditions of a representative, indirect political culture and an inward, hierarchical set of organizational structures aligned with it. The result, even for those governments leading the world in online service delivery, is a profoundly defensive ethos where information control and communication are most often used as shields against the forces of transparency perceived to be threatening or disruptive. In short, as noted above, "the culture of secrecy is deeply engrained."

3.2 Open Source Software

In many respects, there are similarities between strains on the traditional organizing ethos of government and the challenges confronting traditional private sector approaches to computer software design and deployment. The emergence of an open source software movement is illustrative of an inherent belief in openness as a defining governance principle: a community of software design experts shunning secrecy in favour of openness and sharing. Within this camp, the aim is the formation of a community of commerce where incremental innovations are encouraged by an open and accessible network of expertise and information-sharing that facilitates broad participation and transforms many software elements into commodities as opposed to specialized, proprietary systems—lessening the risk of supplier dependence and lowering the overall cost of ownership (Koch 2003). Indeed, the momentum toward open source software is more profound than merely an alternative technology solution. It denotes a fundamentally different governance philosophy than the proprietary and secretive natures of traditional market processes that have by and large underpinned the expansion of computer systems and online activities.

Much has been written about how the open source movement is highly participative and collaborative on a nearly limitless global scale due to the Internet itself. Indeed, the Internet owes its creation to a limited form of open source software that emerged in the 1960s within the confines of government networks that relied on a transmission protocol open to all those public sector entities interconnected in what might now be viewed as an intranet (Rosenberg 2000).

While the mainstream expansion of the Internet would occur mainly on commercialized operating systems, the present incarnation of open source software represents what essentially amounts to a free distribution of software that can serve as an alternative form of operating system for digital networks and systems. Much more important than this free access, however, is the fact that the underlying code for the system itself is also fully available to individuals and organizations (thus the term 'open source'). Organizations can therefore adapt the code to meet the specific needs of both their digital infrastructures and their performance objectives.

Such a contrast does not imply, however, that the open source concept is either inherently uncompetitive or unprofitable in orientation (a common misperception stemming partly from the novelty of open source activity and partly from radical elements of the open source community that did view its initial formation through either an anti-capitalist or a libertarian lens). Instead, the open source community aims to transform the ethos of the commercial world:

> The basic idea behind open source is very simple: When programmers can read, redistribute, and modify the source code for a piece of software, the software evolves. People improve it, people adapt it, people fix bugs. And this can happen at a speed that, if one is used to the slow pace of conventional software development, seems astonishing.
>
> We in the open source community have learned that this rapid evolutionary process produces better software than the traditional closed model, in which only a very few programmers can see the source and everybody else must blindly use an opaque block of bits. Open Source Initiative exists to make this case to the commercial world.[5]

While the basic software is mainly free for all (there are some licensing restrictions), implementing open source systems and solutions still requires products and services to make use of this platform (for the most part, though, such products and services are nonproprietary). Indeed, open source software has become engrained in the marketplace of today's digital infrastructure:

- Operating systems: Servers operating on open source accounted for a 16 per cent share of the market in 2003, which is expected to grow to 30 per cent by 2008;
- Applications: By one estimate (SourceForge 2004), there are 80,000 known applications developed and deployed by using open source;
- Objects: There are at least 70,000 open source components available on the Internet for download such that smart developers can create new applications faster and cheaper. (Center for Digital Government 2004, 3)

The existence of an openly accessible community of developers around the world dramatically heightens the pace of innovation that can occur, a point that not only means a greater potential for new ideas but also a much quicker debugging and securing of existing components. Proponents of open source routinely cite its greater resilience to malicious codes, hacking, and the sorts of errors that often hamper traditional proprietary products and solutions. Indeed, today the US Department of Defense deploys open source systems for encryption, firewalls, and e-mail list management (ibid.).

The most common forms of open source technology are 'Linux' systems, so named after Linus Torvalds, a Finnish entrepreneur who founded an alternative operating system on open source principles in the early 1990s that would challenge the more recognized and proprietary Unix version. Linux systems are proving to be widely attractive in the public sector due not only to security but also to the substantially lower acquisition costs and the promise of continually renewed programs and tools via the open community. At the same time, however, doing so requires the ability to use open source offerings and adapt existing systems to new realities. For many large organizations, including many public sector bodies, this reliance on large-scale 'legacy' systems means greater costs and uncertainty in any move to open source.

The founder of Intel, Andy Grove, has thus called open source a power inflection point that marks a fundamental transformation in the accepted business model. Does open source represent a similarly important shift for the public sector? Any response to that question is bound to be contentious, reflecting an ongoing coexistence between tradition and innovation. Change must also be considered at two somewhat distinct levels. First, government organizations — in an era of e-government — face a set of pressures and constraints similar to those of companies in their quest to improve performance, and so many of the virtues of open source are of interest. Yet the transition is complex, dependent on both government's human and technical capacities and its relational abilities to work effectively with private sector specialists making use of open source platforms and applications.

In short, the managerial implications of open source are an increasingly important dimension of the architecture of e-government, as is the ability of public sector bodies to strategically determine when, where, and to what extent open source makes sense (all the while under tremendous pressure by existing proprietary suppliers to upgrade current systems rather than make a leap of faith into something new).

A second level of change, however, involves the nature of decision-making adopted by the open source movement as a potentially more empowered and democratic form of decision-making that could also finds its place in the political sphere (of the public sector). In this view, open source is thus both a precursor of and a proxy for more open government. The collaborative pressures challenging the more traditional corporate confines of Microsoft and other market entities reflect widening pressures for broader and more open and participative forms of governance in a manner akin to the notion of transparency networks described earlier in this chapter. As a result, companies such as Microsoft are also adapting to these new realities — aggressively championing the benefits of a solid and reliable technology partner while also creating new mechanisms to share limited portions of its own source code with customers and the software development community.[6]

Skeptical of corporate power and proprietary control of a technological infrastructure viewed as transcending traditional notions of private property, open source activists in the marketplace are akin in some respects to activists in civil society dissatisfied with traditional governmental processes, thereby questioning legitimacy. This decline of deference to traditional power structures is a movement clearly accelerated by an information and knowledge age—preceding but in many respects highly complementing the Internet's digital dimension of this socio-economic and political evolution (Cherney 2000; Surowiecki 2004).

Accordingly, within the parameters of a networked world conducive to the more collaborative and transparent infrastructure of open source software, the implications for organizational and political processes are more far reaching, resulting in new informational demands and requirements both within and outside government. The coexistence of and competition between open source and proprietary solutions will continue for some time, a reflection of ongoing tensions between radical and incremental change that builds on the status quo.

Such tension is also quite evident in terms of how the public sector manages its information in a world characterized by increasing demands for transparency. Akin to the source code of the software world is the apparatus of cabinet-based government in parliamentary models where secrecy reigns in principle but not without a growing number of political, legal, and media-based challenges to its sustainability as a model of information containment. Indeed, growing pressures both inside and outside government for a rethinking of the role and governance of information management reflect the advent and pervasiveness of transparency networks and information in flows in an environment far removed from that which conceived the conventions of secrecy.

3.3 Information Management

Existing freedom-of-information policy frameworks now common throughout the developed world are indicative of both the challenge and the potential of information management. On the one hand, governments have recognized (often prodded by public opinion) and enshrined the importance of some level of openness as a foundation for democratic governance—a sentiment solidified by a decision of the Supreme Court of Canada in 1997: "The overarching purpose of access to information legislation... is to facilitate democracy. It does so in two related ways. It helps to ensure, first, that citizens have the information required to participate meaningfully in the democratic process and secondly, that politicians and bureaucrats remain accountable to the citizenry" (Reid 2004, 80). That said, the pursuit of this ideal has a place within the 'culture of secrecy' that has developed over decades of cumulative efforts to either resist or pay little attention to notions of openness (ibid.). Indeed, the ongoing experiences of access-to-information frameworks are indicative of the tentative and cautious paths chosen by many governments as a result of such pressures. Whereas 2005 will mark the first-ever access-to-information law to come into full force in Germany, unease stems from large security-related exemptions to information-sharing requirements and a fear that the organizational mechanisms of government in place to respond to such requests will face unworkable demands in attempting to determine what information can be available or to justify limits relating to security or other matters deemed inappropriate for release.[7]

A key issue here is the perception that access to information is a threat to government and that, as a result, every request for government information must be treated with care (Roberts 2005). Moreover, the very existence of such requests—and the system for processing them—are indicative of just how little information is made available on a regular basis by government organizations—in terms of internal operations such as policy development processes, internal research and analysis, minutes from committee meetings, and so on. This latter characterization may appear odd and out of sorts with tremendous quantities of information made available online by governments around the world. The challenge—common to any organization or institution but becoming increasingly complex due to the size of the public sector and the sheer volumes of paper and electronic resources produced during any given day or month—is the more daunting task of being able to identify accurate and relevant information when called upon.

In an institutional environment predicated on suspicion of scrutiny and exposure, the result is an immensely complex and costly apparatus to manage the interface between external requesters and internal holders and providers of information—one becoming ever more unsustainable as multiplying electronic channels of communication and data generation overlap with traditional paper-based files and archives.[8] Moreover, current systems are often not catering effectively to the typical citizen since the technical and organizational complexities of both the information production processes and the requests themselves require a level of sophistication and resources beyond the casual observer.[9]

A result of this high cost of participation is an increasingly intense media-centric system that further reinforces the secretive, defensive, and adversarial nature of current freedom-of-information policies:

> At the same time, the increasingly critical and adversarial attitude toward government is bound to have an adverse effect on the willingness of governments and bureaucrats to disclose information because of the apprehensions about the political repercussions of disclosure in a climate where information will be mostly used to fuel attacks on the political and bureaucratic processes. The difficulties of operating transparently in a political environment of distrust and criticism will be further exacerbated if the media and opposition politicians appear to use access-to-information provisions mainly as a tool to search for potentially damaging information that can be used to publicly embarrass the government of the day.[10]

The advent of mainstream Internet adoption and e-government agendas brings about at least the potential for envisioning an alternative approach—one more readily axed on proactively and routinely disseminating information before any such request is made (ibid.). While exceptions can be maintained where warranted (though ideally within reduced and well-articulated boundaries), this type of cultural shift would represent a major increase in the availability of more tacit forms of information (i.e., those otherwise and often currently regarded as privy to internal processes and not appropriate for public consumption). Such an approach would be less costly, more manageable, and more consistent with the very contours of the information age that government leaders regularly espouse as laudable.

While one major challenge is clearly political direction, the technical and organizational requirements of such a change are also highly complex. What becomes essential to any such system being workable is a coherent, responsive, and reliable set of policies and mechanisms for recording, storing, archiving, and sharing (when appropriate) information resources. The list of requirements for an information management system axed on openness rather than secrecy is long:

- a reward system that encourages a culture of openness, collaboration, and trust;
- policies, procedures, and standards implemented and updated on a regular basis;
- across all levels of government, harmonization of information management policies, standards, and practices, including those associated with access-to-information and privacy legislation;
- government information resources that are clearly identified, documented, and navigable based on standard approaches to the development of directories and/or databases and the use of controlled vocabularies and naming conventions;
- an information management infrastructure ensuring that considerations of access are built into the government's business processes and related applications that address both internal and external access requirements;
- a technology infrastructure that addresses the diverse access needs of the Canadian public and supports multiple mechanisms to deliver information in response to its requests (e.g., Internet, fax, telephone, etc.);
- a workforce that understands the potential value of information from an 'access' perspective and is trained with the appropriate skills to implement information management practices to manage information throughout its life cycle, thereby providing better access; and
- specialists who provide coaching and training in information management to government institutions.[11]

The challenge is compounded by the archaic and uninteresting perceptions that surround much of the information management infrastructure (e.g., records management and archives) in government — a situation that, according to Canada's information commissioner, has led to information management "almost becoming an oxymoron" (Reid 2004, 83). Despite such justifiable concern, a counterview is emerging about the potential for more electronic and digital forms of 'routine disclosure and active dissemination' that could prove more technologically and socially aligned with the spirit of e-government (Mitchinson and Ratner 2004).

Indeed, there is evidence that governments are beginning to make use of greater opportunities to both share information and link this sharing to the requests of citizens. The City of Vienna, Austria, for example, has established a Citizen's Request Management System that now processes more than 4,000 cases per month: each case is initiated by a citizen's request, and the responsiveness to any such request and the tracking of it are accessible to both employees of the government and the citizen requesting the action. Although the primary emphasis is service-oriented — not unlike the '311' movement in North America[12] — Vienna's system is also used to engage citizens in consultations on a variety of policy issues before elected officials (as well as a means to initiate a discussion of issues not currently on the political agenda).[13]

Similarly, many jurisdictions, such as the County of North Jutland in Denmark, are fostering online platforms for political awareness and discussion that link the public and formal political institutions and promote greater transparency in the decision-making process.[14] More recent converts to democratic governance such as the Baltic nation of Estonia are adopting such mechanisms to foster more open dialogue and shared understanding between the government, civil society, and industry.[15] Similarly, the Internet can facilitate wider and more direct forms of performance reporting — providing information directly to the citizenry that, in turn, becomes the basis of public education and engagement.[16]

The potential for this latter claim, however, is highly uncertain due to the pervading culture of communications that is more consistent with efforts to contain, control, and shape information rather than share it in an open fashion. Accordingly, online channels may well be viewed primarily by governments in power as new and necessary tools to convey a message and the most positive 'spin' as possible on government operations and decisions. Such is the 'contradiction in reform' unfolding in the United Kingdom, where the Blair Labour government is credited with both introducing the country's first comprehensive access-to-information law (which has come into application in 2005) and fostering the most sophisticated communications and media relations apparatus in the history of the UK public sector (Roberts 2005).

While this latter characterization may reflect to some degree the mentality of the British prime minister and his political operatives, historical comparisons are nonetheless made difficult due to the evolution of the political and media environments over time (an evolution that has augmented the tensions between the insular traditions of Westminster actors — notably the prime minister, cabinet, and central agencies — and the increasingly open and networked era of multiplying sources and flows of information and opinion).

The emergence of weblogs is a case in point. As they catch on, they capture more attention. *Time* magazine declared 2004 "The Year of the Blog" (due in part to its significance at the American presidential nomination conventions). New blogs are continually being created: one recent survey suggests that perhaps as many as 8 million Americans have one, catering to the more than 30 million online readers in the United States alone. In essence, a blog is an online platform for publishing, communicating, and discussing that allows 'bloggers' to have their say on any given issue or theme deemed worthy of attention. More recently, 'vloggers' have been added to this virtual spectrum, bringing a video dimension that may offer content ranging from a corporate focus (Microsoft operates a vlog for software designers, attracting 900,000 viewers a month, according to *BusinessWeek*) to the provocative and absurd.

The growth of blogs and vlogs is in many ways akin to the open source software movement. Aided by expanding broadband, individuals can network more freely, join groups of like-minded members, and express themselves in innovative and uninhibited ways: blogging is thus viewed by many as a grassroots orientation, often with the aim of circumventing mainstream traditional power structures in both industry and government.[17]

In the political world, blogging is showing some early signs of what may well become an important new presence. Any key public policy issue is likely to have blogs devoted to it, and with the rising interest in e-democracy the potential of blogging for partisanship and policy-making is beginning to attract serious study. One of the first serious efforts to examine the democratic potential of blogging comes from a leading UK think tank, the Hansard Society. This group created a citizens' jury to analyze the perceptions of potential bloggers and the potential for their use and integration in more formal democratic processes. In fact, part of the impetus for studying the politics of blogging in the United Kingdom came from several parliamentarians who created their own blogs.

The results of the study are decidedly mixed. Many participants felt that blogs seem to be devoted more to specialized constituencies than to mainstream appeal. Perhaps the most important observation, however, is that a higher frequency of broadcasting was taking place rather than two-way dialogue. In other words, blogs are more about publishing and communicating than listening and debating. The central message behind blogging's appeal cannot be ignored: many people want to have input on issues that matter to them, and there is a widening refusal to rely on existing, formalized channels for information as a basis for doing so.

Paradoxically, this relentless expansion of both the production and the sharing of information may also create more reluctance by the public sector to expose itself to such scrutiny, as traditions of communication and control reign despite their futility in withstanding these new pressures. Governments are clearly not alone in this regard since the boundaries limiting public knowledge continue to crumble in a manner that creates discomfort for an elite class that has grown accustomed to being safely insulated within private venues. The resignation of a CNN executive in early 2005 for remarks made in a closed session of the Davos annual meeting of the World Economic Forum is a good illustration: although traditional media outlets chose not to cover the story, consistent with the ethos of Davos that encourages frank and unreported discussions, the executive's remarks became the subject of numerous weblogs that snowballed into a public crisis and the individual's resignation.[18]

There is also some evidence that governments are seeking ways to deploy new technologies not only to manage the architecture to access-to-information requests but also to improve surveillance, oversight, and filtering capacities for materials and requests deemed politically sensitive due to either content of the files in question or the stakeholder initiating the inquiry (Roberts 2005). Westminster-style governance models are particularly prone to such behaviour (ibid.), although similar concerns have long characterized debates in Washington, DC, particularly as of late in light of the dramatic extension of homeland security initiatives and the corresponding effort to curtail the release of government information (a theme discussed in the preceding chapter and returned to below).

Workable and effective forms of transparency are therefore dependent on the interface between external pressures and demands and the internal governance processes that must exist to facilitate timely and reliable measures to respond regularly and proactively to a changing environment (Mitchinson and Ratner 2004). The problems encountered to date by governments with freedom-of-information laws are indicative of not only cultural resistance but also organizational neglect in terms of not strategically addressing the more serious and holistic governance requirements of democracy and management in a more open and digital age. Moreover, new security-related actions undertaken by governments over the past several years are more likely to represent a solidification of traditional limits to government openness — despite the widening efforts of organized interests to overcome these limits (Roy 2005a).

3.4 Secrecy and Complexity

Secrecy
The public sector equivalent of Microsoft's proprietary codes underpinning its operating system may well be national security — in terms of the need to gather information, undertake action, and wherever possible resist exposing both the sources and the operating processes for doing so. The willingness and ability of governments to remain faithful to such a characterization greatly depend on the tolerance and trust of the citizenry — attributes shaped by a number of technological, political, and socio-economic variables.

Since September 2001, the rush by governments in the Western world to respond has led to the introduction of various forms of anti-terrorist strategies and legislation that arguably serve as the greatest expansion of government authority in modern history — particularly in the realm of information gathering. Introduced in the aftermath of September 11th, the Patriot Act in the United States serves as the focal point for such reforms — providing a bolstered legal framework for extended government authority in many segments of personal information that had otherwise been regarded as beyond the purview of the state. As noted in Chapter 2, in terms of US government technology spending, the activities of the Departments of Homeland Security and Defense massively — and individually — outweigh the investments made in the president's e-government strategy focusing on other aspects of technology deployment, such as systems integration and service delivery.[19]

With respect to the discussion of transparency, these financial resources are likely to solidify and bolster the already secretive nature of the defence and security sector to the point where it becomes a protected enclave trumping the public's right to access-to- and freedom-of-information principles (Roberts 2003). Thus, the expanded security imperative of the early twenty-first century represents at least a partial reframing of the Internet as an optimistically-laden infrastructure of commerce and freedom toward the view that the Internet can and must be viewed more suspiciously as a network of potentially threatening movements and activities. Whereas the former image is consistent with empowering and liberating perspectives on the information society, the latter suggests a more traditionally familiar typology of information scarcity and control.

Nonetheless, the implications for public sector transparency within the evolution of e-government in such a context are varied and complex since they must be viewed from two potentially contradictory vantage points. On the one hand, governments in many jurisdictions appear to be bolstered by higher levels of public support for security-related measures, to the point where issues such as privacy (and the protection of personal information) and openness are viewed as secondary to the overriding aim of ensuring public safety (Hart-Teeter 2004). At the same time, however, the pressures arising from a more informed and interconnected public and set of civic movements continue to shape public expectations and the rhetoric of government leaders alike in favour of more open, accessible government (particularly in the context of a public sector online).

One possible result of such conflicting pressures is a somewhat schizophrenic set of institutions and organizations in terms of information policies and management philosophy more generally.

Moreover, it is reasonable to presume that, within the existing structures and systems of parliamentary democracy (or similar regimes such as that of the United States), the overriding political attention devoted to anti-terrorism and public safety measures as of late serves to reinforce the potential for placing limits on more openness in government (a theme discussed more fully in the preceding chapter). This focus is nonetheless out of step with the broader personification of an Internet society as one in which organizations of all sectors must be more responsive and proactively engaged by inviting rather than resisting scrutiny — and by working with the widest possible range of stakeholders in order to collectively define the governance relationships and practices driving the organization in question.

How public sector organizations address and manage such divergences depends not only on these outer policy priorities and pressures (e.g., in response to Internet growth and terrorism) but also on the inner processes deployed by governments to act accordingly. Within the security sector, for example, an excessively secretive culture shapes government interactions not only with external stakeholders but also negatively between departments and agencies fearful of the consequences of sharing information or knowledge viewed as proprietary to a given unit (Roberts 2004).

Complexity

Beyond specific security matters, the relationship between transparency and organizational complexity more generally is also an important element shaping e-government, and it is worthy of further exploration. Chapters 1 and 2 revealed the manner in which both service delivery and security-related dimensions of e-government rely increasingly on technical and organizational interoperability to facilitate more citizen-centric, government-wide capacities (for serving, monitoring, or protecting citizens). With respect to transparency, the question that must be asked is whether or not such government-wide capacities are sufficiently understood by the public and whether or not such an understanding is both relevant and important. Put another way, do citizens understand how the public sector functions, and to what extent does the emergence of e-government shape such an understanding?

In terms of service delivery, it is not uncommon for project champions both inside and outside government to insist that "the citizen does not care about how governments are organized internally and how they process information and undertake decisions—their only or perhaps primary concern is getting good service." Such a viewpoint is analogous in some respects to online, citizen-centric banking, in which the typical customer accesses his or her entire portfolio of products and services through an integrated portal, caring little about the organizational architecture that facilitates this one-stop, integrative experience.

In terms of security, a similar sentiment is that the primary concern of the citizen lies with safety and the prevention of harmful or disruptive acts—with far less attention accorded to how government ensures such an outcome. In both cases, across service and security, it is the outcome that weighs more heavily than the set of internal process considerations of one sort or another undertaken by the entity to deliver or provide such an outcome. In short, understanding how government is organized is unimportant to the public.

Yet here there are important and consequential distinctions between government and business in terms of the expectations and actions of customers and citizens—and the accountability requirements that result. In the private sector, the conditions of competition and choice that define a customer's connection to any private firm (or an investor as well) are more conducive to performance-based accountability than is the case in government, for several reasons. First, the actions of any single company impact a specific subset of the citizenry, and thus they are proportionally more manageable. Second, consumers and investors in the marketplace are more tolerant of risk and errors since they possess (in reasonably well-functioning market conditions) some mobility in moving elsewhere. And third, corporate governance regimes are far more concerned with the reporting of outcomes than is the case in the public sector.

Although a case can certainly be made (along the lines of the argument made by Tapscott and Ticolls 2003) that corporations face rising levels of scrutiny over a variety of operating and process considerations previously shielded by corporate walls, this trend alone is unlikely to lead to a convergence of expectations and pressures on both sectors, particularly when the public sector begins from a dramatically opposite starting point in terms of a primary and overriding concern for process (with performance-based considerations being introduced to government in a manner that is arguably comparable to the wider set of process-based issues facing business).

Moreover, the ability of citizens to hold their governments to account in a democratic context depends on more than the transactional encounters with the public sector as a service provider. Not only is information the lifeblood of accountability (a point underlined by the Supreme Court of Canada), but also the notion of accountability carries an important learning component in terms of generating capacities for social learning and collective judgment that underpin a government's ability to deal with increasingly complex and multifaceted policy problems (Paquet 2000; Juillet and Paquet 2002). In other words, a government's ability to address complexity depends on the public's capacity to appreciate it, whereas a misleading or overly simplistic presentation of how government is actually exercising its duties is therefore detrimental to both public confidence and collective learning.

With regard to e-government and transparency, then, there is a counterintuitive possibility that the development of a more digital and complex organizational architecture to address service and security agendas is actually reducing the degree of openness in public sector operations. While governments are doing more to provide more information on their objectives and priorities, such as service improvement and security, they are providing little insight into the sort of horizontal initiatives required to achieve such outcomes and the level of difficulty and change embedded in the models being put forth.

The consequences for accountability are important — particularly given the general claim that e-government can be a driver of greater transparency that will, in turn, enable improved accountability. The extent to which accountability is improved, however, greatly depends on how it is viewed and on what basis it is applied. One of the conundrums of the complexities associated with the increasingly horizontal governance dimensions of e-government efforts in service delivery and security is that often the managerial accountability for such initiatives joining individual units conflicts with the political accountabilities separating them.

The difficulties of achieving shared forms of accountability — more horizontal and less vertical — are thus a major organizational challenge confronting e-government efforts (Fountain 2001). They also represent a major and related barrier to transparency in terms of the accuracy and relevance of government explanations about how government works, since invariably the political accountabilities — the basis of such explanations — do not adequately address government-wide dimensions to major strategic objectives such as service integration or security or other policy matters transcending multiple units (Lindquist 2005). Instead, they tend to reinforce the uniquely defining responsibilities of individual ministers and ministries.

In short, the major issue to be underlined here is the degree to which political accountability mechanisms (traditionally vertical in structure and orientation) can be adapted to reflect the extent of organizational complexity and horizontal collaboration required to facilitate government-wide capacities where required (as discussed in Chapter 1). In many jurisdictions, it is evident that e-government has been adopted as a strategic, government-wide goal — communicated in an open and forceful fashion — without an accompanying effort to publicly explain the sort of organizational changes likely required to achieve the potential sought.

These organizational changes depend directly on political leadership and the degree to which accountability mechanisms — balancing process and performance — can be forged to accommodate these new realities. So far, the absence of this accommodation is reflected in the general frustration of public sector CIOs (see Chapter 1), and rarely is the CIO a senior position with cabinet-level status.[20]

In terms of what sort of political mechanism is required, there are two avenues. The first is to foster collaborative linkages between ministers for shared interests and integrated agendas, with due consideration given to processes for resource allocation and results reporting. The second approach is a more traditional reversion to centralized leadership within a single political appointee for an enlarged and consolidated bureaucratic portfolio.

This latter approach has clearly been the one adopted with respect to homeland security and public safety (Henrich and Link 2003; Roy 2005c). Perhaps partially unavoidable given the crisis-driven context surrounding this issue, it is also reflective of the public sector mentality of centralized leadership that goes hand in hand with ministerial accountability (and even the dominance of the central agencies serving the prime minister or premier). In short, the lines of leadership and accountability of the public sector are structurally and culturally tilted toward clarity over complexity, centralization over more collaborative forms of coordination. When coupled with the traditionally secretive nature of security operations, and the potentially centralizing tendencies of information technologies, there is nothing automatic about an e-government-led transformation of structures and accountabilities (Allen et al. 2005).

Therefore, while this security-led reversion to centralization and clarity may be invoked by some within government as an improvement by some measure of transparency (i.e., being able to more easily identify the person — minister — responsible), such simplicity comes at a potential cost. First, it presumes an unwillingness or inability by the citizenry to both appreciate and grapple with complexity. Second, and as a result of the first point, this shielding of complexity in favour of simplicity and clarity may well inhibit the sort of new governance mechanisms required — more complex and adaptive — from emerging due to an ongoing cleavage between political and organizational accountability. Moreover, the enlarged organization that results from centralized consolidation will likely be prone to the sort of dangers from inefficiency and mismanagement that characterize excessive bureaucracy — a point underscored by concerns emerging from cases such as the US Pentagon.[21]

Despite the strong focus on security in North America and elsewhere since 2001, governments are beginning to confront the challenges of more complex governance. The Australian government, for example, has publicly spearheaded an ambitious and far-reaching amount of research on government-wide capacities in many policy fields while also considering the specific evolution in government operations and accountabilities presented by e-government:

> To accommodate citizens' increasing expectations for e-government to simplify interactions with government and to hide the complexity of the bureaucracy needed to manage the complex policy issues of our time, integrated services that cross agency and jurisdictional boundaries are necessary (Barrett 2002a; National Office for the Information Economy 2002).

To coordinate the operation of these integrated services in some equitably governed approach will require creation of organizations with unique ownership structures, novel governance structures, and subject to innovative accountability regimes (Barrett 2002a). Importantly, these organizations will be different to, and more complex than, current inter-governmental arrangements, because of the likely involvement of private sector partners (Barrett 2002b, 2003; Painter 1998c) and because of the detailed administrative nature of their operation, where daily transactions span multiple jurisdictions (Turner 2004, 136).

The quotation is instructive since it attempts to strike a balance between the need to hide bureaucracy in a transactional, service-oriented manner and the need to address the separate and overlapping democratic accountabilities at play (in this case across different levels of government, but the point also applies in equal measure to separate ministerial units within a single government). It is hard not to conclude that to shy away from complexity in such an environment may well be comforting in the short term, reinforcing cautious tendencies embedded in status quo governance arrangements, but it is unlikely to foster a level of appreciation conducive to the creation of more ambitious and innovative governance models that will invariably prove necessary.

Performance Management and Public Reporting

Providing information online is not only a transparency issue in the context of e-government but also one element of and a critical prerequisite to expanding public engagement activities (Riley 2003). The shift to more performance-based management systems that is prevalent in the public sector today is closely aligned with issues of public engagement. Holding governments to account on the basis of results and outcomes rather than strict interpretations of rules and compliance measures presumes both a level of acceptance by the public in moving in this direction and an accompanying capacity for comprehension and contribution to such a system (either directly or indirectly). There are, therefore, important informational requirements that must be met to realize any such shift.

Whether the preceding risks of simplistic clarity trumping the realities of complexity are countered or compounded depends to a large degree on the sort of information provided by governments to the citizenry. An effective system of public reporting must also outline both the objectives and the measures by which progress toward these objectives can be gauged. While this type of reporting is increasingly being undertaken indirectly by organizations outside the public sector,[22] governments are only beginning to exploit the potential to provide the information that they hold on their own operations to outside stakeholders, particularly in a manner conducive to focusing on performance.

Lee (2004) argues that the convergence of performance information and e-government in what he terms an evolution toward 'e-reporting' represents a potential and fundamental transformation of traditional means of public reporting. He highlights one such example in the form of an Iowa-based Citizens Initiated Performance Assessment (CIPA):

> First, CIPA helps officials focus on outcome measures and citizen concerns. This enhances public accountability and the result-orientation of public services. Second, CIPA shows the importance of public communication.... Third, managers should prepare for comparative performance measurement as many citizens are interested in knowing how well their city is performing relative to others in the neighbouring area. Fourth, many performance measures should be reported at the neighbourhood level to enhance the relevancy to citizens. Finally, public reporting of performance measurement is important. Cities should consider the usage of technologies, such as the Internet, to do this cost effectively.
>
> Many cities have been collecting performance data for decades. CIPA is simply a change in perspective by managers and elected officials by engaging citizens so that the public can influence the bases on which government services are evaluated. (Lee 2004, 11)

Despite such potential, Lee's research finds highly uneven levels of effectiveness due to varying practices and degrees of commitment by governments. Although the US federal government is found to be providing much more performance information than state and local counterparts, Lee questions the relevance, packaging, and presentation of such materials in manners conducive to public access and understanding. It is these latter elements of e-reporting that are essential to strengthening government accountability and public trust (either through indirect monitoring and electoral processes or through more direct forms of public action initiated by the citizenry of the government itself).

The reluctance by governments to do more online reporting can be explained by a number of factors. First, there is the inherently insular culture of government with respect to information management (a theme examined in the previous chapter but nonetheless underlining here a linkage between transparency and trust). Second, such a defensive may well extend beyond the managing of information and translate into a lack of enthusiasm for enabling the public or other stakeholders to know more about the organizational activities of any specific government body. Such reluctance — arguably another related aspect of transparency — is ascribable to many organizations in all sectors facing the prospect of more scrutiny from outside interests.[23]

Underpinning such factors is the reality that, in most jurisdictions, e-government strategies are being devised from within the governments in power rather than in concert with all concerned stakeholders. Therefore, while the service flavour of citizen-centric governance may be genuine, it is by and large separate from a philosophy of engagement that, to implement in a genuine manner, would require more far-reaching changes to not only the internal architecture of government organizations but also their broader institutional structures and cultures within which these organizations act.

Here lies a key distinction between customer relationship management and citizen engagement. Whereas the former encompasses tools such as focus groups, feedback surveys, and polls (some of them online) deployed by public managers in their role of serving public service customers, the latter is more dependent on collaborative engagements involving efforts to share power and foster learning. Undertaking the latter requires more proactive systems of information gathering and reporting to enable stakeholders and the public to contribute to this more collective and discursive process (Wilhelm 2000; Kossick 2004).

A meaningful strategy of timely and integrated performance reporting online also offers the potential to empower legislators to better undertake their role as key stakeholders in democracy. Although this potential often translates into another example of reluctance by governments in power to move in such directions (for fear of exposing themselves politically), such a defensive may well be gradually overcome not only by the strengthening calls for more participative forms of public engagement but also by proponents of democratic reforms aimed at bolstering the traditional 'representative' bodies of the public sector.[24]

In this respect, there is some important common ground between those seeking more participative democracy and those preferring a refurbished representational model. Both avenues, to be effective in improving democratic performance, require stronger informational capacities not only within the public sector's executive branch but also across the legislative and public arenas. E-government, then, as a means to improving collective accountability, means shifting beyond the 'service and communication' mindset that is so pervasive with respect to online service delivery and focusing with equal vigour on engagement and consultation.

3.5 Conclusion

The main challenges identified in this chapter stem from the fact that the Internet-driven focus on transparency extends far beyond merely providing more information to those who may or may not be seeking it. Instead, it is the very nature of power and governance that is shifting as information becomes less scarce and more readily available. The challenge for organizations is to become less insularly concerned with containing and shaping information and more able to share it with all relevant stakeholders — and to be less defensive and more proactive in doing so. The challenge is also to become more participative and collaborative — both internally and externally — and less reliant on vertical authority. Finally, the challenge is also one of embracing new forms of complexity rather than relying solely on clarity.

While such observations cannot be said to apply everywhere, the lessons from the e-government experiences of many jurisdictions suggest that at least initially e-government proponents understood the necessity of this wider transformation and sought to embrace it. Progress has been slowed by two sources: first, the inertia against such change, especially reinforced when horizontal efforts are not supported by collaborative political engagements to support them; second, the crisis-driven rise of security as a major political issue and the corresponding reversion to a traditional mindset of clear and centralized authority.

As a result, the e-government transformation under way is in some ways less a transformation and more a transition, particularly in terms of political leadership and the democratic institutions shaping the roles and interactions between politicians, public servants, and the public. Such a reform trajectory is consistent with those claiming that ICTs of any sort will likely continue to reinforce existing power structures within organizational systems, at least in the absence of a sharp crisis (Kraemer and King 2003). Whether or not growing public unease with the functioning of the public sector—and the defensive culture within government in resisting openness—constitutes a catalytic set of forces for such a crisis remains an important and open question that must be examined within the specific confines and traits of a given jurisdiction.

Alternatively, if pressures for more transparency are indicative of a broader transformation, then it is through wider engagement and expanded participative capacities that such deeper changes are likely to occur. E-government must also become about broader institutional innovations with respect to democratic governance in order to both restore and bolster trust in such systems, and more and more governments seem to be prepared to at least entertain the prospects for such participative reforms.

Transparency thus becomes an important plank in constructing the e-government foundation that invariably involves more complex governance systems that must encompass both managerial and political change. The balance between central coordination and decentralized autonomy is more than an internal design issue: it is the basis for a new organizational ethos that must be not only communicated accurately and faithfully to all stakeholders (including the public) but also crafted in concert with them. Thus, transparency is also tightly tied to leadership, engagement, and the existence and maintenance of trust—the fourth and final dimension of the e-government transformation. Transparency and trust are therefore closely interrelated, both dependent on more participative capacities for engagement that are the focus of Chapter 4.

Chapter 4
Trust

Trust is a multifaceted concept in terms of how governments seek, retain, and deploy legitimacy and support in their pursuit of policies and actions tied to the public interest. Democratic legitimacy – recognition and consent granted by the citizenry to the political institutions – is a central and fluid concern in the e-government era. Driving this fluidity is a growing body of evidence pointing to declining public confidence in government, heightened suspicion and cynicism toward traditional authoritative bodies, and a shifting of sociopolitical and civic activity to organizations and venues outside the traditional state apparatus. In light of such trends, proponents of e-democracy seek new opportunities for more direct and continual forms of public participation. While calls for such expanded engagement predate the Internet, online connectivity is a powerful vehicle to both distribute information and power and share decision-making. Within the public sector too, trust is a key enabler of governance innovation and reform, as horizontal and networking arrangements involve greater employee empowerment and engagement than hierarchical controls. Indeed, of the four dimensions, trust is the most pervasive in underpinning not only the specific technical and policy requirements of service and security efforts but also the ability of governments to work in concert with all sectors in a collective, innovative, and adaptive manner.

The chapter begins with a general consideration of why trust matters as an essential piece of the e-government puzzle. Section 4.2 examines its more specific application to public engagement and the shift – underpinned in part by online connectivity – to more participative democratic ties between citizens and governments. The importance of employee engagement in terms of external information flows and of disseminating and reporting information online is then considered in section 4.3. Trust's role as a key variable in public sector reform and employee engagement – the new relational and skills challenges facing public servants – is the focus of section 4.4. How these new skills and capacities translate into stakeholder engagement and a basis for collective engagement is the final topic in section 4.5. Part One then concludes with a summary of the major themes and issues emerging from the first four chapters that will serve as a basis for an assessment of e-government in the Canadian public sector.

4.1 Why Trust Matters

The notion of trust is extremely complex—one that is said to be both ubiquitous in our society and difficult to define and understand in the abstract (O'Hara 2004). So much about trust depends on context, whether political, economic, social, organizational, cultural, or technological. Most dictionary definitions of trust refer to traits such as integrity, confidence, and certainty extended by one or more individuals to another person or thing (e.g., an organization or institution): the result is a condition in which one is (relatively or entirely) free from doubt. Trust is intertwined with governance in dealing with two critical aspects of coordination and organization: change and uncertainty on the one hand, and cooperation or collaboration on the other hand.[1] The increasingly fluid context of a globalizing, interconnected, and interdependent world means that trust lies at the heart of the search for good governance.

In regard to change and uncertainty, although there is much rhetoric in the business and political worlds about embracing change as a positive, enjoyable process, the reality is that, for most people and organizations, change is uncomfortable (Stevenson 1998). Order and rules, in contrast, facilitate routine and certainty, which are necessary for civilized and predictable patterns of working and living, and a key purpose of bureaucracy continues to be underpinning such patterns, rendering them both recognizable and respected—or at least subscribed or deferred to in some manner. In a relatively stable environment, large organizations can function well with this sort of system—provided that there are reasonably successful outcomes to underpin the credibility of the existing order or sufficient incentives or limitations in place to limit dissent. As such, what is particularly central to such an order—which breeds hierarchy and control—is deference to authority and expertise (Essex and Kusy 1999). In the public sector realm, such is the basis for representative democracy.

In today's world, the notion of trust in government policy making and political decision making is multifaceted and complex. For example, in equating trust with political support, Parent et al. (2004) nonetheless distinguish between specific and diffuse forms of trust—the former in reference to specific outputs, and the latter in terms of overall political objectives and governing ideology. Such a differentiation underscores the potentially different ways in which citizens may judge government — across precise forms of public sector activities, the political agendas of those in power, and the overall stability and functioning of their democratic institutions. Both bases of trust are relevant for e-government: much of the service mentality of online delivery methods, for instance, is predicated on specific forms of support.

With respect to moving government online, for instance, questions surrounding the level of trust and confidence of citizens in the digital technologies themselves are pervasive in specific ways since online service delivery can be successful only insofar as a sufficiently large and ideally growing segment of the population believes that transactions conducted online are as reliable as other forms of communication and interaction (Bryant and Colledge 2002). For such reasons, during the initial emergence of e-government, trust could be viewed primarily as a set of technical challenges, notably privacy and security, tied to ensuring a safe and functional architecture for moving government online (Galindo 2002; Mullen 2004).

In contrast, broader debates about the nature and form of democracy are tied to the perceived legitimacy of both the overarching political objectives being pursued and the manner and appropriateness of how governments translate these objectives into specific actions and decisions. In other words, diffuse support is closely tied to the degree to which the citizenry should be prepared to defer to the judgments of elected leaders or engage in some mechanism to contribute more directly to such decision-making processes.

The more that authority is questioned (and deference is less of a given), the greater the likelihood of unease with existing political institutions whose structures and procedures stem from an era of select forms of suffrage, limited quantities of information, and a clear delineation of boundaries and responsibilities for authorities vested with powers to govern over the affairs of a given polity. Ironically, for political leaders, it may well be the case that higher levels of wealth and education lead to more trying circumstances for holders of public offices as an 'expectations gap' forms between the citizenry and those representing it: "In the stable democracies, political institutions and elites are probably no less trustworthy than in the past. Rather, the decline in trust in institutions probably reflects a more general decline in respect for authority that has come with the development of post-material cultures. When people no longer worry for their survival, they do not need to cling unquestioningly to the authorities they hope will ensure their survival. Instead, as material well-being increases, trust in political institutions and elites is likely to decline as publics begin to evaluate their leaders and institutions by more demanding standards" (Warren, cited in O'Hara 2004, 253). These new standards are based less on tradition and inheritance and more on reputation and relational capital developed through experiences and encounters over time. In this less deferential and more complex environment, Shaw (1997) identifies three imperatives of trust generation that organizations must strive for to be successful: achieving results by following through on commitments, demonstrating concern while respecting the well-being of others, and acting with integrity by behaving in a consistent manner.

It is within such a context that different claims are made about the ability of e-government to emerge as a catalyst for increasing levels of trust in the public sector. Importantly, in this regard, the e-government agenda has been based on a lofty set of more visionary objectives, put forth by proponents both inside and outside government, that goes far beyond service delivery and encompasses nothing less than the relevance, responsiveness, and performance of a public sector that has adapted to a digital age (OECD 2003).

In this manner, it is both appropriate and necessary to gauge the more diffuse attributes of trust and support linking the citizenry and public sector bodies that collectively comprise the institutions and mechanisms of democratic governance. Raising the bar on matters of trust in such a manner may result in the need to become more modest in expectations, as there would seem to be more potential optimism for improving trust than actual evidence of such a correlation (Coleman and Norris 2005; P. Norris 2005).

Technology and Trust

Although trust is multifaceted and many of its determinants predate the e-government challenge, as the Internet permeates widening spheres of activity — particularly in developed countries — the presence and impact of digital technology itself are likely to rise in prominence. Beyond the issue of trust as an enabling condition for online service delivery, how citizens perceive the digital infrastructure surrounding them and the degree to which they understand it are profoundly central concerns of democratic legitimacy.

For instance, one study of American public opinion in the context of homeland security and new technological deployments shows a deep suspicion and a lack of understanding about new technologies that, in turn, generate offsetting support for higher levels of public sector activism and regulation (Strickland and Hunt 2005). A key problem lies in the lack of public understanding since the citizenry is thus unable to express any coherent view of the acceptable limits of technological use and the appropriate regulatory boundaries across both the public and the private realms (ibid.). The absence of transparency in the realm of security generally accentuates such problems, suggesting that much deeper levels of both awareness and engagement are required to forge a collective degree of confidence and support in more digitized forms of public sector activity.

Kearns (2004) underscores trust as an essential element of e-government's capacity to generate value for citizens, despite little attention being paid by governments to matters beyond more narrow and specific invocations of trust tied to security and privacy. Identifying public trust in government as a potential source of value is a useful place to begin. Yet this point applies more generally, and this chapter is predicated on the notion that trust is an essential component across a broad spectrum of relational governance challenges both inside and outside government: they include both inter- and intra-organizational dynamics with the public sector, engagements between the public, private, and civic sectors, and matters of citizenship and political participation. Given its central focus in the growing interest in e-democracy, this latter challenge is examined first.

4.2 Public Engagement

Democratic legitimacy, the recognition and consent granted by the citizenry to its political institutions, is both a central and a fluid concern in the e-government era. Driving this fluidity is a growing body of evidence pointing to declining public confidence in government, heightened suspicion of and cynicism toward traditional authoritative bodies, and a shifting of socio-political and civic activity to organizations and venues outside the traditional state apparatus (Coe et al. 2001; Evans 2002; Gross 2002; Courchene 2005). An additional danger is the risk of complexity circumventing transparency and further eroding the confidence and trust of the citizenry in its political institutions (English and Lindquist 1998; Lindquist 2005).

Proponents of e-democracy often invoke an urgent need to rebalance representational and participatory dimensions to current democratic systems.[2] This reconsideration is fuelled in large part by the Internet's potential to distribute both information and power more widely, facilitating a broader conversation across all stakeholders and the public. Of course, such pressures for reform precede the Internet, as the case for more participatory governance has been made forcefully both prior to and in parallel to e-democratic discussions. Here the notion of citizen engagement implies a more meaningful and ongoing democratic role for the public beyond merely electing representatives: experimentation with such forms of participation has been occurring for some time (Graham and Phillips 1998; Yankelovich 1999). A related emphasis on distributed and collaborative forms of governance and social learning also involves participatory and relational mechanisms that are separate from the widening imposition of digital technologies: as a result, some view digital technologies as secondary to social ones (Paquet 2004).

Nonetheless, the Internet is a powerful venue for a more widely informed and better educated citizenry, within which lies a growing segment of the population that is disgruntled with many forms of traditional authority and governance — democracy being no exception (Slaton and Arthur 2001; Geiselhart 2004; Palfrey 2004; Edelman 2005). The open source software movement, the rise of the knowledge worker (working both within and with the learning organization), civic networking, and new social movements are all dynamics that, while not dependent on online connectivity, are highly consistent with the aspirations of Internet enthusiasts (and increasingly enabled by virtual communications and networks). As such, the erosion of public confidence reflects neither widespread absence of knowledge nor interest but a weakening attachment to traditional public sector institutions that are viewed as overly rigid, unresponsive, and out of step with contemporary society (Cherney 2000; Allen et al. 2001; Juillet and Paquet 2001; Pavlichev and Garson 2004).

It is in such a context that the Internet offers an instantaneous and potentially ubiquitous infrastructure for democratic life—one that in theory should be less reliant on representational forms of decision-making and more conducive to direct public input. Despite this potential, any systemic introduction of more digital forms of democracy would constitute a major revolution in the structure and functioning of the public sector apparatus (Fountain 2002). Difficulties in structuring such a conversation, and indeed questions surrounding whether online exchanges can facilitate meaningful venues for democratic decision-making, are significant design issues with technological, socio-economic, and political dimensions (Barney 2000; Norris 2000; Fountain 2002; Lenihan 2002a; Oliver and Sanders 2004).

There is, nonetheless, widening experimentation with democratic initiatives involving online capacities (Gibson 2002; MacIntosh et al. 2002, 2003; Geiselhart 2004; Hozler et al. 2004).[3] Based on his review of a number of such examples in the Swedish context, Gronlund (2003, 68) points to relational tensions between the bottom-up and participatory nature of political engagement and more top-down processes of service and implementation: whereas the top-down perspective is about politics as design, the bottom-up perspective is more evolutionary and organic.

One source of unease and resistance in terms of democratic engagement lies within the public sector: who should undertake and be responsible for consulting the public? While elected officials have typically served as the public in governing processes (complementing this representational role with specific and formal forms of outreach such as public hearings—most conducive to participation by expert witnesses and stakeholder representatives well-versed in such rituals), the more recent expansion of public involvement has tended to be by the public service itself, creating new and direct ties between public servants and citizens. The appropriateness of such ties is often contentious since elected officials may view such a trend as a circumvention of their role and a threat to their influence (such frictions will be particularly prevalent in government systems, such as the Westminster model, based on indirect or representative democracy[4]). Indeed, e-democracy need not be about direct public involvement, for it is possible to envision an e-democracy project construed as a means to better enable elected officials to both connect to and more effectively serve their constituents.[5]

The lack of broad social and political agreement over both the desirability and the purpose of e-democracy is thus rooted in both historical disagreement about the appropriate nature of democracy and more contemporary pressures in this new century personified by the Internet. Yet, this sort of separation of issues may well be giving way to a convergence between democratic reform generally and e-democratic experimentation specifically, the commonality being democratic adaptation and legitimacy in a more digital and interdependent world (Wilhem 2000). Such a convergence, however, need not imply consensus on which institutional changes are appropriate and which tools and strategies are best in facilitating stronger democratic performance (Oates 2003).

In a manner not unlike the evolution of service delivery (with respect to mechanisms if not purpose), the emergence of a multichannel system of democratic engagement seems to be unavoidable as more digital and direct forms of democracy are likely to emerge at different speeds in distinct manners across various segments of society. While the most politically engaged are quick to adapt to online opportunities, including more participatory ones both individually and in concert with other citizens and movements, those least inclined to participate currently and historically may well find themselves further marginalized in a democracy more online and, at least partially, more participative (Weber et al. 2003).

This variant of the digital divide—democratic engagement at varying speeds via different channels—is a problem for both existing governing processes (since the most affluent, educated, and/or mobilized are the least likely to be satisfied with the status quo) and prospects for reform (since pursuing reforms requires a mechanism for public dialogue and agreement that will be subject to existing societal cleavages as well as the fear of generating new ones). These sorts of tensions tend to inhibit institutional change given that the common denominator across disagreeing parties will tend to be maintaining the status quo in the absence of either a crisis or a significant political consensus.

The risk in this sort of environment, particularly one that is increasingly open, digital, and interconnected, is that participation will continue to evolve largely outside formal democratic structures and processes: "Public debate and discourse is in danger of migrating away from institutions of government. Historically, in democracies, public debate was 'localized' to afford a locus of meeting and debate. Networking has removed the physical constraints of venue, and created an alternative and more convenient locus for a widely distributed public...especially in the under-25 age range, which is increasingly feeling disenfranchised from conventional democratic institutions, seen by this age group as irrelevant" (Dwyer 2004, 121). Difficulties in coming to agreement not only about the end point but also about the process and mechanism for exploring electoral reforms are a case in point. Similarly, the crafting of and subsequent stymied ratification of Europe's proposed new constitution (nonetheless supported in many countries) are likely reflective of not only the document itself but also the relative legitimacy accorded to a highly traditional process of ruling elites forging an agreement and then seeking public endorsement.[6]

These sorts of difficulties once again underlie the ongoing tensions between transition and transformation in an e-governance era: whereas some would prefer to largely maintain the tradition and stability of existing approaches (allowing for a minor technological retooling where appropriate), others await more significant renewal. Across both currents, those exercising political power at present must attempt to balance the shorter-term constraints and challenges of governing with longer-term questions of legitimacy, participation, and adaptation.

4.3 Employee Engagement

The ability of government to more effectively reach out to and engage with citizens in consultative and participative mechanisms hinges on both the individual skill sets and managerial structures and cultures shaping the actions of public servants. In terms of structure, what matters is the extent to which managers have the appropriate degrees of authority and incentives to undertake such action. The sort of collaborative and consultative engagements that characterize the new work environment of more innovative, citizen-centric organizational forms (taken here to mean both serving and engaging citizens) demand both human training and technological tools of a far different sort than has typically been the case within the public sector hierarchy — insofar as such directions are being genuinely pursued (Allen et al. 2001; Kamarck 2004).

Yet there is nothing natural or unavoidable about an evolution toward a more digital form of organization that is more participative in empowering its employees. Much depends on the nature of political leadership in the public sector and the manner in which new technologies are used to either reinforce existing authoritative structures (or invent new ones) or abandon them in favour of more flexible and collaborative decision-making processes. In viewing the latter track as consistent with and a necessary enabler of the sort of internal horizontal networking within government and partnering outside it, techno-optimists envision a dispersion of power, liberated forces of creativity and innovation, and an empowerment of front line workers to better find and define solutions for clients (Goldsmith and Eggers 2004).

In contrast, skeptics point to the potential for technology to heighten surveillance and reinforce control in a manner akin to a digitized sweatshop. This passage is notable for both its view of the dehumanized employee from "the dark side of IT" and its publication source (*CIO*, a professional publication devoted generally to bettering, advancing, and managing technology):

> It is increasingly clear, however, that for many other employees, the management gurus prophesying that IT will democratize today's workplaces are just as wrong as Taylor was. IT can be used not only to liberate human beings but to control them. In industries employing unskilled workers, such as retailing, IT has created top-down control to a degree that Taylor could only have dreamed of. Instead of working for small organizations, many retail employees work for giant firms that dwarf even the behemoths of the industrial era.
>
> Even so, technological developments now on the horizon seem likely to increase, not decrease, restrictive top-down management. New sensor technology such as radio frequency identification (RFID) devices will inexpensively monitor truck drivers, salespeople, field service technicians and other offsite personnel who have traditionally worked out of their bosses' sight. As such employees are monitored with increasing intensity by new technology, the amount of "management by stress" in American workplaces seems likely to rise. (Hoops 2004)

Such comparative visions are hardly new as they align themselves well with the parameters of 'theory y' management and 'theory x' management respectively, guideposts in historical theories of management based on either empowerment or control. Whereas the former, typically associated with the spirit of new public management and knowledge-age organizations, values the individual's capacity for judgment and creativity in undertaking decisions (within limitations devised by a more flexible authoritative structure), the latter invokes classic principles of bureaucracy and hierarchy that are consistent with the vertical tendencies of ministerial accountability in the public sector (Savoie 2003).

The implications of each trajectory for interpersonal and interorganizational trust within the public sector are starkly different in each camp. Bureaucracy by and large mitigates the need for fostering intra-organizational trust, preferring instead coercion and control enforced in a top-down chain of command. The sort of trust within such a rigidly defined organization has less to do with participation and engagement and more to do with deference to specialization and authority. As the above quotation implies, although much of the new organizational movements consistent with the Internet era (and the open source software community, for instance) promise to break down such tendencies, there is much about information and communication technologies that can reinforce them as well. It is indeed notable that one of the largest areas of public sector activity — domestic security and anti-terrorism — has traditionally relied on such militaristic traditions that have largely extended to the law enforcement and intelligence communities.[7]

Alternative schemes — often simplified into a broad and encompassing category of new public management and learning organization models — have instead attempted to overcome the confines of bureaucratic structure by explicitly embracing more flexible and varying patterns of authority and decision making that encourage both individuality and more spontaneous and organic forms of joint action between individuals and organizational units (unlike the bureaucratic approach of essentially codifying such action and controlling it as much as feasible). The postbureaucratic organization must therefore become more collaborative (Nelson 1998; Kearns 2004). This emphasis on collaboration explains the application of the term 'social capital,' as a proxy for trust, to organizational and managerial dynamics in a more knowledge-driven and digital age that are based more on collaboration than on traditional forms of public sector coercion and control (Agranoff and McGuire 2003; Allen et al. 2005b).

Much of the rhetorical optimism of the e-government project is clearly hinged on an empowered public service capable of generating and making use of such social capital within itself and extending to collaborative relationships across civil society and the private sector (Eggers 2005). Within government, Lenihan (2002b) asks whether the traditional departmental model (emphasizing a hierarchical chain of command) should be viewed as extinct — ultimately to be replaced by a network model of decision-making. In embracing this latter alternative, the Korean e-government road map places front and centre the importance of public sector reform and the transformation of internal work processes to enable collaboration both within governments and externally with citizens and stakeholders (Obi 2004).

Despite such attention, little effort has been made initially in designing e-government to systemically understand the impacts of the Internet on public sector employees and the degree to which the working environment is being adapted in manners conducive to more individual empowerment and organizational innovation across all levels of the organization (Heeks and Davies 1999; Kernaghan and Gunraj 2004). Early work examining the impacts of technology on the public service revealed a three-way partitioning in many jurisdictions: front line workers feared automation and job redundancy, and senior managers were routinely unaware of digital innovation since it had very little impact on their traditional routines and practices (Kieley et al. 2002). Between these polarized perspectives, middle managers revealed the highest level of interest and acceptance in using technologies to seek out innovative work patterns and solutions (ibid.). Such patterns reflect the emphasis today on the importance of mid-level creativity in driving organizational adaptation: in particular, the importance of virtual communications across organizational boundaries is essential to knowledge management and collaboration in more successful enterprises (Ferry 2003; Tapscott and Ticoll 2003; R. Smith 2004).

Such findings are also reflective of the way in which e-government has typically evolved within most jurisdictions and the efforts of central agencies to devise government-wide capacities. As discussed in Chapter 1, the novelty and limited authority of the CIO position (or its equivalent) make such efforts difficult to achieve, while they also prioritize technological alignment and innovation over organizational and managerial change, since these latter realms have often been devolved in some manner to individual departments and agencies (Schelin 2004) — their separateness, in turn, reinforced by the overarching vertical lines of political accountability. The familiar reaction to this perceived absence of sufficient leadership is to call for a further centralization of authority within central agencies with government-wide authority for financial and managerial processes (Kearns 2004).

The problem with such an approach is that such a reaction can lead to a further entrenchment of centralized authority within the very central agencies that are the least conducive to organizational innovations tied to the deployment of new technologies. If this happens, then e-government may erode the stock of trust or social capital within the organization — the very ingredient necessary to enable creativity and innovation to take place. Here again it is pertinent to underscore a theme first introduced in Chapter 1: how e-government creates managerial and organizational pressures that may, at times, conflict with previous reform eras. Much of the influence of new public management on public sector reforms throughout the 1980s and into the 1990s featured calls for smaller, devolved, and nimble organizational units (structured as such within either large systems such as national governments or smaller, subnational jurisdictions).

As such, many governments at all levels created 'agencies' from what had been traditional line ministries, the difference being extra degrees of managerial autonomy to create systems and solutions with less interference from centralized and what had often been perceived as stifling authorities. Employees within such bodies typically enjoy greater degrees of freedom than their counterparts in more traditional government departments (which, in turn, are more traditionally reliant on a bureaucratic culture), and public sector managers leading such bodies typically do so with greater levels of visibility and direct accountability for results than the traditional senior government manager. Within such devolved boundaries, greater degrees of trust are granted to public servants as a basis for a new form of moral contract (in place of hierarchy) to better address complexity and uncertainty via more flexible, adaptive, and collaborative means (Paquet 1997; OECD 1999; Langford and Roy 2005).

This dichotomy of trust generation across macrolevel systems and more individualized organizational units—and how it may be under strain today—is highly consequential in shaping public sector capacities in tune with e-government. One important variable is the potentially contradictory tendencies between a technological apparatus that is becoming increasingly standardized and thus centralized across government (i.e., interoperability) and this managerial imperative to devolve authority and flexibility to those units of the organization most able to align process and performance within the confines of their specific mandate. The point is not to suggest that such a balance is out of reach. The vision of a federated enterprise that is central to e-government is sensitized to the necessity of achieving coordination across both such levels, and there is evidence of its feasibility in successfully deploying new technologies in a manner sensitive to striking such a balance (Culbertson 2005). Accounting for this balance and determining the appropriate human capacities and organizational arrangements that result require a level of strategic awareness of how and why digital technologies are shifting from a supportive role (in storing information and facilitating basic and routine forms of electronic processing) to one that is more central to overall performance capacities (Weil and Broadbent 1998).

One useful framework for understanding this shift is provided by Wilson (1997, 190), who distinguishes between the following seven levels of information management, each one reflecting a different use of IT:

> Level One: Compliance—the use of IT to automate the basic recording requirements of the organization;
> Level Two: Operational support—the use of the recorded data to assist with the management of day to day operations;
> Level Three: Added customer value—the use of information systems to add value to the organization's products, services or relationships with clients;
> Level Four: Competitive advantage—the use of information systems to achieve a leap in competitive advantage and to sustain that advantage;
> Level Five: Strategic insight—the use of information systems to support a new form for the organization;

Level Six: Transformation—the use of information systems to make a fundamental revision to the organization, its business, partnerships, products or services;

Level Seven: Knowledge net—the use of information systems to create virtual organizations which bring together employees from anywhere in the world to undertake a particular assignment and which, when that assignment has been completed, cease to exist.

As one progresses down this list, each subsequent level implies a more technology-savvy workforce to make use of the more sophisticated set of digital tools available to individual workers, as well as a more nimble organization structurally that allows for innovation and creativity to take hold in a manner that can allow for the higher levels of deployment. Although the rhetoric of e-government is often couched in the transformation potential of levels six and seven, in reality the sort of online service delivery initiatives reviewed in Chapter 1 reflect an attempt to penetrate the third and fourth levels (within a public sector culture that has traditionally viewed digital technology as a level one and level two issue). In terms of trust, these higher levels of organizational transformation thus require the dissemination of trust across all units and levels—both vertically and horizontally—of the organization.

Creating a portal to provide integrated information sources and downloadable forms is a good example of a level two or level three deployment, with the implications for skills and training limited to a small cadre of website designers and customer service managers. Leveraging this portal to integrate service transactions across departments and agencies via a common interface with the citizen-customer augments the challenge both technically and organizationally with corresponding skill requirements for a much larger set of service agents and managers joined by these shared processes.

The field of domestic security and public safety is also indicative of the challenges brought about by escalating levels of technology use and organizational change. This policy field perhaps more than elsewhere must reconcile the tensions between the desire to deploy new digital tools and information systems to better combat threats to public safety (and in doing so deploy them across various public sector bodies at one time focused on separate mandates and missions), with the corresponding implications for training and skills, and the traditional culture of hierarchy and secrecy that reigns within these public sector bodies. Indeed, level seven on the above chart personifies something of an ideal scenario for a system of transnational governance to combat terrorism and crime, whereas individual countries are struggling to adapt their own unique systems to the augmenting opportunities and challenges associated with reactions and innovations spanning the range of the other six levels.

In sum, public sector managerial reform in an era of e-government must reconcile the human dimension of engaging employees across a set of technological, organizational, and socio-political variables (Halligan and Moore 2004). Whereas the first set (technological) treats trust as essentially a specialized issue of the digital apparatus itself, the second set (organizational) recognizes the need for employee buy-in (itself a form of trust measured by social capital within the organization). The third set of variables (the socio-political factors) extends the realm of trust to include key external stakeholders and the broader citizenry—and their combined levels of confidence and faith not only in technology itself but also in the public sector's abilities and trustworthiness in making use of it in an effective and responsible manner. In this respect, employee engagement is also interconnected with the ability of the public service to engage the public and external stakeholders.

External Outreach

In terms of external outreach efforts for public and stakeholder engagement, the mentality and internal capacities within the public service for consultation and collaborative action will shape the ability to effectively and genuinely share decision-making power in a more open and flexible manner than the traditional bureaucratic prescription of exercising orders as dictated by authoritative structure. The opportunities of an expansion of public consultation and citizen engagement processes in a meaningful way (i.e., beyond the cynical interpretation of merely being seen to do them) are tied to better enabling public sector authorities to devise policies and processes in the most efficient and effective manner possible (thus, early input and buy-in by those stakeholders affected are likely to minimize costs and difficulties through implementation—and ongoing consultation can facilitate learning and adjustment quickly and effectively).

Consultation is more likely to succeed when purpose and execution are well aligned with objectives and outcomes (Oates 2003). The creation of trust is essential in enabling such positive linkages to be realized. In contrast, the absence of such clarity and connection to results is a recipe for cynicism by those 'consulted,' with the result being a further decline in trust. There is thus an intuitively reasonable assertion that follows: smaller and more focused organizational units within the public sector are more likely to foster the conditions for effective consultation than any such process devised to do so on a government-wide scale.

The early emergence of e-democratic initiatives within existing governmental structures, particularly at the national level, is instructive here. Efforts have been made in many jurisdictions to better coordinate consultative activities of various departments and agencies via a centrally administered, integrated portal that is meant to improve accessibility for the citizen to such processes across government. The risk of such measures could well lie in the costs associated with the pursuit of standardization and uniformity: more efficient communications on a macroscale may well be less creative and effective than more tailored consultations undertaken at the microlevel in response to highly specific issues and circumstances.

The importance of balance is paramount, but so are legitimate concerns about the evolving e-government project in a centralized fashion. Although such a characterization applies less empirically to e-democratic initiatives since governments have mainly been less active on this front (in comparison with service and security initiatives), an incremental expansion of e-government into public consultation may risk excessive centralization and the stifling of innovation if not balanced by offsetting design measures to preserve flexible capacities across different components of an overall system of government.

How such issues play out may also vary across different levels of government. Many of the dangers and problems associated with excessive centralization are partly due to a level of bureaucratic entrenchment and organizational complexity that characterizes large national governments more so than in smaller and more localized settings. Indeed, e-democracy appears to be a fledgling movement based more on local experiments than on national initiatives—despite mixed findings at the local level in terms of the overall level of systemic interest and adoption.[8]

There is thus likely to be some ongoing tension between the attributes of more localized conditions of democratic governance — including geographic proximity, familiarity, and less organizational complexity — that have shown themselves to be more conducive to trust both within localized governments and across their communities and the greater visibility and resources of national-level authorities (Paquet and Roy 2004). The resulting intergovernmental dynamics of e-government's evolution are therefore highly important.[9]

More currently, the difficult alignment issues between organizational design and the managing of people represent an important aspect of the public sector's ability to generate trust intra-organizationally. Such trust is consequential not only in shaping the performance of public servants internally — in working with one another — but also in forming their capacities to extend outward and engage the public in more participatory and collective governance processes that are necessary to become more customer and citizen-centric. Therefore, new forms of political support must be envisioned in order to build the requisite amount of trust between stakeholders — both internally and externally. Such new forms involve collective engagement.

4.4 Collective Engagement

Much of what is required to reframe governance has been recognized. Lenihan (2002a), for example, points to two metaprinciples that must take hold: collaborative and inclusive governance. Similarly, Hunold (2001) invokes a more deliberative democracy via wider openness and participation across the citizenry, public service, and elected officials. An important direction is fostering stronger and wider deliberative mechanisms from within government to acknowledge, be more inclusive of, and benefit from the expanding set of discursive networks outside government (Castells 1996; Oliver and Sanders 2004).

In this manner, more deliberative and more virtual forms of democracy must become mutually reinforcing — made to work within shared boundaries of democratic engagement. Demographics will make this tie more essential as the first generations of those not knowing a time without online commercial, familial, and civic engagements will see no valid reason to exempt the political sphere from this reality (Cherney 2000). Yet governments cannot lose sight of the uneven capacities within the citizenry that drive the existence of a digital divide. Less a technology challenge than a socio-economic and cognitive one, making e-government and e-democracy compatible requires a forceful and explicit commitment in addressing four sets of complex issues: "(1) The antecedent resources one needs to bring to the table in order to participate in political activities via, say, a computer terminal; (2) the opportunity to access or to be included in a particular online political exchange; (3) the ability to deliberate on substantive policy issues by subjecting one's ideas to public scrutiny; and (4) the design or architecture of a network or forum in which new information and communication technologies induce universal, deliberative and robust political dialogue" (Wilhelm 2000, 10). This quotation is instructive in underscoring the fact that digital democracy involves a complex set of challenges extending far beyond securing Internet access and providing opinions online. Facilitating new discursive capacities is essential, and such capacities are highly dependent on many levels of trust—in the technological infrastructure hosting the dialogue, in the fairness of the process used, and in the level of relevance of any such deliberation in shaping decisions and outcomes in a verifiable and meaningful way. Accordingly, digital democracy is a process of collective engagement predicated on responsibilities as well as rights in defining the relational covenant guiding participation and contribution.

E-government—including its e-democratic components—must therefore be viewed as an evolutionary process intertwined with the social and economic fabric of any jurisdiction served by it. Since governments are both the largest user and the chief regulator of technology for any jurisdiction, be it a community, province, or country, the repercussions of their actions and priorities are of great significance. The interdependence of e-government, e-business, and e-society represents a collective governance challenge for all citizens and stakeholders, since the capacity of jurisdictional units to adapt new technologies for the betterment of all aspects of working and living is likely to become an increasingly consequential and important source of competitive advantage in determining levels of development and prosperity in a globalizing world (Fukuyama 2004; Roy 2006).

The UK-based nation of Wales provides a compelling illustration of this vision. Within the confines of the expanded identity and authority devolved to the region from the central UK government, efforts are under way to ensure that this nation within a country (in a manner akin to its Scottish cousins) utilizes e-government as a collective, strategic lever to help foster the conditions for prosperity in the twenty-first century. These efforts have recently been conveyed in the form of an *e-charter for the people of Wales,* developed jointly by the Society of Information Technology Management and the Welch Local Government Association.[10] The charter aims to provide a visionary blueprint for the participation of all segments of Welch society in the digital transformation. Eight principles guide how online capacities can underpin both economic development and political engagement.

The principles are relational in embedding how different stakeholders can expect to create both efficiency and value from their service and civic interactions with a more digitally enabled and online public sector. The principles covered by the charter include council, community resources, the citizenry, business resources, joint services, universal access, online services, and jobs (whereas joint services include customer orientation, online services are more residency - focused).

As local governments, the makers of the charter challenge the Welch government 'to set out its vision for e-services for all the people of Wales and ensure that the support and resources are available to make this vision a reality.' One of the most important aspects of this challenge is to integrate this stakeholder-based agenda for e-government with the broader national objectives developed by the Welch government. Accordingly, the charter seeks to integrate government reform with the economic, social, environmental, and cultural objectives developed by the Welch assembly.

Development of the charter is more a point of departure than an achievement in itself. Nevertheless, it underscores the importance of viewing e-government as a diffuse and dynamic process that is inclusive rather than a service improvement initiative tied exclusively to improving the performance of a single government (at any one level). In putting forth this charter, local governments in Wales are challenging their region-state to develop a vision that is sensitive to the weaknesses and successes of different Welch communities in pursuing innovative forms of governance by deploying broadband access and e-government tools. As such, the document accompanying the charter highlights the many ways in which local authorities are facilitating experiments in both online service delivery and e-democracy.

While these communities are hoping for more resources and assistance from the Welch government, they are also trying to ensure that the Welch central authority does not forge ahead with its own e-government strategy insensitive to the knowledge and learning that already exist within their jurisdictions. Thus, prospects for a transformation of the Welch nation (akin to a small Canadian province) rest not only on central direction but also on localized support and collaboration, and this view raises important questions for Canadian governments at all levels:

- Is the scope of e-government being expanded beyond specific service delivery strategies in order to encompass a more holistic view of collective governance for all sectors?
- Are the federal and provincial governments developing e-government in a manner that is both sensitive to, and supportive of, local realities?
- Finally, is there a meaningful intergovernmental dimension to public sector activity in facilitating answers to such questions?

Whether there exists in Canada the potential to provide more affirmative and constructive responses is one of the key issues examined in Part Two.

4.6 Conclusion

As the fourth dimension of government's ongoing digital transformation, trust is simultaneously the most fluid, pervasive, and contested. In a linear manner, situated within the confines of service and security, trust may be viewed as an enabler of online delivery mechanisms—insofar as users have confidence in providing information and completing transactions via Internet-based channels. In the absence of trust (either from inexperience and uncertainty or from demonstrated failures), citizens will conduct their public service activities via more familiar platforms.

At a second level, the trust of the citizenry accorded to those in power will determine the ability of governments to initiate both administrative and policy reforms. Often this level of trust is in flux, cultivated in normal times by government performance but equally shaped by external events shifting public perceptions and political values. The reframing of security since 2001 — and the enlarged confidence interval accorded to governments in order to both prepare for and counter terrorism — is a case in point. Even prior to the terrorist bombings of July 2005, the UK government had embarked on its plan for a new national identity card with a level of public support that would have been unattainable in 2000 (the plan itself would never have been proposed).

For skeptics of a broader government and an increasingly virtual security blanket, the concern is that this heightened support for government action is in fact a measure of distrust and fear in the public at large. Moreover, how governments are responding — with larger bureaucracies devoted to public safety — may well reinforce hierarchical structures and a command and control managerial culture far removed from the collaborative networks envisioned by optimistic proponents of digitally enabled organizations.

This tension between collaborative efforts to foster government-wide integrated service offerings on the one hand, and the more heavy-handed responses to security threats on the other hand, remains a central aspect of e-government's evolution in many countries today. Such tensions also exist with the public sector in terms of organizational change and the degrees of freedom accorded to public servants to function in both vertical environments (within their chains of command) and new horizontal arrangements more networked and potentially collaborative (Malloy 2003).

At its most diffuse level, whether trust is accorded to political institutions and democratic mechanisms holistically by the citizenry is a question rooted in a complex equation involving openness, engagement, and accountability. The Internet's inherently liberating and empowering orientation coupled with a general decline in deferential authority (and, in the case of democracy, representational power) underscores a view of e-democracy that is much more participatory and responsive than those systems now in place, even as the precise nature of the participation remains highly contested across a wide range of views. Similarly, whether public servants can and should be trusted to lead public engagement exercises is both a managerial and a political issue since it impacts the role of the government official to operate directly in concert with the citizen while also potentially altering the traditional, representational relationships between politicians and their constituents.

Finally, the ability of the public sector to adapt itself to new realities to maintain a strong democratic fabric has critical repercussions for its ability to help orchestrate trust in governance at a systemic level that includes all sectors (notably industry and civil society). Countries that are the most transparent and free of political corruption also tend to be those with the strongest levels of investor confidence in corporate governance, and governments' moral capacities to both regulate markets and effectively partner with the private sector are enhanced as trust pervades and lubricates the system as a whole. Conversely, governance failures in one sector are likely to infect other sectors and pollute the governance culture of the jurisdiction as a whole.

Trust is therefore fragile and contagious, and e-government's emergence must be viewed as not only dependent on trust to meet the specific objectives sought by governments of today but also important in whether or not trust in the governance of a given jurisdiction as a whole is likely to be maintained and improved over time.

Looking Ahead

Fundamentally, the challenges confronting governments today stem from the four dimensions of change examined in the first portion of this book: service, security, transparency, and trust. How these dimensions co-evolve, and the degree to which they are either embraced or resisted, determine how e-government is currently defined and pursued as well as its future potential.

The many variables examined in Part One render the e-government equation a complicated one. The path ahead is likely to be contested and uneven. Prior to examining Canada's own path, we can first summarize many of the lessons emerging from the discussions of Part One that offer a point of departure for both describing and assessing the e-government efforts of any one country. The first two lessons underscore the importance of horizontality and collaborative governance in the context of e-government.

- The rise of online connectedness as a driver of e-government heightens the need for horizontal coordination to transcend internal organizational boundaries, and this point applies to both service delivery and security-related processes.
- Such horizontal governance requires both technological and political reforms to align performance objectives, decision-making processes, and accountability mechanisms in a suitable manner.

The great challenge of working more horizontally is the need to complement separate functional organizations with integrative mechanisms to facilitate shared outcomes. Often this integration runs counter to ministerial arrangements that are more vertical and silo specific, although the increasing attention paid to service transformation efforts and domestic security reforms (and other cross-cutting policy agendas) has at least mobilized awareness and effort. Although for many managers, politicians, and citizens alike e-government is a term that denotes the technological aspects of such challenges (i.e., the notion of interoperability, largely as it pertains to service transformation efforts), the meanings and implications are much broader and more profound.

Accordingly, while the terminology is evolving and use of the term 'e-government' is disappearing in many jurisdictions, it is doing so precisely because of the fusion of interrelated technological, organizational, and managerial agendas. Terms such as 'integrated service delivery,' 'federated enterprise architectures,' and 'smart systems' in fields such as public safety, anti-terrorism, and health all encompass a similar reliance on capacities for information-sharing and coordination that are dependent on the alignment of digital platforms and decision-making mechanisms. Perhaps the greatest source of uncertainty in such efforts is the loss of political clarity and control, as even the term 'horizontal' is misleadingly simplistic since governance patterns are more likely to be varied and networked as they adapt to shifting contexts and circumstances.

The resulting challenge of 'networked management' is dependent on embracing interdependency, and it is a significant departure from the bureaucratic model of public sector management—as well as many facets of new public management that have sought interagency competition and decentralized autonomy (Keast et al. 2004). Organizing and managing interdependencies are therefore central to the public sector's digital transformation: information and communication technologies create feasibility, but in order to generate results their deployment requires organizational and political change. Such change is nothing short of a cultural transformation in public sector operations.

Such changes are also more complicated by a world where internal comfort levels created by relative secrecy are increasingly challenged by an environment predicated on information-sharing and openness. Therefore, the third and fourth lessons are that

- governance is increasingly under pressure to become more transparent and participative, with resulting pressures for democratic reform certain to intensify, and that;
- such pressures may nonetheless encounter resistance within existing political structures and cultures.

Here is a source of tension between many of the reforms engineered by governments in the realms of service and security and the changing external environment that includes the citizenry and a diversifying and empowered set of stakeholders seeking to either monitor or influence government. Service delivery reforms are often predicated on the view that citizens do not wish to bother with government organization, and security is increasingly premised on the notion that citizens cannot have access to much of the information and process-driving decisions.

Such intent, while not without justification in some instances, does not shield the government from greater scrutiny and exposure, further reinforcing a risk-averse culture and placing at risk the level of public trust required to govern with legitimacy. At the same time, much as intra-organizational innovation and more horizontal models require trust through participation and engagement, the same is true of democracy where the compact of representative decision-making is under pressure to give way to more direct forms of public and stakeholder involvement. This conundrum is directly tied to the final lessons of Part One:

- Public confidence and trust in government are central to shaping e-government and e-governance reforms, representing critical determinants in the ongoing capacity of the public sector to adapt.
- The chronological and managerial comfort zone derived from pursuing e-government as a primarily incremental transition may be increasingly at odds with pressures for more holistic innovations in the very nature of democracy itself.

This latter point suggests that the sort of service initiatives and security reforms put forth by many governments may not suffice. Although important and innovative in many respects, they fall short of being transformative. As some scholars have observed, if unaccompanied by significant efforts at political and institutional reform, e-government may do little more than reinforce the existing tendencies of a particular state system (Karakaya 2003; Wilson and Welch 2004).

This mainly incremental trajectory not only implies limited democratic reforms at the institutional level but also important constraints organizationally within the public sector, since the horizontal and networked governance mechanisms are more likely to be stymied from emerging due to an absence of public support and understanding and a corresponding tendency of politicians to therefore view public management and accountability issues through the traditional prism of vertical control and hierarchical authority. Conversely, in jurisdictions where the citizenry is satisfied and confident with the performance and adaptiveness of political institutions, governments will, in turn, enjoy more degrees of freedom to pursue innovative models both organizationally and politically. Performance outcomes in the realms of service and security sought by individual governments are therefore intertwined with, and dependent on, the capacities of their political systems to reconcile the new demands for transparency with the new determinants of trust.

Although many such determinants of trust are unrelated to the advent of e-democracy, the Internet's role cannot easily be understated.

As more and more commercial and civic pursuits encompass an online component, it is not obvious why the political sphere should be exempt (particularly when governments — mainly via executive branch organizations — have proven so keen to exploit cyberspace as a means of improving service and security). The growing body of democratic experimentation encompassing online mechanisms supports this view.

Nonetheless, it remains the case that there is no uniform view across the citizenry in any country as to the appropriateness of e-democratic solutions and the speed at which they should be adopted. Governments must therefore attempt to reconcile the demands of early Internet adopters as well as the opportunities for democratic enhancements with the unease and varied preferences and capacities of different segments of the population as to the conduct and channels of political organization and decision-making.

In sum, the fundamental e-government challenge entails a balancing act — between technological, organizational, and managerial innovation both within and across public agencies and institutional renewal involving the production, organization, and sharing of power in an informational world of heightened personal empowerment and socio-economic and political interdependence. To what extent this balance has been achieved in Canada is therefore the focus of an investigation to which we now turn.

Part Two
The Canadian Experience

By adopting the four dimensions of e-government introduced in Part One (service, security, transparency, trust) as a lens through which to examine Canada's public sector, the next three chapters present the manner in which e-government has evolved across all levels of government over the past decade. With such a wide scope of activities, the purpose is not to provide a detailed inventory of every relevant initiative undertaken by governments during this time but to map out the major contours of how e-government has been defined, interpreted, and pursued. While our primary focus is that of federal and provincial governments, Part Two also explores the municipal reality as a distinct e-government experience as well as the interrelations across government levels in a multilevel environment where the evolving meanings of federalism, politically and technologically, raise important issues about the organization and performance of the public sector as a whole.

Federally: Chapter 5 provides both a review of the major e-government initiatives at the federal level and an assessment of the results achieved to date. What is also important to gauge is the degree to which progress has been sufficiently balanced across the four dimensions in order to enable internal organizational change and external institutional adaptation. Nationally, Canada provides a useful basis for examining e-government. One of the most advanced countries by measures of economic wealth, quality of life, and Internet access and affordability, Canada has been aggressively bolstering its use of digital technologies to realize the promise of e-government.

On the service delivery front, Chapter 5 will reveal some of the reasons that the Canadian government has enjoyed praise as a global leader in electronic service delivery. Despite this acclaim, however, many barriers to stronger progress have arisen, and 2005 marks a key turning point as the foundational strategy of Government Online, created in 1999, yields to a more ambitious, integrated, and multichannel vehicle for service transformation—namely, the creation of Service Canada.

Security underpins much of these efforts—and here as well the federal government has begun to make headway in both designing and implementing, in concert with its private sector partners, a 'secure channel' that is not only central to underwriting the online delivery of federal services (particularly those involving financial transactions and personal information) but also potentially of use by other levels of government in the pursuit of their own specific service objectives (as well as interjurisdictional offerings). Moreover, the expanding realm of the security mindset since September 2001 is also an important variable here in terms of resource allocation, political attention, and the underlying purpose of deploying digital technologies in an interconnected environment.

The interrelated agendas of transparency and trust are also examined—and what is revealed is a government captured by a predominantly reactive mentality responding to either crises or the more incremental but steadily rising demands for more openness and participation. Unlike service delivery, certainly nobody would laud the Government of Canada's efforts in democratic reforms tied to transparency and openness on the one hand and trust, participation, and relational capacities on the other. The consequences of this reluctance are important—both at present and in looking ahead.

Provincially: An examination of the evolution of e-government provincially reveals both similarities and contrasts to that of the federal level. Operating within the same parameters of Westminster parliamentary government, and spurred by the same forces that encouraged the federal inception of GOL, most provinces have undertaken electronic service delivery efforts that have much in common with federal initiatives. Indeed, while the federal government may often enjoy greater recognition, provinces have not only kept pace but also, in many areas, are leading in both developing an online presence and reorganizing the backroom functions of government to better integrate services in a multichannel environment. In doing so, new models of public-private partnerships often discussed in Ottawa are delivering results provincially (though not without considerable challenges).

With respect to service delivery and security, many of the key challenges that occupy federal public servants can also be found provincially, and the ability to overcome them varies across the country. No single province has transformed its service delivery architecture in an ideal manner. In comparison to the federal level, however, the pace of change is more diverse and, like the federal experience, more incremental than radical.

Nonetheless, with regard to transparency and trust, and the pressures and opportunities to embrace innovations of a more democratic sort, there is a more notable differentiation between federal and provincial developments. Although once again perhaps more incrementally than radically, many provinces have begun to explore changes to both the electoral and the decision-making architectures of their governments, in some cases seeking ways to embrace examples of what might be termed 'digital democracy.' Yet it is important to acknowledge that certainly not all of the democratic changes contemplated or introduced at present can be characterized as e-democracy, for many such reforms may have little direct connection to the Internet or digital technologies. Nevertheless, there is a correlation between the nature of these changes and the broader transformation of social, economic, and political activities taking place in an increasingly open, informational, and networked environment.

The provinces, as a network of ten similar yet distinct governance regimes, offer further insight into not only adapting new service and security agendas within the contours of e-government but also reforming the parliamentary model into a more participative and democratically consultative system. While examples from various provinces across the country will serve in this review and analysis, Ontario and British Columbia will be featured as two case studies with which a better understanding of reforms at the provincial level can be developed.

Locally and intergovernmentally: Two recent initiatives illustrate both the potential for new collaborative relationships across governments and the cultural and structural tensions of Canadian federalism that may limit such potential. The consequences for municipalities — seeking to develop their own versions of e-government at local levels — are profound.

The first initiative is the Collaborative Senior's Portal (www.seniorsinfo.ca), an intergovernmental partnership between the City of Brockville, the Province of Ontario, and the Government of Canada.

The portal's main purpose is to facilitate a one-stop resource for senior citizens that can provide information on all public services and significant issues, regardless of jurisdiction. By entering this site, residents thus find information and appropriate links on a range of issues, from local housing options and medical service centres to federal passport applications and provincial forms for death notification and certification.

The portal personifies the vision of e-government, particularly its service delivery emphasis as initially conceived by federal leaders when such seamless approaches to governance became a central objective of the GOL agenda. In a more citizen-centric world, particularly in cyberspace, life events and outcomes should drive the organization of the public sector online—rather than departmental boundaries and jurisdictional lines. At the same time, the senior's portal reveals the primitive stages of online intergovernmental activity. Although the portal does offer an efficient and user-friendly set of informational resources (quickly linking the user from one appropriate part of the public sector to another—often a different government level), this information-sharing role is not complemented by any integrative capacities for processing citizen requests or transactions that may transcend various governments or, in many cases, different parts of a single government.

Can one envision a day when a single act of data entry is digitally shared across governments to facilitate the completion of all administrative tasks? The technological requirements for doing so are relatively straightforward. What is much more complicated, of course, is the political and organizational alignment for creating such an interoperable administrative architecture. Indeed, one measure of progress toward such an outcome is the provincial change-of-address feature (on the senior's portal as well as on the province's main webpages) that enables citizens to simultaneously enter an address change for a driver's licence, vehicle permit, and health card. For municipalities, experiments such as the senior's portal raise the spectre of whether or not local governments should be directing their e-government efforts—often with a more limited set of resources than at other levels of government—at achieving better and more integrated services within their own domain or working with provincial and federal governments to achieve more integrative outcomes.

The second initiative to consider is the international Kyoto Accord on carbon emissions and climate change—and Canada's efforts to reduce greenhouse gases. The environment is an area in which all levels of government can legitimately lay claim to playing a role. Not only did the federal government negotiate the terms of Canada's entry into the Kyoto protocol, but it also regulates and promotes many aspects of industry across the country, all the while asserting authority across numerous environmental matters. Yet provinces share such authority on many matters—controlling natural resources—and both government levels shape the transportation infrastructure of the country and, as a result, the availability and mix of transit methods both between and within communities. On the front lines of planning and development, municipalities are no less influential.

Despite this interdependence, the process of developing a Kyoto strategy has been largely devoid of intergovernmental collaboration and coordination. Local governments are constrained to devise smart growth plans that are either contingent on various funding outcomes controlled elsewhere or subject to significant change as new funding opportunities arise. Moreover, the funding allocated to such local supports pales in comparison to the billions of dollars being deployed via the federal government apparatus. Kyoto discussions are therefore most often framed largely as a federal mix of federal promotion, regulation, and intervention—a strategy forged almost exclusively within the confines of the federal cabinet and its lead departments.

While Kyoto is not thought of as e-government, it should be. The nexus between community growth and energy and environment planning, transportation and the organization of work, and digital connectivity is at the heart of how a global issue such as climate change rests on local governance capacities. On an issue that has featured significant interest and mobilization by civil society, it seems intuitive that an array of municipal engagement efforts could serve as a highly useful input into what is characterized as a 'national' (as opposed to federal) strategy for climate control. Yet too often such capacities are overshadowed by national politics and federal and provincial processes with little coordination between them.

The implications for the ability of governments at all levels to not only collaborate with one another but also engage and mobilize citizens and communities are important, a microcosm of the sorts of challenges likely to be more prominent and complex as more online and participatory forms of democracy take hold. The Kyoto experience illustrates how the traditions of federalism do not naturally give way to a more integrative and seamless digital order despite the technological capacities to act in new ways, and the broader implications of this dilemma are fundamental to viewing e-government as a prism for the public sector as a whole.

Building on a storyline introduced in Chapter 6, these intergovernmental dynamics are examined in Chapter 7 through the prism of e-health, not unlike Kyoto in many respects politically and certainly more recognized technologically as a critical example of e-government. Despite the formal confines of provincial jurisdiction, health care's evolution in a digital environment encompasses important national and local considerations that raise questions about the appropriateness of traditional federalism in the public sector for emerging twenty-first-century realities.

Chapter 5
Government of Canada

Under the rubric of a Connecting Canadians agenda, the federal government launched its flagship e-government initiative, Government Online, in 1999, promising to make use of cyberspace as a means to both share information more widely and transform service delivery over a five-year period. A centrepiece of this effort has been the creation of a 'secure channel' in order to facilitate online transacting, while departments have been encouraged to forge innovative schemes to integrate service offerings within the thematic clusters provided for by the central portal. Progress has meant overcoming significant governance barriers that have nonetheless spurred further efforts to realize interoperability and a federated enterprise architecture for the government as a whole. The importance of such themes was enhanced by the aftermath of 9/11 when the purpose and players of information sharing shifted but the organizational and technological process requirements remained. 9/11 also reinforced a culture of secrecy that is often at odds with the government's own rhetoric about wanting to be more open and accessible through online channels. Similarly, despite flirtations with the notion of a 'democratic deficit,' the realms of transparency and trust have by and large created discomfort for a governing and political context shaped by scandal and a minority Parliament. The result is an overriding focus on service and security measures that seek to expand the use of digital technologies while minimizing political risk changes institutionally that would reorganize and share power in new ways. In short, e-government is ostensibly viewed as a means to preserving and deploying power.

The chapter is organized in the following manner. Section 5.1 examines the evolution of online service delivery as a central tenant of the government's efforts to realize more citizen-centric forms of governance. Section 5.2 then considers the evolution of the security agenda both as an underlying requirement for service objectives and as a separate but partially related agenda for public safety, surveillance, and domestic responsiveness to threats such as international terrorism. Section 5.3 explores the interrelated themes of transparency and trust and their influence on democratic reform debates – including experiments and reforms that have emerged in recent years at the federal level. Section 5.4 concludes with a more collective assessment of these various dimensions of e-government at the federal level.

5.1 From Government Online to Service Canada

The impetus for the major components of the federal e-government strategy arose from a broader effort, Connecting Canadians, that was crafted in the mid-1990s and led by the federal Department of Industry. In the speech from the throne on October 12, 1999, outlining its objectives and priorities, the Government of Canada stated that, "By 2004, our goal is to be known around the world as the government most connected to its citizens: The Government On-Line Initiative (GOL) was launched to meet this commitment. The goal of GOL is to provide Canadians with electronic access to key federal programs and services. The initiative focuses on grouping or 'clustering' online services around citizens' needs and priorities, rather than by government structures" (Coe 2004, 6). The government has often showcased citizen satisfaction surveys with online delivery channels,[1] and Canada's reputation internationally has also been bolstered by international observers, such as Accenture Consulting, that ranked Canada as a global leader — recognition largely predicated initially on the government's main portal (www.gc.ca) that, in the spirit of integrated service delivery, is grouped according to clusters of services and specific client groups.[2] The federal government's objective is to ensure that the 130 most common federal services are online by 2005 (when the GOL program formally ends, giving way to a broader service transformation effort reviewed below). By 2004, some 122 of these 130 services were 'identifiable' online (meaning access to some information about them was featured on government webpages; the remaining services are internal to government and therefore not conveyed publicly online).

Most of these offerings, however, are informational rather than transactional. The ability to complete services and make payments remains much more limited. Some examples of this latter functionality include change-of-address features, online processing of tax returns, business registrations, submission of select statements of employment, and a variety of purchases for government publications. Indeed, online processing of individual tax returns is perhaps the most significant example of success, with nearly half of all tax returns submitted online in 2003-04 (a figure expected to surpass the fifty percent mark by 2004-05).

With regard to 'transforming services' across departments and agencies, progress has been difficult to achieve. The government aims to have seven of sixty-three informational services integrated across separate yet interrelated sources of government activity (including in at least two cases of sources that come from other jurisdictions). With regard to fully transactional services, the government had realized fully integrated transactions across government departments in only two of sixty-seven cases by 2003, with the aim of increasing this level to six by 2005.[3]

One of the main barriers to realizing more integrated service stems from the difficulties in getting departments to work together in sharing information and combining authority to realize more citizen-centric processes. The vertical structures of separate departments serving individual ministers largely translate into autonomy over interoperability: "silos continue to reign" (Coe 2004, 18). Coe's examination of GOL pilot projects — interdepartmental experiments to integrate services — reveals a widespread lack of shared accountability to facilitate collaboration: "When managers were asked whether accountability is shared among partners for the successful implementation of GOL projects, the response was a unanimous no" (ibid.).

In her review of GOL, the auditor general underscores a similar absence of a coordinated architecture required to balance vision and planning: "With only high-level expected outcomes, there is no clearly defined end state for GOL. The government will have difficulty measuring progress and performance toward 2005 objectives" (Auditor General of Canada 2003, 10). Such findings are indicative of the growing need for more rigorous collaborative mechanisms and performance frameworks to both facilitate shared action and gauge progress, particularly in service delivery agendas that transcend traditional reporting relationships (Public Policy Forum 2003; Stowers 2004).

This point will only grow in importance since realizing the sort of citizen-centric service integration implied by a web presence that clusters services (pledging to transcend organizational boundaries to do so) is dependent on a process of building new governance capacities that face many potential hurdles. The chief information officer of the Government of Canada (2004) lists the following issues as core challenges in this regard:

- capacity of the public service (know-how);
- funding and sustainability of GOL initiatives beyond 2005;
- governance and accountability for integrated services;
- moving to common infrastructure; and
- privacy and security.[4]

These internal and external assessments underscore both the breadth of change required in moving forward and the modesty of GOL achievements to date. In recognition of this modesty and the necessity of more significant reforms that are required, during the course of GOL the government developed a parallel though closely related initiative known as Modernizing Services for Canadians (MSC). In essence, MSC not only acknowledges the challenges confronting GOL but also recognizes that online service delivery must coexist and align effectively with other service delivery channels, such as telephone and in-person facilities.

Beginning, then, within the department that was the largest provider of domestic programs and services to Canadians, MSC represented a three-year business transformation initiative (2002-04) undertaken to "renew HRDC policies, programs, services, and service delivery by focusing on what citizens need in a way that supports citizens' full participation in the workplace and community." By building a new citizen-centred foundation, MSC aimed to change the focus of HRDC from the business of conducting transactions to a new emphasis on building relationships with citizens: "it is transforming the current complex delivery network into a single integrated service delivery network that provides seamless, multi-channel service to Canadians."[5]

In May 2002, the Treasury Board approved the Year One Business Plan for MSC that focused on global research and internal preparation and planning and ultimately led to the development of a blueprint for citizen-centred services to Canadians. Central to this blueprint is the MSC vision: *to transform service to Canadians by focusing on what citizens need in a way that supports their full participation in the workplace and community.* The vision for serving Canadians, businesses, and communities included four fundamental objectives: (1) ensure the integrity of social programs; (2) move from the delivery of separate government programs in silos to seamless citizen-centred service; (3) work together as a collaborative networked government; and (4) demonstrate accountable and responsible government.

Although initially rooted in a single federal department, MSC began as one of the largest business transformations ever undertaken in the Canadian public sector, aiming to transform

- the HRDC service delivery network across the country, which includes ten regions, more than twenty-three call centres, web and kiosk service delivery; 122+ processing centres; 320 HRCCs (100 main and 220 satellites); Service Canada delivery (229 sites); and 2,330 third-party delivery partners;
- all services and programs delivered by the department, including transactions amounting to over $70 billion in benefits to Canadians; and
- the nature and the management of the work of HRDC employees and managers (which number approximately 25,000).

Priorities during the second year of MSC concentrated on the implementation of enterprise management for service delivery and corporate services and setting the stage for more simplified, seamless, and integrated service to Canadians—one specific example being the E-Payroll initiative involving a partnership between the lead MSC department (formerly HRDC) and the Canada Revenue Agency.[6] Several other changes were introduced in year two, notably the technical and organizational platform to further integrate service delivery across all channels—phone, Internet, and in person. An example of this is the creation of an enterprise-wide Internet delivery capability. Prior to MSC's introduction, HRDC had 170 distinct Internet sites, each of which was managed independently. In year two, the management of the Internet channel was brought under one roof, and the 170 websites were consolidated into one. The government estimated that these reforms will generate efficiencies of about fifteen percent of annual Internet infrastructure costs.

As part of MSC moving forward into its third year, the government was obliged to address the issue of identity and authentication (in recognition of the fact that at present no government-issued form of identification was designed for integrative service delivery purposes). Accordingly, a major review of the registry of social insurance numbers (SIR) was undertaken in collaboration with the other departments and provinces with the aim of reducing errors and bolstering record management capacities to ensure the consistent identification, authentication, and validation of individuals who require services, apply for benefits, or receive financial benefits. The integrity of the SIR is an important element of the foundation required to enable greater interdepartmental and intergovernmental cooperation in service delivery (the security features of GOL and subsequent initiatives are discussed more fully in the next section).

In developing these new capacities, the federal government sought private sector assistance. Engaging private sector companies essentially revolved around three components of preparation for service transformation: learning from the best practices around the world (via leading companies with global reach across diverse public sector clienteles) and building support across government through education and preparation; actively engaging the private sector companies in the management and governance of MSC initiatives; and leveraging the early experiences of pilot initiatives within a single department (HRSDC) in terms of integrated, multichannel service delivery.

These early efforts are important elements in fostering a foundation for service delivery transformation. Preparation can be viewed in three interrelated ways.

- First, work to date has demonstrated the potential of integrated, multichannel service delivery strategies via early results from pilot initiatives (reviewed in part one of this case study) in terms of service improvements and cost savings.
- Second, significant organizational capacities have been developed (across IM/IT, HR, change management, and performance measurement) within the federal government that are necessary elements of the foundation for pursuing the service transformation agenda, both within the lead MSC departments and on a government-wide basis.

- Third, in moving forward to leverage these opportunities and capacities, MSC has been instrumental in laying the groundwork for a more ambitious government-wide effort at service transformation (Dutil et al. 2005).

The nexus of the first and second points underscores the significant dimensions of undertaking an enterprise-wide approach to service transformation for the Government of Canada. Traditional accountability structures that reinforce individual ministerial accountability and thus separate organizational structures (or silos) have shaped for some time the decision-making culture of government. Shifting to a citizen-centric approach on a government-wide scale is thus a major effort, one that also underscores the importance of viewing the service transformation agenda not as a technology project (i.e., electronic service delivery within a multichannel environment) but as an encompassing agenda for organizational adaptation and performance improvement (Charih and Robert 2004).

The formal creation of a new Service Canada model in 2005 marks the transition to realizing the goals of convergence and better government-wide coordination capacities to realize citizen-centric service delivery.[7] Service Canada may also signal a shift in approaches toward working with the private sector. The MSC initiative, along with much of the GOL apparatus, has essentially been crafted through an insourcing approach where government has sought to make use of private sector expertise in building in-house capacities (notably the secure channel, reviewed in the subsequent section). Although international research on various contracting strategies undertaken by national governments in developing e-government capacities (notably the choice between outsourcing versus insourcing such systems) has not revealed any clear evidence of an optimal contracting regime (Dunleavy et al. 2003), there is a growing view within both government and industry circles that more innovative forms of partnership will be required to realize the more ambitious service transformation objectives sought upon transitioning from MSC to Service Canada.

The companies involved in the MSC experience clearly did so in the hope of wider levels of experimentation in subsequent phases of service reforms, and HRSDC and SDC have been actively engaged in the development of a strategic partnership framework to scope out this potential, learning as well from many provincial and international service delivery models that have featured innovative arrangements between government bodies and the private sector involving performance-based compensation schemes, risk-sharing mechanisms, and a greater overall degree of collaboration than is typically found in traditional contractual relationships (Dutil et al. 2005; Langford and Roy 2005).

At the same time, however, the Government of Canada faces considerable challenges in reforming procurement within a context shaped on the one hand by questionable contracting practices from the past (e.g., the federal Sponsorship Scandal) and growing relational frustration between government entities and private sector companies working in concert on technology-laden initiatives (Brown 2005). These themes are thus returned to in a more forward-looking manner in Part Three.

5.2 From Secure Channel to Secure Nation

In line with both the growing importance of a digital infrastructure across government operations and the emergence of new threats (Chapter 2), security issues have risen dramatically in prominence. Certainly, security and privacy have been recognized as fundamental to the online service delivery agenda. The strategic focal point of security within GOL has been the 'secure channel,' as defined by the Government of Canada:

> Secure Channel is a portfolio of services that forms the foundation of the Government of Canada's (GoC) Government On-Line (GOL) initiative. Secure Channel's primary goals are to provide citizens and businesses with secure, private and high-speed access to all federal government's on-line services, and to provide an environment that enables and encourages departments to integrate with federated common services.
>
> For the GoC, Secure Channel is the common infrastructure that provides secure and reliable network services for all federal departments. It also offers additional services for security, registration and authentication that enable departments to meet their 2005

GOL goals and deliver the most commonly used services on-line. It is the critical link between government programs and Canadians. Without the common infrastructure and services provided by Secure Channel, and the assurances it provides with respect to security and privacy, Government On-Line's Service Vision of client-centric, cross-government service anytime, anywhere cannot be realized.[8]

The secure channel is a crucial platform required to expand the online capacities of the federal government for online service functionality — particularly the processing of financial payments and the completion of transactions required for an exchange of personal, confidential, and/or sensitive information. By 2004, the secure channel had been deployed across all federal departments and agencies as the basis of a new government-wide network infrastructure; it also allowed for the small but growing base of online service offerings summarized above. Among other initiatives planned, the secure channel is expected to allow for the first-ever availability of the national census online in 2006.

The challenge in the next phase of the proposed service transformation for 2005 and beyond effectively involves the formation of a governance mechanism to align the Service Canada vehicle and its reliance on the secure channel in a government-wide effort. Such an agenda represents perhaps the largest proposed overhaul of the federal machinery of government in recent memory — since a 'shared services' model is envisioned to better coordinate and facilitate cross-departmental activities.[9]

Major governance issues pertaining to organizational structures and accountability mechanisms across the federal government present themselves (as well as a set of related intergovernmental issues[10]). It is in fact the significance of the task at hand that may well explain the high levels of secrecy and caution that have pervaded the next steps of the service transformation agenda throughout 2004 and into 2005. Although such a commitment was announced in the 2005 federal budget in March 2005, details were vague.[11]

For much of 2005, proponents of Service Canada within the public service faced uncertainty and resistance from cabinet and central agencies. Ongoing political uncertainties, tied to a minority Parliament and an expected election by early 2006, have slowed progress, casting some doubt on both the precise timing and the details of any eventual restructuring. Such sensitivities are compounded by the secure channel's (and all of the technical dimensions of the government's shared digital infrastructure) housing within Public Works and Government Services Canada (PWGSC), the most scandal-plagued department in recent times (albeit in unrelated areas of communications and contracting[12]).

From one perspective, the potential benefits and risks associated with these various efforts at horizontality (e.g., Service Canada as the external interface and shared platforms for both IT infrastructure and support services[13]) stem from what is a centralizing reform aimed at consolidating many functions from across previously separate departments into a common body. Ideally, this unit can then provide better service functionality to all units in government in moving toward a federated architecture of common standards and shared systems where feasible (while still allowing room for tailored technology solutions within departments when necessary). Clearly, however, the realization of such improvements relies on many variables, chief among them the degree to which more efficient and effective working relationships can be designed (through central imposition, contractual competition, or collaborative arrangements) among participating units (many of which may well find their own reasons for resisting a loss of autonomy).[14]

Upon deploying the secure channel as a platform for online services, a critical set of issues pertains to information management and the handling and privacy of personal information of individuals and organizations transacting with the government via the Internet. The centrepiece of the external interface to the citizen-customer (i.e., user) of such service offerings is the 'e-pass,' defined by the federal government as "a secure, privacy friendly, portable common service solution that is helping to standardize electronic service delivery across government."[15] A description of its use reveals the connection between identification, authentication, and encryption in providing a high level of assurance to the public user:

> The first time someone wishes to engage in a secure electronic transaction with a federal program or service (or if the person chooses to register for a separate epass for each program with which he wishes to have secure electronic transactions), the program redirects the

individual to the Government On Line Certification Authority, which issues the potential user an epass. In addition to a user identifier and password created by the applicant, each epass contains a randomly generated anonymous identifier, known as a Meaningless but Unique Number (MBUN). An epass also contains the mathematical formulae for encrypting and decrypting information. Encryption/decryption services protect electronically transmitted data against unauthorized interception or alteration. (Ibid.)

While the secure channel represents the common infrastructure available for all federal departments and programs, it remains the prerogative of individual units and their managers to determine the appropriate level of authentication required (allowing for variance across mundane information flows deemed a low risk and more sensitive types of information) and ensure that privacy requirements are met. In other words, it is an example of an attempt to facilitate interoperability through both centralized direction in developing the shared infrastructure and autonomy in its application to specific services.[16]

To be able to expand the realm of online service offerings — particularly those involving capacities to complete transactions fully — one concern is identity management and the fact that none of the currently accepted forms of government-issued identification, federally and provincially, was established with service delivery use in mind. Accordingly, use of the social insurance number became a key focus of MSC development efforts (and will now serve as the basis for further efforts by Service Canada).

As governments seek to expand their online usage, and in light of the post-9/11 expansion of the security imperative, the issue of what constitutes a proper identity and how it can be verified is increasingly central. Based on international trends toward so-called 'smart cards' (some examples of which were reviewed in Chapter 2), the federal government has publicly mused about the possibility of a new national identification card, while some provinces have flirted with a similar integrated mechanism for their own jurisdiction.[17]

In place of any encompassing solution at either level, both levels of government agreed instead to form a new Federal/Provincial/Territorial (FTP) Council on Identity that would forge a consensus framework on standards and policies pertaining to identity management by all public authorities in Canada. Yet by late in 2005 there had been no publicly available information about this council (indeed, the status of the initiative appeared in limbo). There is little question, however, of the growing need for this sort of dialogue in light of the widening interest in intergovernmental coordination to facilitate both service- and security-related objectives.

With respect to privacy and the government handling of personal information of its citizens, although the issue is not exclusive to electronic service delivery, the advent of e-government and GOL — coupled with growing concerns about incidents pertaining to the mishandling or theft of information[18] — has done much to raise the profile of such issues. Indeed, the federal Office of the Privacy Commissioner has reported that most of its activity in recent years pertains to GOL and electronic service delivery initiatives (Bloomfield 2004).

At the heart of the federal privacy framework is the Privacy Impact Assessment (PIA), a mandatory tool now part of any new program or service of the federal government that involves the handling of personal information (electronically or otherwise). PIAs perform the following roles.

- They act as an early warning and planning tool.
- They forecast and/or confirm the impacts of a government proposal on the privacy of individuals and groups.
- They provide a mechanism to assess a proposal's compliance with privacy protection legislation and principles.
- They provide a framework for the development and implementation of actions and strategies required to avoid or overcome the negative impacts of the proposal on privacy. (Bloomfield 2004)

While privacy assessment is part of departmental reporting to the Treasury Board, another key stakeholder is the Office of the Privacy Commissioner (OPC), an independent ombudsman who serves as the guardian of the privacy rights of Canadians.[19] Privacy laws require that any department or agency undertaking a PIA must do so in concert with the OPC. With respect to PIAs pertaining to GOL and electronic service delivery initiatives, the OPC has registered a number of sets of issues that it sees as common pitfalls revealed through the assessment process, including proper notice, client authentication, user ID and password management, desktop security, use of shared computers, third-party service providers, transaction monitoring, and database access controls.

The framework for privacy assessments remains at its infancy, and these sorts of potential weaknesses have not had a major impact for two reasons: the relatively cautious approach to online service delivery and limited forms of transacting minimizes the scope of any risk, and over the past few years larger and more politically sensitive privacy matters pertaining to a broadened security agenda and cross-border data flows have overshadowed the micromanagement of information by instruments such as the PIA.

Terrorism and the Border
For Canadians, the tragic impacts of 9/11 were felt first and foremost in terms of the loss of human life. Along with the feelings of sympathy and support directed toward American neighbours, the loss to Canada was felt directly from the twenty-four Canadian citizens killed that day. More peripheral but equally crucial responses to the initial attacks also underscored the closeness of the two neighbouring countries.[20]

In the days that followed, an additional and hugely significant collateral threat to Canada took shape, albeit one economically-oriented. The threat was underscored by two occurrences: first, stories circulating in the American media that at least some of the hijackers entered the United States by way of the Canadian-US border (a theory that would prove unfounded); second, the seemingly endless line of trucks extending back some thirty-six kilometres from the Windsor-Detroit border crossing (joining Ontario and Michigan). The first point threatened to expose Canada as a weak link in US security, whereas the second image underscored the economic catastrophe that could result from being cast in this manner.[21]

As a result, it is difficult to overstate the sensitivity of Canadian authorities to American views and actions. According to Meyers (2003), the United States forged ahead with the securitization of its borders and 'dragged' Canada along with it. While such a characterization would be disputed by some, there is little question that many conditions warranted a response by Canadian authorities that would be in line with US action (both in replicating and aligning to it). Accordingly, in the aftermath of 9/11, plans that had already been under way were fast-tracked to create a 'smart border' accord of some thirty points to reinforce security while facilitating mobility, a balance achieved in large part through technological innovation: indeed, bilateral interoperability and biometric potential are prevalent themes of the accord.[22] The Government of Canada reinforced this bilateral focus with a major financial commitment to border security in late 2001.[23]

Within the country, the legislative centrepiece of Canada's response to 9/11 came with Bill C-36, the country's first official Anti-Terrorism Act, thereby legislatively defining terrorism for the first time in Canadian history and greatly expanding the powers and means of federal authorities to prevent such activities in the future.[24] Underwriting this expansion is also an enhanced degree of secrecy in many aspects of law enforcement and legal proceedings, the focus of which has been the subject of much debate in the legal community, not unlike debates surrounding the Patriot Act in the United States (Allman and Barrette 2004). Complementing this legal authority is recognition of the importance of digital security in order to underpin organizational interoperability, ensure the resilience and integrity of government information holdings (to be heightened in both volume and strategic value), and address the risks and realities associated with the transnational scope of terrorist activity (Brown 2003).

In short, digital security would be reframed from being viewed primarily as a facilitator of service delivery (the main impetus for e-government up to this point) to that of a central tenant in the war on terror (Hart-Teeter 2004). As in the United States, however, the technical and organizational capacities of the Canadian government for doing so were quickly shown to be suspect—and greatly in need of an overhaul (Kernaghan and Gunraj 2004; Roy 2005a). For instance, with respect to IT security generally across government, there is evidence of longtime neglect. In a 2002 audit of government IT security, the auditor general reported serious shortcomings and followed up with a 2004 report that described progress as unsatisfactory.[25]

Along with these technical difficulties one must add the considerable challenges of organizational and managerial coordination across government. The auditor general again concludes that horizontal coordination has been inadequate: "gaps and deficiencies point to a requirement to strengthen the management framework of issues that cross agency boundaries, such as information systems, watch lists, and personnel screening" (Auditor General of Canada 2004, 39). For instance, in an effort to create an Integrated National Security Assessment Centre in 2003 to "use intelligence from many sources to produce timely analyses and assessments of threats to Canada" and distribute this information accordingly, the difficulties of establishing a collaborative mechanism overrode the importance of its role.[26] In a separate study, the Senate Standing Committee of National Security and Defence conducted a review of security readiness and emergency preparedness, noting similar concerns and quoting a senior official's assessment of what is required: "an unprecedented level of cooperation inside and outside of government" (Standing Senate Committee 2004, 14).[27]

The response to such deficiencies came in 2004 via Canada's first-ever National Security Policy to gather all security sectors under a more integrated and coordinated framework: anti-terrorism, policing, border control, and cybersecurity are the purview of a single minister.[28] The American Department of Homeland Security served as a reference point for what would become Canada's Department of Public Safety and Emergency Preparedness Canada (PSEPC), "created to secure the safety of Canadians while maintaining the benefits of an open society. It integrates under one minister the core activities of the previous Department of the Solicitor General, the Office of Critical Infrastructure Protection and Emergency Preparedness and the National Crime Prevention Center."[29] Within this new body and under the shadow of 9/11, the Government of Canada's Advance Passenger Information/ Passenger Name Record (API/PNR) program is designed "to protect Canadians by helping to identify high-risk/would-be travellers: The Canada Border Services Agency (CBSA) is authorized to collect and retain information on travellers and to keep it for customs purposes under section 107.1 of the Customs Act. API is basic data that identifies a traveller and is collected at the time of check-in."[30]

Governments invoke necessity as justification for such actions in light of 9/11 (underwritten by shifting public support toward broader security measures). At the same time, such undertakings face at least four important concerns by critics (often different groups or constituencies most interested in a subset of such issues). They are

(1) infringement on the privacy rights of Canadians; (2) the secrecy surrounding government operations managing such initiatives (and by extension the related information sources); (3) the potential for 'function creep,' where information gathered by one part of government for one purpose (in this case anti-terrorism) invariably finds its way into other processes tied to other purposes; and (4) the possibility for errors or mishaps due to mismanagement of information and identities in particular.

The interplay of these four sets of concerns shapes much of the debate surrounding national security strategy. For example, although the first point is partially mitigated by a variety of legislative safeguards addressing privacy concerns, as well as the independent privacy commissioner (reporting to Parliament and therefore the public as opposed to the government), the same commissioners are often among the most active critics of government action, underscoring problems associated with secrecy, function creep, and identity management.[31] The potential for error and mismanagement within the security apparatus is a prevalent theme of the most recent auditor general findings (Auditor General of Canada 2004, 2005).

In sum, many governance and technological aspects of the service delivery and security dimensions of e-government are closely intertwined. Not only are they both increasingly reliant on cyberspace as a critical component of their operations and interactions with citizens (and others), but also their abilities in making use of new digital technologies require public acceptance in one form or another. Thus, misuse of an online tool by security authorities can chill the willingness of many citizens to share their personal information with other government authorities — and, in turn, to accept that such information may be widely shared across government in the name of convenience and better service.

In this manner, the fortunes of service and security reforms are closely interrelated by the need for a more sophisticated digital apparatus that nonetheless must be well aligned with internal management and organizational processes on the one hand and external political realities on the other. The federal government's capacity to navigate this terrain depends, therefore, not only on its internal competencies but also on its efforts to maintain the support and confidence of the citizenry.

5.3 Transparency and Trust

The close relationship between transparency and trust reframes the e-government equation from a predominantly internal, incremental, and administrative set of challenges toward more cultural and institutional variables. At the same time, these internal and external dimensions remain intertwined: the evolution of Service Canada and national security efforts are both destined to be shaped by how matters of transparency and trust impact existing institutions within which they operate. Although the Internet and digital technologies are not alone in shaping debates, online connectivity facilitates new and wider platforms for informational exchange and knowledge mobilization. Hence, it becomes increasingly difficult to ignore pressures for more participation and engagement and the consequences of these pressures for internal governance reforms.

In some ways, the Government of Canada has proven open to this enlarged spectrum of debate. The public service in particular, in its own efforts to remain modern and adaptive, has recognized the importance of a broader governance renewal hinged, in some measure, on the potential of digital technologies. For example, public servants working within the Government of Canada developed this quotation as one element of their centrepiece for a new vision of twenty-first-century governance: *"Representative democracy in Canada has not been replaced, but it has become more participative. Democracy is no longer just voting every four or five years, but a continuous, engaged, informed and collaborative dialogue involving all players"* (E-Government Policy Network 2004, 9). In 2001, then Clerk of the Privy Council Mel Cappe lauded GOL as a key initiative but underscored that e-government is a much broader concept than online service delivery, one that "must be regarded as a new model of government, one that is born of and relevant to the new emerging society—a society that is increasingly digital and global in its interaction." Cappe went on to underscore the necessity of forging new relational governance mechanisms both within and outside the public service, networks based less on structure and more on collaboration and stakeholder engagement. Within this vision, according to Cappe, electronic (or digital) tools are complemented by changes to enable citizens, elected officials, and public servants to adapt to these new realities.

Prior to entering the Martin cabinet as Treasury Board president, Reg Alcock led a small contingent of parliamentarians who recognized the need to insert the legislature into such debates. Appearing frequently with laptop in tow, Alcock would speak at public forums about e-democratic ideals and the potential for new forms of engagement, much as he served as a champion for the Crossing Boundaries initiative that has continued to serve as one of the few vehicles engaging public officials themselves in such discussions. Yet ministers past and present (including Alcock), once in office, have proven to be far more fixated on managing and steering the public service in specific directions than on improving parliamentary capacities and rethinking democratic governance more broadly. Alcock himself acknowledged this point in an address to the e-government community in May 2005, underscoring the difficulty of reforming organizational structures and systems.

Paul Martin's own interest in empowering Parliament has likewise waned since the 2004 election brought about a partial realization of this objective in the least enviable manner from his point of view: minority status in the House of Commons has undoubtedly raised the prominence of this chamber and the antics and manoeuvrings of its members. Just as important, Martin's democratic reform agenda put forth in his pursuit of his party's leadership never extended beyond the realm of Parliament. In other words, at no point did Martin reveal much interest in more participatory democratic measures involving the public (beyond strengthening the role of elected members in a manner that would enhance their visibility and importance in the eyes of the citizenry). Although there may well be some legitimacy to such limits for some (i.e., defenders of a representational democratic model), this perspective on democratic reform continues to be at odds with the expanding efforts of the federal public service to engage citizens directly, complementing traditional forums with online channels to do so.

Increasingly, then, the public service and elected officials are sending mixed signals about the importance of both public participation and online democracy. The reluctance by the government to entertain bolder reforms appears to be consistent with the cautious, incremental approach undertaken in terms of service delivery reforms. In both cases, the rhetoric implies major cultural shifts and structural realignments, whereas the actions undertaken most often represent the smallest possible deviation from tradition. The problems with this approach may well prove more costly in terms of democratic reform since public attitudes toward the federal government are more sharply negative in terms of politics and parliamentary forums than they are with respect to more operational matters of service delivery (Zussman 1996; Sims 2001; Segal 2005).

Within such contexts are four major challenges that shape what may be characterized as an inertia leading away from significant institutional change at the federal level today:

- the inherent operational secrecy of internal reform efforts geared to service improvement and security agendas that make wider use of digital technologies that decouple such reforms from experimentation with wider or new forms of democratic engagement (Roy 2005a);
- the weak information management capacities of the federal government and the inherent resistance to greater openness that accompanies such weaknesses (Reid 2004);
- the inherently adversarial nature of existing parliamentary processes and the absence of meaningful, proactive information reporting that results, particularly on integrative outcomes (Lindquist 2005); and
- the related political culture of spin and communications management that reinforces inward control and outward suspicion by those in power (Roberts 2005).

The origins of the first point stem from a service-driven focus on e-government on the one hand and an ongoing reluctance for democratic innovation on the other. The emphasis on political clarity and organizational outcomes over complexity and uncertainty fuels a mindset within government that limits what citizens need to or should know. However, this mindset sharply conflicts with the widening persona of an Internet era that lends itself to greater inquisitive tendencies — particularly in probing traditional forms of authority. While the customer of government services online may appreciate quick and efficient transactions online, the same person as a citizen may well come to expect a fuller knowledge of how government operates either directly or indirectly (and such perceptions are fuelled by assertions of political leaders who promise greater openness and accountability).

The second and somewhat related point speaks to the inwardly proprietary culture of information management that characterizes the parliamentary model of government. The emphasis on information containment begins with the principle of cabinet secrecy and is reinforced by the adversarial dynamics of Westminster-style politics. In the case of the Government of Canada, this engrained culture of withholding information to the greatest extent possible permeates both the core public service and the outer sphere of agencies, Crown corporations, and foundations that serve the public interest on behalf of the federal government. In response to growing criticism about such a culture, the federal government has sought to expand its openness, albeit in limited and qualified ways such as making use of the Internet to provide 'proactive disclosure' of travel and hospitality expenses of senior officials and, in some cases, contracting activities of the department.[32]

Yet these new and gradual measures fall far short of the sort of cultural transformation called for by Internet enthusiasts as well as a variety of stakeholders and scholars converging on calls for greater openness (Tapscott and Ticoll 2003; Courchene 2005). The absence of planning and performance information about Service Canada and the secure channel (the former in terms of its proposed creation during 2004 and 2005, the latter throughout its development within the context of the GOL initiative) is indicative of the soundness of such critiques as well as the potential for mischaracterization and contention to emerge from what little information does invariably leak out.[33]

Although some agencies — notably the Canada Revenue Agency — have made important strides in recent years in developing more rigorous forms of planning and performance reporting to both Parliament directly and the public via the Internet,[34] the government as a whole has made little systemic effort to link performance management with online efforts to improve reporting capacities to Parliament and the public. Although the self-reporting style of communicating results in the most positive fashion may at times serve to enhance the image and brand of the Canadian government (GOL is a case in point), the absence of a more neutral, objective, and balanced form of information offsets any such benefit, leading to a further erosion of public trust at worst and stymied collective learning between the government and its stakeholders at best. A recent study of Canada's access-to-information system reveals how this culture of information control extends beyond the shaping of the message to actually resisting release of information in the first place: the use of IT has even become a tool to better monitor, filter, and in some cases stymie external requests for information (Roberts 2005).

Not only is this communications-oriented mindset a key factor in the growing cynicism and declining confidence of the public in its governments, but also the quality and performance of the public service are at risk. The absence of wider political innovation coupled with increased centralization (both politically and technologically) stymies public servants from acting creatively and collaboratively, both with one another and with outside stakeholders. The inability of shared accountability to take hold in GOL projects provides testament to this point, as does the relative absence of a sufficiently robust human resource dimension of the overall GOL framework that saw the most significant amounts of funding allotted to online content of information and service offerings and the underlying technical infrastructure, notably the secure channel (Charih and Robert 2004). This absence is all the more striking in light of the CIOB's own acknowledgement that the capacity of the public service remains a key barrier to broader service transformation improvements.

Here again the pursuit of Service Canada marks an important test of the willingness of the government to both invest in and engage its employees in moving forward while introducing systemic reforms to transcend traditional departmental barriers and reinvent policy-making and service delivery processes for a more collaborative era (Savoie 2005). Despite some progress within limited initiatives under the rubric of MSC (the precursor to Service Canada), there is much about the manner in which senior managers responsible for Service Canada have chosen to communicate the initial announcement of this shift that implies only the most incremental margins of reform in terms of the impacts on people and processes:

> The next step in this process is to reorganize the service delivery functions and some strategic corporate services within our two departments to form the appropriate infrastructure for the Service Canada initiative. This will also mean some changes to the organization of the policy and program branches and corporate areas

within HRSDC and SDC. In addition, most of the transactional shared services — Human Resources, Financial and Administrative Services and Systems — will become part of the Service Canada initiative.

Reporting relationships will not change for the majority of employees. However, some of you will have a new manager within a new or restructured organization effective May 30, 2005.[35]

That deputy ministers would take the first opportunity to reinforce the status quo for most reporting relationships is hardly a sign of significant organizational renewal. Based on the above assessment, this caution can be ascribed to the general disinterest of cabinet in reforming the machinery or governance of the public sector compared with more visible policy initiatives and issues — a tone set by the Prime Minister's Office that is more conducive to reinforcing interministerial frictions, rivalries, and delays than new forms of concerted actions and integrative and collaborative mechanisms.[36]

These primarily political limitations should not overshadow the fact that public servants have largely been responsible for the realization of e-government progress to date (as defined primarily through the service delivery lens). Although political support initially by then Minister of Industry John Manley was an important catalyst, since then a growing community of CIOs, service managers, and policy developers has maintained the momentum and sought to move the agenda forward in what more recently has become a sort of political vacuum where the term 'e-government' has lost some of its lustre to other political priorities.[37]

The service transformation effort continues, but the present political atmosphere dictates that subsequent changes are likely to be modest and incremental rather than bold and experimental. In this manner, the absence of more activity in the realm of information openness and democratic innovation is directly linked to service delivery and security, since these latter agendas are thus more likely to be pursued through modest changes to existing political and bureaucratic structures. Accordingly, such modesty also means that the public service will be less creative and more controlling and directing — in other words, a highly restricted space for managerial and organizational innovation within the confines of public sector organizations.[38]

These sorts of pressures limit and shape what it means to be citizen-centric externally, reinforcing a culture of communication and information control. The extension of this culture into cyberspace is evident in the efforts of the government to utilize online platforms as a direct channel to convey the good intentions and business of those in power, providing an exclusively positive portrayal of government operations.[39] Moreover, the government's consultative claims in pursuing online reforms are shrouded in the service delivery mentality—since the input of citizen-customers is sought through user surveys, polls, focus groups, and other methodologies arguably more image- than performance-based. The government is careful to frame the results of such exercises in the most positive manner possible.[40]

As a result of this orientation, the federal consultation portal—as a more genuinely democratic experiment in shared decision making and policy formulation—has floundered due to an absence of both political and organizational capacity to make use of it.[41] The message to Canadians visiting the site (the government 'is committed to finding new and innovative ways to consult with, and engage Canadians') is a stark contrast from the more mundane reality of what the portal provides—a set of links offered as a partial inventory of ongoing activity. The site is technologically primitive, vastly overshadowed in terms of resources, importance, and use in comparison to the literally hundreds of monthly announcements pertaining almost exclusively to positive outcomes or new initiatives associated with government action of one sort or another.

The limited use of public consultation and political oversight with respect to national security is also illustrative. The government would undoubtedly point to many new outreach mechanisms involving citizens and stakeholders to guide security efforts as evidence of embracing a more participatory mindset.[42] However, such mechanisms have been mainly introduced in the aftermath of the strategy's formulation and in the midst of implementation (arguably in response to growing criticism of the absence of consultation during these stages), limiting sincerity and effectiveness accordingly.

There remains little effort to instill within national security circles an open and public dialogue that could be used to help foster wider degrees of public and collective learning to guide governmental action in this era of new threats and opportunities. The government's plan to create a new Parliamentary Committee on National Security was mired in secrecy and delay throughout much of 2004. Although establishment of such a committee marks an important political innovation, there is much about the committee rules that suggests a determination to preserve as much secrecy as has traditionally characterized the security and intelligence operation (the notable innovation being the extended purview of select parliamentarians to oversee such matters).

The Legislature's Limited Presence Online

With so much of service and security managed from within the executive, and a communications apparatus tightly aligned with the prime minister, cabinet, and central agencies, it is not surprising that the legislative branch has by and large been further marginalized by the e-government movement. Although Parliament maintains its own website that features a significant amount of information on members and their activities, there is little about Parliament online that denotes a qualitatively different approach to political life: in other words, the websites serve as little more than windows of information on the traditional mechanics of parliamentary democracy. Indeed, in comparison to the huge amounts of resources directed at the government's flagship portal (the centrepiece of service and communication), the appearance of the legislative branch is unavoidably primitive.[43] E-democracy is by and large absent.

One important exception, however, is an early effort by the Parliamentary Sub-Committee on the Status of Persons with Disabilities to undertake an e-consultation on the issues before the committee. The thirteen-week process, launched in December 2002 (the first-ever online consultation by a parliamentary committee), sought to both inform citizens and obtain their views on the Canadian Pension Plan Disability Program, and it yielded some encouraging results in terms of interest and participation: "During the consultation period there were almost 190,000 page requests on the web site, almost 1,500 people participated in the issue poll, 135 stories were submitted and almost 30 people offered solutions. When asked about their experience in post-consultation follow-up, more than 90% of participants said they would participate again" (Coleman and Norris 2005, 72). The committee view is that this process — coupled with traditional consultation mechanisms — added an important degree of legitimacy to the final report and recommendations.

Two important lessons can be drawn from this e-consultation, which merits both recognition and praise for its efforts to broaden public participation. First, much as with service delivery, online consultation channels should be viewed not as a replacement for more traditional approaches but as a complement in a multichannel environment. Second, a more aggressive use of such mechanisms may hold merit in encouraging participation, improving legitimacy, and strengthening the outcomes of such committee proceedings. The Sub-Committee on the Status of Persons with Disabilities underscored this second point with its own recommendations based on its initial experience:

> Given the success of the pilot project on e-consultation in complementing its regular committee study of the Canada Pension Plan Disability and providing Canadians with information as well as involving them, the Committee recommends that:
>
> Each committee of the House of Commons considers putting in place an information-based website. Such a site could include common elements (e.g. information about how Parliament works, how committees operate and how to contact the committee) as well as information specifically related to an individual committee's mandate, activities and background information related to its specific studies;
>
> The House of Commons and Library of Parliament be given appropriate additional resources to put in place information-based committee websites with the capacity to facilitate e-consultations;
>
> The House of Commons and the Library of Parliament should put in place an overall framework or suggested course of action to guide any future e-consultations; and
>
> Where circumstances warrant, other committees of Parliament consider including e-consultations with Canadians as one of the options in carrying out a study.[44]

A key limitation of the exercise, rooted less in the application of online channels and more in the systemic use of consultation in the parliamentary model, is the indirect incorporation of the input gathered from the exercise into the recommendations made by the committee. While its report is effective in describing the process of consultation in addressing the issues at hand, there is an element of communications in the self-validation derived by what was heard:

> The broad range of Canadians who responded to our e-consultation—all types of life experiences, age, gender, occupations and geographical locations—clearly indicates that this process reached a good cross-section of individuals and advocacy groups with an interest in the CPP(D) program. Those who sent us their stories or submitted solutions to the Subcommittee confirmed that we had gained access to a wealth of first-hand knowledge about what was important, what worked well, and where improvements could be made. A very important lesson for all of us was that when people are asked their views, they will respond in a thoughtful, constructive, and open way. Despite the "decline of deference" and the perceived irrelevancy that envelops many parliamentary institutions, Canadians, when they believe that they will be listened to and that their views may make a difference, take up the challenge. And this they told us directly. (Ibid.)

Importantly, the committee underscores the key litmus test in determining the credibility of public consultation—namely, whether the public is, in fact, 'being listened to.' Although there is no reason to doubt the sincerity of those who participated in this consultation, and the resulting value for committee members, there is little evidence in the committee's reporting of its deliberations and recommendations to demonstrate clear links between its views and findings and the consultative learning process underpinning such outcomes. Such links require greater care and attention—particularly as parliamentarians seek greater participatory capacities with the public, both offline and online. This experiment also underlines the need for (1) a much wider effort to recalibrate the representational processes of Parliament for a greater degree of power sharing with the citizenry and; (2) a strategic consideration and recasting of the roles currently played by executive and legislative bodies respectively in seeking public involvement.

5.4 Conclusion

The federal government's pursuit of e-government has been shaped primarily by a service and communication mindset on the one hand and the widening security lens of the past several years on the other. Both facets of reform share a widening use of ICTs and online capacities in ways that seek to deploy new governance capacities to respond to rather than engage the public. Accordingly, the political emphasis in terms of the message conveyed to the public is the downplaying of internal organizational complexities in favour of more integrated, citizen-centric outcomes. Such outcomes, however, have been both slow to evolve (in the service realm) and increasingly contested politically (with respect to security), contributing to an expectations gap between the objectives sought and the results achieved.

Although information technologies and online connectivity are becoming pervasive across the service and security realms of government operations, a major difficulty with this path is that, in the absence of bolder reforms, the legitimacy and adaptive capacities of the public sector are placed at risk — as the widening canvas of e-governance and engagement appears increasingly at odds with democratic tradition and matters of transparency and trust.

Within the Westminster parliamentary model, there are increasing signs of recognition of the need for more public engagement, but such signs are more indicative of reluctance and caution within existing institutions rather than an appetite for reform. The difficulties are compounded by the pressures of transparency imposing themselves on the public sector, creating the conditions for a seemingly accelerating series of scandals and mismanagement. This more reactive form of transparency provides testament to the view that, while it is arguably unlikely that governments are erring more often now than before, their failures are now more likely to be exposed and to greater effect. As a result, trust and cynicism are related in a negative spiral.

Such difficulties suggest that e-government, if unaccompanied by significant efforts at political and institutional reform, may do little more than reinforce the existing tendencies of a particular state system (Karakaya 2003; Wilson and Welch 2004). With a widening view that the Westminster parliamentary model may be out of step with the nexus between digital innovations and social and political expectations, such an embedding of the status quo is worrisome.

The extent to which the provinces are faring differently in balancing service delivery and security reforms that are primarily internal and incremental and more outward and holistic pressures for institutional adaptation is the focus of the next chapter.

Chapter 6
The Provinces

In some respects, the provincial e-government experience resembles that which has transpired federally. The focus on online service characterized much of the initial effort, underpinned by the need for an appropriately novel and modified governance architecture capable of facilitating security and interoperability across traditionally separate program and departmental structures. An e-government subsystem unto itself, health care systems – and the advent of e-health – exemplify both the potential for revolutionary change and the risks and barriers in realizing such change. Similarly, the Service Canada model under development federally is more established in many provinces, although there are variants in its purpose and form across jurisdictions at this level as well. Given their shared parliamentary governance model, the provinces face many of the unsettling pressures also arising federally from within the realms of transparency and trust. At the same time, however, there is some evidence of more oxygen being accorded to debates pertaining to democratic institutional adaptation, such as electoral reforms and more meaningful forms of citizen engagement. The degree to which such changes denote e-democratic experimentation remains unclear in many cases, as provincial governments appear to be only slightly less skeptical than their federal counterpart about the potential for significant democratic renewal tied to digital transformation. Nonetheless, distinctions between these levels may be important in anticipating future reforms.

This chapter begins with an examination of the main contours of e-government strategy and organization as they pertain to the realms of service and security. Section 6.2 then undertakes the same task from the perspective of the interrelated dimensions of transparency and trust: given the greater scope of provincial activity and the potential for distinction from the federal experience, this perspective is accorded more attention than was the case in the previous chapter. Finally, section 6.3 offers an assessment of the provincial experiences to present by drawing out a number of key lessons.

6.1 Service and Security

There is much about the federal government's experience that is familiar to provincial efforts to introduce online service delivery. While the portfolio of services offered differs according to provincial and federal responsibilities, the underlying philosophical shift of becoming both more customer-centric and technologically enabled is equally prevalent. If the outward philosophy is similar, so too is the more inherent belief that process and administrative reform are issues of little interest to the average citizen (viewed primarily as a customer in this mindset), who is more concerned with convenience and outcome.

The following quotation from the Government of Ontario's online presentation of the main pillars of its e-government strategy is indicative:

> The government of Ontario is proactively moving towards becoming an e-Government, a government that will be able to meet the challenges of the 21st century... . The current focus of attention for e-Government in Ontario, as in many other jurisdictions, is what we call *electronic service delivery,* or ESD.
>
> To make e-Government happen requires a complete re-design of the internal operations of the government and the operating systems of the broader public sector. Our I&IT Strategy guides these efforts. However, much of this re-design work is, and will remain, invisible to the general public. More visible will be another area of e-Government: *citizen engagement.*

To realize such outcomes, the sort of horizontal integration and multichannel alignment pursued by the federal government is also a primary focus of provincial government efforts. Although the pace of progress and the mechanisms deployed vary considerably, three key challenges stand out: (1) the introduction of new service delivery models to make use of online channels to deliver information and services (in a manner that coexists with traditional channels); (2) the creation of enterprise-wide mechanisms to better share information, promote common standards, and ensure interoperability across separate ministerial departments and agencies; and (3) the formation of new models of public-private sector collaboration in order to realize potential benefits from these organizational reforms.

A key organizational issue encompassing all three challenges lies in devising the leadership and governance capacity, typically via a CIO-led body, to respond to all three challenges in a coherent manner — and one that finds an appropriate balance between centralized control and flexibility and autonomy. In many respects, these three challenges are intertwined insofar as their collective pursuit shapes the e-government architecture for government-wide change.

In some cases, such as Service New Brunswick (SNB), a lead agency (in this case a Crown corporation) is empowered to foster new online capacities by addressing all three challenges simultaneously. Thus, SNB has pursued its mandate with strong leadership from the premier's office, creating a de facto central agency to more or less impose interoperability on all line departments through a single external interface (Langford and Roy 2005). In serving citizens, SNB is regarded by many as an innovator in its use of a public-private partnership to develop new delivery channels in a manner that will ideally generate benefits for government and its stakeholders as well as the private sector entity (CGI) engaged in this effort (ibid.).[1]

SNB now conducts more than forty percent of its transactional business online, and it is expanding into a variety of other collaborative projects with companies designed to jointly develop solutions for New Brunswick that can be marketed and sold elsewhere. Federally, SNB is regarded as a model of interest in regard to the creation of Service Canada (discussed in the preceding chapter), although a number of uncertainties and distinctions present themselves, not the least of which are differences in size, jurisdictional coverage, and organizational complexity between a small province of just under 750,000 citizens and the Government of Canada, which serves more than 30 million individuals nationally.

At the other end of the provincial spectrum in terms of size is Ontario, with more than 12 million citizens, a population that far exceeds many of those countries typically ranked highly in global surveys of e-government progress.[2] Accordingly, the scale and complexity are more akin to those of the federal government, creating a similar set of challenges in terms of forging government-wide capacities. Much like the federal government, Ontario has moved gradually over the past decade in creating its own CIO structure and set of government-wide initiatives to pursue new models of service delivery.

The election of a Conservative government in 1995 spurred cost-cutting pressures that fuelled interest in both eliminating government-wide redundancies and deploying IT to improve efficiency and customer service. A significant challenge in doing so lay in the considerable operational autonomy vested in line departments, including IT planning and management. The Government of Ontario thus adopted its formal e-government plan in 1998 (Information and Information Technology Strategy), and it included a more rigorous pursuit of cross-agency cooperation within a set of measures designed to create an integrated and thus more interoperable organization (in line with the vision presented above).

The new organizational model that largely remains in place today features "The creation of a corporate CIO function with defined responsibilities for strategy, policy, controllership, architecture, common ICT infrastructure, standards and security as well as the human resource and procurement functions relating to ICTs. The corporate CIO was designated the 'owner' of the government's ICT strategy — a key enabler to driving transformation in the Ontario government" (Culbertson 2005, 25). In an acknowledgement of both the limits to centralizing authority and the need to ensure flexibility and adaptability across different parts of government, this corporate CIO is complemented by a set of seven 'cluster' CIOs, each cluster representing a set of departments with similarities in mandates and potential synergies in terms of their digital infrastructures.[3] These cluster CIOs therefore have dual reporting relationships to both the deputy minister of each department within the cluster as well as the corporate CIO. Collectively, the cluster ministries and the CIO establish a memorandum of understanding on how the cluster will operate — a mechanism that seeks to allow sufficient flexibility to balance the mandates and needs of individual departments, the similarities and synergies to be forged within each cluster, and corporate or government-wide directions and objectives (Culbertson 2005).

Assessments from within the Ontario public service are mixed, much as they are by those who have examined this approach. Internally, there is little question that the establishment of this federated architecture of corporate and cluster CIOs has enabled senior management to develop a government-wide vision that is translating into a rebalancing of vertical autonomy and horizontal cost-sharing.

For instance, in addition to this IT infrastructure, the province has established a Shared Services Bureau to centralize all support services from individual departments within a common entity empowered to realize cost savings and service improvements through specialization and 'client' relationships across the government internally.[4]

It is important to underscore this distinguishing between digital technologies on the one hand and other forms of administrative services on the other. Whereas the latter group is more fully centralized, the management of information and communication technologies remains very much a shared function between a central corporate body (the corporate CIO) and the clusters and individual departments. This shared approach is largely based on recognition of the need for some level of autonomy and specificity between units such as the Ministry of Health on the one hand and the Ministry of Natural Resources on the other. At the same time, some public servants bemoan that the result of this flexibility can often be duplicated bureaucracy as major IT decisions require approvals from internal ministry authorities as well as the corporate level (via the cluster CIO).

Although a definitive assessment of what remains an ongoing work in progress is premature, one informed scholarly observer credits this two-tiered approach with providing, at the least, a strategic framework for thinking holistically about the purposes and priorities behind the dispensing of nearly $1 billion annually in IT-related activity (Borins 2004). Not unlike the federal GOL effort, however, the provincial auditor has underscored the difficulties in both tracking and coordinating electronic service delivery initiatives across government (Office of the Provincial Auditor of Ontario 2004).

Unlike the creation of a new and more autonomous SNB model in New Brunswick, an existing line department had been tasked — until quite recently — with managing the delivery of common and shared services both online and via other channels such as call centres. Accordingly, the Ministry of Consumer and Business Services was the lead actor in forging integrated service offerings in a manner that resembles to some degree the basis of MSC at the federal level: "One of these new initiatives is ServiceOntario, which was announced in the spring 2004 budget. The ministry is leading this multi-year, multiministry, interjurisdictional initiative. The premise of this initiative is to improve access to government services to all Ontarians, including people with disabilities. The initiative will transform the face of government service delivery in Ontario. In the following years, ServiceOntario will enable one-stop access to government services and information in-person, by phone or online."[5] Situating the 'ServiceOntario' portal as a basis for integrative services within a line ministry (Consumer and Business Services, itself within the Economics and Business IT Cluster) was thus an alternative example of facilitating interdepartmental capacities, at least for those issues where an integrative service model would be appropriate.[6] This line ministry functioned without any direct authority over other departments; however, collaboration can be facilitated both within the cluster by a common CIO and across government by the corporate CIO. Perhaps for this reason, upon shuffling his cabinet in July 2005, the premier's restructuring of various ministries led to the fusion of Consumer and Business Services with the central agency, Management Board Services (a body whose mandate is by definition government-wide).

It seems, then, that the Province of Ontario responded to one of the main strategic design quandaries in terms of e-government and internal governance reform — namely, the relative importance of fostering e-government delivery capacities on integrative scales (i.e., across departments) versus the deployment of online service delivery within more unique and specific departmental mandates. There is some tension here between the vision of e-government and portals that reorganize service offerings in a citizen-centric manner (i.e., based less on boundaries than on shared outcomes) — thereby creating organizational pressures for centralized integration and the potential for more separate innovative service delivery models based more on uniquely tailored solutions within departments and agencies.[7] Ontario's most recent changes suggest a nod to the former — corroborating the rising pressures of e-government for a more centralized management architecture to foster an 'enterprise-wide' architecture for more integrated service outcomes.

The Province of British Columbia

The evolution of e-government in British Columbia features a less centralized model than that of Ontario, one nonetheless relying on a strengthened CIO position that has evolved into an equally important platform for government-wide strategy over the planning and deployment of a digital infrastructure and IT-enabled tools to improve service.[8] The CIO for the province is responsible for overall direction setting for the e-government framework, including following seven 'central foundations' as identified in the current e-government plan from 2004 to 2007: privacy, authentication, electronic records management, security, common user interface, interoperability standards, and e-government management and central funding (Government of British Columbia 2004b).

In contrast to Ontario, there are no CIO clusters in British Columbia. Instead, each ministry has a CIO equivalent to oversee departmental planning and implementation, and this group in turn reports to the government-wide CIO, a deputy minister-level position situated within the Ministry of Management Services, the body responsible for government-wide infrastructure and administrative management (akin to Management Board Services in Ontario and the Treasury Board Secretariat federally). Although staff in the CIO office point out that deputy minister status is testament to the level of authority and direction, it is noteworthy that the current e-government plan calls for stronger authority and additional resources to improve government-wide performance.

Such calls, however, are complemented by an emphasis on the importance of pursuing more individualized electronic service strategies for each department: "The CIO will not dictate ministry e-service priorities, rather he will work with ministries to develop foundation applications in time frames and with priorities that complement ministry plans" (Government of British Columbia 2004b, 22). Much of the progress in terms of online service delivery, with currently over 500 services offered online, reflects the separate but coordinated efforts of line departments fostering delivery methods for their own purposes.[9] This heightened level of coordination also reflects the CIO's emphasis on fostering a government-wide electronic infrastructure: "In 2002, BC opted to include IT infrastructure as a shared service and established a three-year goal for IT infrastructure consolidation, an aggressive schedule when compared with other jurisdictions in North America" (ibid., 6).

Overall, the emphasis of the current CIO structure in British Columbia is a more collaborative and less formalized set of horizontal mechanisms than is the case in Ontario. On the positive side, there is evidence of growing acceptance of the need for government-wide approaches and solid progress toward achieving a stronger set of organizational and technological capacities for the government as a whole. Moreover, the encouraging of innovation by ministries has paid dividends in terms of new and varied examples of service delivery. Yet concerns lie in the degree to which a common portal will be sufficiently supported with interdepartmental sharing mechanisms to further integrate services (a stated objective in the e-government plan) and the degree to which current resource and authority levels of the CIO office will be sufficient in creating the 'foundation' for better overall e-government performance.[10]

A somewhat unique aspect of British Columbia's e-government plan and CIO authority (insofar as it is distinguishable from Ontario and most other provinces) is the level of attention accorded to expanding a digital infrastructure outside the core public service (in a fashion not unlike that of Alberta[11]). The construction of a communications network consisting of high-speed data and voice lines has connected all core government offices across the province, and plans are in the works to extend the network to all segments of British Columbia's extended public sector (e.g., health care authorities and schools). Moreover, the province has established a new agency, NetWork BC, to expand broadband Internet access to all rural communities unsupported by market services.[12] Such moves indicate a provincial trend to seek broader alignment between e-government as an internal reform agenda and a wider lens of digital transformation for the jurisdiction as a whole.[13]

An additional and important distinction between Ontario and British Columbia lies in the role of the private sector, much more aggressively welcomed and pursued by the latter province. Indeed, over the past few years, many dimensions of the provincial government's IT infrastructure have been shifted to the private sector through outsourcing and partnership arrangements.[14] In comparison, the McGuinty government in Ontario has generally been more cautious about private sector involvement, a reaction in part to a shift in ideology away from almost a decade of Conservative governments—a period that featured a number of controversies about public-private partnerships and IT projects in particular.[15]

Despite Ontario's caution, the necessity of significantly reforming procurement systems is widely viewed as a critical issue in shaping provincial efforts at fostering more integrated, multichannel service delivery systems and achieving better public sector governance generally (Mornan 1998; Jordan 1999; Langford and Harrison 2001; Allen and Roy 2002; Kieley et al. 2002). Much like the federal government, the Province of Ontario responded to its own unease in late 2004 with an external review of IT management and procurement in order to probe both root causes and potential solutions.

The presentation of the technology sector's leading industry association, the Information Technology Association of Canada (ITAC), to the Ontario review panel offers insight into the current situation in terms of both challenges and potential avenues for reform:

- many business transformation projects have not met expectations in terms of schedules, costs, and requirements;
- IT-enabled transformation projects are seen as high risk;
- the reputation of the IT industry and its customers as a whole is impacted by these troubled projects; and
- this has occurred in the private sector as well as in government. (ITAC 2004)

In its presentation, ITAC offers a study of IT project failures for which the top three causes are a lack of clear links between the project and the organization's key strategic priorities, including measures of success; a lack of clear senior management and ministerial ownership and leadership; and a lack of effective engagement with stakeholders. In terms of making headway in such an environment, ITAC suggests a range of improvements that, while varying in scope and purpose, tend to converge around the creation of more flexibility and trust between industry and government. Indeed, the invocation of trust as a key relational component of such partnerships calls into question the extent to which the internal transformation of public sector governance can and should be viewed as separate from more externalized matters of transparency and trust (a theme returned to more fully below).

ITAC points to the Province of British Columbia, which has been among the most aggressive subnational jurisdictions in encouraging public-private partnerships, as an example of the type of procurement to partnering reframing that is required:

The Province of British Columbia has developed a Joint Solutions Procurement Process for the evaluation and selection of vendors in large IT projects. Its basic principle is to engage the private sector bidders in a joint discovery of the risks and benefits of the initiative to assess the capacity, commitment and capability of the private sector bidders. The procurement process follows defined gates where information is disclosed and discussed and the field of potential vendors is finally reduced to two. The final stage engages the finalists in competing bids based on a range of criteria relevant to the business outcomes sought by the government. (ITAC 2004, 13)

This type of procurement approach — emphasizing results and outcomes and innovative solutions for achieving them — is consistent with a lessening emphasis on static, upfront measures of cost and price and a greater reliance on more performance-driven and collaborative-based project management. Although rather novel, the BC government is committed to using such an approach in the future formation of IT partnerships. Similarly, it is this type of approach that will likely be required within the contours of the next phases of the federal service transformation — and the emergence of a new Service Canada model to more aggressively pursue citizen-centric service delivery on a government-wide scale (as discussed in the previous chapter).

With respect to impacts and performance outcomes to date, several important observations can be made: first, there is no dramatically discernible difference in the level of service delivery sophistication across these provinces at present; second, despite this early uniformity, provinces have nonetheless made more headway than their federal counterparts in achieving integrated service delivery outcomes and organizational reforms required to underpin them; and third, as a result of this provincial-federal contrast, the provinces are to some degree serving as both a model for current federal reforms and a basis for pursuing service integration on an intergovernmental scale.[16]

Indeed, e-government has driven the emergence of an alternative apparatus of federal-provincial relations that nonetheless remains in its infancy. Stressing integration, collaboration, and interoperability, the CIO Council (comprising federal and provincial representatives) and the related Institute for Citizen-Centric Service Delivery are important vehicles in conducting the research and preparation required to move in such directions. Their findings, outputs, and reports are the basis of an annual Lac Carling Summit in Quebec (the first such meeting was held at the Lac Carling resort), a venue inclusive of municipalities and private sector representatives as well.[17]

Currently, the infrastructure for intergovernmental service integration remains limited, overshadowed both federally and provincially by internally focused reforms, and the difficult co-evolution of this form of digital federalism and the more traditional practices of autonomy and conflict have been well illustrated as of late by the example of Ontario. The head of the Ontario public service has spoken publicly on the importance of a new provincial-federal agreement protocol for service collaboration, whereas the premier's message over this time period in 2004-05 was fixated on fiscal imbalances between Ottawa and his province (such intergovernmental themes are explored further in the subsequent chapter).

Security and E-Health
The security dimension of e-government at the provincial level is in many respects both similar and closely connected to what has been transpiring at the federal level, albeit with some important distinguishing traits.

Clearly, the shared emphasis on delivering services online is a driver at both government levels. Identity management, authentication, and safe and resilient channels of information-sharing, -recording, and -transacting—all hallmarks of the federal government's secure channel initiative—are equally prevalent in the provincial domain. Yet the secure channel at the federal level—in essence an insourcing effort to make use of private sector expertise to nonetheless build the required capacity in-house—has by and large not been a model replicated by provinces. The chief reason for this distinction is the greater willingness of many provinces to engage in partnerships and outsourcing arrangements with the private sector in pursuing service delivery outcomes.

Accordingly, service and security concerns have become more interwoven into the fabric of such partnerships, with results to date that provide both comfort for proponents of this direction and ammunition for those more suspicious of or hostile to it. Some comfort is derived for proponents of greater partnering from the growing experimentation in new service capacities that feature significant roles for the private sector without serious problems or flaws pertaining to security. Moreover, many provincial officials concede that such a role for industry has helped to facilitate greater security capacities than otherwise would have been the case.

This point is testament to two key, interrelated aspects of a partnering and outsourcing emphasis: engaging leading competencies from specialists not easily available within existing government resources (human and financial), and doing so through innovative collaborative schemes that integrate service and security outcomes with performance-based incentives to ensure that the partnership can be beneficial to both parties. Such trends are discernible internationally, and although many provinces remain at early stages of such efforts there is evidence of a growing willingness by provincial governments to introduce more flexibility and creativity into procurement systems to realize such outcomes (Langford and Roy 2006).

Nonetheless, critics counter that we remain in the early days of these sorts of partnering arrangements that could well be laying the seeds from which future discontent and problems may grow. Two arguments are typically invoked: first, the volatile and uneven set of experiences with private sector involvement to date; and second, more specific matters of security pertaining to the handling of confidential public information.[18]

This latter point became a notable topic of political and public discussion in 2004 when the provincial privacy commissioner raised the prospect of US technology companies working with Canadian provincial governments (via their Canadian subsidiaries) being bound by US federal government laws under the Patriot Act to share public information with American security organizations. Politicians and company executives alike were quick to deny such allegations, but the story was given new life by media reports that federal officials concurred with the BC assessment and consequently had been quietly undertaking efforts to develop new safeguards for their own contracting purposes to shield this potential occurrence from taking place.[19] It is at the same time important not to exaggerate the impacts of this debate, welcomed by many stakeholders. In British Columbia, in fact, the provincial government quickly adapted its contracting provisions without dramatic repercussions for its aggressive use of public-private partnerships (and the issue received no significant amount of media or political attention during the provincial campaign of April-May 2005).

In large measure due to arguments centring on the safeguarding of public information, the application of e-government to health care — a provincial jurisdiction — is to some degree unique unto itself. Unlike more transactional personal and corporate services deemed less contentious in nature, the health care system is viewed as particularly ripe for both revolutionary digital innovations and significant risk. As a result, more than elsewhere caution has been viewed as the appropriate mentality in proceeding. More to the point, e-government has by and large emerged as a parallel existence within the realm of health care (denoted by the label 'e-health').

Although the promise and evolution of e-health have much in common with other public service areas, the size of the resource allocations, the critical importance of the issues and outcomes at play, and the political sensitivities shaping debates surrounding the management of health care all converge to underscore the uniqueness of this area — particularly at the provincial level.

In Ontario, a provincial E-Health Council has been formally established to build on the various initiatives and programs that have emerged since the late 1990s. The purpose of such an office is essentially to provide a CIO capacity for the health care system as a whole in order to guide system-wide reforms pertaining to new technologies.[20] The Government of Ontario defines e-health as 'achieving better health outcomes by transforming health systems and business practices through the investment in and more comprehensive use of information and information technology.'

In many respects, the pursuit of e-health in such a manner encompasses many of the previously reviewed governance challenges that pervade service and security dimensions of e-government: interoperability and the balance between central coordination and flexible responsiveness comprise a particular challenge for a large and diverse province that operates without regional health authorities (on an annual health care budget of roughly $30 billion). To what degree information-sharing and digital innovations should be pursued on a provincial or local scale is an important variable and a major factor for security considerations — since the greater the system in terms of geographic and demographic coverage, the greater the complexities in creating a networked architecture that is robust, reliable, and responsive.

Moreover, over time, one can expect the logic of connectivity and interoperability to at least create stronger incentives for national mechanisms—of either a more unilateral federal nature or stronger intergovernmental forms of collaboration. Indicative of the latter path is the recent formation of the Canada Health Infoway, a federal-provincial research entity accountable to both levels of government that has been given the mandate of "Fostering and accelerating the development and adoption of electronic health information systems with compatible standards and communications technologies on a pan-Canadian basis with tangible benefits to Canadians. Infoway will build on existing initiatives and pursue collaborative relationships in pursuit of its mission."[21] At present, the work of this research body is being complemented by provincial governments seeking to introduce pilot initiatives involving electronic health records in their own jurisdictions. The optimistic interpretation of this arrangement is based on the view that the joint accountability structure of the national Infoway body (to both federal and provincial levels) ensures coordination rather than repetition in terms of research and resources—and to date there is little evidence to suggest otherwise. An example of the sort of localized changes hoped for by e-health proponents is on display in the City of Laval, Quebec, where an intergovernmental partnership has resulted in the formation of a shared digital infrastructure across various segments of the health care system that improves diagnostic and processing capacities, thereby improving service for users of the system.[22] Ontario's e-health efforts, as well as their local and intergovernmental repercussions, are examined more closely in the next chapter.

In sum, there are pressures rooted within service and security dimensions of e-government that to some degree converge around the notion of extending visions of seamless governance and interoperability beyond any one level of government. From the service delivery side, there are opportunities jointly recognized by provincial and federal officials as being consistent with the logic of citizen-centric service now subscribed to. The message has often been reinforced by the public pronouncements of political leaders at both levels since e-government's inception (despite the periodic contradictory or overshadowing messages coming from these leaders with respect to other aspects of federalism).

This logic feeds a mutually reinforcing concern about security — as do many aspects of the global environment today, ranging from terrorist activities (both online and offline) to the no less consequential and partly related realities of technological interdependence that now characterize public sector operations — predominantly within countries but also across national borders. Despite this attention and recognition, mounting evidence suggests that traditional divisions and an ongoing separateness between federal and provincial governments continue to exert an important influence (the specifics of which will be examined in the next chapter).

If service and security dimensions of e-government feature similar objectives and agendas (even as the speed and scope of change vary), differences between federal and provincial levels become more pronounced when examining matters of transparency and trust. While both government levels face similar pressures transcending any one jurisdiction or country, there are signs that many provinces may be prepared to embark on a path of broader democratic reforms with potentially important implications for the evolution of parliamentary and more participative forms of democratic governance in Canada.

6.2 Transparency and Trust

From one vantage point, the manner in which provincial governments have responded to the pressures associated with the dimensions of transparency and trust deviates little from the path of the federal government. This interpretation owes itself to the e-government chronology beginning with electronic service delivery — while acknowledging the potential for broader democratic change with a mix of rhetorical interest and structural trepidation.[23] Indeed, at both levels, there has been a long-standing interest in public consultation that precedes the more recent emergence of e-government, yet at the same time, throughout much of the 1990s, there was little distinguishing evidence from either level to suggest that such an interest had been vigorously transformed into broader institutional reforms by political leaders in office.[24]

More recently, however, an expansion of provincial initiatives and reforms has begun to lay out a path that is more distinguishable from what is transpiring federally. While generalizations across all provinces would be misleading, the network of ten jurisdictions may therefore offer a more robust laboratory of democratic and digital reforms. In terms of the most visible shifts in democratic style and structure, British Columbia and Ontario will once again remain the primary focal point, particularly since initiatives adopted as of late by both of these jurisdictions are being closely watched across the country. A bit of background on both provincial polities is useful in explaining the current reforms of these jurisdictions.

In British Columbia, the election of the provincial Liberals to office in 2001 — and the days and months leading up to this change in government — served to crystallize the absence of transparency and the decline of trust in provincial politics and administration. The previous NDP government, led by Glen Clark, had staggered toward the election through a series of episodes: (1) the presentation of a provincial budget suspected to be overly optimistic in its assessment of the deficit; (2) major cost overruns in the construction of new, high-speed ferries that were continuously denied but long suspected and widely acknowledged outside government;[25] and (3) an RCMP investigation of the premier himself involving alleged networks of unfair access and preferential treatment to associates of the premier who, in turn, were suspected of involvement in illegal business activities.[26]

There was also growing public disenchantment with an electoral system (a first-past-the-post model in line with Westminster practice) that produced majority governments viewed as greatly out of proportion to actual voting. The system had benefited the NDP in the election of 1996 when the party narrowly formed a majority government despite winning proportionally fewer votes than its Liberal opponent.[27] Moreover, the system would produce a less surprisingly partisan but decidedly lopsided outcome in 2001, giving the Liberals seventy-seven of seventy-nine seats in the provincial legislature on the strength of 57.62 percent of the total vote cast (versus two elected members for the NDP, 21.56 percent).

Sensing the public appetite for new directions, the BC Liberal platform of 2001 included a number of measures proposed to increase transparency, improve accountability, and strengthen the overall level of trust in government. The most prominent of these proposals was undoubtedly the creation of an independent citizens' panel to consider alternative electoral models and make a proposal that would be binding in a provincial referendum that coincided with the May 2005 general election. This date of the provincial election and referendum was well known in advance due to another measure enacted by the Liberal government: fixed election dates (thereby removing an element of secrecy and surprise from the governing party). In addition, open cabinet meetings were promised, albeit on a highly limited scale, through televised sessions, including the new cabinet's first such meeting in 2001.[28]

Across government, the BC government moved to increase openness and accountability via stronger performance reporting mechanisms for provincial departments and agencies. The new system introduced a more stringent set of requirements for annual performance plans for each ministry, while the Budget Transparency and Accountability Act provided for the adoption of generally accepted accounting principles for the provincial budget as well as a more regular process of public reporting on governmental finances.[29]

The Ontario election of 2003 featured a highly similar set of circumstances, both in terms of problems facing the Conservative government in power (albeit under a new party leader and premier) and solutions proposed by the opposition (and now governing) Liberals, led by Dalton McGuinty. Under McGuinty, the Liberal Party platform featured a number of initiatives similar to those adopted by British Columbia and presented in an integrated agenda that came to be known as democratic renewal.[30]

Once again, the absence of transparency in the budgetary context of the province played prominently during the election. The last budget introduced by the previous Conservative cabinet led by Premier Ernie Eves had been widely criticized for significantly underplaying the size of the projected deficit. Upon taking office, the Liberals requested a public review of provincial finances by the provincial auditor, a move that led to a dramatic restating of the projected deficit as well as a number of recommendations for increasing the transparency — and thus the credibility — of the budget-reporting process.[31] Ironically, such moves would create a veritable straitjacket for the new government in terms of its ability to meet its election promises (which featured most prominently a tax freeze along with rising investments in core public services, notably health care and education), although the motives of the newly governing Liberals for introducing such measures were by no means above reproach.[32]

Concerns over declining levels of public trust were also overtly addressed by the Liberal Party platform as a matter of primary concern. To stem this tide, a number of ideas were put forth, including real-time, online disclosure of donations to political parties and a pledge to increase the voter turn-out rate by ten percent for the next provincial election (to be fixed, following the BC example). A citizens' assembly was also proposed, albeit more cautiously than in British Columbia.

Indeed, this latter example points to the significant emphasis on public participation that was even more apparent in the 2003 Ontario Liberal platform than in the 2001 BC version. Whereas British Columbia focused predominantly on engaging citizens to review and perhaps revise the electoral process, the Ontario Liberals spoke of expanding public engagement via citizens' juries and other consultative mechanisms on a variety of issues during the course of governing.

With respect to the impacts and outcomes of these various changes, there can be little doubt that both provincial agendas remain works in progress — and the degree of change realized to date should not be exaggerated. In both jurisdictions, the first mandates of these two new governments saw much more attention and debate devoted to contentious matters of public finance and government restructuring than to issues of e-government and democratic reform. Notwithstanding the very different directions plotted out by both governments,[33] the commonality of their experiences underscores the tensions between the difficult realities and choices of governing: once in power, is it better to make use of the earned electoral mandate to do 'what's right' (ideally a determination shaped by the electoral discourse), or can such responsibilities be shared with stakeholders and the citizenry at large? In short, should government be expected to deploy power or share it?

For Ontario's governing Liberals, the focal point of their first year in office proved to be their precarious fiscal situation, yet they were anxious to begin practising their new style of politics centred on citizen engagement. The result thus became an inaugural exercise in citizen engagement on budgetary directions of the new government — a rather daunting nexus of the most high-level and politically contested decisions on the one hand and efforts to involve the public on the other.[34]

Indeed, the inaugural consultation exercise faced many hurdles. Many participants in the citizen panels that were formed would go on to report that it seemed odd and counterintuitive to be asked to shape the government's agenda so soon after an election: had the election not served as a notable, sufficient, and ultimate example of public consultation?[35] Other participants resented the absence of tax cuts as a legitimate scenario for discussion during the engagement process.

Instead, the options for discussion presented included the following four approaches deemed complementary avenues to developing a budget framework: (1) raise additional revenues; (2) streamline government operations; (3) foster conservation; and (4) change government service delivery. Quantitatively, all four categories received favourable ratings from forty to fifty-five percent of participants prior to the engagement sessions, levels that increased once again for all segments to levels of seventy-two to seventy-six percent (Canadian Policy Research Network 2004). It is not unreasonable to question the usefulness and direct applicability of such results for crafting a budget, and many observers would be quick to suggest that the exercise may have served as a political tool designed to engineer support for 'raising revenues' (from forty-two percent in favour prior to the sessions to seventy-six percent in favour following them).

Despite such qualms and the difficult setting of a government facing intense media coverage of a government quickly backtracking on its election promises, there is much in the actual process of consultations that is more commendable. Overall, the set of representative, regional discussion forums organized by consultation experts generated a thoughtful and sincere attempt to grapple with high-level issues of what government should do to shape Ontario's future in the most effective manner possible.[36]

Clearly, however, the weakness of the process stems from precisely this high-level focus that invariably clouds the crucial link between participation and outcomes (a link that is arguably the central determinant of whether public consultation augments or erodes trust). The tenuous nature of this link was confirmed by the centrepiece of the government's first budget: the creation of a new health care levy for all citizens, thereby breaking the government's pledge not to raise taxes. At best, the only indirect role played by the prebudget public engagement process was the ascertaining of a general expression of support for investing in core public services. Even this link would further erode in the aftermath of the budget that featured intense media coverage and the premier and minister of finance rallying to the traditional political posture of leadership entailing tough decisions.[37]

Despite these troubled beginnings, the Government of Ontario has continued to pursue its democratic renewal agenda on a variety of policy and process issues.[38] The appointment of a minister responsible for the agenda, and the corresponding creation of a new secretariat led by a deputy minister,[39] have added both a political presence and a corresponding impetus within the public service to take seriously the notion of engaging the public on matters of public policy. These organizational changes — and the growing set of smaller but more positive and influential experiences with consultation — have undoubtedly created the beginnings of a cultural shift within the Ontario public service. While citizen engagement has been for many years one of the four main components of Ontario's definition of e-government, there is a growing feeling within the government that perhaps for the first time the component is a serious matter.[40]

In terms of e-government and online engagement, any such link was minimal during year-one budget consultations (the reliance on traditional town hall meetings was coupled with a website of information on the budget process and an invitation to provide input via this site). Yet, as the repertoire of consultation experiences has grown, so has the reliance on and sophistication of online channels as a means of engagement. Some observers of the election itself noted the more technological-savvy operatives working in the Liberal ranks (leading to a much more effective use of the party website, for instance), while the consultative mindset of this group once in power quickly translated into an internal 'intranet ideas campaign' to seek advice from public servants directly on creative ideas for improving government operations and performance (Borins 2004).

One of the first examples of citizen engagement involving online consultations by a government ministry featured a process linked to the formulation of a new provincial policy on rent control. A multichannel consultation process was designed and implemented by the Ministry of Municipal Affairs and Housing, and the publicly reported internal assessment of the process was highly encouraging in terms of the effectiveness of using the Internet as a legitimate means of involving stakeholders and citizens.[41]

Indeed, in 2004 alone, this ministry conducted five consultation exercises with online components on a range of issues, reporting that the average cost of implementing such an exercise online was $22,000, inclusive of internal and external costs.[42] Ontario government managers reported only a modest uptake of interest in and use of online channels, due in the case of rent control review to the uneven level of Internet access by key constituents, who preferred to use traditional mailing, but on the whole the findings from these pilot experiments have been regarded as sufficiently encouraging to warrant an expansion of such activity in the future.[43]

In contrast to this participatory emphasis, the first term of the BC Liberal government brought a much more modest effort to expand the consultative capacities — online or otherwise — of the executive branch. Priority was given to both achieving and reporting on outcomes pertaining to contentious decisions, notably those involving public sector cutbacks in light of the provincial deficit, a sluggish provincial economy, and the introduction of significant tax cuts. The philosophy of the BC Liberals was largely predicated, therefore, on the view that public trust could best be preserved and restored by greater openness and consistency in pursuing the promised agenda. This perspective is clearly more aligned with a stronger preservation of representational democracy, simultaneously facilitated and yet partially tainted by growing concerns over executive branch dominance.[44]

The response to such concerns came in the creation of an independent citizens' assembly to examine prospects for electoral reform. The assembly brought together 160 members randomly selected from a province-wide pool of volunteers, and their deliberations continued until late 2004, when the assembly unanimously endorsed the Single Transferable Vote (STV) system as their choice to replace the current 'first-past-the-post' process more in keeping with parliamentary tradition. STV essentially involves a more proportional system based on larger electoral districts with multiple representatives from each district (based on population). Citizens thus rank their candidates in order of their preference, and votes are then transferred among the candidates as the lowest performers are dropped from the contest until the required number of representatives for the given district is determined.[45]

Failure of the model to garner sufficient support from the province-wide referendum that coincided with the May 2005 provincial election (the system required sixty percent approval by the voting public from no less than sixty percent of all current provincial ridings) obviously came as a heavy blow to assembly members and proponents of the process (conversely, political reaction was more muted since the two main political parties remained neutral on the issue). What seems clear from the exercise is that, despite the apparently laudable aims of removing politicians from the reform process, the very independence that underpinned the assembly's work then became a liability in its efforts to persuade the public about the merits of its choice or even the existence of the process to begin with (opinion polls pointed to widespread apathy and a lack of knowledge about the referendum and its implications rather than any strong and shared objection to STV).

In other words, the assembly lacked the resources and the capacity to communicate its efforts to the citizenry at large, particularly at a time when political coverage revolved around partisan election agendas and the antics of the government and its opposition in jockeying for power. Ironically, the very apathy that was a factor in the assembly's creation undercut its ability to galvanize interest and support (although its disbanding in December 2004, six months prior to the election and referendum date, leaving a void of communication and information awareness activities, sealed the fate of the proposed reform).

Since British Columbia's creation of the assembly had been closely watched by many provinces (arguably serving as a catalyst for various electoral reform initiatives in New Brunswick, Prince Edward Island, and Quebec), the implications of this failed attempt will be felt elsewhere in the country. The Government of Ontario has already committed to pursuing a similar model of citizen engagement for considering electoral reform, and there is thus an opportunity to learn from the BC experience. A key lesson seems to be not only to empower any such body with a decision-making capacity but also to ensure that the body is given the resources and the means to communicate its results — either directly through its own activities or indirectly via existing political institutions and current members.[46]

In addition to electoral reforms and online engagement, one other area of activity discernible provincially pertains to online transparency and the potential for strengthened accountability — namely, results and performance reporting by governments. What distinguishes provinces from the federal government in this regard is a stronger emphasis on integrative reporting that seeks to focus on key measures of progress for the government as a whole (as opposed to planning documents and annual reports by separate agencies and departments, a common tool used at both levels). For instance, Ontario's 2004 progress report offers a streamlined summary of benchmarked activities (e.g., comparing objectives sought, measures taken, and progress achieved in four key thematic areas: education, health, the economy, and working together[47]). The Province of Nova Scotia has produced a much lengthier annual accountability report (2003-04) that nonetheless clusters results around six 'core business areas.'[48]

The strength of such reporting efforts lies in the effort to regroup information on various government entities into a synthetic and more performance-based framework that goes beyond the traditional budgeting updates by government and reports to citizens in a fashion not unlike corporations reporting to shareholders.[49] This type of information not only offers the potential to better inform citizens about executing their own roles (be they voting or partaking in consultative mechanisms of one sort or another) but also provides a public dimension to the sort of horizontality that is increasingly part of internal government operations.[50] Moreover, researchers in British Columbia have discovered that performance reports are highly valued by legislators who view them as important tools in facilitating transparency and capacities to better exercise their own accountability functions over government (McDavid and Huse 2003).

One of the difficulties underscored by the views of legislators, however, which also pertains to the public at large, is the trade-off between simplicity and ease of use and accuracy and relevance that imply more detailed information. Clearly, such integrative reporting cannot replace the need for more agency-specific performance information, another important distinction between reporting environments in the public and private spheres (in the latter, corporations generally provide integrative reporting for the entity as a whole rather than separately issued updates by division or unit). Moreover, the manner in which such information is received by the public—as either communications material aimed at bolstering the government's image or a genuine effort to gauge progress against a promised agenda—is unclear.

The overriding service and communication apparatus that prevails in the executive branch of parliamentary government undoubtedly reinforces the view that such reporting is about orchestrated information management more than an effort to strengthen democratic oversight.[51] As provinces follow Ontario's lead, then, in exploring institutional reforms aimed at greater levels of citizen engagement, questions pertaining to the source, credibility, and objective of government information flows are likely to rise in importance, as are tensions between the engrained culture of communications within government and efforts to forge a more consultative mindset and set of mechanisms.

6.3 Conclusion

From recent and ongoing provincial experiences, four key lessons stand out. The first lesson is that pressures to reform democracy are building, and they will continue to gather steam; such pressures cannot in all instances be linked in any direct fashion to the rise of online connectivity, but there is an association between a citizenry with augmenting capacities to both observe and scrutinize the political process and the Internet's ability to promote awareness, share information, and facilitate discussion and exchange in ways that go beyond traditional media channels.

The growing interest in online consultation by governments at all levels (despite variances) is indicative of such a linkage, and one can expect to see more citizen involvement in governing in the future both online and through more traditional forums (with the balancing and alignment of the two a key managerial challenge for new public service capacities aimed at lessening the overall focus on exercising power and introducing a greater measure of power sharing).

The second lesson pertains to information management and dissemination and the ongoing tensions faced by governments between deploying web-based channels as a communication means versus a more consultative purpose. Within present institutional structures, governments face a conundrum of often being responsible for the process requirements for expanded public engagement (i.e., the sharing of timely, relevant, accurate information) while serving as the key stakeholder in seeking input or sharing decision-making authority in some manner. Although provincially there are signs that e-government is facilitating a stronger focus on reporting results (of use to both legislators within the public sector and stakeholders and the citizenry outside it), the offsetting risk of a predominant service and communication mindset is that such reporting is viewed more as imagery and spin than as a genuine effort to strengthen accountability and learning.

The third lesson, in terms of redesigning democratic processes and mechanisms and making use of public involvement to do so, is that framing such a task within the parameters of electoral reform may be insufficient to galvanize the interest and support of the broader electorate — beyond those chosen for the task. The absence of a 'digital democratic' component in British Columbia may well be indicative of the need to frame democratic reform in larger terms, particularly if more progress is to be made in engaging young voters for whom digital communication is becoming 'virtually' ubiquitous across most segments of their lives. Although one can legitimately expect a sufficient level of commitment and democratic literacy on the part of most citizens — and developing a stronger level of civic responsibility may well be part of any solution — democracy is increasingly in competition for attention, particularly in a more digitally interconnected and visual world.

As a result, exercises in generating ideas for democratic change should perhaps be framed in more general terms, with the precise parameters of change as an area open for public deliberation. Such a lesson may be particularly relevant for a government such as the Province of Ontario that has committed to raising voter turn-out and democratic interest more broadly across younger segments of the voting population (although the voting age itself may also be open for reflection[52]). Formation of a nonbinding youth panel, for example, to explore possible avenues for creating online democratic mechanisms is a case in point: if nonbinding, the question for participants and the public at large will be to what degree it offers a legitimate opportunity to influence political leaders and reform existing democratic institutions and processes.

This latter point underlines the fourth lesson—namely, the digital accentuation of a marginalized presence and role for the legislative branch in parliamentary democracy. The path in British Columbia has been an eventual alteration of the manner in which the composition of the legislature is determined without much of a short-term focus on its current role. Similarly, beyond a like-minded openness to democratic reform, the Government of Ontario is directing most of its innovative focus on the executive's capacity to engage the public—and doing so online aligns the already leading presence of ministers and ministries on government portals—versus the mainly educational web presence accorded to legislatures with much less democratic engagement assigned to it (and without the service functionality that drives online service delivery).[53]

Legislatures in Canada are particularly at risk. American state legislatures, for example, are outpacing their Canadian provincial counterparts in terms of technological adoption and deployment, a point underscored by a recent 'digital legislatures survey' compiled by a prominent e-government monitoring organization.[54] Although not a federation formally, the United Kingdom has promoted a strong local, regional, and subnational orientation to e-democratic experimentation through elected officials and electoral bodies, seeking to align learning from such experiences with recognized state leaders in the United States, such as Minnesota.[55] A much wider e-democracy lens is also apparent across Europe—facilitated by EU interest and support—that is rooted more in bottom-up experimentation than in national imposition (Gasco 2003; Gronlund 2003; MacIntosh et al. 2002, 2003).[56]

Through sharing similar parliamentary structures and cultures, there is also much to be gained from comparing the federal and provincial levels, particularly in terms of what one level can learn from the other. With respect to the evolution of e-government, there has been a similar chronology of key stages of reforms across most of the four dimensions of change.

Many aspects of electronic and online service delivery reflect a common set of challenges and objectives—notwithstanding differences in the core service offerings from distinct jurisdictional responsibilities. As with previous phases of public sector reform, there is some evidence that the smaller provincial jurisdictions are better able to undertake organizational restructuring in a manner conducive to balancing government-wide interoperability and efficiency with a set of more individualized departmental capacities. The absence of a more robust intergovernmental architecture is a shared concern across both of these levels (and a theme that we return to in the next chapter). Although the provincial focus on security matters has not been the growing fixation that it is federally, efforts to underpin online services and internal electronic systems with a secure architecture are proceeding in a cautious manner, particularly with respect to key policy jurisdictions such as health care.

With respect to transparency and trust, many provinces are demonstrating a willingness to entertain democratic reforms to introduce a more participatory flavour to the representational institutions of parliamentary democracy: online experimentation in both performance reporting and public consultation is also gaining ground. Yet provinces are also struggling with voter apathy and executive dominance, which limit current experimentation with links between governmental bodies and the public, without any offsetting role for the legislature.

In short, the provinces have pursued e-government as a service strategy in a largely incremental manner within the confines of existing institutional structures—while showing some early signs of openness to wider democratic change. A significant variable in the future evolution of online service delivery is whether or not stronger intergovernmental mechanisms can be forged to integrate services across various levels of government. Similarly, any democratic reform agenda should invariably raise further questions about not only whether more public participation is warranted and how but also whether democratic engagement across various government levels can and should be coordinated in a manner akin to more seamless service delivery processes.

To address such issues, it is first necessary to inject the municipal presence into the equation to ascertain how e-government is evolving locally and to consider the intergovernmental ramifications of e-government for the future of Canada's public sector as a whole.

Chapter 7
Local and Intergovernmental Perspectives

The local perspective on e-government involves two interrelated vantage points on public sector governance. First, there are municipal governments pursuing their own e-government strategies both proactively and reactively within the realms of service, security, transparency, and trust. Second, there is the matter of how citizens and communities co-evolve and interact from the front line of a public sector that seeks more seamless governance arrangements across jurisdictions and inclusive of all levels of government. This latter emphasis on interdependence and seamless coordination that defines what technologists refer to as a federated architecture (for the public sector as a whole) often runs counter to the traditional structures and culture of political federalism, a challenge further complicated by the situating of local government within the provincial domain. The challenges of health care governance are illustrative in this regard: although formally a provincial jurisdiction, the advent of e-health creates pressures for reconciling local, provincial, and national dimensions of health care's adaptation to a more digitally and politically interdependent world.

Section 7.1 of this chapter dissects the aforementioned dynamics within the realms of service and security, comparing local governments' pursuit of such objectives with those of provincial and federal governments and examining more closely how intergovernmental relations are evolving in a digital environment. Section 7.2 provides a similar undertaking within the realms of transparency and trust. Section 7.3 then considers how various federalist and multilevel systems of public sector governance are adapting to the e-government age, situating and critiquing Canadian arrangements within these comparative contexts. To probe more deeply into the Canadian environment, Ontario's recent experiences with e-health are examined in section 7.4 as an e-government subsystem within the confines of Canada's multilevel polity. Section 7.5 then concludes this chapter with a summary of the main findings.

7.1 Service and Security

Like their provincial and federal counterparts, Canadian municipalities have actively pursued e-government agendas over the past decade. A review of municipalities around the world reveals a sophisticated online presence via portals that are highly informative, easy to use, and functional in a variety of ways (Lenihan 2002d; Moon 2002; Melitski et al. 2005; D. Norris 2005). Indeed, at first glance, there seems to be little difference with respect to the quality of the online portal between many large cities, provinces, and the federal government. In short, municipal e-government is well under way.

With respect to purpose and performance aims sought through municipal portals, there is a recognizable emphasis on service functionality that reflects the citizen-centric principles so engrained in federal and provincial online service delivery strategies. For instance, most municipalities have organized their online portals around streams of common services defined by user type (e.g., resident, business, visitor, etc.) while also offering a set of 'life events' or 'key topics' to facilitate quick and convenient navigation.[1] For less obvious requests, site maps, search engines, and alternative inquiry methods (e.g., telephone or e-mail follow-up) are common characteristics of local government websites.

In terms of specific offerings, portals are being utilized to offer a variety of services to local citizens. For instance, many municipalities now accept the online completion of various permits, registrations, and reservations. Examples include applications for business permits, online payment of property taxes, pet registration, and recreational and other facility reservations.[2] As with other government levels, the completion of financial transactions online is limited but growing, albeit in a manner correlated with population size.[3] Many municipalities allow for online payment for items such as parking violations, but the processing of larger amounts is more sporadic. In some cases, municipalities are able to circumvent the need to create such an in-house capacity (where the creation and maintenance of a secure architecture comprise a significant expense) by relying on indirect channels of online payment: Vancouver residents, for example, can pay their property taxes online via their financial institutions.[4]

The early stage of e-payments across Canadian municipalities is not out of line with trends elsewhere, notably in the United States (Melitski et al. 2005). The unsurprising correlate of size reflects not only a larger and more sophisticated municipal government in terms of digital infrastructure but also the external attributes of the communities being served, as the concentration of broadband Internet access and use in urban dwellings creates some pressure for moving in such a direction relative to rural and remote areas in particular (Hudson 2001; Malecki 2003; Scott 2004).[5]

Beyond providing information and common services for their citizens online, municipalities also post-employment opportunities on their websites and in some instances allow online applications to be submitted. In larger communities, residents can also tailor their online experience to specific needs and neighbourhoods to receive information on local construction projects, community events, e-mail notifications of parking restrictions, and traffic webcam updates.

As many of these examples imply, then, the primary impetus behind e-government strategies locally is stronger customer service, better communication, and greater efficiency, an orientation also found south of the border in the 2004 Digital Cities Survey in the United States: "The survey of 183 city mayors, managers and chief information officers found that the growing use of information technology is chiefly focused on 'service-oriented, business-driven and cost-effective' outcomes. City leaders, however, are facing increasing challenges to expand and maintain the use of information technology due to escalating budget pressures as well as public expectations for self-service."[6] Although such pressures for greater self-service and public responsiveness are reflected in the widening deployment of online channels, as with other levels of government, the reality remains a multichannel environment in which subtle incentives may nonetheless be emerging to encourage Internet-based transactions.[7] The emergence of '311' systems in North America is a good illustration of both the need and the potential for alignment across different service delivery channels—notably the telephone and the Internet.

The City of Calgary is Canada's pioneer for 311. To develop a world-class presence on the Internet, a strategy for Calgary on the Web was proposed in December 2000 to ensure the creation of a strong and flexible web presence that supported sharing of information through universal access to efficient, effective products and services.[8] Development of the portal would prove instrumental in solidifying the profile of e-government and IT management at the political level, thereby creating an important foundation for more recent initiatives, such as 311.

Accordingly, in his 2005 state of the city address ("Building on Big Ideas"), Mayor Dave Bronconnier delivered a public commitment to the 311 concept as a means to continually improve municipal performance in terms of a timely and leading-edge approach to citizen service. Not unlike the 911 emergency response system in simplicity and form, 311 is being developed as a direct and single point of access to municipal government—regardless of the call's purpose. Not only are the multiple blue page listings displaced as a result, but also through interoperability and a multichannel service architecture local government can better coordinate response actions and managerial capacities to both gauge and improve performance: "3-1-1 will provide our city managers better tools too. They will know exactly how long it takes to respond. They'll know where resources are being underutilized, and where resources are stretched. And we can adjust service to improve. 3-1-1 is as much about accountability as it is responsiveness at City Hall. It's the new kind of thinking that Calgarians want for the 21st Century."[9] In 2003, Calgary led a coalition of Canadian cities in submitting an application to the CRTC to approve the designation of the 311 code for access to municipal nonemergency services—in a manner similar to the use of this code in several American cities.[10] The Canadian 311 application, filed in October 2003, requests that 311 be assigned for noncommercial, municipal government use across Canada with requirements for local governments to seek application and obligations for telecommunications carriers to route 311 traffic once the new system is in place.[11]

As with all municipalities that have adopted the goal of deploying 311 codes in their communities, the potential extends beyond the introduction of a new telephone number. 311 denotes a shift toward a model of citizen service via transparency and empowerment accorded through not only the single-point access to all municipal services but also the ability of citizens to then track the processing of their requests by the municipal authority. Calgary officials view 311 as an enabler of a self-service approach where citizens can leverage the existence of multiple digital channels that can be complementary. An initial telephone inquiry leading to a work order, for example, can subsequently be tracked via the Internet (and many less complicated requests for information can similarly be diverted to online channels, even if the initial inquiry comes via a call centre).

Calgary's portal and the 311 system are therefore complementary means to an integrated objective: better service outcomes. The city adopted a framework of four guiding principles in its current development of 311: access twenty-four hours a day, seven days a week; responsiveness and consistency; accountability; and centralized capacities for information management. These four principles reflect the coordinating tensions of achieving interoperability on a government-wide basis to better connect externally in a more citizen-centric manner.

Having issued a request for proposals in 2003, the City of Calgary selected Motorola from the fourteen companies that submitted proposals; Motorola's track record with several large US municipalities was an important factor in its selection.[12] The city's contract with Motorola is based on an exclusive set of licensing agreements until 2008 managed within a budgetary envelope of approximately $10 million (a figure that includes both commitments to Motorola and all internal costs associated with the service transformation process).

On May 18, 2005, the new system went live, and city staff began fielding the first calls and service requests from citizens.[13] As testament to the planning that underpinned the launching of this new system, city officials forecasted an initial uptake of 43,500 calls in the first two weeks of operation, and the actual result was approximately one percent below this level. City officials report no major surprises following the launch, an outcome credited to the significant preparation that preceded it.[14]

Alignment between a 311-phone-based network and a municipal portal is an important step in achieving a more citizen-centric governance model, and many municipalities are hopeful that an effective use of 311 coupled with its alignment to portal-based capacities can result in both service improvements and efficiency gains. While there is some evidence to support the service improvement potential, whether efficiency can translate into cost savings for local governments remains more uncertain, as municipalities that remain in the start-up phases of their systems are reluctant to provide many details about the cost structures and business plans underpinning them.

One reason for this reluctance may often be confidentiality clauses enshrined in the partnership agreements with private sector vendors such as Motorola providing the 311 infrastructure. Although the overall budgetary framework is public knowledge through the municipal budgeting process (where, comparatively speaking, IT spending and planning are much more readily available for public scrutiny than the larger budget activities of provincial and federal governments), disclosure of specific contracting features such as gains sharing and incentive structures is often more limited. Although recent experiences from other cities, notably Toronto, suggest that such a lack of openness may well be a source of problems if secrecy and unscrutinized financial dealings compound, defenders of such practices engaged in 311 projects would resist such comparisons, pointing to the considerable usage of rigorous project management techniques and mechanisms of political oversight and monitoring.[15]

Indeed, while sound financial management is an important guiding principle sought at all government levels (despite the well-documented challenges of doing so in terms of IT-based initiatives), current 311 experiences seem to confirm an early and ongoing trend of service transformation efforts involving digital technologies — namely, that short-term cost savings are rarely if ever realized and should not be viewed as a key objective (Roy 2003; Langford and Roy 2005). It is also important to underline the much smaller financial spending budgets, even on a per capita basis, that constrain the e-government activities of municipal authorities,[16] and there is some evidence to suggest that the cost pressures rooted in such constraints coupled with the smaller, more nimble organizational structures of local governments (in comparison to those of other levels) explain the reduced failures of large IT projects and e-government transformation initiatives in relatively more contained environments, such as specific agencies or subnational units (O'Donnell et al. 2005).

One reason for such findings may well be both an overall reduction in the risks associated with initiatives in such an environment (with respect to size and scope) and, partly as a result, greater degrees of freedom by municipal authorities to undertake more flexible and adaptive relationships with the private sector than is typically feasible for more senior, larger orders of government (Dutil et al. 2005).

Such flexibility may also be facilitated by the potential for greater experimentation and learning across municipalities, since a much larger number of smaller governments pursue similar aims through varying strategies: this type of diversity is evident, for instance, in the underlying mechanisms for secure transactions being used in different cities and communities.[17] Many attributes of the 311 movement suggest a level of horizontal coordination of this sort across local governments,[18] and there is widening interest in examining the potential for intermunicipal collaboration of a more formal type in the pursuit of shared objectives.

Along with the potential for greater horizontal links, the emergence of 311 underscores the persistent intergovernmental quandaries that are more vertical. Despite the rhetoric of a more seamless public sector that permeated the federal GOL initiative at its inception, municipal activities are not unlike provincial and federal activities that demonstrate a primary concern with their own service apparatus, while intergovernmental processes for more collaborative and integrative mechanisms remain primitive and widely underdeveloped.

Although the formation and recent activities of two intergovernmental coordinating bodies (the CIO Council and the Service Delivery Council) underscore the growing effort to foster such mechanisms, it is questionable whether there is the political will to do so.[19] A case can be made that there are, in fact, two versions of federalism shaping the public sector at present: the first—and by far the more engrained and prevalent of the two—is a mindset axed on competition and independence (as governments and their political leaders jockey for fiscal resources and political visibility), whereas the second is a movement under construction built around the principles of collaboration and interdependence.

The implications of the relative weakness of this second approach may well be magnified by the municipal 311 experience. As a federal government official recently acknowledged in Canada's pre-eminent e-government forum, 311 should be a wakeup call for provincial and federal governments engaged in their own service transformation efforts. What happens, the official asked, when a citizen dials 311 with an issue that is partly or fully provincial and/or federal in scope?[20] The illusion of seamless intergovernmental coordination will be a weakness of the public sector that owes its exposure to the very efforts of government leaders in drawing attention to it as a critical objective in line with public expectations.

Although a case can perhaps be put forth that a small amount of inconvenience stemming from jurisdictional separateness may well be warranted and accepted by the public during a transitional phase as a new architecture is put in place, the difficulty stems from the growing costs of separateness in terms of not only lost opportunities for service integration but also more pressing areas where intergovernmental capacities are of great urgency.

The Front Line Security Gap

A 2004 report, *National Emergencies: Canada's Fragile Front Lines*, prepared by the Senate Committee on National Security and Defence, exposed the disconnect between reality and polity in Canada: "Emergencies are local. The governments that design and control anti-emergency strategies, however, are federal, provincial and territorial. Canada's constitution presents a formidable challenge to the development of a swift and comprehensive approach to dealing with national emergencies. The Committee believes that the best way to serve the citizen is by listening to first responders' needs and wants to avoid suggestions that there is a hierarchy of greater and lesser governments."[21] Despite such a view, most indications from the realm of homeland security suggest that the federal government views itself very much as a 'greater government,' one focused more on an expansion of its own capacities than on fostering new coordinating mechanisms across government levels. Canada's much-vaunted, first-ever National Security Strategy (the details of which were reviewed in Chapter 5) is more accurately a federal security strategy with an array of promises to reach out and 'inform' other levels of government of progress: even beyond the vagueness of such intentions, the emphasis on federally-led consultation exercises underscores the mindset at play.[22]

Such an approach is not unlike that which characterized the federal introduction of GOL and the development of its secure channel backbone: the recognition accorded to interjurisdictional potential simply did not factor into initial planning stages and early governance design work—a move that has resulted in widespread resistance by provinces to downstream participation in the channel as well as rising provincial unease that a similar process is unfolding with the example of Service Canada.[23]

In fairness to the federal government, more intergovernmental dialogue and concerted action between provincial and federal governments have been acknowledged as important elements in fostering a national security framework.[24] At the same time, however, not only have such overtures to the provinces occurred largely after the formation of the federal government's action plan, but also there is little evidence of a willingness by these two levels of government to incorporate the municipal presence: "OTTAWA, January 24, 2005 — Federal, provincial and territorial Ministers responsible for emergency management met today and announced a number of measures to improve Canada's emergency preparedness."[25] Persistent criticism by and growing concerns among municipalities, underpinned by the Senate committee's findings, seem to have at least sensitized federal leaders to this issue. In a May 2004 address to the Federation of Canadian Municipalities annual conference,[26] the deputy prime minister acknowledged the Senate study (referred to above) and pledged to rectify many of the shortcomings revealed in it. In an effort to laud the importance of local government as a partner in security, however, the example offered by the minister served to underscore the severity of the challenge. The initiative invoked was the Joint Emergency Preparedness Program, a $5 million annual commitment of *matching funds* to help finance the purchase of equipment, the development of emergency plans, and the conducting of local training. In light of the annual operating budget of Canada's largest city alone, in excess of $8 billion, the limited scope of such financing becomes apparent (more so in comparison with the billions in new spending within the federal government apparatus).

A comparison of Canadian and US efforts to support local responders in domestic security efforts is equally revealing. South of the border, more than $2 billion in new, unmatched federal funds has been dispersed to local authorities to bolster security capacities, an amount that clearly dwarfs Canadian levels on a per capita basis. Despite this considerable funding base, the US experience also underscores the ongoing difficulties plaguing municipal efforts to both navigate state and federal processes and ensure that the local capacities are adequate to make good of such funding once arrived.[27]

For municipalities in both countries, the limited presence and status in security efforts stem from two complementary sources: first, ongoing federal-provincial (or state) frictions and a general preference by federal authorities to be leading national priorities; and second, provincial and state concerns about this growing federal activism extending to the municipal domain, thereby creating new federal-local government relationships that threaten to circumvent formal provincial jurisdiction over matters of local government. The result is a weakening of the national security architecture in two interrelated ways: weak local capacities for first responders, but also the absence of the local perspective within the federal arena, where so many of the program decisions are made.

These problems are unquestionably more pronounced in Canada, however. In the United States, many states (in many cases making use of the new federal programs) have put in place collaborative mechanisms to strengthen, work with, and support local initiatives (while seeking to align these mechanisms with federal programs). Pennsylvania's underlying philosophy of transcending government boundaries in a bottom-up manner is indicative of this emphasis on building local capacities: "Emergency responsibility lies at the municipal level."[28] Although only one policy statement of intent, the broader coupling of significant resources and greater sensitivity to local and intergovernmental capacities is an important contrast to the current evolution of domestic security efforts in Canada.[29]

In brief, there is little sign of a fundamentally new approach to intergovernmental relations in both fostering synergies through integrated or even more coordinated services and creating a more locally embedded and responsive domestic security framework. In an environment where the governance of service delivery and domestic security are increasingly interwoven with their growing reliance on digital infrastructures, the prevailing mentality of national planning may be increasingly out of step with the need for more concerted action and stronger local capacities.

7.2 Transparency and Trust

With regard to transparency and trust, municipalities have been no less determined than other governments to make use of online channels of communicating in order to provide timely and accurate information to their citizens (Lee 2004). Although the depth of this commitment varies in part due to population size (as the larger cities have many more issues within larger and more complex operations), the quality and quantity of information available via local governments online seem comparable to other government levels (Melitski et al. 2005).

Whether or not such openness is being pursued to alter and strengthen local democratic capacities is a more complex notion. It bears noting that, relative to the Westminster-based model provincially and federally, municipal governments have generally been viewed as less rigidly constrained by representational democratic structures and partisan politics and more open to public participation and more grassroots forms of stakeholder engagement (Barnet 1997; Graham and Phillips 1998).

The formation of budgets seemingly supports this comparative view since locally political negotiation, community mobilization, and discursive processes are much more readily apparent at the municipal level. There is also some emerging evidence of this distinction carrying over into the realm of online government. For example, in coming to terms with a 2.93 percent property tax increase in its 2004 budget, the City of Vancouver undertook a public consultation strategy (including public meetings, a local opinion poll, and online questionnaires in English and Chinese) to explore the relative preferences of residents between service cuts and modest tax increases (beyond the level of inflation).[30]

At the same time, municipalities tend to provide much more detailed and citizen-friendly accounting of their budgetary processes and financial results than is typically the case provincially and federally. Along with extensive details outlining the crafting of its $7.1 billion operating budget for 2004, the City of Toronto provides an online budget simulation for residents to experiment with shifts in financial allocations across municipal priorities; its purpose is also to provide a public education vehicle on council's priorities for 2005 and 2006.[31] While municipalities have not been free of corruption and mismanagement, local residents, businesses, and community groups generally face fewer barriers in both understanding municipal spending priorities and engaging in decision-making priorities that shape such priorities into policies and plans (Ho 2002; Vivian 2004). The Internet certainly seems to be capable of reinforcing these sorts of political dynamics through a greater sharing of information and knowledge regarding both operational and political processes (Lee 2004).

Despite such potential, the evidence is not indicative of a strengthening of participative governance capacities locally via online channels (Gattinger 1998; Justice et al. 2004; D. Norris 2005).[32] There is even some basis for a counterview that reforms tied to e-government may well be centralizing not only administratively but also politically, favouring key figures such as mayors at the expense of other stakeholders both inside and outside government.[33] This view is particularly prevalent in postamalgamation urban dwellings where the creation of larger 'local' entities has been accompanied by both organizational changes to reinforce central control and an altering of politics as a smaller number of elected officials are forced to serve larger populations in a more representational manner than has typically been associated with more localized and community-oriented politics.[34]

Indeed, across both Canada and the United States, there appear to be few signs of a widespread appetite for e-democratic reforms emphasizing participation and engagement. This point may be viewed as potentially counterintuitive to democratic reform expectations given the fact that local governance processes are often viewed as relatively more open, accessible, and flexible than provincial/state and federal apparatuses. Yet, in response to the question of why e-democracy is not more central to local government in the United States, Norris's own surveying of American officials reveals this explanation:

> Part of the answer is found in the definition of e-democracy provided by the focus of group participants. Theirs is an "in practise" definition, as one would be expected from local government practitioners, in which operationally and functionally e-democracy means the electronic delivery of information and services and the ability of citizens to contact and interact with government electronically. Furthermore, they believe from their experience that this results in making government more open, transparent, responsive and citizen-centric. This operational definition, while at odds with the definition I provided earlier, however, is highly consistent with what their local governments have actually done to deploy e-government. But it does not encompass e-democracy as extensive e-citizen participation, e-referenda or e-voting. (Norris 2003, 16)

Such findings are equally relevant in Canada. Although the Internet is beginning to immerse itself in the consultative efforts of cities and communities in some instances, such examples are recent and rare, and they do little to negate the primary service orientation of municipal e-government. Two underlying sets of factors help to explain this municipal reluctance to explore wider democratic reforms, particularly online. First, within municipal structures, there are limited resources and an organizational leadership intent more on making use of those resources to manage service outcomes than on experimenting democratically. Second, there is a prevailing sense that local citizenries are at best mildly interested in an expansion of democratic activity at the local level — viewing it as less important than efficient and responsive service.

Moreover, as with most provincial/state and federal governments, there is no obvious organizational placement for e-democracy (or democratic engagement more broadly). With CIO-type structures focused primarily on internal operations, and updating and reforming these operations to better 'serve' the municipal client base, the already challenging emphasis is primarily on deploying limited resources to meet the performance aims already agreed to by or in concert with the elected officials. Accordingly, most municipalities assign public consultation responsibilities to communications departments despite the dramatically different purpose and focus.[35]

Limited signs of overt interest by the citizenry may, for some, call into question the view that proximity matters greatly to the facilitation of meaningful forms of more direct and participative democratic engagement. Alternatively, it may well be that local processes are partially, albeit increasingly, overshadowed in cyberspace by the instantaneous coverage of politics at provincial, federal, and international levels (along with widening opportunities to partake in discussions and activities related to issues at these different levels, if not directly via online democracy that is plugged into formal political institutions, then indirectly through new channels and forums such as weblogs and the like). The overlaying of demographic factors of such a claim is increasingly viewed as important in terms of a fluid distribution of attention spans and activity preferences among those younger generations most likely to be digitally connected (Cherney 2000; MacIntosh et al. 2002).

Fiscal federalism may also play an important role. The underpinning of dramatically larger technology investments federally than elsewhere crowds out interest in and attention to local affairs, much as it may also shape the actions of municipal governments influenced not only by the prevailing service and communications culture of provincial and federal governments but also by a growing envelope of potential funding opportunities allocated on the basis of federal interests and objectives rather than more localized dialogue and governance.

What results is a rather insular focus on incremental adaptation, applying digital technologies on what remain important and legitimate aspects of governing a locale. What is lost is a higher degree of experimentation to broaden dialogue and find new ways to augment civic participation in local governance via e-government reforms that emphasize engagement over service.

7.3 Federalist Capacities and Design Tensions

Parallel to the evolution of e-government in recent years has been a widening view that Canada lacks a meaningful strategy to realign resources and priorities across the federation in a manner conducive to and supportive of the rising importance of localization (Paquet 2000). Blake's (2002) concern, for example, is that any emphasis on local capacities and engagements is largely rhetorical, lacking meaningful investments in structure, education, and cultural change. The lack of political and strategic integration in a more territorial-aligned framework for economic development in Canada was highlighted by the OECD as a major impediment to stronger governance, an alternative viewpoint but one that complements the front-line security gap: "Deficiencies in local governance remain the Achille's heel of local and rural development. More sustainable solutions must evolve from the grassroots local communities. Without changes in decision making capacities at that level, it will prove difficult for economic development policies to transcend the federal/provincial jurisdictional issue and become more effective" (OECD 2002, 6). Such recognition has spurred recent discussions about a new fiscal deal for cities and communities. Internationally, Canadian municipalities lack both financial and decision-making autonomy and recognition as well as a capacity to influence decisions intergovernmentally (Barnett 1997; Wong 2002; Bradford 2004; Paquet and Roy 2004). The governance of a country such as Denmark, comparable in population to the largest of Canada's provinces, features taxation powers structured inversely to the residual property tax feature of local governments in Canada: income tax in Denmark is predominantly localized.[36]

A similar set of financial structures characterizes Switzerland, where local 'communes' enjoy not only significant taxation powers relative to other government levels but also the ability to restructure their electoral and decision-making systems, both individually and in concert with other local communes. An alternative system in the Netherlands features more nationalized taxation mechanisms that nonetheless enable the transferring of a substantial level of resources to local governments via unqualified grants (thereby empowering local governments with the authority to budget these resources in a locally decided manner). Italy's most recent e-government strategy carries an explicit commitment to fostering local, regional, and national capacities in a complementary manner, backing up this commitment with significant funding arrived at through a cross-jurisdictional dialogue.[37]

In part shaped by these experiences elsewhere in Europe, the newly established Scottish executive has sought to empower local governments in Scotland with expanded degrees of freedom, experimentation, and consultation. The 2003 adoption of the Local Government in Scotland Act specifies a broadly based 'power of well-being' that enables local authorities to act in any manner they see fit in terms of bettering their jurisdiction, and in doing so local government is appointed as the primary decision-making body in coordinating such efforts with other public sector mechanisms (e.g., regional development agencies, health boards, etc.). Even within the more similarly structured federations of Canada and the United States, municipalities south of the border enjoy a wider array of financial mechanisms and in many cases a general 'home rule' power that provides municipalities with wider degrees of freedom within state-level legislative frameworks than is the case for Canadian local governments under provincial control (Vander Ploeg 2002).

Yet even the manner in which this agenda has focused largely on federal largesse and new infrastructure spending is indicative of ongoing neglect in terms of thinking strategically and intergovernmentally about federalism and governance: "Although the federal move is to be applauded, it also draws attention to the increasingly curious absence of provincial governments from the national debate over cities and an urban agenda. Given that provinces are a much larger player than the federal government on the municipal stage, and will remain so, their very modest role to date is both puzzling and troubling.... At issue, then, is the need for a strategic framework upon which can be built a new relationship between the municipal and provincial governments.... And, we need to think about more than the need for more money."[38]

How this nexus between fiscal resources and local capacity is addressed will ultimately determine whether or not localities in Canada are able to achieve the spirit of what it means to be a *smart community* where localized learning and collaborative action are enhanced through a mix of proximity and connectivity (Eger 1997; Coe et al. 2001). Technology alone may well be insufficient (Polese and Shearmur 2002), but if technology can be an enabling force for greater dialogue and engagement, the opportunities for mutual trust and collaborative initiative are enhanced (Evans 2002; Hampton and Wellman 2003). In aligning activities rooted in cyberspace and traditional geography, the central importance of proximity remains clear for many proponents of broader public involvement: "Participation must be seen more broadly and more powerfully as an opportunity to strengthen local democracy, empower citizens to influence the quality of life in their communities, and educate citizens more broadly about economic forces and trade-offs at play within their communities and beyond" (Lukensmeyer and Torres 2003, 13).

There is little evidence in the Canadian context of e-government facilitating such efforts to empower local processes. Instead, federal and provincial government initiatives have targeted specific needs, as denoted by the current federal program Broadband for Rural and Northern Development, an ongoing, competitive funding mechanism of limited proportions for smaller communities seeking broadband.[39] Yet such federally administered activity only reinforces Blake's aforementioned criticism that, rather than local capacity-building within communities, resource deployment will be shaped primarily by the bureaucratic and financial inertia of federal processes, controls, and reporting requirements, as well as a federal desire for extending national visibility and reach via cyberspace (Gibbons 2004; Paquet and

Roy 2004).[40] The implications are important in terms of whether citizens and stakeholders are likely to perceive local engagement as a worthy cause — since top-down governance mechanisms are unlikely to foster meaningful capacities at the local level (Bailey 2003).

The tendency of e-government in Canada to implicitly reject notions of devolution and subsidiarity that more prominently shaped federalism debates in the early 1990s can be seen as an extension of the logics of interoperability, security, and shared and integrated services that are so prevalent within provincial and federal governments. The heightened pressure for more centralized governance mechanisms within each government to coordinate such measures has largely been replicated intergovernmentally as the secure channel experience of provincial trepidation toward federal control (reviewed in the previous chapter).

There are two additional variables that must be recognized as more unique design tensions between federalism and e-government: the first is the distribution of financial resources, and the second involves shifting notions of community and identity in an increasingly digitally connected and politically interdependent world.

Debates surrounding fiscal federalism (i.e., the composition and distribution of taxation and spending across and between different government levels) underpin both provincial grievances and demands on the one hand and pressures for a new deal for municipalities on the other hand. Intuitively, a larger resource base with which to invest in digital technologies shapes the intentions of any single government — since it seeks to both equate and align its technological sophistication with political and operational ambitions. For a federal government spending at least six times as much money on technology on a per capita basis than the City of Winnipeg, the culture and behaviour of the federal public service will be shaped accordingly (reinforced by politicians elected federally and thereby keen on federally-led activities). Here the view that cyberspace offers an emerging frontier of connectedness between all citizens and their national government is an enticing vision to guide such efforts (Marshall et al. 2004).

Such dynamics involve more than relative taxation and spending power, however (as Gibbons attests in the passage above). The fluidity of identities also reshapes the attachment between citizens and their various governments. The Internet — and a broader digital infrastructure of information, imagery, and communications on a global scale — allow individuals and groups to forge new ties and identities in a manner less restricted by national space (Kotkin 2000; Courchene 2005; P. Norris 2005). However, these new patterns of association, mobilization, and identity also appear to be capable of coexisting with more traditional identities and affiliations rooted in national citizenship.

Whereas in the previous decade it was not uncommon to hear pronouncements about the end of the nation-state (as Czechoslovakia succumbed to such pressures in a laudably less violent manner than other federal states, such as Belgium, that seemingly flirted with a regional-linguistic dismantling), the nation-state appears to have reasserted itself. In the case of Belgium, in fact, the emergence of e-government is one such example of a unifying force for a national project that nonetheless remains sensitive to regional autonomy and intergovernmental coordination.[41] In a manner that would seem to be a reversal of the devolutionary flavour of the late 1980s and early 1990s, national identities have proven more resilient than anticipated some fifteen years ago: in a more open and virtual world, the self-images of many countries are shifting, becoming smaller and collectively more unified (though not without divisions) than in the past.

The reason for this latter claim is the changing relationship between geographic size, population, and identity based on relative stature in an increasingly globalized environment. For example, the historical rhetoric of Canada as the world's second largest nation in terms of land mass is increasingly overshadowed by the view that Canada is a small player in a large and increasingly uncertain and competitive global order. The pronouncements of political leaders emphasizing national challenges of economic competitiveness, political clout, and, in the case of the Olympic games, athletic excellence serve to reinforce the mindset of a relatively small nation of just over 30 million people struggling to maintain a level of performance and prosperity in world that may well approach the 10 billion mark in the coming decade.

The challenges facing municipal governance systems and formal bodies of local government are thus twofold. First, the distribution of identities across national, provincial, and local planes may well be shaped by patterns of resources and visibility that inherently favour national authorities. Second, there may be a cleavage or differentiation with a locality between the notion of a geographically defined community on the one hand and the formal municipal authority on the other—meaning that localized communities may be strengthening in a manner that is largely disconnected from municipal institutions (Andrew 2002). These challenges are interrelated since citizens will be less inclined to both pay close attention to and involve themselves in the participative intricacies of a level of government viewed as relatively less powerful and influential than other government levels. It is, in fact, telling in this regard that the recent explosion of interest in citizen engagement has largely been rooted in more provincially- and federally-led initiatives, directly or indirectly, via think tanks and research groups associated more with these levels than with municipal authorities.[42]

What remains absent, however, is the possibility of strategically assessing the relative potential for citizen engagement to occur at each government level—and how the public sector as a whole can best accommodate, facilitate, and make use of an expansion of participative capacities across all levels in a more concerted (and possibly more digital) manner despite evidence that citizens would be welcoming of democratic and governance innovations tied to both electronic reforms and a devolution of power to strengthen municipal and local authorities (Commission on Legislative Democracy 2004).

Recent polling by the Centre for Research and Information on Canada confirms this view, pointing to a considerable decline in levels of trust accorded to provincial and federal governments (the latter more than the former varies considerably across the country) and much higher levels of trust at the municipal level.[43]

Federated Engagement and New Forms of Power Sharing

Over the past two decades, many of Canada's largest cities, as well as a number of smaller communities, have witnessed political amalgamations underpinned by the common objective of both simplifying and unifying municipal governance.[44] Efficiency and clarity were often the guiding principles of such exercises, designed in many cases to replace multitiered systems with single councils and an elected mayor to oversee a strengthened municipal administration.

What may well have been sacrificed in this movement is more creativity in devising local capacities for self-governance and adaptation, thereby further distinguishing local democracy and government from provincial and federal levels. Although municipal governance remains distinct in many respects, there is much about 'big city' politics—and as we have seen in the preceding chapter with respect to initial e-government strategies, for example — that increasingly resembles other government levels. In particular, democracy is gradually becoming less grassroots and participative and more representational.

The City of Toronto is a case in point: forty-four elected councillors (in addition to the mayor) serving a population of roughly 2.5 million is a parameter that conjures up images more in line with provincial legislatures than a 'local council.' Although officially nonpartisan, what is increasingly parliamentary about such a body is a growing professionalization of a political class that must, by necessity, act more indirectly for their constituents than could otherwise have been the case under previous models of multitiered local governments. Moreover, as with the recent evolution of federal and provincial forums, the concentration of power in the mayor's office, although not as absolute as that of a prime minister or premier in majority, is an important feature of many cities — a principle aspired to by many of those designing the new models put in place.[45] The City of Toronto is hardly a unique case, however, as urban centres such as Ottawa, Gatineau, Calgary, Winnipeg, and Halifax are but a few governed by a single council with a relatively small number of elected officials for a growing and diversifying population.

As the democratic architecture of cities becomes more formally representational, it is therefore not surprising to see the imposition of the 'service mentality' that pervades provincial and federal reforms — without much in the way of evidence to suggest that municipalities are either benefiting from stronger participative capacities or doing much to foster them. In short, despite the relatively more open and accessible nature of municipal governance, in comparison to provincial and federal levels (the specifics of which were discussed in Chapter 6), there are reasons not to be hopeful about a local democratic renaissance — particularly in light of the concentration of resources and thus digital capacities at provincial and federal levels.

7.4 Federated E-Health in Ontario

The Government of Ontario defines e-health as achieving better health outcomes by transforming health systems and business practices through the investment in and more comprehensive use of information and information technology. In terms of the realms of service and security, Ontario's e-health efforts may be simplified as a set of three major directions (in line with the parameters of e-health laid out above): (1) efforts to create new e-health competencies and capacities within the core bodies of the provincial government with health care responsibilities; (2) efforts to realize interoperability and an EHR-type infrastructure to better serve the public user at the community level and in doing so balance province-wide systemic reform with the localized dimension of health care organization, accountability, and delivery; and (3) efforts to address the particular circumstances of remote parts of the province, notably northern regions and communities.

Regarding the first direction, a provincial Office of E-Health was formally established in 2004. This new office is akin to a central policy unit guiding the overall evolution of e-health within the core provincial public service and across the extended health care system. In this latter realm, the office works closely with its predecessor organization that has since become an autonomous public agency, Smart Systems for Health (SSH), a provincial body focused on developing and introducing IT-based technological solutions in health care (and in doing so working more directly with health care practitioners and their communities[46]). Similarly, SSH spawned the Ontario Health Information Standards Committee (OHISC), another body that predates but now complements the work of the e-health office by attempting to facilitate interoperability across different segments of the extended health care system through recommendations and policy guidance for health informatics data management systems and the technical standards required to underpin their use.

The purpose of the e-health office today, then, is essentially to provide a CIO capacity for the health care system as a whole in order to guide system-wide reforms pertaining to new technologies. The head of this office reports directly to the deputy minister responsible for the provincial Ministry of Health and Long-Term Care (the appointed department head who, in turn, reports directly to the political minister).

The e-health office also serves as the secretariat and coordinating body for the Ontario e-Health Council, a forum that is actually a collection of four separate councils with specific areas of focus (continuing care, laboratories, physicians, and hospitals). Four additional councils have been proposed, and their status is under consideration by the government (pharmacies, public health, regional integration, and program integration). It is these councils that comprise the extended and comprehensive network of sectors, professions, and organizational bodies that comprise Ontario's health care system. The council mechanisms are meant to reflect the separate needs of groups such as physicians on the one hand and hospitals on the other. At the same time, however, the danger of fragmentation is apparent to many observers: "While the e-Health Council format provides valuable support for projects within each sector, it may also cause the creation of virtual silos that may impede or restrict the sharing of important information. To prevent this, the region must be aware of what is going on within each sector and work cooperatively to share projects" (Health Care Network of Southeastern Ontario 2005, 4). The latter segment of this quotation — the invocation of a regional concerted approach — underscores one of the most central quandaries facing e-health in Ontario: namely, the geographic alignment of health care operations and delivery across central (provincial), regional, and local dimensions. Identified above as the second major direction of provincial efforts, the now familiar problem is striking the balance between system-wide coordination that is demanded if interoperability is to be realized and a requisite level of flexibility and autonomy that permits individual organizations and subnetworks of health care providers to act in innovative and client-centric ways.

In the case of Ontario, this challenge is somewhat unique in comparison with other provinces since there are no regional health care authorities with formal decision-making autonomy between the province as a whole and community-level care providers and facilities such as physicians, clinics, hospitals, and the like.[47] The provincial e-health office and the provincial CIO structures represent the province-wide perspective on health care matters, whereas locally and regionally a variety of largely informal, advisory bodies (district health councils) promote coordination and dialogue for specific subprovincial zones while also providing input to the provincial government.

Whereas the formation of such movements represents a bottom-up emergence of governance mechanisms to address shared externalities, both positive and negative, the province has also responded with a formalized strategy to instill more local coordination through the creation of a province-wide set of Local Health Integration Networks (LHIN). The purpose of these bodies is to facilitate interoperability and integrated health care delivery in a collaborative manner without imposing a new layer of centralized, regional authority on the system. Even those engaged in e-health acknowledge that "the impact of the LHINs on Ontario's e-Health agenda has not yet been defined" (Health Care Network of Southeastern Ontario 2005, 7). Indeed, an important governance design question is the shape of relations between the new LHINs network and the proposed e-Health Council on Regional Integration.

There is now an expectation that the LHIN will become a vehicle to promote a shared services approach to a more common IT infrastructure that, in turn, can facilitate system-wide perspectives on resource planning and delivery within a given jurisdiction (Government of Ontario 2005). In doing so, however, it is clear that the provincial government is walking on eggshells in attempting to facilitate provincial guidance and stronger local coordination in a manner that is not interpreted as a threat to key stakeholders with their own territorial and operational autonomy. Hospitals are one key stakeholder group. Their views pertaining to the LHIN model would see strong support at first glance but also be conditional on the LHIN not undermining their own governance structures and authority: "The hospitals of Ontario and the OHA (Ontario Hospital Association) are strong supporters of increased integration of the health care system and believe that efforts to improve integration should build on current system strengths and successes. Hospitals also support the establishment of LHINs that will focus on engaging communities in health system transformation by enhancing and supporting local capacity to plan, coordinate and integrate the delivery of health services at the community level. In addition, the OHA fully endorses the government's commitment to maintaining local independent governance including the voluntary role of hospital trustees" (Ontario Hospital Association 2005, i). The backdrop of this position is the contentious relationship between hospitals, health care groups generally, and the previous Conservative-led governments in power from 1995 to 2003 that preferred a heavy-handed approach to government restructuring (driven less by an interest in e-health and more by an overarching agenda of tax cuts and spending reductions[48]). In health care specifically, a number of hospital consolidations were imposed across the province, leading some hospitals to fight such moves (e.g., smaller hospitals fused into larger ones), while others positioned themselves as larger health care centres with more responsibility and autonomy. Importantly, the absence of regional authorities in Ontario meant that power throughout this process and since then has been shared between the province centrally and individual hospitals locally. Hospitals are members of voluntary local and regional networks (whose existence as a precursor or partner to the LHIN remains unclear) since such mechanisms are horizontal and of no threat to their own self-governance capacities.

With respect to e-health, the hospitals have positioned themselves not only as supporters of the LHIN model as a complement to their own authority but also as critics of the province's lack of more forceful and political interest in IT-led transformations of the health care system as a whole (Ontario Hospital Association 2005). Part of this interest may no doubt be ascribed to a genuine attachment to the potential of e-health to improve medical systems, but it should also be viewed as a position that complements the hospital's own agenda in seeking more direct funding from the province to invest in its own operations through autonomous governance structures.

From the lenses of transparency and trust, there is evidence to suggest that the foundational e-health work being undertaken by the province is not translating into wider public learning and support. Public opinion research in Canada suggests that it is in Ontario over the past three years where the decline in confidence accorded to the provincial government has been the steepest.[49]

Here the question of whether the Government of Ontario is acting transparently with respect to health care reform is an important one. At one level, for those stakeholders and informed observers engaged in e-health areas, there is ample information about the strategies and mechanisms currently being deployed (and the rationale for doing so). Yet, at the same time, the absence of more political attention devoted to e-health and both the opportunities and the risks associated with new digital technologies suggests less a desire to withhold information or mislead the public than a preference for a form of positive-laden clarity (i.e., the message of government succeeding) over a willingness to embrace uncertainty and complexity. The risk of such a direction, however, is a further erosion of public legitimacy and trust since such efforts are viewed as manipulative and politically deceitful at worst, incomplete at best (Paquet 2004; Reed 2004; Reid 2004).

At the community level, arguably the mesolevel of governance analysis (between the province and the individual citizen and autonomous health care providers that comprise the system's microlevel), this loss of legitimacy at the provincial level is coupled with weak capacities locally. The creation of the LHIN raises the issue of whether or not such a mechanism will be sufficiently empowered to orchestrate a level of systemic change on a subprovincial level (i.e., the fourteen regions each denoted with an LHIN). While the OHA and the province view the LHIN as an important vehicle for community mobilization and engagement in health care transformation (a view supported by the increasingly participative determinants of governance legitimacy and positive change), it is also the case that the public must be convinced of the usefulness of doing so. A weak regional mechanism with little authority to instill change may well undermine the credibility of the system, viewed once again as a vehicle for provincial intervention and communication as opposed to genuine consultation and engagement (Woodward 2003).

The Government of Ontario provides a counterargument based on the necessity of incremental change — since such a network is at the least a starting point for organizational dialogue and public consultation, particularly across a diverse province where the needs of different regions are varied and diverse. Yet it is perhaps telling that creation of the LHINs seems to be a centralized process closely controlled by the provincial government, suggesting that, while there may well be some potential for new organizational synergies to develop, the case for public interest mobilization is much less evident.[50]

An important question emerging from these developments is whether or not Ontario needs a more formalized regional component of health care governance, particularly one that is directly and democratically accountable to a localized citizenry. Although a new regional health care authority is one option, so is the utilization of stronger local and municipal governments already in existence. It bears noting that in many European countries sharing a strong public sector orientation to health care, particularly across Scandinavia, it is regional governments as opposed to national authorities that are primarily responsible for health care organization and delivery. In these countries, the national government (akin in some manner to the province in Canada) sets a broad policy framework and serves as a partner in funding arrangements, but regional governments are primarily responsible for operational planning and delivery.

In the short-term, this sort of scenario in Ontario faces major hurdles since the LHIN boundaries do not easily align with those of municipal governments. Moreover, since municipalities have not historically dealt directly with health care, the establishment of local or regional health care governance via municipal bodies poses a number of questions (which extend beyond the scope of this chapter). At the least, however, there is a need in the immediate term to contemplate (1) whether or not the LHIN will be sufficient to orchestrate interoperability and systemic innovation within a largely provincial (macro) and professional and organizational (i.e., doctors and hospitals, the microlevel) framework; and (2) how such a localized network will both mobilize public engagement and facilitate stronger community capacities for e-health adaptation and health care reform more generally within existing political structures at the provincial and municipal levels.

Perhaps the greatest challenge facing Ontario's government with respect to systemic reform is how one should define the 'system of health care,' particularly in an era characterized by the emergence of e-health. Digital technologies can and should be viewed as an instrument of local innovation (at the interface of health care organization and delivery), much as they also facilitate the opportunities for coordination and systemic change at province-wide and pan-Canadian levels. What sort of strategy is best able to achieve success across these varying levels?

While the Province of Ontario is beginning to create many aspects of a solid technical and organizational infrastructure for e-health, what remains problematic is the political landscape. What is therefore required is a much stronger exploration of the means by which public and community engagement can be both expanded and leveraged as a means toward creating the conditions for (1) a higher level of trust among the province's citizenry (which at present is highly skeptical of the government's message of reassurance and incremental improvement) and (2) stronger forms of public engagement at the local and regional levels to orchestrate the sorts of shared processes required to underpin complex change with mechanisms for socializing learning, shared risk, and collective change.

Abelson and Eyles (2002) rightfully point out that public participation is essential to orchestrating change and adaptation by improving the quality of information (through transparency of not only politically filtered outcomes reporting but also more pervasive, upfront accounting and consideration of challenges and choices), greater debate around directions and options for improvement, and strengthened accountability mechanisms to oversee the public interest (and, by extension, nurture and strengthen trust in the overall system).[51] As the Canadian public seems to be increasingly willing to look to local government structures for a greater role in governance generally, the challenge for e-health as a whole in Canada is to complement national research and infrastructure development with strengthened mechanisms for localized delivery and accountability.

Rectifying this absence with an e-health strategy based more on direct political and community engagement (ironically enough, virtues espoused by the Government of Ontario in its own democratic renewal agenda) may well be the most central requirement facing the province at present.

7.5 Conclusion

In taking a step back, then, to consider the potential for a digital transformation of the public sector as a whole (inclusive of federal, provincial, and local levels), there are three sources of inertia that limit the potential for significant and positive change to occur. The first such source is the widening disconnection between the rhetoric of more integrated and seamless governance across jurisdictions and the ongoing reality of separation. The potential for acting more interdependently remains constrained by the structures and politics of independence (Jaeger 2002).

With respect to the four dimensions of public sector reform, this danger is most applicable within the interrelated realms of service and security. Portals such as the seniors' initiative rooted in Brockville or the public safety portal—coupled with the laudatory pronouncements of government leaders—invite speculation of an environment shaped less by boundaries and more by outcomes. Yet there can be no real progress in achieving fundamentally more concerted outcomes than is currently the case without a significant degree of intergovernmental innovation and collaboration. Moreover, to be effective, such a process will invariably require a more meaningful municipal presence than is currently the case.

The second source of inertia is the structural inhibitors now being placed on a wider movement of bottom-up reform — particularly in the realms of transparency, trust, and democratic renewal. Without some mix of devolution (to further empower municipalities) and collaboration (to interlink all government levels more strategically in designing policies and processes), it will likely remain the case that federal and provincial political forums will overshadow local democracy. Indeed, as Ontario's e-health experience suggests, there is a risk that municipal governance will be further marginalized in an online world, particularly from the perspective of democratic interest and engagement.

This danger also underscores the connections between the four dimensions of governance reform reviewed throughout this book. The front line gap, for instance, eluded to above also extends from primarily public capacity questions (about service and security) to overarching matters of democratic accountability and legitimacy (rooted more within transparency and trust). Security efforts are a case in point. Despite growing efforts at interoperability within and between various law enforcement and intelligence-gathering agencies (in manners often transcending federal, provincial, and municipal boundaries), the absence of a corresponding political mechanism to guide such actions should be a concern.

Therefore, the front line gap not only places communities at risk in the event of particular occurrences (when resources and capacities may be lacking) but also limits the ability of the citizenry to counter what might otherwise be an excessive degree of secrecy with a culture of public engagement and specific and effective mechanisms of oversight.

The third source of inertia is perhaps the most immediate challenge facing municipalities: namely, the widely varying capacities of local governments to both invest in and deploy a digital infrastructure — including both municipal operations and community-wide networks for online access and engagement. This particular version of the digital divide is highly geographic across the country, with a widening gap between the presence and usage of a digital infrastructure in large urban settings versus smaller, often more rural, communities. In the spring of 2005, the Federation of Canadian Municipalities estimated that roughly 1,300 communities remained without broadband Internet access.[52]

In short, an important requirement of Canada's digital transformation of the public sector as a whole is a conversation that links democratic renewal, fiscal federalism, and the growing need for new and more regularized forms of intergovernmental collaboration. What is particularly crucial at the local level is municipal creativity to strengthen the alignment between traditional notions of place, new community-based identities, and public sector engagement. Diversity is thus less an advantage than an essential and obvious requirement for progress: the multicultural environments of the largest cities will differ in democratic form and culture from more homogeneous jurisdictions, and the interrelationships between core urban centres and surrounding regions encompass a level of diversity across the country (and indeed within many provinces) that excludes uniformity as a serious proposition.[53]

A meaningful decentralization of taxation authority would challenge local governments to craft solutions for their own jurisdictions – and citizens would take notice. Municipalities may also choose in some instances to pool their interests and resources into new regional mechanisms (which could serve as a basis of unified efforts not only to broaden and improve Internet access for the population at large but also to share administrative functions relying on an expensive and sophisticated digital infrastructure). As an alternative, a key component of any 'new deal' for cities and communities should be to transfer new funding sources to municipalities without conditions, making it clear, however, that local governments would now be expected to take the lead in devising their own digital capacities as a means not only to serve their constituents more directly but also to partner more strategically with provincial and federal governments in devising a multilevel governance approach (i.e., a federated architecture) that is respectful of a strong, front line municipal presence.

To realize the promise of both more seamless and more responsive forms of e-government, a strong municipal dimension is paramount.

Realistically, however, the impetus for strengthening local and regional governance capacities is unlikely to emerge from vested interests provincially and federally. Tensions rooted in ICT deployments and online connectivity between the necessity of national, centralized actions and systems on the one hand and more localized, proximity-based initiatives on the other represent a set of issues that must be more forcefully inserted into a basis for reforming Canadian governance to meet the new realities of a more digital, connected, and interdependent environment.

Part Three
Looking Ahead

The first decade of e-government in Canada has not been without considerable effort. At all levels, governments have devoted substantial resources and attention to making use of digital technologies and online connectivity in ways that would have been unthinkable for the most part in the early 1990s.

The Canadian assessment of such efforts, however, reveals only modest and incremental progress in specific aspects of reform, notably service improvement, a pace and scale out of step with the rhetoric of digital renewal and a widening schism between the citizenry and their public institutions. What is missing is a sense that a new governing style or real institutional innovation has occurred. Although some early signs of democratic reform are gathering force at the provincial level, they are doing so in a relatively cautious and timid manner, overshadowed in many cases by health care debates, federal scandals and minority politics, and the various crises that come and go over the course of governing.

Such a context lends credence to the views of those e-skeptics who claim that the impacts of any forthcoming digital revolution are greatly exaggerated and that, instead, the pace of change will be modest and incremental, safeguarding—for some—the inherent stability of the public sector that is one of its defining traits. Yet it would be a mistake to subscribe to such a view outright for two reasons. First, the nature of the scandals emerging in Ottawa as of late are, if not driven by, at least indicative of a set of pressures associated with the painful imposition of a new culture of openness and transparency. This new culture has much to do with an underlying and expanding digital infrastructure of both traditional and new media channels for communication and information sharing. Second, the precise contours of e-government are becoming harder to pin down in terms of specific initiatives (such as GOL), but they are also becoming more subversively engrained in most aspects of public sector operations—ranging from national security and health care to environment protection and economic development.

The first point suggests that much of what is transpiring in Ottawa (and to a similar degree in many provincial capitals) is an inability by existing institutions to easily adapt to the new realities presenting themselves. There is thus much about the recent agenda that is worrisome, especially in terms of its reactionary form. The implications of this point will be explored more fully in Chapter 8.

The main focus of Part Three, however, is to look ahead and contrast what is unfolding in the Canadian public sector at present with what could and should be transpiring. In doing so, three sets of transversal issues emerge that build on the four e-government dimensions adopted throughout this book but also go beyond them in seeking to pinpoint the main determinants of public sector governance reform, both internally and externally.

Here it is useful to return to the definition of e-government provided at the outset of this investigation: continuous innovation in the delivery of services, citizen participation, and governance through the transformation of external and internal relationships by the use of information technology, especially the Internet. Whereas service security denotes dimensions of relational fluidity internally, focusing primarily on the organizational machinery of government, transparency and trust are more centred on the institutional roles and relationships of democracy and how they are shifting due to the advent of the Internet as a new digital, socio-economic, and political infrastructure.

The first set of issues, examined in Chapter 8, is organization and accountability. Although accountability issues permeate all aspects of democratic politics and public sector management, their invocation here is primarily from the perspective of the public service, the roles and responsibilities of public servants and their relationships with elected officials, particularly ministers of the executive branch. The increasingly horizontal nature of service and security agendas is a key driver here, and the 2005 creation of Service Canada is a case study that merits closer attention in terms of how it is evolving at present—at its inception—and some of the main lessons that can be drawn from the preceding analysis as well as some important parallel experiences of other countries. Essentially, this chapter argues that Service Canada's success rests on resolving some key accountability quandaries shaping how individual departments and ministers operate separately and collectively in pursuing the objectives of service integration and transformation.

This discussion of the internal organizational dynamics of the public sector cannot be sufficient without recognizing its interdependence with how accountability extends beyond the executive branch to include the legislative branch and the citizenry at large. Accordingly, the second set of issues, explored in Chapter 9, is participation and engagement — and the implications of the emergence of a more participative and direct democracy for existing institutional arrangements. In light of changes and pressures rooted in the closely related dimensions of transparency and trust, it is important to ask whether or not the ceremonial traditions and contraptions of Parliament can remain the focal point of democracy in the twenty-first century and whether there is at present an appropriate balance with respect to digital technologies and online presence between the executive and legislative branches (such a balance constituting the allocation and conduct of political power).

As shown throughout this chapter, while Canada may cling to the status and recognition of having achieved some limited prominence in e-government as an agent of service improvement (a status owed to models at all three government levels), the country is lagging in terms of political willingness and experimentation in ways to digitally refurbish both existing representational mechanisms and more novel and participatory ones. Such reluctance threatens to further erode the legitimacy and performance capacities of the public sector at all levels. Indeed, a major theme of e-democracy that must be addressed is the need for a new intergovernmentalism that can reconcile opportunities in cyberspace with those stemming from proximity and place-based communities: collaboration and strategic alignment more than competition are therefore called for between all government levels to ensure that federalism and e-democracy coexist in a positive manner.

These two sets of issues — organization and accountability on the one hand and participation and engagement on the other — allow for a consideration of the main contours of digital transformation for a polity denoted by national boundaries (albeit with multiple government levels). Yet there is much about the Internet and e-governance that transcends such boundaries, and accordingly the final set of issues, addressed in Chapter 10, is transnational in scope. Continentally and globally, the emergence of online connectivity and digital interoperability carry the potential for more open commerce and the necessary level of social mobilization and political engagement required to complement widening markets with workable governance arrangements. Conversely, the post-2001 security fixation has recast somewhat the transnational equation by inserting a much more prominent security variable that shifts the priorities and actions of national governments within their own jurisdictions as well as with one another.

For Canada, these pressures are felt most acutely at the continental level as security and border management have reshaped bilateral relations (and to a lesser degree trilateral ones with Mexico under the NAFTA umbrella). While traditional trade matters such as beef and lumber remain visibly prominent, a new set of issues has arisen concerning the handling of Maher Arar, the processing of personal information of Canadians via American subsidiaries, and aggressive efforts by government agencies in both countries to realize more interoperable and integrative continental mechanisms for the rebalancing of personal freedom, open commerce, and public safety and anti-terrorism — concerns that have transformed the American polity over the past half decade.

These issues represent a highly consequential linkage between the e-government dimensions of security, transparency, and trust. Whether the public supports a continental security regime (bolstered not only by new technologies but also by new political mechanisms, as has been argued lately), whether there is sufficient political oversight of security arrangements both within this country and across our borders, and how the public's views on such questions will evolve are key determinants of whether or not e-government evolves in some form beyond national borders.

Globally, too, such matters are central, underscored as of late by increasingly tense debates about the governance of the technological nucleus of the Internet itself and America's preference for unilateralism versus rising pressures for multilateral governance. This debate in particular, central to a sustained expansion of online activities, demonstrates how matters of transparency and trust and the emergence of e-democracy more generally face familiar political and jurisdictional quandaries stemming from the familiar confines of national interests and domestic politics.

Chapter 8
Organization and Accountability

The notion of accountability is central to public sector governance, and it is therefore a fundamental determinant of e-government. Much of the resistance to broader institutional change may be attributed to the imposition of pressures from within the realms of transparency and trust on models of organization and accountability created in a time of limited information flows, relative secrecy, and highly indirect and strictly representational forms of democracy. Yet even the pursuit of reforms tied to service and security has exposed the limitations of tradition and the need for alternative governance mechanisms within the public sector and beyond it. This chapter focuses primarily on the former perspective, situating the federal flagship initiative, Service Canada, as an important illustration of the need for more collaboration among both departments and ministers, more visibility and performance responsibilities for public servants, and a more politically nonpartisan set of mechanisms for managing information flows as a public resource and the lifeblood of transforming the Westminster model of ministerial accountability into one more appropriate for a more open, interdependent, and digital era.

Section 8.1 summarizes the main forces of resistance to change that are particularly prevalent within the federal government. Section 8.2 addresses the urgent need to reconceptualize accountability arrangements away from a strict interpretation of Westminster customs in order to adapt managerial and political relationships to an emerging era of more direct and shared forms of public accountability. Section 8.3 considers the ongoing tension between procurement reform and collaborative relationships between industry and government that are at the very crux of e-government's emergence: the importance of transparency and new relational capacities for engagement and execution is offered as the basis of reform. Section 8.4 then extends the realm of the accountability challenge to consider the central role of information, how it is currently managed and contained within the executive branch, and the need for a new strategic and more politically neutral mechanism to oversee the processing and disseminating of this critical public resource.

8.1 A Recipe for Paralysis

For better and for worse, Ottawa and the federal government serve as the focal point of politics and public sector management in Canada. Money plays a large role, of course, as nearly $200 billion in annual spending plans — accompanied with burgeoning budget surpluses — have a way of attracting attention. Even key areas of provincial domain — notably health care — become subsumed in federal-provincial discussions, reflecting if not solely a federal fixation then at least a 'national obsession' with federal-provincial relations. To underscore this point, recent debates about better supporting cities and communities have been largely framed and formed around new federal spending commitments to be allocated on the basis of federal-provincial agreements.[1]

Along with attempts to overtly expand its authority by directing funds to other levels of government, the federal apparatus has inwardly expanded as well, with key implications for the relationship between technology and public administration. As discussed in Part Two of this book, financial spending on a digital infrastructure within the confines of federal authorities in order to support service delivery and security efforts dwarfs anything that is happening provincially and locally. For such reasons, present federal plans will do much to shape the future of the public sector as a whole, and these plans are not without some worrisome features.

Since its inception, central to the e-government vision federally is the notion of service. As a guiding principle, this emphasis on service essentially involves doing more things and doing them better to please a citizenry viewed largely through the prism of being 'customers' of public service providers. To reinforce this service mentality, communication thus becomes an essential tool to make customers aware of the service efforts being made by public authorities. These one-way flows — providing service and communicating this message — are also the means by which ministers may be seen to be delivering on their own specific agenda, thereby deflecting attention away from scandals and crises that may or may not be rooted in their own action or organizational domain.

Thus, service and communication become means to both preserving and deploying power. In a political context shaped by scandal and adversarial exchange (the two feeding off one another particularly well within Westminster institutions), what often results is a form of 'political spin' that greatly reduces the legitimacy of the message being conveyed by governing authorities. The harder a government tries to portray itself as doing more to serve citizens, the more it risks being viewed as attempting to either market itself in the best possible light or, worse, manipulate or divert public attention away from its political difficulties.

Two other elements must be added to this mix: secrecy and simplicity. With respect to the former, the more governments feel threatened and in need of controlling their responses, the more political leaders may feel the need to shield their intentions until they can be cast (i.e., announced/spun) in the best possible light. The danger of such an approach is obvious, for the announcement is cynically received as an attempt to deflect or refocus public attention.[2] A corresponding reflex of governing in such an environment is simplification: to frame a particular initiative in the most appealing and reassuring manner possible, objectives, means, and accountabilities must be clear and conducive to media sound bites.

In sum, for a government to be seen to be serving and responding effectively, clear and effective communications are necessary. But it is the very nature of this clarity, simplistic and politically subjective, that fuels both cynicism and criticism politically, further eroding trust in government. At the same time, the implications for management and governance within the public sector are equally important. After all, ministers are the interface between externalizing communications and politics in such a manner and internalizing the processes and decisions that must follow.

Indeed, it is this interface that is becoming particularly ill-suited to the changing realities of governing. When more openness, consultation, and collaboration are called for, and when complexity is invariably a large part of the governing agenda, traditional control mechanisms are insufficient. What often results is a mindset of risk aversity and a reasserting of command and control structures—the very sort of leadership and organizational philosophy most out of tune with the new managerial and governing requirements that governments themselves often underscore as central to their future success. Similarly, with the terminology and focus of e-government shaped by service and security orientations and a control-minded mindset, the pursuit of interoperability is more likely to be sought in an aggressive, secretive, and confrontational manner than by more collaborative means.

Such is the daunting context within which the federal government now seeks to launch its new Service Canada vehicle on the one hand, and a government-wide approach to shared IT services on the other. As outlined in Chapter 4, the former entity is to group together most federal services in an attempt to improve multichannel service delivery via a single citizen interface, whereas the latter builds on a previously more supportive role played by subunits within PWGSC. It is indeed probable (and understandable within the logic sketched out here) that ongoing delays in final decisions pertaining to the autonomy and scope of Service Canada that have persisted through 2004 and much of 2005 are reflective of the difficulties of embracing complexity and change.

To effectively fulfill its mission, Service Canada requires either an unprecedented level of interdepartmental coordination or outright restructuring and bureaucratic fusion. The former option would entail new collaborative mechanisms to transcend ministerial and departmental boundaries — along with a form of managerial and political leadership to underpin and report on the execution of these mechanisms. The latter option would bypass these requirements by fusing all relevant units into an amalgamated entity — underpinned in this case by a more recognizable and centralized chain of command (likely a single minister). As explored in Chapter 5, the latter option is more in keeping with recent security efforts in both the United States and Canada since 9/11. Much as it is proving unworkable in the security realm, it would be equally out of step with what is required for truly bettering service delivery capacities of the federal government.

In other words, the formation of Service Canada is, in itself, not necessarily a misguided venture. Unless one is prepared to reverse and discredit the entire logic of service improvement that both predates and makes use of an e-government platform (in what is now an established multichannel environment with online use destined to rise in the future), creating a government-wide entity to facilitate service clusters, interoperability, and innovative models of information sharing and processing is undeniably a sensible proposition. Moreover, this type of entity is enjoying various and evolving levels of success in many jurisdictions.

Nonetheless, Service Canada is a critical test case for both the federal government's own rhetoric of what is entailed in fostering an effective e-government infrastructure and the wider spectrum of research on organizational design and human leadership in a postbureaucratic, customer- or citizen-centric era. It is a test case for creating a truly networked architecture of interoperability that strikes a coordinating balance between shared objectives and some degree of central authority on the one hand and flexible capacities for achieving these objectives on the other. Flexibility is paramount since most of the potential partners of Service Canada will maintain partially unique and separate agendas reflecting their own status, mandate, and ministerial domain.[3] Collaboration is essential, even as it is underpinned with formalized interunit mechanisms such as contracts, service agreements, and the like.

For many politicians (and many longtime public servants serving them), the implications of such an approach are excessively messy, uncertain, and risky when viewed through the prism of clarity and communications. The other danger stems from those who view such an agenda as an infringement on their own political and/or managerial autonomy. Both dangers are accentuated by vertical notions of ministerial accountability that shape both budgetary processes and political aspirations.

One potential path to alleviate both forms of resistance is centralization of a more traditional and recognizable sort. Service Canada thus becomes a new agency with its own minister and operational responsibilities hived off various departments and amalgamated into a single set of structures. Doing so requires political intervention from the centre, and this type of intervention is not unfamiliar to many current and past restructurings of federal government operations. In fairness, however, even traditionalists recognize that such measures are unlikely to suffice in an organizational, political, and technological environment increasingly demanding horizontal processes to forge meaningful policy agendas and, by extension, service delivery agendas (Savoie 2005).

The result is a form of paralysis along this continuum between a flexible and collaborative entity on the one hand and a more centralized and autonomous unit of authority on the other. For many, the attraction of the latter is its easy fit with tradition, both politically and organizationally, despite being increasingly out of step with the more fluidly integrative and networked requirements of today's environment. By extension, the largest unknown with the former lies in not only publicly explaining and internally operationalizing the complexities involved but also envisioning a political architecture of shared accountability appropriate for such processes.

8.2 Networked Accountability

For some longtime observers of Canadian public administration, many current problems are indicative of a breakdown of traditional controls brought on by various reforms put forth under the guise of 'new public management' and related movements. According to this view, what has resulted is a breaking of the traditional 'bargain' between elected officials—notably ministers—and public servants (the basis of this bargain being anonymity, job security, and merit-based promotion for the public servant and full duties and visibility associated with public accountability—via Parliament—for the minister). Savoie (2003, 266) notably laments the loss of traditional boundaries and controls and the resulting erosion of clear lines of accountability: "Hierarchical organizations are useful: inspired by the military model, they encourage central planning, discipline and accountability. In addition, employees have some authority and rules of behaviour designed to prevent chaos, and these provide the basis to blame someone when things go wrong and when the rules are not followed. The new policy environment groups together numerous departments, agencies, and stakeholders to pursue shared objectives in both policy formulation and program delivery. The individual public servant meanwhile is lost in the crowd."

As Savoie acknowledges, whatever the past strengths of the traditional model of ministerial accountability, one cannot merely reach back and call upon tradition to resolve emerging challenges. Such a tradition dictates a public service that operates according to the guiding principles of "employment security, merit-based advancement, and anonymity," the basis of the traditional 'bargain' between politicians (notably those serving in cabinet) and public servants (ibid.). The growing imposition of horizontality as not only desirable but also essential—coupled with the dispersal of information and power across an extended public sector of think tanks, academics, special interest groups, and other stakeholders—renders this traditional bargain unworkable in moving forward.

A new bargain has yet to be successfully defined, and a primary culprit in Savoie's analysis is the philosophy of new public management. Driven by the application of business models to government, such an approach has sought a separation of politics and management, leaving the latter realm for a public service left to its own devices and facing the worst of two worlds: an absence of performance objectives akin to the profit motive of the private sector and a loss of anonymity in terms of operational failure through a weakening of the doctrine of ministerial accountability (as ministers appear to be increasingly prepared to place distance between themselves and the public service).

Accordingly, Savoie's prescriptions—although recognizing the existence of multiple forms of accountability ("co-accountability" is the term deployed)—are predicated largely on the preservation of ministerial accountability, albeit in an updated and more flexibly interpreted manner.[4] Of central importance is a bolstered legislative branch to better hold the executive to account and a near-irrefutable willingness by ministers to effectively account for actions and decisions within their domains (while not necessarily accepting responsibility for the actions of officials but answering for such actions and undertaking remedial measures as required). Accordingly, in Savoie's interpretation, the accountability of the public servant is best enforced not in a public or political manner (i.e., holding officials overtly responsible for their duties) but in a direct, more traditionally secretive fashion via ministerial review and action that nonetheless maintains the anonymity of the public servant.

Traditionalists may take heart in such a view, but they are swimming against a forceful current. The notion that public servants are any more deserving than politicians—or any other group of decision makers in today's society—of being shielded from transparency and more direct lines of accountability is a nonstarter—it is also dangerous. Not only is it unlikely to be feasible in an age when information is increasingly available, but also any such emphasis can only lead to a reinforcement of the insular culture of secrecy that is already so pervasive in the public sector.

To flourish, institutions and organizations must be able to adapt to and be reflective of the times in which they operate. Savoie's hope that a bolstered set of adversarial mechanisms within the parliamentary model—coupled with stronger controls over public servants expected to act within the strict confines of ministerial orders (except in blatantly unethical or illegal matters)—will lead to a rejuvenation of confidence and respect among public servants and Canadians at large is unlikely to be realized. Trust is increasingly based on direct engagement and reputation cultivated over peer-like encounters and interactions (rather than deference to rank or role as traditionally determined), and to deny the public service the authority and indeed the responsibility to reach out to stakeholders beyond their ministerial leaders is to restrict innovation and marginalize their role beyond salvation.

To underscore this point, one must also consider the individuals likely to become senior public servants. Savoie's analysis largely ignores digital technologies as an independent and consequential variable, relegating it to minor status as one of many factors used to justify models of new public management that emphasize business-like solutions for the public sector. Although distinguishing between the public and private sectors is a worthwhile measure, such a marginalization of e-government merely underscores the degree to which the public administration community has paid scant attention to the nexus between technological and managerial reform in government (Kernaghan and Gunraj 2004).

This point is central to human resource management and the recruitment and retention capacities of a public sector not only in need of renewal but also facing the imposition of turnover via demographic stealth (Moritz and Roy 2000). Although there is much imperfect about current methods of rewarding and promoting individuals to the senior ranks, it is unhelpful to envision future recruits—insofar as they are to be among the best and brightest of today's younger generations—reverting to an ideal 1960s prototype of a public servant (Lindquist 2005).

Such issues are central to e-government's permeating evolution across the public sector, changing not only service delivery methods but also broader issues of structure, culture, and accountability (Allen et al. 2005). Central to this shift is how people behave, and younger people today (especially the most educated), with their near-ubiquitous and continually networked set of digital devices for managing and communicating information, represent the future cadre of public sector managers. Along with this somewhat more positivist view of realigning public organizations to the sorts of individuals likely to inhabit them as employees is an equally important danger in preserving public service anonymity. The danger lies in the widening security-technology nexus (discussed conceptually in Chapter 2 and applied federally in Chapter 5) that promises to continually extend the veil of secrecy across larger segments of the federal government apparatus rooted in a traditional culture of secrecy yet increasingly reliant on digital computer systems and virtual networks that reinforce this tradition and extend it in new directions.[5]

There is a strong case to be made that many of the present difficulties plaguing federal operations stem more from Canada's reluctance to embrace bolder reforms than from any present deviations from tradition — particularly with respect to the role of public servants and the manner in which they are held accountable (Hubbard and Paquet 2005). In many other Westminster-inspired models of parliamentary democracy, senior public servants are truly beginning to be held accountable for results based on their own decisions and authority: in other words, management based less on process rules and responsibilities and more on outcomes and achievements (Aucoin et al. 2004).

In the United Kingdom and New Zealand, for example, many department and agency heads are recruited, appointed, and compensated (and at times removed) on the basis of performance contracts that signify a distinct sphere of autonomy. Nevertheless, accountability of the public servant in charge of managing the agency remains within the confines of policy and political objectives laid out by the government.

In Sweden, a similar level of managerial autonomy is complemented by flexibilities that are the basis of a 'contractual' and 'networked' approach to pursuing aims both vertically and horizontally as circumstances dictate:

> Owing to the increased need for cooperation between different administrative units, *networked administration* represents an appropriate organizational paradigm for modern administration. The

term refers to administration composed of independently managed units that rely on functions and resources provided by other such units or private companies, and form part of permanent and temporary cooperative structures.

Forms of collaboration among administrative units vary according to country and administrative tradition. The Swedish model of cooperation may be summarized as a *contractual model*. Accordingly, an administrative unit decides for itself whether external services and functions are sufficiently attractive for the unit to use them or pay for this use. (Swedish Agency for Public Management 2004, 2)[6]

The pursuit of 'agency' reforms is illustrative of such design choices and hugely important to the future of e-government (e.g., the emergence of Service Canada, the pursuit of internally shared services, and procurement and partnering decisions externally). Many countries have sought to transform 'departments' into 'agencies' through significantly enhanced degrees of both autonomy and more explicit managerial roles for public servants. In contrast, the Canadian experience with such reforms — particularly at the federal level — has been timid, precisely due to an unwillingness to move away from a strict and traditional interpretation of ministerial accountability.

The most notable if partial exception to this trend is the Canada Revenue Agency (CRA), a body that perhaps, not coincidentally, has enjoyed perhaps the greatest progress in establishing online delivery channels that enjoy significant use among its clientele.[7] Even here, however, despite an additional margin of both freedom and responsibility for senior management of the revenue agency, the doctrine of full ministerial accountability remains in place, representing a form of Canadian compromise between tradition and innovation.

Such a compromise is unsustainable, as is the traditional model of ministerial accountability itself. In his analysis of the HRDC grants and contributions scandal and the implications for accountability, Good (2003) points to ongoing tensions between three forms of accountability relationships inherent in the reforms of recent decades: for control, for assurance, and for learning. He underscores that, despite widening interest in the latter type, Canadian public administration and its reform in recent times most often reflects competing forces between the first and second types. Accountability for control, of course, emphasizes traditional top-down authority and risk aversion, whereas accountability for assurance invokes the public servant acting as an agent of the principal (minister) in seeking to meet expectations and achieve objectives in a manner focusing somewhat less on rules and more on outcomes: importantly, public servants may accept responsibility but not answerability in a political (i.e., parliamentary) context. Accountability for learning, in contrast, emphasizes continual improvement and adjustment for bettering both the individual and the organizational capacities of the public service to meet increasingly complex challenges. Collaboration is valued more than control, and knowledge is viewed as the central lifeblood of a more organic and adaptive form of governance akin to a world of distributed power (Agranoff and McGuire 2003; Paquet 2004; Eggers 2005). Importantly, while acknowledging its growing recognition in public sector circles today, Good underlines that its potential is often stymied by the adversarial nature and structure of the political environment that seek to reinforce blame and clarity over adjustment and complexity.

And here lies the central conundrum for public sector reform provincially and federally: accountability for learning cannot take hold unless one is prepared to entertain broader changes to the parliamentary regime, including—most importantly—exercising and applying the principle of ministerial accountability and its implications for the roles of and interrelationships among politicians, public servants, and the public.

Including the public in this mix is essential since an increasingly digital, networked, and knowledge-rich world is one where the meaning of citizen-centric governance is about not only serving but also including the citizenry in a new system of learning governance comprising both representational oversight mechanisms and direct public engagement. As Paquet states, "It is not sufficient to develop a new more encompassing cosmology.... One must also design new organizational forms capable of taking advantage of the new ICTs and the new network thinking, and also likely to provide more effective social learning" (2004, 199).

The implications for the creation of a new entity such as Service Canada are important. As many experiences from other jurisdictions have shown (including many provinces), the success of such an integrative mechanism designed to explicitly transcend vertical boundaries depends largely on a dynamic and collaborative leadership model categorically different from the traditional department. The senior manager in charge of such an entity must have the latitude and incentives to foster new organizational arrangements—and must be directly accountable for the results. Much of the research conducted for Service Canada has therefore focused on such models elsewhere, notably Australia's Centrelink agency—roughly equivalent in scope to the tripartite Modernizing Services for Canadians agenda that arose from within HRDC and has since facilitated Service Canada's initial partnering with HRSDC and SDC.[8]

Digital technologies are determinant for two reasons. First, the imposition of service and security objectives demands interoperability within government, leading to either a greater emphasis on networks and collaborative arrangements or the imposition of more centralized, control-oriented mechanisms. Second, the skills and capacities of public servants to work in such new patterns can be greatly enhanced or further confined by a digital infrastructure. Much depends on what form of accountability is sought (control, assurance, or learning). There should be little question that, if Service Canada is to play a role as a catalyst for innovative governance arrangements that are citizen-centric and by definition less constrained by traditional practices and controls, an emphasis on learning is the most appropriate.

Central to improving accountability and performance in such a fashion is the need for a form of internal engagement that seeks to instill trust within the public service via more openness, responsibility, and room to focus on performance. The cultural shift implied by this form of engagement is no small task for any public service. For example, a recent survey of 50,000 federal public servants in Australia revealed that only about ten percent of employees were 'fully engaged' in making use of their skills and discretionary efforts to achieve their organizational objectives: while some ten to fifteen percent were clearly disengaged, the survey revealed that a full three-quarters of employees were ambivalent or in the middle (and as a result 'up for grabs' in terms of whether to become engaged or not). The study found that the top five cultural traits of an organization that carry the maximum positive impact on engagement are communication, reputation of integrity, culture of innovation, culture of flexibility, and customer focus.[9]

The first two points — communication and integrity — speak to the need for participation and dialogue within the public service in a manner more akin to today's environment. Whereas in the past the integrity of a public servant was largely derived from loyalty to cabinet, this sort of authoritative imposition of direct control is more likely today to convey a sense of distrust among senior managers (i.e., expected to follow orders and remain anonymous) and a dispersed culture of ambivalence within the rest of the organization. In other words, the type of managerial innovation required demands a meaningful and leading role for managers — precisely the sort of activity acknowledged to be of least interest to political leaders (Savoie 2003).

Creating a citizen-centric culture of innovation and flexibility, then, requires a stronger degree of autonomy for public servants themselves, a level of autonomy that must be matched with the accountability requirements to orchestrate resources and solutions in a performance-driven manner. The evidence to date largely suggests that, while there is a certain amount of organizational fluidity and restructuring under way within the federal government (driven by service and security aims), resistance to an internal cultural shift in both participation and accountability, the sort of attributes inspired by the transparency and trust dimensions of today's digital transformation, remains firmly entrenched.

The common misconception in envisioning such reform is to view any direct and open empowerment of senior managers as a dangerous weakening of the doctrine of ministerial accountability and thus the stability of the system as a whole. Yet the role of elected officials in the executive branch remains central to such a system in a number of respects. First, authority must be vested in this new entity and the personnel leading it, and here ministerial accountability remains a function that can 'coexist' with alternative forms of managerial accountability (Aucoin et al. 2004). Creation of the blueprint and direction of resources to achieving it are in large measure political decisions: the execution of decisions becomes the realm of managers. In other words, defining governance remains a political function — within which managers must be held more to account for their actions (Aucoin and Jarvis 2005).[10]

There can be little question that at times the two will overlap, creating frictions and leading to public exchanges between officials and ministers on matters of knowledge and appropriate behaviour. Nonetheless, it is precisely the openness of such exchanges that will do more to preserve the nonpartisanship, professionalism, and effective performance of a public servant than a secretive chain of command leading to a simplified (yet far less revealing and useful) voice of a highly general form of answerability through a minister.

At the same time, ministers must also learn to collaborate with one another in a more open manner. The challenge of horizontality in the public sector is often hamstrung due to the separate fiefdoms of ministers — traditionally overcome only by strong forms of intervention by central agencies (Lindquist 2005). Accordingly, those operating at the centre face the difficult and often conflicting challenges of remaining on top of all issues at all times while not being overwhelmed and overextended as a result (even if a prime minister's entourage seeks as much control as possible). Overly concentrated power is a well-established feature of debate in parliamentary countries, and the implications are not lost on those seeking to influence the government in raising the profile of an agenda that is cross-governmental: the service delivery dimension of e-government is a case in point.[11] In an era of expanding information, communication, and complexity, such an approach is clearly unworkable, even as the political instincts of those in power aim to slow the damage (often with an eye on political survival). The end result, however, is paralysis.

One necessary response, a basis for learning and results-driven accountability, is to devolve authority to ministers to let them deal with their own agendas. Yet the challenge remains that many of these agendas are intertwined, which is why ministers must act concertedly when necessary, in an open manner, integrating their actions and agendas via explicit governance processes extending from budget setting and the formation of objectives to collectively reporting on shared outcomes. It is precisely the absence of this type of collaborative architecture that impeded the progress of most pilot initiatives under GOL, and the costs can also be viewed on a range of other issues requiring horizontal efforts that make use of multiple pockets of competencies across government but invariably must be made to fit within separate ministerial domains. Accordingly, it is understandably more common for ministers to compete with one another for the affections of central agencies (and those cabinet colleagues overseeing them) than it is to witness the formation of strategic partnerships and alliances in the name of shared objectives (Bakvis and Juillet 2004).

The interpretation and application of ministerial accountability as a system of separately operating worlds — created at one time to provide the clarity in accountability reporting that comes from specialization and division — is increasingly at odds with the governing realities of the current era. The result is that any such clarity comes at the cost of flexibility and capacity within the public service — and legitimacy outside it — as the public intuitively understands the growing cleavage between how its model of government is explained (in terms of accountability) and the patterns of organizational and governance complexity. At the same time, although this cleavage is recognized, the absence of a more accurate portrayal erodes trust and increases cynicism.

This reality forms the basis of the response, therefore, to critics of such a notion as networked accountability for ministers, characterizing such a shift as dangerously complex in blurring accountability to Parliament and the public. Simplistic solutions for complex problems are unlikely to suffice, and there is much about the traditional governing model that underestimates the capacities of the citizenry to embrace complexity and partake in the design of new solutions and mechanisms for maintaining and improving public services and decision-making processes (Paquet 2004; Courchene 2005).

One useful starting point for experimenting with such a new direction is an expanded and revised set of cabinet committees. Already such subcommittees represent partially networked bodies, removed (in most cases and to some degree) from direct prime ministerial involvement and based upon agendas conducive to a subset of ministers interlinked by interests or agendas that transcend any single department or portfolio. At present, however, these committees do little more than act as a filtering device for final cabinet decisions, and they are as secretive as cabinet itself. Even the most politically informed citizens may not be aware of their existence, and there is little collective awareness outside government of their purpose and functioning.

What may hold some merit is rendering such bodies public in their deliberations and aligning their formation with specific horizontal agendas requiring collaborative attention. A subcommittee on Canada's Kyoto commitments, for example, could enjoin the ministers of the environment, natural resources, industry, and health in a task force-like structure designed specifically to achieve results in an integrative fashion. Such a body would be expected to form a strategic plan on the basis of at least a partially integrated budget and set of performance measures based on shared objectives. What is critical for such a model to be effective is ensuring that all ministers partaking of the shared agenda carry equal visibility in the eyes of the public — thereby pooling risks and rewards in a manner that goes beyond merely acknowledging the separate duties and contributions of each participant.

With respect to a new Service Canada model, any new agency must therefore couple a more visible and autonomous level of responsibility for the senior manager (i.e., a public servant) leading the entity and a networked-type board of directors comprising at least a subset of ministers most impacted by and interested in any government-wide effort to better integrate and deliver services. Such a model shares much in common with the Canada Revenue Agency, although important distinctions lie in both operationalizing the stronger managerial role and creating a collaborative interministerial forum to oversee and guide decisions (rather than maintain full and direct ministerial accountability, as is the case with CRA).

Such a collaborative mechanism does remove the need for strong leadership and direction from the centres of power — notably the Prime Minister's Office and central agencies; instead, it calls for a reformation of such leadership. It is a given that any flagship initiative in terms of either policy development or organizational reform requires visible and sustained support to proceed (Lindquist 2005). What an interministerial mechanism does provide, however, is a basis for leveraging such support into stronger horizontal capacities, thereby reversing the built-in resistance within line departments to mechanisms for service integration. Moreover, such a mechanism provides a more accurate portrayal of government organization to the public, a precursor to meaningful forms of performance reporting based on integrative results rather than the more silo-specific agendas of individual ministries and ministers.

Within government, an empowered leadership team of public servants for a new entity such as Service Canada could then draw from such interministerial involvement in forging the new sorts of internal mechanisms required to achieve collective aims. The collaborative political mechanism as such, in turn, translates into a negotiated, contractual-like approach where separate departments are encouraged to work together through budgetary and performance incentives tied to integrated performance outcomes (in an overtly horizontal and thus binding manner).

Much of this argument also finds resonance in domestic security and public safety efforts where the present emphasis on clarity via a single ministerial portfolio with a greatly enlarged flagship department and set of accompanying agencies is likely to prove not only organizationally ineffective but also misleadingly simplistic in its reporting to Canadians (via Parliament). Accordingly, creation of a new Parliamentary Committee on National Security is an important test case for such changes in two respects. First, the degree to which such a body can lessen the culture of secrecy that pervades the national security apparatus (and by extension a growing component of the entire federal government) is an important question.[12] Second to what extent can a single minister (in this case the deputy prime minister) be expected to orchestrate and report on changes and strategies that cut across so many different components of the federal government?

The intergovernmental scope of both service delivery and security agendas would suggest that this logic can also find applicability between governments as well in addressing the current political gap in elected leadership that limits existing mechanisms such as the federal-provincial CIO Council. If the federal government is serious in its commitment to seamless service delivery across jurisdictions, at the least the new Service Canada model will feature a formal advisory board encompassing provincial and municipal leaders (with the eventual aim of fusing their inclusion within a single body of elected officials from all government levels).[13]

The more politically charged security agenda may well call for a new intergovernmental forum to both publicly discuss and publicly report on intergovernmental commitments and shared concerns. For such a visible and at times contentious agenda (in a manner akin to health care), the prospect of a discursive mechanism breaking down into local and provincial lobbying efforts for more federal funding is a real issue, one that cannot be addressed without consideration of participative and democratic reforms and their relative importance across government levels (a theme of the subsequent chapter).

Another critical dimension of both managerial organization and accountability is the growing importance of collaborative relationships between industry and government—central to designing and maintaining a digital infrastructure as well as aligning it with performance objectives. Tensions between procurement and partnerships must therefore be first understood and subsequently reconciled.

8.3 Procurement and Partnerships

Much of the architecture for e-government depends on a widening set of relationships between technology specialists in the private sector and public sector authorities with ultimate responsibility for programs and services. The sorts of procurement reforms being adopted by many provinces of late—emphasizing results and outcomes and innovative solutions for achieving them—are consistent with a lessening emphasis on static, upfront measures of cost and a greater reliance on more performance-driven and collaborative-based project management (Paquet and Roy 2000; Allen et al. 2005b).

In moving toward models allowing for greater relational flexibility and creativity, the ongoing challenge is to further rebalance procurement's control emphasis with the necessity of collaboration. The following distinction is reflective of the tone of the dialogue emerging in many jurisdictions, and it points to the importance of creating meaningful and tangible links that recognize and structure interdependence in an appropriate fashion: "*Cooperation*—Informal relationships that exist without any commonly defined mission, structure or planning; and *Collaboration*—A more durable and pervasive relationship involving shared structures and joint authority, a full commitment to a common mission and pooled resources, risks & rewards" (Mattessich et al. 2001). Incremental reforms to traditional procurement mechanisms have often sought to facilitate some cooperation between industry and government—though even collaboration has often been limited in comparison to an emphasis on process and controls. In contrast, due to growing complexities of new technologies and organizational transformations, strategic relations are increasingly recognized as an imperative for effective public sector performance: indeed, such a philosophy has been driving the BC government's reforms of late, and many governments around the world have struggled to adjust to these new relational quandaries (Andison 2004; Langford and Roy 2005).

A current review of procurement at the federal level underlines the point well, contrasting the public sector's emphasis on a competitive and adversarial culture with suppliers to the approach used by successful companies and, increasingly, governments: "successful private sector companies and other jurisdictions avoid an adversarial approach by adopting more strategic relationships with their suppliers" (PWGSC 2004, 24). Nonetheless, procurement problems have been recognized as a key factor in the underperformance of the GOL strategy for some time (Public Policy Forum 2001).

A necessary starting point for effectively balancing cost-based procurement and performance-driven relationships is a differentiation of the sorts of activities and inputs sought externally. Whereas commodity-type goods (including in some instances technology products such as off-the-shelf software programs and small hardware components such as printers) may lend themselves to more centralized and market-driven approaches (including e-procurement mechanisms[14]), the pursuit of IT-enabled organizational innovations requires a higher level of interdependence at all levels of planning and execution.

Prodded by international experiences and growing provincial reforms, federal recognition of such issues is encouraging. Two key tests of more holistic public sector reform in Canada will be (1) whether political leadership will emerge to oversee a more strategic orientation with industry partners than has been the case to present and (2), if such political support is forthcoming, whether the procurement and partnering functions are differentiated and reorganized to reflect a new mix of competition and control on the one hand and strategic collaboration and relational management on the other (Langford and Roy 2005).

The key to any such reorganization lies in the need to more fully differentiate between the sort of organizational capacities required in government to address the more complex and relational arrangements involving digital technology. Too often procurement reform implies that existing procurement authorities will be retooled to better balance their contractual and control mindsets with more openness to flexible partnerships. This request is both unfair and unhelpful: it is unhelpful since controls remain useful mechanisms for government buying — particularly for commodity goods and transactional services — but also for complex partnerships that still require close monitoring, risk management, and legal protection. The unfairness of such reforms lies in expecting the same individuals and organizational bodies that oversee this control function to be equally conversant and effective in forging collaborative ties.

Collaboration often predates the need for contracting and controls as internal stakeholders sort out their organizational needs and the extent to which external agents are required. Yet even here — in this preparation phase — there is growing evidence of a potential to leverage public-private collaboration to both mutually and creatively define the vision and scope for the changes ahead (Dutil et al. 2005). At the same time as the nature of such collaborative arrangements is increasingly ongoing, the management and execution of the relationship requires a lessening of the reliance on the control function and a greater need for navigation by the parties involved in the processes themselves.

As a result, the ongoing existence of a central procurement authority may remain a necessity, but it alone cannot and should not serve as the collaborative function as well. What is required is a new entity — with a differentiated mandate and a fresh culture to facilitate partnering in a manner that will allow for the definition of a collaborative framework in advance of any involvement by procurement authorities. Moreover, this type of authority should be less 'centralized' and more federated in seeking to align government-wide perspectives on technology requirements with more organizational-specific needs of individual departments and agencies. A network of collaborative agents could serve as a vehicle, organized from within the CIO function rather than from within the procurement body.

Governments have begun to move partially in such directions. Many provinces, such as British Columbia and Ontario, treat technology procurement in a distinct manner — under the strategic realm of the CIO. Other jurisdictions, such as the United Kingdom, have also sought ways to create separate processes and policies for technology acquisition and outsourcing and partnering arrangements. In Canada, particularly at the federal level, much more relational flexibility and innovation are required, along with more openness throughout the process itself.

The increasingly strategic nature of acquiring, deploying, integrating, upgrading, and maintaining digital systems often involves longer-term commitments of hundreds of millions (and at times billions) of dollars. At present, aside from the technical community of experts overviewing vendor selection and contracting mechanisms (as well as those from the private sector proposing solutions), wider public and political scrutiny is exclusively after the fact. Consequently, only those projects and initiatives encountering difficulties generate political interest in a typically controversial manner, further reducing the margin of manoeuvrability for both the public and the private sectors.

Here is a good example, therefore, of a nexus between democratic and organizational reform that can facilitate stronger and more shared degrees of accountability by learning. To draw once again from the federal example, if Service Canada is to eventually embark on a multiyear partnership with the private sector to manage its multichannel delivery apparatus, a citizen's panel should be deployed as a key feature of such a process. A mix of citizens, public servants, and elected officials could then collectively overview deliberation and selection.[15]

Such steps would extend transparency and credibility to the citizenry and ensure a stronger level of buy-in and support for the sorts of investments and changes required once the partners are selected (changes that invariably lead to uncertainty and friction, often the sources of reactionary criticism against initial 'deals' once the implications of the agreements come to light). This sort of openness throughout the process would go a long way toward lessening the importance and suspicion surrounding the intense 'insider' lobbying that often accompanies large government activities involving industry in the lead-up to such a decision being made.

In sum, senior public servants leading a public sector body (likely a new performance-modelled agency) would carry the authority to determine both if and the degree to which private sector involvement is warranted. These senior managers can be expected at times to initiate small contracts in order to leverage outside expertise in preparing for larger organizational transformations involving public-private sector collaboration. Upon embarking on a process of engaging an outside industry partner for a substantial endeavour, the senior managers would work in concert with the 'collaborative' authority to undertake an open selection process—after which contracting authorities would be expected to assist in finalizing the legal contours of the collaborative relationship.

With regard to the federal government at present, one acute risk lies in the potential for a form of hypercentralization of all such functions within the single departmental entity PWGSC. Such a scenario could happen in the following manner: procurement authorities already act under the purview of this body, along with the shared IT services function for government-wide infrastructure and key elements of online service delivery such as the secure channel and maintenance of the main Government of Canada portal (indeed, the management of GOL projects was shifted to PWGSC in 2003—joining the secure channel). Finally, there is no new 'collaborative authority' created; rather, PWGSC is once again asked to reform procurement to rebalance control and relational emphases.

For some, the attractiveness of such a move lies in both the familiar consolidation and the clarity resulting from a single ministerial purview. Yet such moves would only solidify organizational paralysis—not only due to the baggage of recent scandals over advertising plaguing PWGSC (activities that were admittedly separate from most units of this department of direct relevance to this discussion)—and, more importantly, cement an enlarged bureaucracy officially empowered with government-wide responsibilities but in reality unable to develop the credibility and relational capital required to act collaboratively. The only avenue for proceeding would thus be along the familiar terrain of ordaining change from a ministerial decree (the minister of PWGSC but also supported in explicit fashion by the prime minister). In short, vertical integration would trump horizontal collaboration, and the new Service Canada entity (indeed all units of government) would be further handicapped.

An alternative approach—one consistent with networked administration, contractual forms of collaborative governance, and learning-based accountability—is to embed a new partnering unit within one of the two central agencies with strategic oversight capacities, TBS and PCO (the former a more obvious choice if under the realm of the CIO). This unit would help to facilitate government-wide collaboration while leaving most decisions pertaining to technology acquisition and relational management (with either an internal service provider for highly standardized solutions or a private sector alternative for more tailored needs) to individual departments and agencies.[16]

Such a direction is nonetheless entirely dependent on both political support for this sharp deviation from traditional hierarchy and centralization and a CIO with the mindset and skills to act in a facilitating manner.[17] More than the personalities of the players involved, this deviation underscores the need for reframing procurement away from its traditional contours of competition, control, and transaction costs and toward a strategic recognition, understanding, and pursuit of synergistic and relational practices shaped by a collaborative agenda. Entwistle and Martin (2005) define this new agenda in terms of three requirements (or areas in need of more attention and study given their rising prominence in the public sector today): (1) the costs and benefits of high-trust interorganizational relationships; (2) the ways in which partnerships combine the competencies of different sectors; and (3) the extent to which new partnerships transform public service delivery.

A major blockage in moving in such directions in the Canadian public sector context is a cultural aversion to partnering within the procurement authorities due to an exclusive association of contracting vehicles with competitive pressures and market controls. A centralized procurement authority and an effort to impose a shared services infrastructure on the whole of government reflect this association. As the Swedish model emphasizes, a contractual mindset is also conducive to collaboration insofar as it enables empowered units to make their own strategic determinations of their partnering needs (and subsequently forming explicit contracts to suit these choices). For these reasons, any movement down this latter path in Canada requires an organizational and political catalyst that starts from an explicit willingness to distinguish between procurement and partnering and begin to foster the sort of collaborative capacities necessary for more effective relational governance mechanisms.

With regard to risk-sharing and new accountability arrangements between sectors, there is much evidence across the country — particularly at local and provincial levels — of a more collaborative mindset taking hold in seeking shared capacities that are driven by principles such as openness, learning and adaptation rather than a traditional control mentality (Dutil et al. 2005). Therefore what is required, particularly at the federal level, is more oxygen for such emerging innovations and a willingness to systemically support them through the formation of a collaborative culture. The sort of new unit or organizational infrastructure required (separate from procurement) to focus on relational management less rooted in hierarchy is not out of line with the similar requirements of addressing increased horizontality across the public sector—where new forms of central supports, incentives, and skills are called for (Lindquist 2005).

The overarching and most fundamental issue confronting senior officials and political leaders is acceptance of a collaborative agenda as the best enabler of human, organizational, and technological alignment in a more partner-centric, networked world.

8.4 Information, Politics, and Performance

More transparency is a critical feature of the sorts of managerial and governance changes required within the public sector to adapt to the opportunities and pressures of a digital era. Providing higher levels of information in terms of quantity and quality throughout the decision-making process is a critical element of creating a more participative ethos enjoining public servants and politicians alike.

The use of online reporting must become more regularized and operationalized in the culture of the public sector. The opportunity for the public sector is to balance the growing sources of online information inherently critical in nature with a more neutral flow that can serve as a platform for stronger collective learning between government bodies, stakeholders, and the citizenry. Moreover, parliamentary mechanisms could be made to function in a less adversarial fashion than is the case at present, with the emphasis shifted from exposure to pre-emptive consideration and ongoing deliberation and adjustment.

Building stronger capacities to provide more politically neutral and performance-relevant information is an important requirement for realizing e-government's potential to positively marry transparency and accountability. Yet, in serving as a model for other organizations, governments can shape accountability practices across all sectors and, in many cases, strengthen them. A key role in this regard is to serve as an 'information broker' in making use of its extensive information holdings to empower individuals—both citizens and consumers—to make better choices about their own affairs and collective decisions (Eggers 2005).

Already, community profiling about education, crime, pollution control, and so on affects housing prices and the geographic choices of many households. Much of the information available, however, comes not from government sources but from a variety of more subjective providers acting in a manner at least as focused on their own interests as on the public interest. For such reasons, the State of Florida has recently begun making available online its performance-based rankings of all nursing homes operating in the state.[18] In its October 2005 speech from the throne, the government announced plans to create a new integrated information system and website that empowers patients to see for themselves how long wait times are at their local hospital, and whether a procedure is available sooner at another hospital. A flourishing network of such bottom-up and highly focused initiatives carries greater potential for influencing behaviour and systemic performance than more standardized and centralized reporting mechanisms envisioned for a country as a whole.

What is becoming clear is the increasingly strategic importance of information not only as an organizational and individual resource but also as a public good (Lenihan and Hume 2002c). It is no longer sufficient for the executive branch (federal and provincial) to maintain exclusive authority over policies and systems for generating, managing, and sharing information. This point is less a matter of any risk of an Orwellian state apparatus out of control (since there are many forces countering such tendencies both within and outside the public sector) and more a matter of bettering governance—in terms of deliberation, collective decision-making for those processes involving government, and self-governance capacities for those without it.

Within the Canadian parliamentary context, beyond the sort of managerial and organizational changes occurring to reform service and security capacities, a broader revision of the information architecture of the government as a whole is called for (in a manner that aims at better public sector governance but also views government's informational role as a key dimension of the governance capacities of all sectors and the country as a whole). For instance, organizations that serve the public interest by virtue of their informational role (Statistics Canada, the National Archives, etc.) could be regrouped into a more politically neutral or publicly accountable body. Unlike the present independent commissioner model (for areas such as information management and privacy) set up to 'oversee' government and 'protect' the interests of Canadians, this new informational arm would be established to foster new linkages between the government (cabinet and the executive), elected representatives (the legislature), and the citizenry. Accordingly, a shared accountability mechanism comprising all three groups should be created.[19]

The head of this new entity (ideally appointed for a fixed term upon selection through a nominating mechanism encompassing both elected officials and citizens), be it a province or the country, would serve as the 'CIO' for the jurisdiction as a whole — functioning in the truest sense of this orientation toward information.[20] This new body would have an important 'communications' function as well in inheriting a large dimension of the work that has until now been undertaken by executive departments or agencies (e.g., PWGSC at the federal level). Although departments and agencies could continue to maintain their own web presence and communicate information specific to their mandates, a more politically neutral forum would work with government, elected officials, and the public to design standards and mechanisms for online reporting in key areas of the government's agenda, as well as agreed-upon areas of public interest (e.g., health matters, safety concerns, etc.).

The creation of this sort of truly 'public sector CIO' should also be viewed explicitly as an opportunity to foster a more government- and democratic-oriented perspective on the nexus between digital technologies and organizational management. Too often this nexus is an insufficiently creative importation of a private sector set of competencies into the public sector domain — within the executive branch. For this reason, it is not unusual to find public sector CIOs with industry backgrounds. While there is nothing fundamentally wrong with this sort of crossover, many such CIOs often encounter difficulties due to their presumed strong mandate and support from the executive that nonetheless proves insufficient in the face of public sector complexities. A prerequisite, therefore, for serving as a more institutional CIO for the public sector as a whole, should be not only demonstrated experience in managing large organizational infrastructure but also a sound understanding of democratic governance and the interface between political institutions and the public service.

In short, in the future, the public sector apparatus for information management and dissemination should become less the direct and exclusive domain of the executive branch under direct partisan control and more a set of shared governance entities with wider accountabilities to distinguish between government's internal information resources on the one hand and broader political and societal interests requiring more routine and objective mechanisms of dissemination on the other. As with the case of technology procurement, line departments and most special agencies would be left to organize their own information systems (coordinating such efforts with central agency assistance), but the manner in which such information is reported externally to the public would be partially determined and coordinated via a more politically neutral and publicly accountable body.

While some observers would point to the risks for the government in such a direction, the reality is that such risks are lessened since this new body would be more consensual and deliberative — and less adversarial than the present assortment of stakeholders with roles that are largely institutionalized to deploy information (most often gathered with difficulty from unwilling government providers) as a weapon rather than a resource for collective action. In this manner, such a body is a prerequisite to building new mechanisms of accountability inclusive of the legislative branch but nonetheless driven by information scarcity and its use as means for confrontation and blame.[21]

In terms of the online presence of the public sector, such a new body should be reflective of the initial point of contact into the public sector portal rather than the executive branch (as the most heavily promoted and functional Internet address nationally and provincially). Such a move would help to lessen the barriers between the two existing branches of government and partly alleviate the sentiment among elected officials that online government is a channel that circumvents their own visibility and influence.[22] This sort of body could also be the basis for shared governance solutions to not only address collectively the growing quandaries of intergovernmental coordination with respect to information security, privacy, and identity but also enhance the public visibility accorded to such issues and the sort of responses being put forth by governments as well as the objectives, implications, and accountability considerations derived from such responses.

Indeed, many of the changes called for in this section can be envisioned only in a wider template of institutional renewal — one more conducive to not only a better-informed public that functions as the ultimate source of oversight and accountability but also a more engaged citizenry with the means and mechanisms to contribute more fully to democratic governance. This broader and more participatory lens is the focus of the next chapter.

Chapter 9
Participation and Engagement

The main focus of the preceding chapter was the need for rethinking how accountability is understood and practised in terms of the internal governance environment of the public sector – and how this environment responds and reports to the public. In contrast, this chapter emphasizes the external governance environment – and the manner in which the public perceives democracy today as well as its role in contributing to it. Accordingly, this chapter seeks to further the debate on how our political institutions should evolve in order to adapt to the more digitally connected, informed, and participative parameters shaping the authority and actions of government. The main contours of an e-democratic course are sketched out, drawing at times from experiments, reforms, and studies under way in other jurisdictions.

Building on many tenets introduced in Chapter 8, the first half of this chapter is largely concerned with parliamentary democracy as it applies federally and provincially. Section 9.1 summarizes the argument that 'Parliament' is no longer alone, making the case for reframing public accountability toward more participatory and shared orientations. Section 9.2 then examines the case for a renewed emphasis on citizenship to not only empower the citizenry to expect more direct input (as is often the case today) but also shape political participation as a collective responsibility. Finally, in building on these foundational pieces, section 9.3 sketches a template for the emergence of e-democracy by both drawing on the most useful evidence emerging from experimentation elsewhere and laying out the main challenges and opportunities that lie ahead for governments in Canada.

9.1 Parliament Is No Longer Supreme

There is merit in the view that Parliament as an institution must be strengthened if it is to once again play an effective role in scrutinizing government activity. Moreover, the role of political parties is also a central variable that merits further attention, and both of these issues are addressed below. More fundamental, however, is the need to formally reframe Parliament's role away from serving as the exclusive agent for exercising public accountability (in its representational capacity) toward a shared mindset where Parliament (or a provincial legislature) acts in concert with the citizenry in new ways.

The underlying difference is in the premise that the present era requires a form of public accountability based on more than just representational oversight: direct engagement is also a determinant of legitimacy and effectiveness. Whereas parliamentary democracy has functioned as an indirect, representational system in which the citizenry is largely relegated to the role of electing its representatives (and subsequently deferring to their judgment), public accountability today implies a more direct engagement between both the governing executive and the public on the one hand and the legislative branch and the public on the other.

Both such interrelationships must be addressed — along with how the legislative branch then functions to hold the executive to account — in order for a meaningful agenda of democratic reform to emerge in a complementing manner to changes in accountability mechanisms within the executive. Indeed, the public and the legislature share a common prerequisite to enhance their roles, both separately and with one another: information in a more timely, objective, and usable manner than is now the case. Doing so requires a digital infrastructure to both manage information and orchestrate its dissemination with parliamentarians and the citizenry (as discussed in Chapter 8), much as it also requires an e-government focus that extends beyond the realm of providing 'service.'

Without question, the chronology and strategic focus of e-government to date have primarily emphasized better service by the executive to the public (thereby introducing the citizen as client variant of performance accountability, albeit with limited results). Those in the governing executive have been far less interested in mobilizing resources to enhance the digital stature of the legislative branch, and for the most part parliamentarians have done little to draw attention to this neglect (despite some notable exceptions at all levels[1]). At the same time, much of the focus on performance reporting — particularly the potential for doing so online — has similarly emphasized a direct explanatory link from the executive to the citizenry.

When citizens or stakeholders seek information on government activities, the tendency is to visit the websites of government departments and agencies; if more objective or even opinionated assessments are preferred, then a variety of independent bodies, both inside and outside the parliamentary domain, present themselves (the auditor general, officers of Parliament, think tanks, NGOs, etc.). Reasons for visiting parliamentary resources online are usually far less evident (beyond perhaps seeking contact information to enlist the direct assistance of a representative). This point is well underscored by the main Government of Canada portal (the gateway to the executive branch), which carries no prominent link to Parliament beyond an indirect series of selections leading to contact information for Members of Parliament and background on how government functions.[2]

These patterns are reflected in the fact that perhaps the most notable of such actors as of late, the auditor general, is able to disseminate findings more widely and powerfully than ever before — officially tabling such information in Parliament but in reality directing it increasingly to the public at large (both indirectly via the media and directly online). In some respects, this trend is unlikely to be reversed in an increasingly digital and instantaneous media environment: as a result, the role of Parliament will never again be to serve as the focal point for most public deliberation and debate, as was perhaps once the case.

The real questions therefore become what role can Parliament establish for itself in a more digitally interconnected and knowledge-rich era, and how can Parliament serve to strengthen democratic engagement and public accountability in such an environment? A partial response lies in the sort of shifting of resources and capacities from the executive to the legislative branch proposed by Savoie (2003) and others. But such changes alone will be insufficient if unaccompanied by a broader effort to embrace more direct forms of public accountability in a manner inclusive of the legislature (unlike the present trend to view such engagement as an emerging prerogative of the executive).

Although there are undoubtedly many variables in what is certainly a complex democratic performance equation, the digital dimension is a prominent one that cannot be ignored. Both directly in terms of its own operations and indirectly as a proxy for the jurisdiction, it is not enough for 'government' to be online: democracy too must be online and in a manner that preserves and strengthens the legitimacy of Parliament by adapting its purposes and structures to these emerging realities. Part of this project will involve changes within existing institutions, but the very nature of the institutions themselves must be open for reflection and redesign, and an equally large focus must be on shaping the attitudes and expectations of the citizenry.

As we have seen in Part Two of this book, there are early signs of a movement toward democratic reform that encompasses a wider focus on public accountability (and by extension a rethinking of many parliamentary traditions), at the provincial level more than at the federal level. Electoral reform, citizens' juries, more online and transparent reporting are separate elements of an attempt to re-engage the public in democratic life (in manners beyond voting). There is much that is commendable and promising in the gradual formation of a network of experimentation with such innovations.

Nevertheless, an important limitation lies in the fact that, for the most part, these experiments are being forged from within the confines of the governing executive, thereby ensuring that their introduction largely preserves—to the extent possible—existing structures and the use of such structures to formulate a set of conditions for electoral success (although a decision, such as that of British Columbia and the one now under consideration in Ontario, to empower a citizens' body with the mandate to propose electoral reform directly to the public via a binding referendum does denote a rare exception to this point).

Accordingly, in the realm of e-government as it has evolved to date, the result of this mindset is that such reforms are therefore conveyed via the communication—service apparatus—increasingly online but in a manner limited to the executive branch. One of the major consequences of this limited focus has been an extension of the language and mentality of 'rights' and expectations that the public is accorded when being 'served' by government bodies. Far less prominent is democratic balancing of such rights with a set of expectations based on duty and responsibility.

9.2 Rights Cannot Suffice

Whereas the executive focus on e-government has stressed service to the public, the ethos associated with the legislative branch must be more overtly political in emphasizing both the opportunity and the obligation of democratic participation. In other words, the legislature must serve as a catalyst for defining a new form of digital citizenship based at least as much on responsibility as on rights.

The assertion of rights in today's society is obvious enough. Issues ranging from same-sex marriage to linguistic education in Quebec schools are framed as fundamental rights (within Canada's Charter of Rights and Freedoms). There are calls for an environmental bill of rights, a health care patient's bill of rights, and stronger protection for privacy rights. Perhaps most prominently in the digital world is the assertion of traditional property rights by many artists and the recording industry.

This notion of rights also fits well with the service emphasis of so much of the present e-government focus. Governments aspire to be citizen-centric since people 'expect' efficient and responsive organization. At the federal level, the new agency, Service Canada, will attempt to oblige citizens. Locally, municipalities strive to create a new citizen response system based on a '311' telephone code for all nonemergency services. Recently, this discourse of rights has been proposed as an explicit dimension of e-government by a coalition of European cities.[3] The view put forth by this organization is that four types of 'e-rights' should be ensured by a new European e-charter. The four areas include rights to accessibility, rights to education and training, rights to information, and rights to participation.

At first glance, the logic behind such an agenda would seem irrefutable. Not only is there consistency with so many other sectors of activity, but also this package of rights helps to frame the basis of a response to the digital divide. Left to market forces or one's inherited social standing, the benefits from networked societies are likely to become increasingly polarized. People should thus be accorded more rights to extend fairness and equality into the digital realm.

Yet the problem with this movement is the neglect of the other side of the coin—namely, the duties that accompany citizenship. Political leaders and the public seem to be far less interested in defining a set of new responsibilities to coincide with a revised social contract for a more digital era. Whether personal responsibility is in decline is undoubtedly a contested proposition. While governments today may be overtly less demanding of citizens in some instances, others point out that, in many aspects of our lives, more self-autonomy is often demanded of individuals and organizations. Indeed, a shift to self-governance is in many ways consistent with the vision of the Internet as an empowering and liberating infrastructure that threatens traditional hierarchy and authority. People are less deferential—and more trusting of their peers than their leaders. More often than not, this new worldview resonates particularly well with younger generations.

The explosion of downloading music and sharing files online is a good illustration. With industry estimates of more than 2.6 billion files of music, film, and other artistic endeavours shared each month over the Internet, it seems to be the case that many people (and certainly not just the young) are prepared to reconsider their own definition of appropriate behaviour in cyberspace. While recording companies may be technically correct to assert their ownership rights, the recent launching of a few hundred lawsuits against online perpetrators across North America has all the markings of a losing proposition.

It is difficult to envision a more compelling indication of changing attitudes and expectations than such an open and widespread movement to redraw the line between what constitutes unlawful and acceptable behaviour. The global explosion in counterfeit goods is another case in point. Although these examples constitute consumer behaviour, upholding the legal boundaries of the market is also a public interest issue—one made all the more difficult when such boundaries appear increasingly open to reinterpretation. Moreover, the behaviour underlying these examples is bound to extend into the arena of politics and democracy shaping electoral and democratic participation in kind. In short, collective responsibility—particularly via public sector institutions—may well face a steady decline accentuated by the 'choice revolution' closely aligned with the expansion of rights and greatly facilitated by the expansion of cyberspace (Cherney 2000).

Without question, a major drawback in any plan to promote a public duty to participate is the unpopularity of any such message— particularly for those already in or aspiring to public office in the legislature (with an eye on power in the executive). The uphill battle is all the more significant in light of both the message from the executive framed in rights and service and the competitive, market-like atmosphere of electoral campaigns that would seem to compel politicians to 'sell' their package of product-like proposals to a citizenry behaving increasingly like consumers. Such is a significant derivative of the digital age—beginning with television—but one made all the more prominent as of late by the close association and comparisons between e-commerce and e-government.

A Responsibility to Be Engaged

Overcoming the limited focus on rights, choice, and service is unlikely to happen without a concerted effort to do so. Yet one should never underestimate the public capacity to both understand the need for and embrace change, particularly in a system as fundamental as democracy and one where there is widespread dissatisfaction with the status quo. There is much about present public opinion to suggest not only an attachment to the importance of democratic governance but also a desire to engage and participate, and such a foundation for fostering new political approaches is an important starting point (Malkia et al. 2004). In moving forward, a new style of politics—predicated on stronger and more direct forms of both public accountability and public engagement—must therefore become both more digital and more discursive.

The conceptual guideposts for this agenda are transparency and trust. Openness and transparency—already imposing themselves on governments—must be built into democracy in a more proactive, ongoing manner. A more participative form of politics within a more networked and outward-looking legislative branch would then be less predicated on embarrassing the government of the day and more focused on remedial action and new policy and managerial agendas to be put forth for consideration. An expanded system of online performance reporting is thus central to empowering the public and elected officials, although a more regularized effort by governments themselves to divulge more information would paradoxically reduce the risk of sensationalist, after-the-fact exposure that often comes about in the present system.

With respect to trust, as established in Chapter 4, there are strong indications that trust is destined to be less based on deferential notions of authority and increasingly shaped by interaction and performance-based reputation. It is for such reasons that a more participative form of politics must be encouraged, with the importance of participation a central tenet of civic education at all levels of society. Finally, and perhaps most critically, the participation itself must be tied to outcomes in order to ensure legitimacy, and this shift is both the single largest opportunity for the legislative branch to assert itself and the largest challenge. The opportunity stems from the difficulties that arise for governing bodies to share decision-making power when under pressure to perform. The legislature, therefore, which comprises of as many members who are supportive of government as those who are hostile, enjoys wider degrees of freedom to engineer dialogue and table the results of these dialogues within the formal confines of Parliament.

Yet, for this to happen in a constructive manner, not only does the legislature require a meaningful role in policy making, but the very nature of legislative processes and forums must also be adapted. For instance, in the twenty-first century, there is little need for a 'question period' of the sort currently used, the purpose of which is best understood in a now imaginary world without ubiquitous digital coverage of governing institutions. Question period personifies the adversarial and communications-oriented culture of current politics that is precisely the opposite of what is required: its abolition would not be missed for long. Nonetheless, in less dramatic fashion, one could envision a reformation of its purpose and role to facilitate more conversational inquiry to embed accountability and debate in a broader framework of actors and information than the nightly news media can allow.[4]

Such a proposal for abolishing or reforming question period can quickly be extended to the purpose of traditional chambers such as the House of Commons: is it still a relevant and purposeful forum in governing, and what role, if any, should it play? There seems to be little question that the physical presence of Parliament itself is likely to become increasingly ceremonial—and less central to actual decision-making and governing. Already much of what transpires in Parliament—following traditions dating back to a time without widespread electric power—let alone an electronic infrastructure—looks and feels inherently out of step with the present realities of governance that many agree have contributed to a relative decline in stature and influence. If such broad agreement exists, moreover, then even the most strident traditionalists should be open to major revisions to rehabilitate the parliamentary role (as procedural retooling is surely unlikely to suffice in the face of broader societal change).

It is also important to acknowledge that a ceremonial role is not necessarily a trivial one. There is undoubtedly much merit in preserving symbols and structures of tradition that represent an important source of civic unity (however fragile at times) across both the federal and the provincial levels. Where many proponents of parliamentary reform falter, however, is in the belief that such common beginnings must or can largely shape current practices and processes.

There is thus no question that a virtual dimension to parliamentary democracy and public accountability is essential. Such a dimension need not and should not replace traditional dialogue in face-to-face forums (although more and more of these dialogues are occurring and will continue to occur outside formal legislatures). Instead, an online public space must be forged to broaden deliberations to the widest possible spectrum of citizens and stakeholders and link these deliberations to the working procedures of representatives. Although Canada has a notably sparse set of experiments upon which to draw, a growing movement toward online forms of democratic engagement is evident.[5]

The central design challenge in any such system lies in aligning the virtual public space with actual decision making within governing bodies. Such alignment does not imply providing a digital means for plebiscites and referendums on all or even most issues (thereby largely circumventing the representational process); rather, it entails a clear demonstration of how elected representatives have made use of such dialogues. The secondary part of this design challenge is then to ensure that online capacities provide at least as much space for deliberation as debate and one-way communications.[6] Parliament will therefore require a sophisticated technological apparatus to both monitor and at times filter these proceedings, the rules for which must be formed in concert with the citizenry in order to foster a collective measure of confidence and respect while neutralizing the fear that elected officials are somehow censoring the flow of information (Edwards 2004).

The objective should be to create, if not a fourth branch of parliamentary governance (beyond the executive, legislative, and judicial branches), then at least a new dimension—aimed specifically at public involvement—to both complement and interlink with the government of the day and the legislature. As such, a nonpartisan committee of Parliament could begin this process with a democratic renewal mandate—nonetheless requiring it to establish a public assembly empowered with the resources and the mandate to work in concert with elected officials to devise this new public space.[7]

Two other groups of actors must also be highlighted for their centrality in both the current system and the required changes to reinvigorate it: political parties and the media. With respect to parties, their weakened capacities and declining influence in policy-making are key issues, but beyond retooling their abilities to contribute one must also question whether the vehicle of a political party should and can remain the primary means of public engagement in a more networked, citizen-empowered, and interconnected polity. The present party structure personifies the secretive and representational modus operandi that is now in the process of being so thoroughly discredited (particularly within the realm of federal politics). Moreover, in terms of their usage and adoption of digital technologies, political parties in Canada have shown themselves to be particularly uncreative, for the most part content to adopt the Internet as a communications vehicle for political marketing and fundraising.

The steady decline of parties underscores the case for change; today perhaps only two to three percent of Canadians belong to any of the federal parties now in Parliament. Other studies estimate that the average age of partisan membership is well over fifty (Howe et al. 2005). Blogs, chat rooms, and other online venues and tools are undoubtedly part of the new 'Wild West' of the Internet age. Hence, there may well be genuine risk for parties seeking to exploit this terrain to their advantage—but ongoing risk avoidance seems to be destined to merely confirm the present decline. Aside from becoming more digitally creative in a consultative and participative manner, parties must also become more experimental, decentralized, and autonomous from the governing executive bodies.

Yet the structure and culture of political parties also reflect a close alignment of their role and the wider systemic environment within which they operate. Changing partisan behaviour is therefore less a question of providing advice to parties to act differently and more a matter of changing the rules of their game. It is important to go further and explore both modified and new sets of parliamentary and more participatory mechanisms that are more dispersed and—in some instances—virtual as well.

For example, electoral reforms of a more proportional nature can be helpful in generating a greater plurality of voices and interests, only some of which will even be represented by formalized parties in their present guise. Here again the misleading clarity of strong national parties must give way to the embracing of a level of complexity that is not only unavoidable but also potentially helpful in crafting a new set of governance mechanisms for twenty-first-century democracy. The short-term difficulties of adjusting to political fragmentation and coalition governments would be offset by the gradual cultivation of a more collaborative culture within the legislative branch that would also shape the mentality of the executive and the broader governing culture of a jurisdiction as a whole.[8]

A system of more participatory democracy and public accountability will also be one based less on traditional party structures. The exodus of young people away from partisan movements is indicative of both the dispersal of political power and a much greater ease of organization and mobilization in a networked world. In the future, parties that manage to successfully adapt to these new realities will reflect either strong ideological movements framing positions on most issues or moderate coalitions of various civic and private interests seeking to forge a sufficient level of commonality to form an electoral platform.

Importantly, however, such platforms—although important in framing electoral debate—should count for less in a political system more continually deliberative and adaptive to direct public scrutiny and input. Here again the beginnings of a path toward electoral reforms based on greater proportionality are not out of step with this evolution in breaking down the high concentration of power in a small number of parties in favour of both the strength of individual candidates and a wider variety of viewpoints.

Along with the structures of Parliament and political parties, perhaps the other most prevailing blockage to generating a new style of politics is the media—particularly traditional forms of digital media, notably television. Currently, and this point should be carefully noted by online skeptics, e-democracy already exists within institutions, albeit as a matter of television more than anything happening online. Nowhere is this more true than in the United States, where the 2005 presidential election featured more than $200 million of advertising spending, much of it on television commercials. Such a trend—albeit adjusted to a Canadian scale—is one factor that underpins the increasingly 'presidential' nature of federal and provincial campaigns that revolve around party leaders jockeying for the office of prime minister.

Even between elections, however, television media coverage—particularly on a national scale—often seeks to portray political activity in the most contentious, conflictual, and sensational manner possible. Scandals and errors make for the best news—and, in the absence of such drama, the highly charged theatrics of question period make due. In short, the imagery of politics via television conforms to many of the most worrisome trends in today's system, and there may well be much potential in a form of electronic democracy less dependent on television and more aligned and interwoven with the fabric of online learning and exchange.[9] Given the erosion of public trust in the political system and traditional authority structures more generally, and with the ongoing but shifting importance of the media as information intermediaries, it is critical to include their role as a key variable in pending reforms to democratic governance and the manner in which stakeholders interact, learn, and exercise accountability (Nadeau and Giasson 2003).

While it remains critical to preserve the central importance of journalistic freedom and integrity in the functioning of a democratic and open society, nonetheless necessary is a role for the media less driven by television imagery and more engrained in the complexities of the governance of issues and the communities influenced by them. For instance, the concept of civic or public journalism holds considerable merit in making an expanded effort to reframe media coverage toward more constructive and collaborative forms of investigative endeavours that frame issues in a multidimensional manner from the perspective of the citizenry (Ridell 2004). Importantly, the conditions for this type of media involvement are more likely to be crafted locally as opposed to nationally—a theme returned to below.

Although new media such as weblogs are important, both symbolic of the dispersal of power and information and influential in shaping opinions, they also underscore the dangers of a disorganized, purely organic digital environment for democratic politics. While these new actors and their forums mobilize debate and the formation of new special interest movements, their role is often more conducive to the promotion and coalescing of precise agendas on specific issues (often from specific viewpoints as well) than to the dialogues and exchanges required to generate collective action through learning and compromise.

Thus, perhaps the greatest and most pressing aspect of the twenty-first-century project on democratic renewal is to reassert a collectivist dimension to political activity in a manner that our traditional representational forums were once able to do. Defining this dimension in an increasingly digital world must account for not only the frictions between representational tradition and more directly participative tendencies today but also the degree to which our multilevel, federalist system of democratic accountability remains appropriate.

9.3 Charting a Course for E-Democracy

E-democracy should be viewed as both an obligation and an opportunity. It is now an obligatory, unavoidable part of democracy's evolution since the empowering potential of the Internet is consistent with the evolving aspirations of those seeking to create, maintain, and/or expand political freedoms, mechanisms of public accountability, and self-governance capacities. As more and more people move online, particularly the younger generations, it would be nothing less than a crippling blow to the performance and sustainability of democratic institutions if they were to somehow remain without a significant online component.

Although the number of those dismissive of a wider integration of the digital and the democratic are in decline,[10] one problem with viewing e-democracy as a necessity is the largely reactionary manner in which it will be pursued. As has typically been the case in Canada, governments recognize its importance and have no wish to be viewed as uninformed or hostile, and as a result a variety of incremental innovations are explored in a cautious manner to seek a balance between those aspiring to much greater degrees of change and those less concerned with institutional reform than more pressing matters of day-to-day governing.

To break free from such incrementalism, one critical requirement is to engage existing political leaders in a more forward-looking examination of the prospects for and consequences of (both positive and negative) e-democracy. Accordingly, engaging those holding political office at present requires reframing e-democracy into an opportunity to be exploited for the collective benefit of a particular jurisdiction (and by extension for the benefit of those elected to govern). Such a view is not out of step with one aspect of the rationale put forth for e-government initially just a decade or so ago—namely, that the innovative use of ICTs and online capacities by the state would spur positive externalities by example and use for both industries and individuals increasingly confronted with the need to adapt to new digital realities.

The key difference, however, as discussed in many of the preceding chapters, lies in how e-government has been embraced primarily as an apparatus for serving (and more recently securing) the citizenry rather than mobilizing their participation or fundamentally altering the roles and interrelationships between those governing and those being governed. Now that e-government is at least implanted—as a service vehicle and as a necessary component of a modern and well-functioning public sector—the shift to e-democracy becomes a more substantial form of competitive advantage for a city, region, or country seeking to maintain and improve its present standard of living (Lodge 2003).

This opportunistic portrayal of democratic renewal is closely aligned with the growing body of knowledge demonstrating a positive link between participation, learning, adaptation, and collective performance. Moreover, it lies at the heart of the notion of good governance as the centrepiece of prosperity and civic resilience. E-democracy, then, can be viewed as an enabling strategy to both broaden the engagement of the population with a jurisdiction and make use of this broadened engagement as a means to stronger governance. Given that countries and localities tend to distinguish themselves from one another much more in the realm of political culture and democratic structure than is typically the case with service architectures (which nonetheless also vary given the interdependence of all such components), there is reason to believe that over time e-democracy will come to unfold in a much more diverse—and by extension competitive—manner than has been the case to this point.

This competitive view should not negate the ongoing and significant potential of a collaborative approach to the development of e-democracy across all institutions, particularly given the rising importance of international processes in commercial, political, and civic spheres. The purpose and intensity of any such competitive dynamic will also differ in important ways between market and state systems, even as both sectors in this regard face heightened pressure to balance competition and collaboration in new ways (and by extension often being encouraged to embrace certain aspects of behaviour from the other system). Yet a competitive dynamic is both intuitively normal and desirable in an increasingly fluid and dynamic world where new institutional arrangements are sought at all governance levels to address increasingly complex challenges.

One indicator of such a willingness to compete—and an enabler of the ability to do so—is the creation of a forward-looking mechanism to address democracy as a systemic challenge in need of holistic and innovative thinking. In this regard, the people of Scotland are perhaps benefiting from the unique creation of a new Parliament, aimed to be more digitally enabled (and collaborative) than the Westminster-based original. Finland's Parliament has established a Committee on the Future to address longer-term development issues both inside and outside the public sector in a multistakeholder fashion (with digitization serving as the primary motivator in striking such a mechanism).

The Australian State of Victoria created a formal Public Inquiry on Electronic Democracy that reported its findings in 2005—articulating an extensive and detailed agenda for e-democratic development as a critical means to political and institutional renewal in the years ahead.[11] In contrast, the absence of such forward-looking mechanisms would suggest a likely default to incrementalism and ongoing tensions between a public appetite for reform and existing public sector structures (tensions that will vary considerably across jurisdictions in terms of depth and intensity).

The absence of such a mechanism in Canada is worrisome in this regard, despite the important and groundbreaking work of one quasi-formalized body that has sought to fill such a void: the Crossing Boundaries initiative has given an important voice to persons both inside and outside government interested in e-democracy, engaging politicians in what to date remains a unique and almost exclusive manner.[12] Yet Crossing Boundaries remains not only independent of the governing executive but also separate from the formal institutions of Parliament, legislatures, and councils, and it thus cannot replicate the more formal voice of an inquiry such as the example in Victoria, Australia.[13]

More direct political engagement with both elected officials and the citizenry is required to serve as a bridge between existing formal institutions and emerging innovations in participation and engagement that are currently more prevalent outside these institutions than within them. This bridge is also vital since the work of institutional redesign — to be viewed as legitimate and successful in realizing democratic improvement — cannot be the exclusive domain of present holders of political office. Not only is today's current crop of politicians unlikely to be sufficiently capable of envisioning future reforms (since their actions have prepared them to compete for and exercise power in existing structures), but also such direct political control is opposite of the vision of dispersed leadership and shared ownership that is generating the need for change in the first place. In short, institutional change must be a partnership between stakeholders inside and outside the current model, including the public.

The efforts of Canadian provinces to realize electoral reform in such a manner are thus more encouraging than the federal preference for traditional control. The Government of Ontario has gone further in seeking citizen involvement in other sorts of institutional reform (Chapter 6) while also instilling a degree of organizational recognition and resources for the potential for democratic innovation across government (directly linking e-government and citizen engagement). Although in the short-term any promise of reform remains largely overshadowed by traditional politics and immediate policy agendas, the decision to empower a citizens' body with the capacity to propose changes marks an important shift from tradition — one that could have lasting impacts on the political system as a whole.

Electoral reform may also be an overly narrow lens, however, through which to contemplate democratic change. As is evident in Ontario and elsewhere, the focus on electoral processes does little to alter the immediate governing environment and problems identified with it: for instance, there is little about Ontario's democratic reform effort that lessens the eroding visibility and influence of the legislative branch (although conceivably electoral reform could have such an impact). The central importance of the organization of government's infrastructure architecture (a theme discussed in the preceding chapter) remains excluded. Similarly, the digital dimension of electoral reform is typically a narrow conception of e-democracy (e.g., voting online).

A forward-looking body with a more encompassing mandate for democratic and digital innovation is therefore required, one more in line with the Finnish and Australian examples previously noted. Importantly, what such a body would produce as a framework for e-democracy remains highly uncertain — meaning that it would be inappropriate here to present a set of ideas or reforms as a blueprint for the future of political life. Based on the growing body of experimentation both here and elsewhere, however, it is possible to sketch the main parameters of a reform agenda and some of the key elements in need of attention.

Three Sets of Variables

Any template for e-democracy must encompass three sets of interrelated variables that will collectively determine the degree to which digital technologies are effectively aligned with democratic capacities. These three areas are a technical architecture, a political infrastructure, and a protocol or language for an online behavioural culture.

With regard to the technical infrastructure of e-democracy, of overarching importance is the trustworthiness of new digital technologies as a secure platform for democratic activity. In this sense, many of the efforts to date in forging secure channels for service delivery are an important precursor since the technical difficulties in facilitating online voting or dialogue are no greater than those currently being addressed to handle the managing of financial transactions and personal information.

What is unique to e-democracy, however, is the expanded importance of collective perceptions across the citizenry as a whole. Online service delivery remains largely a novel choice — and for the time being the same is true of online democracy. Accordingly, for there to be a significant uptake and use of Internet-based forums and processes to encourage democratic participation (in a manner qualitatively different from the typical transactions of service delivery), the technical apparatus in place must be seen to be beyond reproach and quickly adaptable to the accelerating pace of technological change (to respond to both upgrading improvements and potential threats — threats that multiply in the absence of continual maintenance and refurbishment).

To the extent possible, an e-democratic architecture should be built on the principles of openness and interoperability, both between levels of governments and beyond national borders. Here the growth of open source software is immensely helpful to process design efforts in facilitating the cross-fertilization of technical standards, quality specifications, and performance tracking: in short, learning can be greatly enhanced.[14] While the purpose and content provisions of a formal public sector online forum will by necessity differ from more commercial and anarchistic forms of online activity (for reasons explored below), there is little reason for variance in the underlying technical architecture facilitating connectivity generally.

As governments face resource constraints and rising pressures for skilled workers, a shared platform of open technical specifications reduces the risk of supplier dependence and the formation of internally proprietary solutions to government that over time can fall into disrepair or face escalating costs for maintenance and modernization. Governments must view these technical components of e-democracy not as static, one-time development projects but as an ongoing infrastructure that must evolve alongside the leading practices and emerging opportunities and threats that will continually render adaptability an important imperative for both functionality and performance. Where these technical competencies for ongoing adaptation are housed within the public sector is a key issue. Drawing on the notion of a more politically independent body to oversee the information infrastructure of the public sector (Chapter 8), this type of body—with multipartisan and public oversight—must also serve as the technical foundation for an e-democratic architecture (entailing an important shift of both financial and human resources away from the executive branch of government to this new entity).

In terms of political infrastructure, there are three critical subthemes that must be addressed: awareness and education, interest and involvement, and learning and adjustment.

The importance of awareness and education can often be misconstrued as a strategy for communications (thereby reinforcing the one-way informing mentality that is the basis of the service emphasis so prevalent today). What sets apart this type of activity, however, is the need to raise awareness not about what governments are doing and why but about how individuals can be involved in contributing to the deliberations and decisions of governments. Even without soliciting the active engagement of most citizens, there is tremendous potential for e-democracy to raise the overall level of political literacy across the public at large, already an important impact in creating better-informed voters, monitors, and judges of government actions and choices. "For the aim, in a democratic society, of the cultivation of judgement in governance should not be the empowering of a political elite, but the strengthening of the competence, maturity and self-governing capabilities of the citizenry (Elkin and Sotan 1999). Indeed, every democrat must hold that in the medium- to long-run, only the robustness of the judgement capabilities of citizens can guarantee that those of policy-makers will be similarly stout" (Perri 6 2001, 21). The key shift required is a much stronger assertion of the legislative branch of government and a corresponding citizenship dimension of public sector activity (in contrast to the more customer-centric service flavour of most government sites at present). Also clear is that merely creating an online presence is insufficient: e-democracy also entails an important outreach function by governments to both promote and facilitate the use of online resources and their integration into societal learning.

Education is thus critically important as an enabler of participation. An instructive path of some interest for Canada is the increasingly localized dimension of e-democracy in the United Kingdom and efforts there to integrate civic processes and tools that are online with schools in order to reach the youngest generations of future Internet navigators and voters (Andrews and Cowell 2004). What is important, however, for these generations is not the promotion of online activity in general but the need for a culture of civic engagement to take hold that can create a mixture of incentives and responsibilities to partake in formalized political channels that clearly differentiate themselves in important ways from online commerce and social pastimes such as gaming, text messaging, and the like. A recent UK survey prepared by the Oxford Internet Institute underscores this potential as well as the need for careful demographic segmentation: "The biggest factor ... is age; 98% of school children, including a large chunk of the 25% who are identified as illiterate or innumerate — use the Internet, as do 67% of those of working age. In contrast, just 22% of retirees go online. What we are saying is that it's age more than education: social class or income isn't really that important" (Parry 2004, 5). Such findings underscore the need for different approaches to raising awareness and education according to demographics as well as the unavoidable necessity of managing multiple engagement channels as a democratic portfolio for some time to come. An exclusive reliance on any one medium of communication and engagement by a demographic group (e.g., the young online or the old in traditional town hall meetings) could have sharply negative implications for democratic cohesion and legitimacy as participation and energies are fragmented rather than integrated.

Conversely, if growing proportions of different age categories can be encouraged to make use of a mix of both online and offline formats, then there will be a widening basis for engagement. This latter direction is consistent with research on the formation of communities showing that, while online connectivity facilitates the formation of new ties, its relative strength lies in further contributing to communities that have already formed or those that couple cybermeetings and activities with traditional, face-to-face encounters (O'Hara 2004; Huysman and Wulf 2005).

With respect to interest and involvement, the most significant participative challenge of e-democracy is undoubtedly striking a balance between more direct forms of expression and decision-making on the one hand and wider deliberative capacities for listening and exchange on the other. Here the use of publicly-run and monitored discussion forums has been shown to have a greater potential than more grassroots, organic forums, although there are several caveats: such a potential has been, for the most part, limited to electoral campaigns, and emerging evidence suggests that those most politically engaged offline are likely to be those engaged online—in the absence of more aggressive steps to widen the participative net (Jensen 2003). What is often lacking in between elections is a clear reason to participate, particularly in light of the passive use of online capacities that remains in place in most cases.

A virtual dimension of public sector deliberations and decision-making processes must therefore become more regularized as a demonstrated source of input into the governance mechanisms supporting Parliaments and councils. The recommendations put forth by Canada's Parliamentary Sub-Committee on the Status of Persons with Disabilities (Chapter 5) offer a modest and useful point of departure, although there are growing signs of Canada's laggardness in terms of e-democratic experimentation. In the United Kingdom, the widened lens of e-democracy, although highly localized in experiments and investments, extends to the national Parliament, where an effort led by the House of Commons Information Committee seeks to engrain more digital awareness and practices into the mechanism and culture of Parliament.

After consultation and study, the committee recommended the following set of principles (subsequently adopted by the House Modernization Committee and cabinet and adopted into the current planning efforts of the House of Commons Commission):

A. The House is committed to the use of ICT to increase its accessibility and to enable the public, exercising its right to use whatever medium is convenient, to communicate with Members and with Committees of the House;
B. The House is committed to using ICTs to enhance the professionalism of Members, their staff and House staff in all aspects of parliamentary life.
C. The House is committed to the use of ICT to increase public participation in its work, enabling it to draw on the widest possible pool of experience, including particularly those who have traditionally been excluded from the political and parliamentary process;
D. The House recognizes the value of openness and will use ICT to enable, as far as possible, the public to have access to its proceedings and papers; and
E. The House will develop and share good practise in the use of ICT by other parliamentary and governmental bodies both in the United Kingdom and elsewhere, and will work in collaboration with outside bodies. (Parry 2004, 6)

It is not surprising to find that such a level of political awareness has translated into much more advanced websites and online capacities by the UK Parliament than is the case in Canada.[15] Moreover, the more aggressive efforts of parliamentarians themselves, rather than fuelling complacency, seem to facilitate higher degrees of constructive criticism and citizen mobilization to further improve the United Kingdom's online political presence.[16] In the United States, the Congress Online initiative, sponsored by the Congressional Management Foundation, has been a leading source of research and dialogue on matters pertaining to ICT use and online connectivity across the American congressional setting. A key focus of the work has been on the challenges confronting politicians in a more open and connected environment, the intensity of which in the United States is clearly unparallelled anywhere else in the world.[17]

In terms of learning and adjustment, such attributes apply directly to bettering the performance of governments in power through the sort of new accountability arrangements discussed in the previous chapter as well as a more participative polity. What is equally important, however, is to build learning capacities into the democratic system as a whole, particularly as e-democratic experimentation grows and online dimensions of voting, consultation, and decision-making become more regularized. This point was a key recommendation of the Australian State of Victoria's parliamentary study of e-democracy that argued for the development of ongoing metrics and mechanisms to both gauge democratic performance and facilitate the introduction of new initiatives and mechanisms (in line with technological change, public use and acceptance, and research and results from pilot initiatives).

Building on this political infrastructure, therefore, is the need for a complementary focus on a behavioural culture conducive to wider and more productive forms of participation and public engagement. An explicit protocol is required to sketch out the parameters of civility, respect for diversity, codes and guidelines for online exchange, and management of identities. The notion of identity is central to establishing a matching of the level of engagement sought and the credentials required of an individual seeking to provide input online: whereas a general discussion on a broad topic may be conducive to relative anonymity, a higher form of engagement requiring more specific opinions may well also require a level of self-identification and authentication that is more appropriate for evidence-based deliberation and the formation of policy positions.

Importantly, such a protocol cannot be developed by politicians alone or by government experts in the fields of communication and consultation—since such an approach is unlikely to galvanize the interest and buy-in necessary for widespread adoption. Although provinces are beginning to deploy various forms of citizen involvement to envision institutional reform, the public must be directly engaged in designing a road map for online deliberation, in partnership with elected officials and public servants. Public servants are particularly in need of this form of collective guidance to facilitate the wider development and acceptance of norms for new interactions between themselves and elected officials in online environments. One early Canadian pilot to create a digital Commons features a three-week online discussion forum between a group of students, parliamentarians, and public servants; the last group contributed the least mainly due to uncertainty about their role and freedom in coparticipation with elected officials (MacIntosh 2003).[18]

This relational uncertainty also extends to the need for online facilitators of democratic dialogue and how such facilitation should be organized and conducted (Ridel 2001). A new extension of citizen engagement to involvement in decision-making not only from a content perspective but also from that of process may well be warranted:

> Moderators fulfill important functions. In particular, they contribute to the interactivity and openness of the discussions. However, moderators do not function in isolation. Their position is embedded in organizational arrangements, in which they have to cooperate with other actors, like public officials and representatives of social organizations. The new interface that may come into being in these deliberative arrangements has its own structure of dependencies and biases.
>
> In this interface, moderators have to strike a balance. It seems that independent moderators are in better positions to do this. In many cases, however, citizen moderation is a good option as well. Moderation by civil servants is an acceptable option, if citizens have no reason to question the neutrality of the moderation. (Edwards 2004, 165)

While governments alone cannot define the new protocols of online democracy, political leadership is nonetheless essential in creating a space for such issues to be addressed in an open fashion. A significant number of resources will also be required — a reality that should be viewed less as a barrier to participation (given the large sums being invested in digital infrastructures at present) than a need for reallocation. Rather than directing new funds almost solely to the service and communications apparatus of the executive, a more balanced approach is required to foster the requisite capacities of political bodies to take their places online. At the same time, in a world of finite resources and limited visibility, the abilities of different levels of government to act are clearly not uniform, and questions of intergovernmental alignment remain important considerations for a positive e-democratic evolution.

A Federated Point of Departure

Just as service delivery efforts face significant hurdles in becoming more cross-jurisdictional, so too e-democracy, where—for the reasons discussed throughout this book—the federal government will likely seek ways to exploit its visibility, resources, and apparatus to engage Canadians in a more direct manner. Certainly, provinces and municipalities may well respond in kind, seeking to make use of their advantages rooted in proximity and flexibility and a desire to foster and showcase new models of democratic innovation within their own jurisdictions.[19]

As with service delivery, however, a new intergovernmental approach—of both language and mechanisms—is urgently required to foster a dialogue between governments on the governance of public engagement both generally and via a polity with an increasingly important virtual dimension. In this regard, and much more so than in the service realm, a 'seamless' public sector 'consulting the citizen only once' and sharing such input across the public sector as a whole is an unworkable proposition: different levels of government continue to have separate responsibilities that lend themselves to unique outreach activities. A plurality of such approaches is also a powerful driver of innovation.

Yet there is a growing basis of interdependence across different government levels such as socio-economic development, environmental preservation, human care, and quality of life invariably require more concerted efforts by the public sector as a whole. In terms of a new intergovernmental architecture, then, the collective aim should be a refurbished framework for democracy through promoting democratic engagement and realigning resources and authority in a manner more sensitive to and encouraging of localized deliberation and citizen input. In other words, in terms of building public engagement strategies, the emphasis should be less on federally-led consultative exercises (leading invariably to communicating and 'spinning' positive results) and more on building federal solutions and approaches via ideas arrived at through strengthened municipal forums and intergovernmental bodies designed to strengthen public accountability (through the sort of politically neutral information infrastructure discussed in the previous chapter).

The impetus for such change must come more from elected leaders locally and provincially than from the federal level (although a federal government more open to renewing multilevel arrangements and some level of devolution can only help matters). At present, the gathering lobbying force of mayors, for instance, in seeking more federal funds is a precursor to what should be an orchestrated call for more decision-making autonomy in making use of such resources — and in recognizing the opportunity for locally distinct responses to the present dissatisfaction that pervades this country's democracy. Provincially, the challenge for premiers is to extend the space currently accorded to democratic reform to questioning whether and how democracy is best strengthened through provincial or local experiments in reform.

With respect to the increasingly digital nature of democracy, as municipalities are doing with their service delivery capacities, they must strive to deploy online tools and mechanisms in expanded efforts to entice segments of the local community that are otherwise uninterested in, or disengaged from, formal municipal processes. The conundrum here is that, without a stronger degree of importance attached to self-governance from the provincial level, any such effort will be visibly overshadowed by provincial and federal processes. Similarly, a strengthening set of provincial and federal efforts aimed at e-democracy — without a preceding and underlying municipal component — would further threaten to erode municipal autonomy and identity.

Accordingly, the intergovernmental dimension of democratic reform is essential as a starting point to shape discussions and initiatives aimed at parliamentary adaptation at provincial and federal levels. There seems to be little question that in the short term, due to both the widening spectrum of globalization and the present Canadian political culture shaped by tradition, a massive form of devolution from the federal level is unlikely any time soon.

E-government is an important prism through which the new style of governance arrangements may be identified and crafted as organizations in all sectors seek to foster coordination in a manner that reconciles central authority and flexible autonomy: such is the notion of a federated architecture that is as much political and organizational as it is technological. Indeed, the scope of what must be sought is explicitly multidimensional: technically, it permits decision-making systems within a variety of organizational subunits to join together; strategically and politically, it allows for both action and authority to be facilitated, shared, and coordinated across a multitude of levels and activities (Koch 2005).

Therefore needed is a political mechanism to lay the groundwork for the gradual establishment of a new form of federalism more conducive to the principles of interdependence and engagement than current arrangements. Central to any such revision is a strategic reconsideration of where and how best to orchestrate and share democratic engagement in a more virtual world that is clouding the traditional separation of government levels in favour of more seamless, collaborative approaches.

Importantly, the challenge of forging a federated architecture based on more open and collaborative forms of governance, and the tensions that exist in departing from current practices, also extend beyond the borders of any one country. The emergence of e-governance transnationally, and the implications for Canada, are the focus of the next chapter.

Chapter 10
Beyond Canada's Borders

Many of the forces reshaping domestic structures are also transnational in scope and implication. Much as e-government creates pressures for interoperability within countries, it will also do so in terms of relationships between countries – and both state and nonstate actors. The security imperative presents a conundrum for governments in an increasingly globalizing and digital age of interdependence. On the one hand, the increasing mobility of financial, cognitive, and human resources – both within and between countries – means that no government enjoys a sufficient capacity to act alone in addressing the widening spectrum of security challenges, including terrorist and criminal activity, the use of digital technologies by such groups, and the overall reliability and resilience of a digital infrastructure that transcends any single jurisdiction. This widening technological canvas of shared networks and electronic linkages – which serves as a backbone in the facilitation of more collaborative efforts between governments – thus also provides heightened exposure to new pressures and threats. The governance challenge so prevalent within national authorities – striking a balance between central authority and decentralized, more flexible forms of innovation – also extends beyond national borders as technology and security go further than traditional free-trade flows in generating pressures for strengthened multilateral and bilateral agendas. Yet these agendas – in particular the stakeholders, venues, and governance arrangements to be adopted in their pursuit – remain highly contested.

Within this context, section 10.1 sketches the main characteristics of the transnational environment in terms of governance and connectivity – situating the central role of the United States and the consequences of this role for Canada in a general manner. Section 10.2 turns more directly to the issue of homeland security efforts in the United States, asking whether Canadians have been placed at risk (by drawing on specific examples demonstrating the growing links between Canadian and American governance). Section 10.3 then turns to the future of North American relations in a digital world – considering the bilateral and trilateral pressures that exist currently. Section 10.4 addresses global governance challenges rooted in the widening importance of ICTs *and Internet connectivity the world over; the Canadian perspective on such challenges is also examined.*

10.1 Transnational Fluidity

Distinctions between government and governance can often be fluid, particularly in the domestic environment where a 'public sector' denotes democratically accountable authorities at national or subnational levels (authorities that nonetheless comprise governance processes both internally and collectively). For the most part, however, the absence of formal democratic mechanisms beyond national borders (encompassing transnational polities, with the EU being the only partial exception) ensures that decision-making is primarily about governance arrangements that encompass both state or governmental actors (most often from countries) and a more distinctive 'nonstate' flavour.

Economic and technological integration, personified by the symbolism of the Internet as a unifying force for democracy and capitalism the world over, fuels pressures for new forms of governance that must nonetheless coexist with shifting priorities and antics of countries. The growing presence of multinational corporations and new social movements suggests a departure from a nation-state-centric order of governance, the Westphalian international order that shaped global politics for much of the second half of the twentieth century, and is neither feasible nor desirable (Slaughter et al. 2004). Yet state governments remain powerful actors, and the transition to something new and transnational is under way, although the institutional design of this new order remains uncertain, contested, and fluid (Coglianese 2000).

The emergence of a discourse focused on e-democracy is a good illustration of these uneven and somewhat competing forces. While national governments remain primarily concerned with designing e-government initiatives centred on efficiency and service delivery, the push for alternative forms of democracy, including online variants, has been more rooted in many segments of civil society whose outlook is more global than national (Norris 2005). Invariably, such interests and their mobilizing abilities in an increasingly interconnected world have enhanced the Internet's stature as a new social and political infrastructure for transnational engagement (Geiselhart 2004).

Here the centrality of the Internet is real, underpinning the mobilization of new social movements, the sharing of information and knowledge, and the empowerment of civil society mechanisms and voices that are inherently transnational, often disconnected from any particular domestic system of governance (Preyer and Bos 2002; Norris 2005). While often lacking the resources of private sectors, the growing strength and presence of civil society actors in the transnational realm is a major force in terms of transnational power relations and transnational decision making (Rosenau 2002). Yet questions arise: is such a group representative and of whom, and does it possess legitimacy to instill a degree of democratic accountability in governance arrangements beyond national borders?

Evidence to date is mixed. Some evidence points to a limited but growing sense of global identity that could cement new forms of community, formed loosely by common beliefs and a shared sense of belonging and interdependence (Norris 2005). Perhaps due to the declining confidence in most developed nations across the private and public realms, there is also a de facto higher degree of confidence expressed in transnational NGOs and international institutions relative to domestic actors (ibid.), although many serious questions exist in terms of the structures and legitimacy of civil society actors and their impacts on transnational spheres of governance (Aarte Scholte 2002; Edelman 2005). Yet such findings vary considerably across countries and cultures, and over the past several years the reassertion of national authority through traditional state instruments has become an important variable.

With respect to transnational governance and the extension of a digital infrastructure into the transnational arena, there are three somewhat distinct viewpoints. First, the rising importance of ICTs and online connectivity in such a context can be adopted by global governance proponents as a platform for dispersing information and power more widely — thereby moving the world closer to a set of conditions that may eventually yield some form of global polity. In the interim, current governance forums — notably intergovernmental organizations such as the UN and the WTO — face, at the least, greater calls for transparency and more direct forms of responsiveness to interests aside from member countries (Ougaard and Higgott 2002). Somewhat aligned with proponents of such changes are more radical critics of the status quo, less interested in or coherent about what comes next and more centred on exposing the structural flaws of the status quo as they perceive them.

Second, many stakeholders engaged in global governance processes — most often representing traditional actors such as national governments — worry that the erosion of the basic conditions of bargaining and decision-making that in the past allowed for a reasonable functioning of intergovernmental institutions threatens stability and prosperity (Coglianese 2000). Central to these conditions are rising pressures for transparency and engagement that hamper the traditional style of a transnational governing elite — the anonymity of which has much in common with the traditional model of a nonpartisan public service in parliamentary democracies (the notable difference being a more indirect and diffuse set of accountabilities to both the leadership of the organization and member countries as a whole). The collapse of the MAI and stalled WTO negotiations are cases in point.

Third, there remains an important nation-state-centric camp of those who are skeptical about relinquishing any meaningful amount of decision-making authority to organizations and institutions beyond the realm of national sovereignty (and, by extension, political accountability). Even prior to 9/11, the Bush administration was positioning itself more toward this latter camp, backing away from a series of multilateral commitments and demonstrating a stronger willingness for unilateral action and influence internationally. Of course, the war on terror since 2001 has crystallized this focus on American unilateralism and foreign relations, but it has done so in a rather simplifying manner, dramatically downplaying and often ignoring the implications of ICTs for the evolution of transnational governance, either within traditional venues or by virtue of new ones.

Although homeland security efforts have focused primarily on bolstering national authorities (and the technological capacities of such authorities), nearly as prominent has been the American-led effort to strengthen collaborative networks between countries. At the heart of these networks are the now familiar themes of technological interoperability and information-sharing — reflecting the intuitive notion that, just as terrorist and criminal threats transcend national borders, so too must any effective set of responses. This is not to say that the United States has shown itself to be much interested in creating stronger multilateral forums to address these changes in more politically integrated ways (as some critics of current US policy would espouse). Instead, for the most part, the United States has encouraged an expansion of less formalized and less transparent governance mechanisms in the pursuit of its goals (which remain primarily framed as domestic in terms of securing individuals and infrastructures, even when some individuals — nationals — may be abroad). For Canada, the governance implications of these pressures — both continentally and domestically — are becoming ever more pronounced, and they are the immediate and primary focus of much of this chapter.

At the same time, however, the dimensions of the relationship between ICTs and transnational governance extend beyond the realm of security — preceding it in many cases. The Internet is a highly complex and sophisticated technical architecture that, despite its fleeting, groundless image of eluding ownership and control in a traditional bureaucratic sense, requires governing in order to function. The arrangements and actors shaping the governing of the Internet represent an increasingly critical element of transnational governance, one broadly ignored by traditional international relations theorists and radical activists alike (joined in many cases by a shared ignorance of the intricacies of managing online connectivity, a characterization that extends to just about the entire global population).

The extension of this digital infrastructure of connectivity — and the consequences for technical and at times social and political interdependence — are of great importance to both the global economy and any fledgling notion of a global community. They also represent the extension of the e-government project beyond national borders, in terms of fostering new transnational mechanisms politically and/or maintaining and managing interdependencies in a more virtual and interconnected world.

10.2 US Homeland Security: Are Canadians at Risk?

Along with growing attention devoted to security matters in Canada has been an equally prominent and related set of critical events involving

American authorities — and often some level of concerted action between the two countries. Three such events will be examined here, each of which underscores the growing importance of transnational flows of information as well as the potential for unintended consequences: they are the deportation of a Canadian citizen from the United States to Syria, concerns about the Privacy Act enabling US authorities to gain access to personal information of Canadians, and shifting documentation requirements for cross-border travel.

Maher Arar is a Syrian-born Canadian citizen who came to Canada in 1987, subsequently earning a master's degree and finding employment as a telecommunications engineer for an Ottawa-based company. In September 2002, returning from a trip to Tunisia, on a stopover in New York, he was detained by US security officials, questioned, and eventually deported from the United States to Jordan and then to Syria, where he would be interrogated, imprisoned, and tortured for more than a year. Upon his return to Canada in late 2003, the crusade to shed light on his ordeal and what he alleges to be a groundless campaign against him has resulted in the formation by the Canadian government of an independent public inquiry (or commission of inquiry) to examine this affair.[1]

The inquiry has been set up to review the appropriateness of the actions of Canadian officials in the case and to provide recommendations on a new oversight mechanism for the security-related actions of the Royal Canadian Mounted Police (the federal police service with certain responsibilities pertaining to domestic security). Although the commission's final report is not expected until late 2005, a substantial amount of work has been undertaken since its formation in February 2004. In regard to the scope of this chapter, two major and interrelated points stand out from the first year of the commission's activities: first, the inherent secrecy of national security matters; and second, the inability of the commission to shed light on the role of American authorities despite their centrality to the case.

The first point has been the focus of ongoing legal battles between various stakeholders in the camp of Mr. Arar and the Government of Canada. On repeated occasions, significant portions of government submissions and testimonies have been censored for 'national security reasons.' Moreover, the government overruled decisions by the judge leading the inquiry, who argued for the release of information to the public (in some cases, the government chose to black out portions of the judge's rulings pertaining to the information in question). Finally, after prolonged legal disagreements (delaying the proceedings of the inquiry), the main parties came to an agreement in late March 2005 that seems to significantly relent to the preferences of government authorities by temporarily agreeing to no longer seek public release of the details in question.[2]

The second point reveals the disconnect between political and legal oversight mechanisms within a country and the increasingly transnational nature of security matters. In the Arar case, it has been widely presumed that American authorities deported Mr. Arar based in part on information received from Canadian authorities. Indeed, much of the media coverage surrounding this case focused on this possibility—generating a considerable amount of political and public interest in Canada pertaining to the role of the United States in the handling of this matter and the appropriateness of American actions. Such issues have been largely excluded from the purview of the Arar Commission, however. Jurisdiction cannot be extended to American authorities: although invited to partake in the inquiry, the United States politely declined.

Ultimately, the inquiry may shed some light on the American role as a by-product of investigating the actions of Canadian officials (and the possibility that they cooperated in some manner with their US counterparts). However, it is only due to the sensational nature of this particular case that any such probing is taking place, despite the increasingly regularized practices of information-sharing between authorities in both countries (Barry 2004). The secrecy of such practices—and the more general absence of political oversight on security matters—comprise an important theme of domestic and continental governance that will be returned to more fully below.

It is, of course, both relevant and important that the Arar case unfolded in the aftermath of 9/11 as a result of the more aggressive security policies adopted in both Canada and the United States. Indeed, the second issue involving bilateral information flows of a sensitive and disconcerting nature pertains directly to the US Patriot Act and its potential extension into the personal information files of Canadian citizens.

The issue stems from the outsourcing activities of many governments in Canada (and elsewhere) resulting in functions previously undertaken within the confines of public sector organizations shifting to external specialists delivering that function via a contractual partnership. Outsourcing typically denotes the transfer of technical and organizational resources (often including personnel) to this external provider, and, in the realm of digital technologies and constant pressures for modernizing and improving decision-making and service delivery capacities, this type of collaborative activity has become engrained in the fabric of organizational life.

In the Canadian public sector, perhaps no government has been more aggressive in pursuing this path than the Province of British Columbia. Over the past several years, it has entered into a number of new outsourcing initiatives aimed largely at upgrading the digital infrastructure of the provincial government. Accordingly, many components of the information management architecture within the province rely increasingly on the direct involvement of private companies — and in many cases these companies invariably handle personal data pertaining to citizens of British Columbia.[3]

In 2004, the provincially-appointed privacy commissioner publicly declared that such information could be at risk of being directly sought by American authorities due to provisions of the Patriot Act. The concern stems from the fact that many companies involved in outsourcing activities in the province are, in fact, Canadian subsidiaries of US corporations. Thus, these companies could be obliged in some instances, according to the commissioner (an independent office of the BC legislature), to share their information holdings with US authorities if called upon to do so (due to the invocation of the Patriot Act for a security-related matter). Despite efforts by government officials at all levels in Canada to downplay the significance of this issue (which nonetheless received considerable media coverage), it was subsequently revealed that internal efforts by officials in the federal government confirmed the legitimacy of the case made by the BC privacy commissioner (and as a result ordered a review of federal contracting provisions to ensure safeguards against such unintended transfers of information to US authorities — safeguards acknowledged to be absent until this point).

Although legal experts dispute the reach of the Patriot Act to play such a role in facilitating information gathering in Canada, the significance of any such 'threat' is mitigated by two complementary vehicles: contracting provisions (limiting the actions of American companies working with Canadian governments), and a more implicit protocol of goodwill between the two countries that renders such subversive action not only risky (in generating a public backlash) but also less efficient than other means of bilateral cooperation to ensure that the informational needs of both countries are being looked after: "Regarding the controversy around the US Patriot Act, the ICT Industry believes strongly that it would be inappropriate for US law enforcement authorities to try to obtain personal information on Canadian citizens from an outsourcing contractor... . In fact, US authorities have established arrangements in place with Canadian authorities and there should be no difficulty in obtaining such information for any legitimate anti-terrorism investigation purposes by going through Canadian authorities to get the information at the source" (Courtois 2005, 5). While such a view undoubtedly has merit, many aspects of the Arar affair may limit the extent to which the Canadian public is prepared to embrace this second avenue of bilateral cooperation as a sufficiently reassuring mechanism against an American security apparatus deemed misguided, faulty, or overextended in some fashion. Moreover, such a sentiment is not exclusively a Canadian reaction, for many critics within the United States have led the charge in raising such suspicions and questions.[4]

Despite these bilateral flares, neither the Arar affair nor concerns about the Patriot Act have done much to quell cross-border traffic and the desire of companies and citizens from Canada to seek US access. Indeed, along with economic flows of goods and services, nearly 2 million Canadians visited the State of Florida alone in 2004. This influx is estimated to generate more than $1.5 billion in direct tourism spending—representing Florida's largest inbound source of tourism (as well as the highest levels of foreign direct investment).[5] With respect to travel documentation, requirements have typically been minimal, with various forms of government-issued identification, such as a driver's licence, accepted.

The first barrier erected in the post-9/11 environment to this relative free flow of individuals (at least pertaining to leisure travel, since professional and employment restrictions are more varied and common) focused on Canadian landed immigrants. Beginning in March 2003, landed immigrants in Canada from many countries faced new visa restrictions.[6] Subsequently, in April 2005, the US government announced that by the end of 2007 Canadians entering the United States will require a passport or a similar form of 'secure identifier.'[7] Although the transition period is regarded as a cushion to soften the blow of this important change (in 2002, roughly a quarter of all Canadians held a valid passport), the significance of this change is real.

Ironically, this policy change was announced just a few weeks after the release of a trilateral North American study (under the auspices of the US-based Council on Foreign Relations) that argues for the formation of a continental security perimeter as well as a set of institutions to forge the sort of North American 'community' that might one day lead to less restricted mobility within the continental perimeter along with some form of standardized identification to facilitate such openness while preserving security. These various currents underscore the necessity of interoperability and interdependence on the one hand and the present realities of governing in a more independent manner on the other. As the former set of pressures can be expected to continually intensify, in a manner intertwined with economic integration, how the Canadian polity responds is an important question.

10.3 Continental Interoperability and Governance Quandaries

Security has undoubtedly emerged as the dominant ideological theme shaping relations between Canada and the United States (as well as those between the United States and Mexico).[8] Commercial exchange is now to be facilitated by shared security, and human mobility is now assessed and qualified via the same prism. Moreover, the pursuit of this common security agenda is increasingly informational and digital in scope. Some level of interoperability between authorities must be achieved to facilitate a collective sense of confidence in one another and a basis for joint action. The close alignment of security efforts—including reforms to domestic structures and transborder initiatives—underscores this point. In short, the pursuit of technological interoperability seems to be clearly established as a central tenet of bilateral relations.

Yet the examples of the previous section suggest that this path of convergence may not be without difficulty. From the Canadian perspective, there is ongoing trepidation among many about a path of convergence and integration that could seemingly do more to justify the fears of free-trade critics in the 1980s than rising commercial trade flows have been able to do. In short, continental interoperability conflicts with the traditional notion of national sovereignty.

One potential way to resolve this conflict is to foster a continental 'community,' as some parties have proposed as of late (Pastor 2004). Pastor's efforts largely underpin the trilateral vision endorsed by prominent representatives of Canada, the United States, and Mexico and released by the Council of Foreign Relations at a time chosen in part to coincide with the North American Leaders Summit in Waco, Texas, in March 2005. The trilateral initiative is bold — albeit in an incremental manner — in proposing a set of measures to complement security measures, with a new political dialogue and shared economic investment aimed at the collective prosperity of an interdependent continent.[9] Such a vision is predicated in part on an optimistic interpretation of public opinion polling (included in Pastor's separate commentary referenced as such) suggestive of enough support in the three countries to serve as a basis for the creation of a continental ethos to complement national affiliations and lend credence to the formation of a transnational community.

Without referring to this blueprint itself, the leaders of the three North American countries (members under the NAFTA trade accord) acknowledged elements of it at their summit meeting by pledging the creation of a new trilateral framework, the Security and Prosperity Partnership for North America. Such a commitment is consistent with the trilateral aspirations of the Mexican president, who has been the most aggressive in calling for the pursuit of stronger governance ties in a manner akin to the model of Europe. The significance of the participation of the Canadian prime minister in this joint pledge was tempered by recent commercial tensions between Canada and the United States (notably lumber and beef) and the decision announced just days before the summit that Canada would not partake in the US-led initiative for ballistic missile defence. Moreover, trilateral relations involving Mexico are far less discussed in Canada: the commonality of Mexico and Canada is a historical fixation with US relations and undoubtedly a rather varied set of views within each country over the appropriate scope and pace of stronger ties. Although some Canadians may be open to the notion of a Mexican ally in trilateral negotiations — thereby blunting US power to some degree — other prominent observers take the view that such a third party can only dilute progress that could otherwise be made on a bilateral basis.[10]

Yet nowhere is the absence of a stronger basis for continentalism more apparent than in the United States itself. Since 2001, foreign policy experts have debated the more inward, nationalistic tendencies of the country as well as the outward extension of these tendencies internationally in a more unilateral fashion. Importantly, however, both directions reinforce a bolstered federal government, particularly in the interrelated and technology-intensive realms of homeland security and national defence (realms that by definition extend beyond national boundaries).

Within such a setting, there would not seem to be much room for a serious investment in a qualitatively different (and more integrative) approach to North American affairs. Not only are the southern and northern bilateral agendas very different in terms of issues and concerns between each set of countries, but also, as a result, elected representatives in the United States are far more focused on managing in an incremental fashion each relationship as opposed to forging a deeper form of trilateral community. In short, there is little indication that 9/11 will play a similarly catalytic role in continental integration as World War II did in kick-starting the construction of a more integrationist and unified European agenda. As all proponents of strengthened North American governance acknowledge, comparisons with the European Union (EU) must be sensitive to the unique time durations of each continent (and the almost half century since the Treaty of Rome versus the formation of NAFTA in 1992); the European Union's ever-expanding membership, which now stands at twenty-five countries (versus the three North American countries); and the uniquely powerful presence of the United States not only continentally but globally as well.

Yet recent evolutions in EU governance may also be revealing with respect to the implications of the status quo for North America. First, there is some evidence to suggest that the e-government project in Europe has done more to assert national-level authority and visibility than any corresponding European dimension (Roy 2005b). Second, the recent elevation of security and safety issues within the European Union to the top of the political agenda has exposed the absence of continental capacities to facilitate meaningful interoperability and collaboration across member states (Grabbe 2005). Moreover, the inherent secrecy of this sector — both nationally and at the level of the European Union — may well impede the performance of European security authorities due to a public mistrust that limits the willingness of countries to relinquish resources and responsibilities to this upper governance tier (ibid.). In the North American context, then, such secrecy seems to be compounded by a complete absence of any unifying political links to begin with.

Without grander political ambitions, one can expect the United States and Canada to continue down a cooperative path — with the US model of homeland security continuing to serve as an important reference point for Canadian-American relations and steps that might be taken to give such a model a stronger continental dimension. From the Canadian perspective, this more cautious pace is more in keeping with the present political mood of the country shaped by a minority federal government and issues such as the Arar affair, missile defence, and ongoing trade frictions.

For traditional nationalists in Canada, such a conclusion may well be welcomed as a second best alternative to an even greater degree of separateness preferred by some.[11] Yet it also comes at a great cost. What will be missing in such a climate is a more open and consultative environment for both populations in all countries to consider their collective fate and the degree to which closer continental ties are warranted or not. Instead, for Canadians in particular, their government is likely to continue down a dualistic path that, if not deceptive, will prove to be something less than fully candid: publicly asserting independence while privately pursuing interdependence with US authorities wherever practically possible.

Although one might expect some concern by the citizenry about this dualistic set of tendencies, the reality is that the public within each country has much to deliberate in terms of the actions of its own government. The widening digital scope of security activities merely accentuates a debate in national terms, with ongoing concerns and reforms surrounding the US Patriot Act and its equivalents in Mexico and Canada. In the short-term, such national debates may well continue to temper a more overtly political consideration of new continental arrangements, particularly those involving institutional innovation aimed at more integrative decision-making within transnational bodies.

Yet a fundamental problem remains: namely, that the resulting incremental approach to continental interoperability aligns itself rather well with the already secretive nature of domestic security within each country. The danger of such a path lies in both the expanded realm of secrecy across many aspects of public sector operations pertaining to security that will grow to include a broader set of transborder provisions and the resulting governance apparatus that will become insular and unaccountable, provoking either dangerous overextensions of authority or unintended consequences from mismanagement or error.[12]

The Canadian government is not without some understanding of these pressures, particularly greater calls for more openness and accountability in security matters. Accordingly, a new joint parliamentary committee is being established to provide — for the first time in Canadian history — a mechanism of direct political review of the security community.[13] In addition, the government has created a new body, a Cross-Cultural Roundtable, and it will soon establish a new advisory board on national security matters.

What remains suspect, however, is the extent to which this new political forum can challenge the traditional culture of secrecy surrounding security operations. Although the new parliamentary committee is meant to transcend overt partisanship (with representation from opposition parties in the House of Commons as well as members from the appointed Senate), members will be sworn to secrecy under existing legislative rules severely limiting the public release of information (indeed, in some cases, such rules have been strengthened under recent anti-terrorism legislation). Accordingly, it is unclear the extent to which this new body will serve as a vehicle for expanding public awareness and involvement in security matters — and thus a basis for strengthened accountability. New tensions may also arise in devising a workable relationship and a division of duties between the new parliamentary committee and other review bodies in place, particularly as all of these actors adjust and adapt to the ongoing and potential changes to the security apparatus.[14]

With respect to continental security, the Arar Commission demonstrates the separateness of Canadian and US authorities and their respective systems of review and oversight,[15] and there is little reason to expect a new parliamentary structure to have more success in engaging American stakeholders in such a political review mechanism. Indeed, the deputy prime minister (also the minister of public safety) overseeing this new committee has already stated categorically that information from third parties (including other countries) will be shared with parliamentarians only with the consent of the providing party (an unlikely prospect in the case of foreign governments and national security matters).

This absence of transparency and public engagement is arguably a more severe and consequential issue for Canada than for the United States. Not only is the United States largely driving the homeland security agendas of both countries, but the Canadian government's efforts to distinguish between operational and increasingly digital forms of bilateralism on the one hand (tacitly more aligned in many areas of security interdependence), and political bilateralism on the other (separation and sovereignty to the extent possible), fundamentally limit the political discourse in Canada, invariably emphasizing the more simplistic and divisive latter realm.

The risks for Canada in this type of setting are many. First, in bilateral (and now trilateral) discussions, the negotiating power of Canadian authorities is likely to be weakened by the backdrop of a public that is viewed by its leaders as inherently unaware and suspicious of, or even hostile to, most options entailing closer and more overt forms of collaborative action. Second, the citizenry in turn is likely to become cynical as evidence emerges (most often through errors or contentious incidents exposed after the fact) that demonstrates closer collaboration across borders. Third, in such an environment, the growing digital infrastructure that underpins so much of security operations — both within and between nations — will unfold in an increasingly insular and hidden fashion.

In the context of North American relations, this latter point is central. The implication of such a context is that, rather than engage in an openly political dialogue on the options and choices confronting and linking Canadians and their North American neighbours (a dialogue that would, in turn, facilitate a basis of public learning to guide future decisions), politics and the realities of governing become increasingly fragmented from one another. In an increasingly digital world, the cost of this fragmentation increases as the risks described here feed off one another.

Indeed, one illustration of these costs is the recent foreign policy review exercise conducted by the Canadian government. Billed initially as an important rethinking of Canada's role in the world (and within it the continent), one would expect not only visibility of such an initiative but also a uniquely participative effort to invite all stakeholders to contribute to this new vision. Instead, the review was conducted in an almost entirely internal manner — within the confines of a small number of departments jockeying for position and stature under the watchful eye of the Prime Minister's Office, which reportedly rushed its completion and release in light of unflattering media coverage and political uncertainty. At best, the outcome of this sort of process may shape a number of incremental decisions and policy stances in the short term, but it is unlikely to galvanize the Canadian public into a thoughtful and reflective consideration of future scenarios and their implications for multilateral and bilateral relations (as well as the domestic choices that result).

Lessons Learned and Choices Ahead

The evolution of Canadian security policy over the past few years reveals three major lessons for both Canadian democratic governance and Canada's participation in continental governance relations. First, the US reaction to 9/11 has been the predominant factor shaping Canadian policy and governmental structure. Second, the inherently secretive nature of security policy and the national security apparatus is gradually and incrementally being extended to the continental realm (with digital technologies playing a large role in facilitating this process of interoperability). Third, the governing styles and structures of Westminster parliamentary government may well be particularly conducive to reinforcing this second point, limiting the public discourse on both current domestic matters and prospective continental choices.

Two factors are likely to shape the consequences of these lessons in the short-term. They include, most directly, the viewpoint of the United States and, indirectly, the widening scope of digital technologies and online connectivity.

In terms of the first point, there is little indication that continental governance is a US priority—particularly in terms of establishing new political institutions. The limited attention devoted to both the Council on Foreign Relations' trilateral manifesto for a North American community and the leaders' summit in Waco, Texas, in the days that followed this report underscores this point. This US posture may be ascribable to both a reasonable satisfaction in driving the de facto bilateral agendas now emerging within the realm of security and a large and congested set of domestic and international agendas. The implications of this posture for Canada are both reassuring and worrisome. They are of concern in the sense that current trends and dangers will gather momentum. What is perhaps more reassuring, however, is that Canada has some time to reform its own governing environment and better prepare its authorities and the public at large for more significant bilateral reforms that are likely to emerge at some point in the future.

Accordingly, there may be an opportunity—in the immediate term—for the new National Security Committee of parliamentarians to think outside the box with respect to its role in not only reviewing existing national security arrangements but also preparing, in concert with the public, the groundwork for future reforms. There are many high-level and important issues that will crowd the work of this new body, issues rooted in fundamental concepts such as freedom, rights, terrorism, and domestic and international law. At the same time, the committee would be well advised to tackle two thematic variables in both an explicit and an innovative manner: the continental dimension of 'national security' and the growing prominence of digital technology in today's world, both within and between governments.

In terms of an explicit continental focus, the committee should seek to forge new and direct political ties between elected officials in Canada, the United States, and Mexico. Although any such mechanism would undoubtedly begin with a limited, consultative role, at the least the formation of a publicly recognized and regularized vehicle for political dialogue would begin to lay the groundwork to better integrate continental interdependence and trilateral political review. The sketching of a modest agenda for trilateral action and institutional building offered by Pastor provides—once again at the least—a useful starting point for political dialogue and an exchange of views.

With respect to digital technologies, the main challenge is twofold. First, the new National Security Committee must be equipped with the resources and the will to foster expertise in the intricacies of technical interoperability and its impacts on organizational and political decision-making across government and within the security apparatus in particular. Not only is this investment crucial to shaping the continental dimension of its work in an appropriate manner, but it is equally central to understanding and contributing to national security domestically. Specifically, the committee should seek ways to build on the commitment of the deputy prime minister to lessen the overall culture of secrecy shrouding law enforcement and security agencies.

This focus is particularly relevant to the emerging governance complexities of the dramatic shifts in financial and organizational resources within the realm of safety and security that carry enormous implications for managerial governance and accountability in a restructured public service. The committee has the notable opportunity, for example, to provide a visible and political dimension of the issue of managerial horizontality that permeates national security and information technology efforts but is nonetheless denied any such status (replaced in the former case by an overtly simplistic assigning authority to a single minister for the entire portfolio of agencies, departments, and cross-governmental processes).[16]

The lessening of secrecy also invited an exploration of the potential for greater public involvement in national security matters, both via elected (and in some cases appointed) representatives and in a more direct fashion. Through traditional public consultations, new intergovernmental partnerships, and online channels of deliberation, the National Security Committee could undertake to serve as a catalyst for a broad dialogue on national security arrangements and the implications of these arrangements on the reformation of existing domestic institutions, as well as the prospective creation of a complementary continental agenda in a more open setting.

10.4 Global Governance Challenges

Although most central to Canadian interests directly, the continental governance realm can also be viewed as a subcomponent of the broader global environment and the challenges of extending governance the world over. Moreover, continental and global agendas are intertwined by virtue of their shared transnationality as well as the manner in which the United States serves as the focal point in many discussions and issues at both levels. There is much about e-government, particularly the emphasis on information security and interoperability and new forms of civic and democratic mobilization, that will continue to transcend borders, raising some new and some familiar questions about the degree to which economic globalization requires stronger governance mechanisms politically in order to be sustained and expanded to wider segments of the global population.

Understanding the global governance environment — and how it is likely to change in a more digital era — is also an important precursor for realigning Canadian foreign policy and perhaps even partially rethinking the purpose of foreign policy in a more interconnected world. At the heart of any such reconsideration is a familiar choice — whether to focus on the bilateral (and perhaps trilateral) agenda with the United States, or to attempt to counterbalance the weight and risk of this central relationship with a wider set of multilateral engagements.

Until recently, new global governance pressures tied to ICTs have largely been driven by the changing needs of an expanding marketplace in terms of both consumption and production. The rise of e-commerce has brought about a major step forward toward broader global interconnectedness, at least in terms of market structure, organization, and behaviour (Ronchi 2003). Consumers are empowered to transcend physical space and shop across jurisdictions, while supply chains and production chains are also increasingly mobile and dispersed (ibid.) Along with producers and consumers, a growing class of workers and activists represents the makings of a cosmopolitan citizenry whose aspirations and identities in economic terms transcend national borders (Norris 2000, 2005). Such flows and synergies between communities and countries are regarded as important sources of economic stimulation across jurisdictions (Saxenian 2002).

Along with these competitive pressures for products and services comes a broader need for a more global architecture capable of sustaining and expanding e-commerce. Given that the scope of online commerce is inherently transnational (open to all with access), there is a corresponding need to ensure that common structural rules and cultural standards are in place to facilitate the effective working of this expanded marketplace. At least until September 2001, this market-led expansion of online activity underpinned the emergence of a decidedly unpublicized set of governance mechanisms to facilitate both the growth and the reliability of Internet-based activity (particularly in the commercial sphere) and counter emerging forms of 'economic crime' facilitated by the same technological web: the emergence of the Reporting Economic Crime Online initiative is an example of not only trying to better coordinate information and action across national borders but also doing so in a more citizen-driven manner.[17]

Drake (2004, 1) defines ICT global governance as "the collective rules, procedures and related programs intended to shape social actors' expectations, practises and interactions concerning ICT infrastructure and transactions and content." ICANN is perhaps the most prominent governance body in this regard: "Neither a government nor a for-profit corporation, ICANN is a hybrid that interacts with both and with individuals as well" (Geiselhart 2004, 334). This entity has even experimented with direct and digital forms of democracy in electing members to the board overseeing its operations, although the "ambiguities of legitimacy and lapses of transparency and accountability that have characterized ICANN are typical of other attempts at global governance" (ibid.). Others argue that ICANN's selection also reveals an explicit strategy to bypass traditional bodies (e.g., the International Telecommunications Union) in favour of something new (Drezner 2004).

There is much that is American about this new structure and style—a point not lost on those skeptical of ICANN's ability to serve as a global agent of the public interest:

> The US government maintains policy control over the "hidden server" root server that sits atop the Internet's hierarchical domain name system. The server, which is operated by VeriSign under contract with the US Department of Commerce, contains the authoritative listing of all generic and country code Top Level Domains called the root zone file... . The US government's control of the master root server translates into ultimate authority over much of the institutional organization of the Internet's infrastructure... .
>
> Accordingly, the government has established an MOU with the non-profit Internet Corporation for Assigned Names and

Numbers (ICANN) giving it responsibility for Internet Protocol (IP) address space allocation.... . ICANN, in turn, regulates much of the marketplace through a web of contractual relationships with domain name providers, but remains ultimately answerable to and dependent on the US government.... .

A great many governments around the world are deeply uncomfortable with this unilateral US control, and some even fear the possibility of politically inspired decisions to manipulate, disrupt or terminate their nation's connections to the Internet.... . For its part, the US government repeatedly has stated that it has no intention of transferring its authority over the master server to any entity, although there is some ambiguity as to whether this will remain the policy. (Drake 2004, 18)

In terms of global governance, there is much that is new about the focus of ICANN and other bodies underpinning online connectivity. However, from the perspective of international politics, there is also much familiar about the evolution of roles and the relative power of different players, notably the US government. A case can be made that the current position of the United States and debates surrounding it resembles the free-trade movement in the latter half of the twentieth century: the United States took a leading role in establishing new institutions, notably GATT (which would become the more powerful and assertive WTO), and has since proven more resistant to relinquishing authority to an evolving multilateral movement that seems to require a lessening of national sovereignty and a greater pooling of collective authority in a more multilaterally accountable organizational mechanism.

Although the United States has been more tacit in its resistance to the WTO (in some cases even deferring to its authority and championing its importance, particularly if its own interests are furthered), American resistance to the ITU is more in tune with the US view generally toward the United Nations (the ITU falls under the UN purview). Many American and non-American observers alike would readily agree that the ITU has not shown itself to be particularly adept in playing a leading role in terms of global telecommunications policy, and questions about capacity are prevalent (ibid.). Nonetheless, the issue has further exasperated global tensions surrounding institutional reform and the US role specifically, with even the European Union abandoning the American position in October 2005 as some form of compromise appeared to be elusive in the lead-up to the November World Summit on the Information Society, the second phase of this UN-led initiative designed to broker a new global compact on the governance of the Internet and the world's increasingly shared telecommunications infrastructure (Hermida 2005).

It thus seems that the challenge of crafting an appropriate form of global governance for a global digital infrastructure suffers from many of the same issues shaping international agendas and multilateral governance venues for some time. Yet an important and more recent distinction with respect to digital technologies and status quo arrangements bears consideration — namely, the rising prominence of a security agenda that features heightened collaboration within at least select families of countries and regions. The central role of information-sharing and interoperability between countries aligns with the need to maintain a strong and robust infrastructure globally. A strong case can be made that in the short-term global ICT governance is likely to be less about forging new and strengthened multilateral institutions and more about key countries seeking to balance and maximize their commercial and security interests, with the latter leading to heightened levels of technological and organizational activity between like-minded countries.

One risk of such an evolution is an extension of the sort of secretive and informal governance arrangements that now characterize North America to higher governance planes transnationally (Zinnbauer 2004). Such a risk is accentuated by security and secrecy prioritized over transparency and trust. An additional risk on a global scale is the increasingly secretive and centralized manner in which the Internet itself is being managed, raising issues about not only the agendas of those controlling this infrastructure (and whether such issues constitute sufficient safeguards for a public interest that inherently transcends any single country) but also the potential fragility of the controls underpinning the stable performance of the infrastructure itself.

To manage such risks, two potential avenues present themselves: the first would entail a nearly complete reversion to largely national governance systems, closely guarded by public sector authorities (democratically accountable or otherwise), whereas the second would envision and embrace stronger multilateral institutions to introduce a basis for collective action and more direct forms of accountability between a global citizenry and its governing institutions. Although the first path represents at least the partial choice of a limited number of countries, a few of them large and economically powerful (notably China), processes of economic liberalization coupled with the emerging pressures for digital coordination converge and point to the latter path as the only viable alternative option from the more contested and uneven governance landscape currently in place.

Although American government power and policy remain notable variables in any movement down one path or the other, multilateralists would contend that the present actions of the US government (and others) do not lessen the growing case for more globalized governance mechanisms and responses. The centrality of an e-democracy project aimed at some common basis for global citizenship is one important element (Hayden 2005), one that may align itself with other less overtly political movements that are transnational—such as environmental awareness and even greater stakeholder responsibilities of global corporations.

With the private sector leading the push to expand the reach and acceptance of these new technologies, it is not surprising to find industry as a leading advocate of and a key stakeholder in many of the new governance forums emerging to play such a role. One prominent example is the Global Digital Divide Initiative (GDDI). An offshoot of the World Economic Forum, it is partly an impetus for the responsibilities of global corporations in a global sphere, as underscored by the "CEO Charter for Digital Development," a "private-sector commitment to transparently allocate human, in-kind or financial resources to reduce poverty in developing countries and disadvantaged communities through the use of information and communications technologies" (Hansen and Salskov-Iversen 2003, 19). What is perhaps more revealing in terms of the formation and execution of these initiatives is the equally important role of various actors from within the private sector and civil society, surpassing the contribution and control of any single national government (Selian 2004).

Although such initiatives are raising both awareness and resources to counter what remains by any objective measure a pronounced and ongoing global digital divide (Chen and Wellman 2003), the extension of a digital infrastructure to the developing world would be incomplete in the absence of a much more ambitious set of reforms aimed at trade policies and the sorts of more formalized redistributive mechanisms now in place in the European Union (and called for by continental proponents in North America). In other words, for a global economy to be accompanied by a global community and a global polity, a leap in innovation and cohesion from present arrangements is called for. The more modest question in the short term is whether the growth of a digital infrastructure can contribute to a more open and globalizing dialogue about not only the sorts of reforms called for but even the willingness of different countries and cultures to contemplate them.

A small trade- and continentally-dependent, and increasingly multicultural, country such as Canada finds itself with an interesting set of choices between bilateral relations with the United States and more multilateral perspectives on the rest of the world. It is both unlikely and unnecessary that a choice between the two be made, particularly when economics so strongly dictates the paramount importance of the North American marketplace, whereas demographics seem destined to ensure a population more ethnically diverse and more globally cosmopolitan than an exclusive focus on US relations (particularly in terms of closer political and cultural ties).

However, a major challenge in balancing these two perspectives lies in the growing fault lines between private industry on the one hand (championing a continentalist agenda) and civil society on the other (more varied in outlook but home to a large contingent of those who would prefer some distance between the two countries). As argued in the preceding section, what is essential to reconciling this divide is a public sector more overtly willing to encourage a political and genuine discussion about the intricacies of such debate (as opposed to framing viewpoints as either being for or against the guarding of national sovereignty).

Also highly relevant to Canada's future role in world affairs is that younger people (particularly those most likely to be online and unengaged in traditional political forums and processes) appear to be increasingly intent on maintaining multiple identities and attachments, many of which extend to the transnational domain. Such an outlook seems to hold much promise in encouraging political leaders in Canada to foster new and innovative linkages between Canadian political institutions and those elsewhere. Indeed, the linkages required call for a fundamental rethinking of the purposes, processes, and boundaries defining what has traditionally been regarded as 'foreign affairs' within a national government.

The sort of hidden horizontality occurring across the Government of Canada due to a widening continentalist sphere of activity is also emerging with respect to globalizing issues and agendas as many 'separate departments' engage in activities with an explicit transnational dimension. The most recent foreign policy review (leading to a published strategy in April 2005) is not without rhetorical merit in recognizing many of these currents in and their implications for the need to foster new linkages between a variety of stakeholders both within and outside government due to a recognition that today's issues are too complex for silos (Government of Canada 2005).

Yet the exercise was also a missed opportunity, particularly in terms of process, in failing to engage Canadians as both individuals and stakeholders in a dialogue about the future of their world and Canada's place in it. Similarly, without a sufficient focus on process, there are clearly significant questions about capacity and the seriousness of the government's intent in pursuing these and other ideas that collectively constitute a shopping list form of pledges and commitments involving nearly every region and conceivable issue.[18]

A new and uniquely digital dimension to engage Canadians—particularly young people—should have (and will eventually one day) focused on fundamental questions about process.

- What forms of online channels currently exist in Canada that pertain to concepts such as citizenship, multiculturalism, and global and continental relations?
- How can the public sector—led by a renewed Department of Foreign Affairs—act as both a broker in providing and sharing information and a facilitator in sparking new and more collective dialogues aimed specifically at shaping government priorities and actions?
- What current online mechanisms exist between Canadians and their relatives and fellow ethnic community members living abroad?

- How can such mechanisms be better aligned with more traditional political processes and discussions in Canada, particularly among Canadians rooted more in one of the two founding cultures?

This last question points to the obvious cleavage between national political institutions that are so engrained in the historical traditions of English- and French-speaking communities and so distant from the cultural and demographic realities of growing segments of the country. The fact that the City of Toronto is the world's most ethnically diverse city must represent a political and economic asset in allowing Canada to better prepare its role and convey its influence on a global scale. Yet the limited linguistic orientation of the City of Toronto's website serves to underscore not only its limited impact as an interface with the rest of the world but also the limitations of the municipal authorities' efforts to date to engage various ethnic communities that are often civically organized but in a manner largely outside formal democratic governance bodies.

Here lies the important linkage between globalizing and localizing tendencies that have been discussed for so long but that have prevailed only in limited economic and market applications such as industrial clustering. The implications of a global-local connectedness extend much further into the political and cultural realms, although the present structures of the Canadian public sector are highly unaccommodating in this regard. As argued in the preceding chapter, stronger forms of public deliberation should be as localized as possible—and then leveraged into a broader national debate only after authorities and communities have been both empowered and aligned locally.

The local and regional diversity shaping Canada—and the ability of this subnational diversity to express itself politically—are important sources of input into Canada's ability to both balance continental and global agendas and contribute to governance building at both levels. Such a contribution will be varied and diverse in different parts of the country: British Columbia extends more forcefully into Asia than most parts of Ontario, which are more continentally-oriented (with the notable exception of Toronto); similarly, the relative importance of American and European ties and influences varies across different parts of Quebec and the Maritimes, and this variance is an important reason in itself to both expect and encourage political and municipal bodies to become more internationally assertive and interconnected.

The growing interconnectedness of cities and subnational regions is evidence in this regard, a trend likely to continue to shape transnational governance relations in the future (Safai-Amini 2000; Sassen 2002; Richman 2004). The federated architecture of democracy outlined in the previous chapter is therefore relevant to the future of global governance insofar as it better enables different communities defined by territory, ethnic culture, or some other basis to contribute to Canada's place in the world — via a more flexible and locally sensitive national apparatus that seeks to facilitate and, when necessary, filter such diversity into a more formal Canadian voice, particularly with respect to matters and institutions shaped largely by national governments.

Here too the federal government's foreign policy review paper acknowledges many of these points, pledging, for instance, to make better use of cities and provinces in pursuing international objectives (and, in the case of provinces, promising to establish a new set of 'smart networks' to promote international links among Canadian institutions and their counterparts abroad. The absence of a meaningful intergovernmental architecture to pursue such ties — coupled with an overly centralized and insular federal apparatus (reflecting the manner in which the policy review was managed and formulated) — seems to greatly diminish any such endeavours evolving into meaningful governance mechanisms.

Finally, it is perhaps most telling that the Internet and ICTs are largely absent from Canada's most recent foreign policy statement: no mention is allotted to ICANN, for instance, and, despite the acknowledgement of closer collaboration with the United States on a number of security fronts, the digital infrastructure for doing so does not seem to warrant any explicit recognition or attention. Just as the design and rollout of e-government have been recognized as potentially important levers in facilitating economic competitiveness and attractiveness internationally for a particular jurisdiction, so too must they be recognized as platforms for democratic and cultural renewal as a basis for strengthened participation internationally in more political and civic forums.

Canada's ability to effectively serve as a bridge between the US perspective on multilateral issues and institutions and the views of other parts of the world rests on both strengthened economic prosperity and civic participation. In this sense, although e-government entails important expansions of interoperability both within and between partnering countries (expansions that require open and effective oversight), it also entails the gradual extension of community and political interdependence beyond national borders.

Conclusion

E-government's first decade has been less transformative than transitional, and this assessment holds particular resonance in the case of Canada. Despite the promise of dramatic change and continuous innovation, it is possible to argue that the public sector today looks much as it did some ten years ago when the Internet began its ascendancy to the mainstream of social and market activity.

Any such argument is also partly misleading, however, since it underplays the significant changes and investments that have occurred as governments—like all organizations—struggle to keep pace with accelerating rates of technological change. Online public service delivery is an emerging reality at all levels, and e-democracy, though rather slow to evolve in Canada, is beginning to impose itself as a more regular feature of politics and decision making in many jurisdictions around the world.

Still, many of the changes to date can be characterized as transitional since they have been introduced in a manner that has either sought to explicitly maintain traditional principles and organizational practices or failed to overcome their limitations in order to realize new ones. Although there are pockets of innovation and examples of transformation on a microscale, broader systemic reform has so far remained elusive.

Perhaps, then, the most pertinent question surrounding the public sector in going forward is whether we are therefore on the cusp of a transformation that is now unavoidable and just a matter of time. Whereas the answer to this question should be seen as affirmative, it does not necessarily follow that the implications will be positive. Much depends on the decisions and choices of those in power within the public sector as well as the preferences and actions of the citizenry.

This book has revealed some key design tensions that have emerged thus far in the transition toward a new digital era, tensions that may well become key determinants in whether the path ahead spurs significant renewal—and thus a positive transformation—or stymies it, bringing instead the risk of significant decline and uncertainty.

Centralization and Complexity

With respect to service and security, these primarily internal and organizational dimensions of e-government have been brought by the rise of Internet connectivity across societies—challenging governments to make use of this new cyberspace to become more citizen-centric. Perhaps the greatest risk emerging in the Canadian context is an excessive degree of centralization, both organizationally and politically. In terms of organization, initiatives such as Service Canada—unless underpinned by a new governance regime to effectively facilitate coordination in an appropriately networked manner (with implications for incentives, skills, processes, and accountabilities)—will further centralize authority in the familiar command and control manner typically deployed for key government initiatives.

There is little question that today's organizational context—relying heavily on interoperability to guide and coordinate a set of diverse and dispersed activities—requires an important leadership capacity endowed with the resources and authority to act. Yet it is the very nature of this leadership that is in flux today, although the degree to which it is changing sufficiently in the public sector remains open to interpretation.

Striking a new balance between hierarchy and flexibility, between vertical and horizontal dimensions of accountability, is the nexus of technological and organizational interoperability and innovative leadership. Striking the capacities of the public service in this regard, via initiatives such as Service Canada, entails more than incremental modifications to existing structures and processes. A more networked and collaborative mindset must take hold in order to loosen the forces of bureaucratic and political tradition that are intertwined with vertical hierarchy and control.

Accordingly, politicians must also embrace a more collaborative mindset—particularly ministers, who must begin to operate in tandem with colleagues in more open and integrative mechanisms that transcend objective setting, resource allocation, and results reporting. While cabinet may well need to preserve an element of secrecy in extraordinary circumstances, such changes effectively call for a dispersal of its members and duties away from a concentrated and all-inclusive core across a new and diverse set of political networks based on interdependence, openness, and shared accountabilities.

The dangers of centralization also apply democratically and federally to the relative visibilities and capacities of local, provincial, and federal governments. Across the spectrum of new service delivery and public security challenges, establishing new entities such as Service Canada and reorganizing old ones via shared service models and the like are unfolding in an excessively insular manner driven by a reinvigorated federal government (at least in the context of the past decade) enjoying burgeoning fiscal surpluses and a sense that strong national action in the public interest calls for decisive and direct forms of intervention, particularly in a post-9/11 security context.

In the service and security realms, the absence of a meaningful intergovernmental architecture to make use of the very rhetoric flowing from governments themselves ('seamless and responsive governance across all levels') denotes a major handicap for the emergence of e-government that is gradually evolving—as many pundits predicted only a few short years ago—into just plain (and more all-encompassing) 'government.' Moreover, with respect to democratic renewal and the growing calls for citizen engagement, this top-down mentality—coupled with the more independent structures separating each level of government (in particular federal and provincial)—creates competition, confusion, and public cynicism. Since parliamentary models reinforce communication over genuine consultation, the public is invited to contribute without a genuine link between input and result.

The widening spectrum of democratic experimentation provincially provides some hope, although provinces must also be equally willing to envision a stronger set of participative capacities locally—created and managed by municipal authorities empowered with the purpose and flexibility to do so. Although virtual consultations will continue to grow as a governance feature at all levels of government, it is a mistake not to prioritize localized engagement, where a multichannel environment can best be deployed in a truly citizen-centric fashion.

The new federated architecture of democratic engagement required for the digital age should be inclusive of local, provincial, and federal processes more than is currently the case (despite the frequent rhetoric of collaboration). Although geography and jurisdictional distinctions will continue to matter, they will also lessen — replaced or complemented in many cases by overlapping spheres of issues such as service delivery, public safety, environmental protection, and smart planning that invariably cut across all levels at the same time.

To break free from the dangers of centralization, the changes and innovations required demand a willingness to embrace rather than shy away from complexity. In the public sector, complexity is often the enemy of reform: skeptics invoke the need for clarity in a system that must remain accountable at all times to all citizens. The public must know who is in charge, who is to blame, et cetera. Such a mentality largely explains the perceived necessity from within parliamentary government to assign the most important files to a single minister (however large, complex, and multidimensional these files may be).

The same mentality also explains the growing schism between the realities of governing and the manner in which formal processes and institutions are presented as functioning. There is simply far too much about the operation and governance of the public sector that is either hidden from or just not visible to the public, and the advent of e-government is critical here as both a driver of new initiatives (horizontal committees, service transformation efforts, and new security measures) and a source of contradiction between the rising expectations of empowerment and the public sector's inherent cultural preference for clarity and simplicity.

This schism lies at the heart of public dissatisfaction with all governments and the growing examples of operational paralysis at the federal level in particular. Addressing it requires recognition of two additional design tensions stemming more from the externalized e-government dimensions of transparency and trust.

Community and Deliberation

Fundamentally, to address complexity in a democratic context, participative-based learning must be the basis of a renewed sense of community that reasserts membership — citizenship — as a complementary set of rights and choices on the one hand and responsibilities on the other. The fact that some skeptics call into question the ability of most citizens to play such a role is a reflection less of the intelligence and willingness of most members of the public than of the inertia of the governing mindset — that public participation is an option to be managed rather than a necessity to be embraced.

The digital politics of today (driven by television), so rooted in adversarial contests emphasizing clarity and the breaking down of clarity (as a failure), does little to foster the sort of collective intelligence required for most of today's public interest issues. Indeed, the inverse correlation between heightened transparency (being imposed on governments reacting in kind) and declining levels of trust at present underscores the real possibility that e-democracy could well weaken rather than strengthen the political fabric of our governance systems. The costs of such a weakening in terms of economic development and social cohesion are indirectly as important as the more direct consequences for governments unable to rely on the legitimacy and trust levels required to play a leading role in public interest matters.

At the heart of membership in a community is a willingness to contribute, and in an increasingly mature and participative democracy such a contribution often comes in the form of conversation, the 'magic' of which can be essential to forging enough compromise and agreement to serve as a basis for collective action (Yankelovich 1999). For some, participating in such a conversation is a regularized activity, ideally done in a real-time, face-to-face manner; for others, the anonymity of online discussion and reflection is a preferred route. The underlying challenge of a political community in a digital age is to both foster and align a set of institutions encouraging contributions of all sorts — insofar as they are guided by a sense of civility and a willingness for both give and take that must be cultivated over time.

The importance of community also stresses the need for civility and empathy in politics and government, traits eroded at present by a communications mindset (rooted in television but being transferred online, at least by formal political actors) emphasizing conflict via 'war rooms,' attack ads, and the like. Although the Internet can compound such behaviours and beliefs, it can also broaden political participation beyond the tools and antics of such operatives: the thousands of nonprofit discussion forums and politically neutral blogs are testament to such a potential.

The great challenge for twenty-first-century democracy is to bring such activity into the realm of formal political institutions — revamped from the current structures and freed from the present limitations. The dangers of not doing so lie not in digital technologies leaving behind the public sector but in how such technologies will be deployed. As computer systems, life sciences, and other advanced fields increasingly fuse into one another, their implications for not only political life but also all forms of human activity are destined to be more complex and consequential. To cope and adapt, our societies require capacities to deal with complexity in an open and deliberative fashion.

Lyon (2004) frames the choice that lies ahead as being between morality and management, the latter denoting a technocratic effort to keep up with new technologies and make use of them without the reflective and broadly social capacities for understanding the implications of such deployments. By extension, the danger of such a path is not generating the collective abilities necessary to steer us along an enlightened, informed, and rewarding path.

In its first decade, e-government has come to be adopted by many scholars, activists, and citizens alike as an issue of morality in terms of the appropriate nature of democratic governance for a new century. Yet governments have largely responded with a managerial emphasis, reflective of both efforts to incrementally improve existing operations and a natural discomfort with how, or even if, to embrace broader systemic change. Although political leadership is central to kick-starting any process to transcend this division, the process required to guide our society through the next phases of digital transformation cannot be expected to be the exclusive domain of any one government — or indeed of only the public sector.

Often in the public sector, senior managers or political leaders seek to undertake initiatives to look ahead with new ideas and fresh thinking, and many 'think-pieces' are often commissioned. Although the level of openness and visibility will depend on whether such an initiative is being internally administered or politically managed, the typical process for doing so relies on either in-house or external subject experts to devise an initial vision or blueprint that then becomes the basis for review and deliberation. Even when the consultative intent is genuine, the engagement is thus responsive and framed by the very parties seeking guidance through future uncertainty.

Contrast such a traditionally linear approach with the emerging universe of weblogs and the like. A May 2005 cover story in *Business Week* invites readers to imagine a world where publication and advertising industries are turned on their heads by narrative and visual processes of opinion making and idea sharing occurring utterly out in the open for all to see, unfiltered by editors and executives alike.

Such a grassroots movement is well under way in Korea, for instance, where more than a quarter of the country's population subscribes to 'Cyworld,' an online platform replicating traditional social and economic activities and facilitating new ones. E-mail and text messaging do not begin to describe this cyberforum, which seeks to transcend the physical and digital spheres through three-dimensional, personalized home pages that are literally 'homes' — rooms are furnished and decorated — with transactions facilitated by a cybercurrency.

Although basic access to Cyworld is free, it is operated by Korea's largest wireless service provider, and many of the additional services and activities are fee-driven. SK Communications estimates that nearly all South Koreans in their twenties have subscribed at one point in their lives (Cameron 2005). Cyworld is an extreme but by no means unique example of what has been termed 'smartmobs' by one notable commentator, and it is worth bearing in mind that their presence and influence, particularly among younger generations, remain in their infancy (Rheingold 2002).

The implications of such trends for the future of political activity and democracy — while not easy to predict — are certain to be profound. Indeed, it is this nexus between the uncertain future and the widening participative ethos facilitated by online governance that must be understood: expert commissions and traditional authorities cannot guide the crafting of a future path. Here lies the making of a twenty-first-century equivalent to the royal commission that is urgently needed to broaden this dialogue and collectively and interactively scope out a path for adapting and bettering our system of democratic governance.

Transformative Collaboration

If there is a commonality across the four e-government dimensions that imply an internal organizational renewal with respect to service and security on the one hand (a renewal closely intertwined with political leadership and democratic governance), and a more externalized set of institutional changes on the other (in turn shaping organizational and machinery decisions of governments), it is the challenge of collaboration.

Currently, collaboration is viewed more as a cost than as a virtue — even by many managers and elected officials who routinely espouse the benefits of collaborative activity. Horizontal governance within the public sector must be collaborative to take hold. In doing so, however, running counter to tradition often entails the creation of new mechanisms that remain poorly understood and resisted. Moreover, such efforts may be shunned as overly constraining in a political environment favouring clarity and simplicity in political organization and leadership.

While leadership is a key lens through which the conduct and interpretation of existing actors may be understood, it is also a symptom of the larger organizational and managerial paradigm in good currency not only in government but also in all sectors. Yet it is government more than elsewhere that has continued to rely on the foundational pillars of Weberian bureaucracy, which include hierarchy, clarity, and specialized (or stove pipe) organization. In this largely vertical world, the interface between formal structure and informal culture creates a reflexive preference for top-down management and process control.

The notion of control is fundamental here to understanding the reframing that must occur. All organizations and institutions require some form of control, but the growing interest in new governance systems is testament to the need to view control less as a means to shape every aspect of behaviour (i.e., process control) and more as a basis for coordinated and shared actions orchestrated on the basis of outcomes and objectives. From the perspective of more horizontal but in reality networked governance solutions that are the essence of service transformations and effective security strategies, two fundamental questions remain stubbornly unanswered.

- How can public managers be motivated to share data and, more generally, to work jointly for the public good?
- How can we understand and influence the range of barriers, from psychological and social to structural, political, and technical, that mitigate across cross-agency initiatives? (Fountain 2003, 33)

The first question is arguably more structural and transitional and, as a result, in keeping with much of the e-government experimentation that has occurred to date, the latter question underscores the more culturally transformative challenges of realizing a collaborative environment. A key argument derived from the investigation in this book is that addressing this latter and more holistic scale of change requires much more meaningful reforms to the political apparatus surrounding the organizational mechanisms in transition. It is only if new technologies — and the attitudes derived from using these new technologies in categorically different processes — begin to permeate the institutions of democracy (and relationships between the executive and legislative branches as well as both with the citizenry) that a more meaningful management program can be expected throughout the public service.

Here the implications for e-government to become a new paradigm of governance (one more connected, networked, and collaborative) extend beyond the realm of the public sector. The difficulties of navigating transitional and transformative change are occurring at all levels of society and across the private sector in particular. It is increasingly clear that the evolution of working and living in this digital era is thus far a mixed story of opportunity and empowerment for some and a precarious and high-stress living for others — including many of those described as the professional class of knowledge workers.

Not surprisingly, there are some early signs of a backlash against the 'benefits' of being digitally connected to the workplace and to one another in a manner reminiscent of predictions that the most affluent and fortunate will be those able to consciously disconnect themselves from technology, thereby preserving private or individual space. Indeed, in some limited instances, private corporations are responding in kind. Engineers at Google, for instance, receive a day a week of personal time to focus on pet project ideas regardless of how closely aligned such ideas are to current corporate strategy. Online platforms are then used to share the results of such creativity and spur new collaborative initiatives that have become an important source of innovation for the technology company.

To some degree, governments have much to learn from individual corporations that are reinventing both structure and culture through a nexus of technological and organizational innovation. Yet governments must also preserve their distinctiveness in terms of democratic accountability and the public interest by not only offering specific services but also by serving as a model for working and living in a digital age. E-government must therefore be viewed not only as a new way of operating within the public sector but also a new way of organizing politically and acting in concert with other stakeholders and the public.

This new way entails a collaborative ethos that must ideally render e-government a more participatory model of co-governing between public servants, elected officials, and the citizenry that, in turn, will shape the nature of the government's relationships with other sectors — notably industry. In this respect, more collaborative relationships between industry and government are not about nurturing cozy ties in a technocratic organizational environment — with token transparency on a technical but highly limited scale. Such relationships must generate, preserve, and rely on trust from the public as well as key public servants and politicians.

The difficulties of engineering such changes at the federal level remain an important quandary in the Canadian context. E-government may well turn out to resemble previous stages of public sector innovation in one important respect — namely, the bottom-up pace of change and reform where the relatively smaller and more flexible confines of local and (in most cases) provincial governments allow for more organizational and political nimbleness. As the growing pains of the City of Toronto remind us, however, this case for the promise of localized leadership rests entirely on a sufficiently open environment and an engaged citizenry (the absence of which can quickly lead to corruption and cronyism at a level rivalling anything happening federally).

A path of transformative collaboration (as opposed to transitional change) is therefore likely to require a stronger empowerment of decentralized subunits within federal and provincial governments on the one hand and municipal governments on the other. Collaboration across all of these levels will be required, but as argued throughout the preceding chapters it can come about only through less lopsided governance arrangements more conducive to both intergovernmental partnering and making use of the relevance and importance of proximity that remains as crucial for democratic performance as it does for innovation and competitiveness in Silicon Valley and the many communities attempting to replicate its market-based collaborative model.

In short, e-government's first decade in Canada has been about the search for growing but limited opportunities for public sector reforms denoted largely by the realms of service and security that are most visible and resource intensive at the national level. Pressures associated with heightened transparency and shifting and more complex determinants of trust are exposing the shortcomings of this trajectory, as traditional political and bureaucratic control overshadows the potential for new and more collaborative governance forms.

If e-government is to usher in a positive transformation of both democratic engagement and public sector management, it will entail a truly federated strategy of localized experimentation coupled with a much greater willingness to make use of digital technologies as collaborative and discursive platforms than is currently the case. Such is the truly transformative challenge for e-government's second decade.

Notes

Notes to Introduction

1. New blogs are continually being created. One recent survey by *Business Week* suggests that perhaps as many as 8 million Americans have one, catering to the more than 30 million online readers in the United States alone. In essence, a blog is an online platform for publishing, communicating, and discussing that allows 'bloggers' to have their say on any given issue or theme deemed worthy of attention. More recently, 'vloggers' have been added to this virtual spectrum, bringing a video dimension that may offer content ranging from a corporate focus (Microsoft operates a vlog for software designers — attracting 900,000 viewers a month, according to *Business Week*) to the provocative and absurd.
2. As with the downloading of music and movies, some of these traditional structures perceive the threat and are responding in kind. Apple Computers has launched legal action against a long-time blogger (thinksecret.com) with a history of releasing new product information in advance of the company. The case raises fundamental questions about freedom of expression and proprietary knowledge in a virtual world — one such question being whether bloggers are to enjoy the safeguards of journalistic activity accorded to those in more mainstream publishing outlets.
3. An exception to this claim could be online voting, which involves an e-government application that does little to alter the representational parameters of electoral processes. Accordingly, however, the vast majority of e-democratic visions put forth go far beyond such incremental change.
4. For those readers unfamiliar with the Canadian governance structure, Canada is a federal system with a central government (usually referred to as the Government of Canada or the federal government), ten provincial governments with extensive independent powers, three territorial governments in northern Canada that are more dependent on central government funding, and municipal governments that are creations of provincial governments and have only limited relations with the federal government.

5 Organizations such as Accenture Consulting that have ranked the Government of Canada as the world leader in e-government (as defined predominantly by online presence and service delivery strategies) rely heavily on self-assessments undertaken and shared by the federal government itself. These assessments include citizen satisfaction surveys (e.g., polls and focus groups) used to benchmark the perception and quality of the public's encounter as a 'customer' of government. For examples of this evidence, review the various annual reports of the Government Online (GOL) initiative, leading up to the final report in 2005 (available online at http://www.gol-ged.gc.ca/index_e.asp).

6 This passage was written by John Reid in his final annual report submitted to Parliament in 2005 (although his term has subsequently been extended by the government). For access to this report and further information on the information commissioner, please see www.infocom.gc.ca.

7 Only in recent years has the Government of Canada attempted to measure its overall level of IT spending. In a Treasury Board report prepared in 2004 by the Chief Information Officer Branch, *Government of Canada IT Spending*, the total amount for that year was estimated to be $4.9 billion (inclusive of hardware, software, and associated human resource costs both internally and externally via consultants). This amount represents a four percent increase over 2002-03.

8 As discussed later in the book, the challenge has thus far proved largely elusive. Interjurisdictional service integration was promised within the initial GOL program created in 1999, and it is now once again referenced as a key direction for Service Canada. The reality is that all governments have been sufficiently challenged by their own internal strategies and reforms to neglect this next frontier (although over the past several years a number of pilot initiatives have been undertaken, and within public services dialogues across government levels on issues of shared importance have multiplied).

9 In his first week as Canada's new ambassador in Washington, Frank McKenna caused a political firestorm in Ottawa by stating that Canada was already part of ballistic missile defence by virtue of joint North American defence structures (a view categorically denied by the government during the same week that Prime Minister Martin would announce Canada's decision not to participate in the system). Other examples, such as the proposed formation of joint border security units, also underscore this point.

Notes to Chapter 1

1 Source: Statistics Canada (http://www.statcan.ca/Daily/English/040923/d040923a.htm).

2. The article discusses IBM's plans to rely less on sales of computer products and systems (increasingly viewed as a commodity industry of lower margins and intense competition both in the United States and around the world) and more on strategy consulting and partnering relationships that would see IBM take on the management of increasingly core responsibilities from its clients to better align technological and organizational infrastructures with performance outcomes.
3. This New York City initiative—though large on a municipal scale—is hardly unique: it was recognized as a leading example of a trend of such efforts emerging in cities and states across the country. For a complete profile of all initiatives, see "Effectiveness through E-Payments: Current Learning and Suggested Best Practices," available online at the National Electronic Commerce Coordinating Council (www.ec3.org).
4. Many early proposals for e-government highlighted the potential for massive savings in shifting from paper-, person-, and telephone-based services to online channels, arguing that savings would be quick to materialize as citizens shifted online. While significant savings have been realized in limited service areas, such as online filing of tax returns, adoption levels coupled with government accountability to the population at large mean that in reality online channels must coexist with other service delivery methods (leading to the term 'multichannel service environment'). The experience of the Canadian banking sector, as a leader in developing online capacities, is instructive: after several years of growth since its inception in 1997, surveys in March 2005 suggested a levelling off of online users at roughly thirty percent of the population, down slightly from thirty-three percent in 2004 (surveys from TNS Canadian Facts, a Toronto-based market research firm).
5. Source: www.pweinternet.org (December 2003 survey).
6. A notable and useful resource of perspectives, articles, and commentaries on the digital divide can be found online at www.digitaldividenetwork.org.
7. Source: Statistics Canada (http://www.statcan.ca/Daily/English/040923/d040923a.htm).
8. This logic can also be applied intergovernmentally, as explored later in the book. For instance, in British Columbia, an integrated federal and provincial web presence allows for single business registration for programs and applications across both levels of government.
9. Although the UK government vigorously pursued large outsourcing deals on a national scale (albeit on a department-by-department or agency-by-agency basis), many of the largest outsourcing examples in North America would come initially from subnational jurisdictions such as San Diego County and BC Hydro. The US federal government also entered into several large-scale agreements in the 1990s, notably in military operations, with one such partnership between the US Navy and EDS valued at $7 billion.

[10] Source: CIO Association of BC (http://www.cioabc.ca/About_CIOABC).

[11] To some extent, the emergence of security as a central concern of all governments since 2001 has countered these points by fixating political attention on the need for better government-wide preparedness, a theme examined in the next chapter.

[12] Congressional testimony by Treasury Deputy Assistant Secretary (Information Systems) and Chief Information Officer (CIO) to the House Sub-Committee on Government, Management, Information, and Technology, March 2000 (http://www.cio.gov/documents/testimony_cio_govt_management_it_mar_2000.html).

[13] Such a characterization does not imply uniformity in such a shift, as some jurisdictions may well be beginning from a point of extreme autonomy and centralization. Specific case studies of federal and provincial governments are reviewed in Part Two.

[14] Adopted from Wendell C. Lawther's report *Contracting for the 21st Century: A Partnership Model*, IBM Endowment for the Business of Government, January 2002 (www.businessofgovernment.org).

[15] San Diego was ranked number one in the country among county-level governments for online service capacities in 2004 by the Center for Digital Government.

[16] For example, the Government of Ontario followed such an approach by creating a Shared Services Bureau for administrative matters, while leaving information technology under the domain of a corporate CIO overseeing both government-wide and separate departmental infrastructures (the specifics of this case and others are examined in Part Two).

[17] In Ontario, pertaining to shared administrative services, such an approach was discussed and eventually abandoned due to fears of unworkably diverse arrangements across different parts of government.

[18] The UN-sponsored Global E-Government Readiness Index (2003) illustrates this point with the following ratings (of 1.000) across different regions: North America (0.867), Europe (0.558), South and Central America (0.442), South and Eastern Asia (0.437), Western Asia (0.410), Caribbean (0.401), Oceania (0.351), South-Central Asia (0.292), and Africa (0.246).

[19] The study identified five major trends: "i) eGovernment advances are diminishing; ii) The pace of progress of a number of early leaders has now slowed to the point where many other countries have caught up; iii) eGovernment leaders are reaping tangible savings. Governments' initial objectives for their online programs were to provide service improvements and alternate channels of delivery. Cost savings were a hoped-for result rather than a certainty. Now we see a decided trend that the focus for many

governments is specifically on the cost savings potential of eGovernment; iii) Promoting take-up is taking hold, but the challenge remains. Our citizen survey shows that eGovernment currently is far from being used to its full extent; iv) the integration challenge is changing. Interest in horizontal integration has been apparent for some time; what is new are decided efforts to integrate vertically—across national, state/regional and local levels of government; and v) personalization is emerging. Some governments are working to maximize the amount of services that can be matched to citizens' interests and needs based on a minimum amount of confidential information" (http://www.accenture.com/xdoc/en/industries/government/gove_egov_value.pdf).

[20] The rankings are based on a composite score based on three separate indices: a web measure index (the core of e-government as defined in this chapter since the focus is on quantifying the existence of information and services online in each public sector jurisdiction); a telecommunications infrastructure index; and a human capital index. The report is available online at http://www.unpan.org/egovernment3.asp.

[21] Over the past several years, the OECD has sponsored a series of studies and venues to bring together the collective experiences and challenges of member countries. A useful synthesis of what is termed 'The E-Government Imperative' outlines a set of issues and priorities that applies to all member jurisdictions notwithstanding many institutional variations among them. The report is available online at www.oecd.org/dataoecd/60/60/2502539.pdf.

[22] In November 2004, Microsoft announced the creation of the Solutions Sharing Network (SSN). According to its press release, "Microsoft Corp. today announced it is delivering the Solutions Sharing Network (SSN), a global initiative that provides an online, community-based capability to promote increased communication, deeper information exchange, and collaboration between government organizations, academic institutions and other public sector agencies. SSN enables Microsoft's global public sector partners and customers to share their unique IT solutions, architectures, best practices, application source code that the governments own and have contributed to the project, and research to increase efficiencies and reduce long-term development costs." Such an initiative can also be viewed as a partial response to the open source challenge—essentially, new software codes of a nonproprietary nature, the development of which is facilitated by the Internet's inherent networking capabilities. This theme is returned to in Chapter 3 (www.microsoft.com/presspass/press/2004/nov04/11-08SSNPR.asp).

Notes to Chapter 2

1. Source: http://www.securitystats.com/.
2. Source: http://www.caida.org/analysis/security/sapphire/.
3. Source: http://www.deloitte.com/dtt/cda/doc/content/Global%20Security%20Survey%202003.pdf.
4. Source: http://www.cba.ca/en/content/stats/040622-delivery%20channels%202003-leaj.pdf.
5. Of relevance to security-related matters is the bolstered public support for stronger governmental action and the relatively higher levels of trust accorded by the citizenry to law enforcement authorities versus other governmental actors. For instance, a 2003 Statistics Canada survey of 25,000 individuals revealed an 82.1 percent confidence level (either 'a great deal' or 'quite a lot' in police compared with other groups such as banks (68.1 percent), major corporations (45.8 percent), and Parliament (42.8 percent). *Globe and Mail*, July 7, 2004.
6. Source: http://www.infoway.ca/ehr/glossary.php?lang=en&section=E&#Electronic_Health_Record.
7. In the United States, identity theft is reported to be the fastest-growing crime in the country, having already harmed nearly 60 million Americans (www.csialliance.org). The Better Business Bureau of Canada estimates an annual cost of $2.5 billion to Canadian consumers, and the total annual cost to the Canadian economy has been estimated at $5 billion.
8. Because biometrics can be used in such a variety of applications, it is very difficult to establish an all-encompassing definition. The most suitable definition of biometrics is "The automated use of physiology or behavioural characteristics to determine or verify identity" (www.biometricgroup.com).
9. The British government has introduced legislation to establish a new agency by 2008 that would issue both passports and a national identification card, with the card being compulsory for all citizens by 2013. The card would feature a biometric chip with an identifier unique for each individual, and its purpose is to facilitate better and more integrated access to government services for citizens while also enabling authorities to counter identity theft, fraud, and domestic security threats. Many European countries already use similar cards, and there is general interest in and growing commitment to biometrically enabled forms of identification for both passports and domestic mechanisms in many countries around the world, including the United States and Canada.
10. The US federal government had adopted an e-government agenda axed largely on improved service delivery prior to September 2001. However,

service transformation projects managed by OMB have had trouble securing even modest funding levels for pilot initiatives over the past several years, whereas the president's proposed 2006 budget calls for $41.1 billion for the Department of Homeland Security, within which the use and deployment of information and communication technologies (ICT) feature prominently (for budgetary details, see www.dhs.gov).

[11] Prior to 9/11, the federal government focus on cybersecurity was indirect and fragmented across various e-government and e-commerce initiatives. In February 2003, the president tabled the country's first 'national strategy to secure cyberspace,' elevating the issue within the executive branch in both the White House and the Department of Homeland Security.

[12] Indeed, many scholars distinguish between information and knowledge management, underscoring the latter when organizations refine and make use of information to facilitate learning and the pursuit of specific objectives. Accordingly, knowledge management is a useful prism to examine and understand many aspects of defence, intelligence, and homeland security (Desouza and Vanapalli 2005).

[13] This estimate was reported by GlobalSecurity.org, an American observation and research group devoted to security, defence, and intelligence matters.

[14] Main findings of an August 2004 report by the Office of the Inspector General (OIG-04-31). The report underscores the challenges of deploying information technologies in a uniquely large and fluid organizational context (similar concerns have been raised by the Canadian auditor general with respect to Canadian authorities: see Section Three). It is also noteworthy here that mismanagement and weak comptrollership are charges made regularly by critics of the Pentagon (both inside and outside Congress), the point being that it is hardly unusual to witness large bureaucracies facing operational difficulties with such huge amounts of dollars (and DHS faces the additional pressures of an accelerated and politically charged formation period).

[15] One of the most prominent critics of the Patriot Act has been the American Civil Liberties Union, which nonetheless saw fit to restrict its concerns in this manner: "The Patriot Act is a 350-page law that contains about 160 provisions. The ACLU and our ideologically diverse allies inside and outside Congress have zeroed in on fewer than a dozen that we think went too far too fast, that have not been shown to have either been necessary or effective in countering terrorism... . Section 213 it turns out, the so-called sneak-and-peek provision, according to the Justice Department itself, has mostly been used for non-terrorism investigations. Section 215, the so-called library records and other tangible records provision, where people are so concerned about having their library records searched secretly without their knowledge, we're told hasn't even been necessary, that libraries are

voluntarily turning over information to the government or ... under different authority." Nadine Strossen, quoted from PBS's *The News Hour* (http://www.pbs.org/newshour/bb/terrorism/jan-june05/patriot_4-5.html).

16 In 1999, for example, 126,809,769 pages of government information were declassified. By 2004, this number dropped to 28,413,690. "Secrecy Report Card: An Update," April 2005 (www.openthegovernment.org).

17 The *Globe and Mail* in Canada reported in March 2005 that, at a recent technology convention in Seattle, security experts held a contest inviting hackers to manipulate the search engines Google and Yahoo to find confidential information on citizens and organizations. They did just that: using Google for about one hour, contestants gathered information on nearly 25 million people (of potential use for fraudulent activities). In its corporate response, Google said that its service is "a reflection of the Web. Although we aggregate and organize information published on the Web, we do not control the information itself nor do we control access to it." Yahoo responded in a similar manner: "we continually optimize our Web search to provide users with a comprehensive and relevant experience by indexing content that is part of the public domain." Indeed, there is no evidence that either company is somehow directly at fault, but the nature of the incident as well as the corporate responses will reinforce for many the suspicions of O'Harrow and others.

18 The United Kingdom has recently adopted a plan to introduce a new, mandatory identification card, along with biometrically-enabled passports. Indeed, pilots are already under way in Scotland, and over the next several years the plan will be complemented by the creation of a National Identification Registry (a database holding personal information on all citizens designed to enable stronger authentication of identity, thereby reducing fraudulent activity, and—from the perspective of national security—augmenting surveillance capacities).

19 The International Civil Aviation Organization (www.icao.int) is the leading intergovernmental organization examining biometric standards for travel documentation. Of course, the fledgling biometric industry is a key proponent as well.

20 Congressional testimony by Karen Evans, Administrator for Electronic Government and IT, OMB, October 16, 2003.

21 The home page for the European Union is www.europa.eu.int. The domain name 'int' typically denotes an international organization (i.e., intergovernmental, autonomous from national governments), although in April 2005 the European Union announced the adoption of 'eu' as its registered domain name henceforth available to all European organizations.

Notes to Chapter 3

1. Here's an illustration: "Mexico's federal government established Compranet for government procurement as part of its efforts to curb corruption by automating procurement processes. By facilitating a process of bidding and reverse bidding online, it seeks to make government purchasing more efficient and transparent. The system allows the public to see what services and products the government is spending its resources on and what companies are providing them with these services. There are more than 6,000 public sector tenders logged daily, and more than 20,000 service-providing firms are regular users. Other countries in the region are looking to imitate Mexico's successful Compranet."
2. In parliamentary democracies, the executive branch comprises the head of state, cabinet, and the public service (among other actors), whereas the legislative branch comprises chambers with the public's representatives responsible for holding the government (i.e., cabinet) to account.
3. For evidence of this point, see Savoie (2001) for a Canadian perspective that nonetheless is predicated on majority government in Parliament. The corresponding and widening interest in electoral reform is a theme returned to in Part Two of this book.
4. For instance, the auditor general of Canada typically gives a press conference upon initially releasing her reports (formally 'tabling' them in Parliament). Conversely, some commissioners routinely complain publicly that Parliament pays insufficient attention to their own efforts.
5. Source: www.opensource.org.
6. In 2005, Microsoft created its Solutions Sharing Network: A Global Initiative for the Public Sector, designed to facilitate openness and knowledge-sharing across jurisdictions (with 'code sharing and code reuse' identified as benefits of membership).
7. In preparation for an expanded implementation of such legislation in the United Kingdom, the British government has gone as far as making a public appeal to the media to "not humiliate us" in the first days and weeks of the new law (http://admin.corisweb.org/index.php?fuseaction=news.view&id=116056&src=pub).
8. Such systems are not hugely expensive by narrow measures of direct financial spending, but their total cost must account for the complete infrastructure of direct personnel and indirect time commitments by those responding to the system across government departments and agencies (where staff can be called upon to prepare responses that must then be reviewed and approved by various layers of management before release to the requesting party).

⁹ The existence of government online does little to alter this reality since many jurisdictions do a poor job of providing clear and efficient access to freedom-of-information mechanisms that are often dispersed within government departmental sites (e.g., the Government of Canada's main portal page does not include a direct link for access to information requests alongside the extensive description of programs and services and official reports available).

¹⁰ Source: http://www.atirtf-geai.gc.ca/paper-infopolicy-e.html.

¹¹ Source: http://www.atirtf-geai.gc.ca/paper-future2-e.html.

¹² '311' denotes a new phone number for municipal services adopted by many US cities (and currently under development in Canadian municipalities; see Chapter 7) that is the basis for a customer response system (which can also be accessed online). The main purpose is to facilitate both a single point of contact for all nonemergency services (routed through 911) and tracking mechanisms and performance reporting to improve openness and responsiveness.

¹³ Source: http://www.wien.gv.at/english/vcrm/.

¹⁴ Source: http://www.nordpol.dk/english/.

¹⁵ Source: http://tom.riik.ee/.

¹⁶ Online performance reporting as a basis for public engagement is therefore examined in the subsequent chapter, pertaining to trust.

¹⁷ As with the downloading of music and movies, some of these traditional structures perceive the threat and are responding in kind. Apple Computers has launched legal action against a long-time blogger (thinksecret.com) with a history of releasing new product information in advance of the company. The case raises fundamental questions about freedom of expression and proprietary knowledge in a virtual world—one such question being whether bloggers are to enjoy the safeguards of journalistic activity accorded to those in more mainstream publishing outlets.

¹⁸ The CNN executive at the centre of this episode—having just arrived in Switzerland from Iraq—reportedly made comments implying not only that American journalists were being targeted by insurgent groups in Iraq but also that the American military undertook similar actions aimed at journalists from countries deemed hostile or unfriendly (the executive then retracted this claim fully or partially—the precise nature of the remarks remained disputed by various observers and sources).

¹⁹ "Lawmakers continued their recent tradition of appropriating only a small amount of the Bush administration's e-government fund request in the fiscal 2005 omnibus spending bill. For fiscal 2005, administration officials requested $5 million in directly appropriated funds and authority to use $40 million in federal agency fees collected by the General Services Administration. But

lawmakers appropriated $3 million, and they rejected the administration's request for permission to draw from the GSA fund" (http://www.fcw.com/fcw/articles/2004/1206/news-egov-12-06-04.asp).

[20] Strong political leadership for IT management has been underscored as a critical success factor in facilitating progress down the e-government path. Despite this view (and the symbolic sponsoring of such strategies by heads of government in many jurisdictions), the CIO function is often not only political but also subordinate to senior public servants in central agencies with broader managerial responsibilities, such as the Treasury Board in Canada, the Office of Management and Budgeting in the United States, and most Canadian provinces.

[21] "Despite years of modernization efforts that cost taxpayers billions of dollars, thousands of accounting, personnel and logistics systems at the Pentagon remain 'fundamentally flawed' and have led to logistics and pay problems for forces serving in Iraq, according to a new report by the U.S. General Accounting Office. The problems, primarily a lack of management oversight and investment control, stem from 'long-standing' challenges to the Pentagon's business modernization efforts, GAO auditors told members of Congress yesterday. For example, more than 200 inventory-control systems at the Defense Department still aren't integrated, offering little or no visibility of the Pentagon's $1.1 trillion in assets, according to GAO. In addition, the Pentagon has no standard process for identifying critical business systems, nor does it even have a standard definition of what constitutes a business system. 'These problems have left the department vulnerable to billions of dollars of fraud, waste and abuse annually, at a time of increasing fiscal constraint,' GAO auditors told Congress. The Defense Department's IT management blunders have also adversely affected U.S. military units and service members, including those fighting in Iraq and Afghanistan, according to the GAO"

(http://computerworld.com/managementtopics/management/itspending/story/0,10801,94392,00.html).

[22] Examples include the e-government surveys reviewed in Chapter 1 and the various surveys and rating schemes produced by nongovernmental organizations such as the international watchdog organization Transparency International.

[23] An additional factor in explaining this reluctance is simply the novelty of the Internet for exploring online potentials for performance reporting.

[24] In fairness, some governments themselves are introducing parliamentary and electoral reforms both in Canada and elsewhere; the experiences of the federal government and Canadian provinces are examined in Part Two. For a good review of electoral reform studies and pilot initiatives (mainly in the

United Kingdom and other Westminster countries, as well as presidential system comparisons), see the Electoral Reform Society (www.electoral-reform.org.uk).

Notes to Chapter 4

1. This view is closely derived from Barbara Misztal's synthesis of sociological theories of trust that presents three purposes of trust in modern society: making things predictable, bringing people together, and helping them work together (reproduced in O'Hara 2004, 70).
2. An exception to this claim could be online voting, which involves an e-government application that does little to alter the representational parameters of electoral processes. Accordingly, however, the vast majority of e-democratic visions put forth go far beyond such incremental change.
3. Ann MacIntosh heads the International Teledemocracy Centre at Napier University in Edinburgh, Scotland (www.teledemocracy.org), the world's first research institute created to both study e-democracy and contribute to its evolution. The centre has undertaken a number of pilot initiatives with local Scottish governments as well as the Scottish Parliament (notable for its efforts to incorporate e-democracy into its deliberative processes).
4. Since the United States has had more experience with direct democracy, particularly at state and local levels, there has traditionally been a more vibrant debate about its relative strengths and weaknesses. For a good overview of direct democracy concepts and theories and their application in the State of Arizona, see www.uapress.arizona.edu/samples/mccund-ch4.pdf. In Canada, conversely, the Crossing the Boundaries initiative is notable for its efforts to engage elected officials in a dialogue on democratic reforms appropriate for a more digital age (www.crossingboundaries.ca).
5. In a fashion similar to that of e-voting, such an approach has not been overly present in e-democratic literatures and experiments — perhaps due in part to the low rates of technology adaptation by politicians themselves (Coleman and Norris 2005; Mahrer 2005).
6. There is, in fact, much support for such a view on the weblog of the European commissioner for institutional relations and communications, a position created to improve the European Union's image and outreach capacities across European member countries. The Swedish-born commissioner, Margot Wallstrom, contributes regularly to the blog and invites frank and open discussion on issues of interest to citizens. The website of the blog is http://weblog.jrc.cec.eu.int/page/wallstrom.
7. This point does not imply that reforms to such systems have not been pursued. During the 1990s, for example, the US military and those of most

ENDNOTES 307

Western countries began governance renewal efforts designed to foster organizational learning and decision-making capacities based more on empowerment, collaboration, and adaptiveness (Paquet 1997).

8 Most early e-democratic experiments are found at subnational levels (Clift 2004). Examples include the first binding referendum to include online voting in a Swiss canton in January 2003, local elections in Great Britain in 2004, and Canada's first pilot with online voting in 2003 municipal elections in Markham, Ontario.

9 They are examined empirically in Chapter 7 and returned to more prescriptively in Part Three.

10 Source: http://www.carmarthenshire.gov.uk/attached_files/simons/E-Charter%20for%20Wales.pdf.

Notes to Chapter 5

1 The results of such surveys are summarized and made available in general form in the annual reports for the GOL exercise. That these types of instruments constitute 'public consultation' is a point returned to later in the chapter.

2 There are three main subselections from the main portal — Canadians, non-Canadians, and businesses — the logic being that the sorts of information and services required by online visitors generally fall into one of these three camps. Accordingly, with just a few clicks, users are more likely to find the information that they seek.

3 In 2004, the six bundled services included online reservations for national parks, export/import control systems, employment insurance services, federal business incorporations, and Aboriginal employment services. In all such cases, the intent is to offer a single point of online contact to complete transactions in these service areas, thereby not requiring any further processing of paper or providing of information via telephone.

4 Source: Government of Canada, "From Government On-Line to Service Transformation," presentation, Ottawa, Ontario, January 2004.

5 These quoted captions are from internal MSC planning documents made available to me by MSC managers. They have also been used as a basis for a case study focusing on the private sector's role in collaborating with the federal government's lead department (then HRDC) responsible for MSC (Dutile, Langford, and Roy 2005).

6 From MSC planning documents: "Employee payroll, earnings and income related information constitutes the single most important set of data required to administer government programs in Canada (including EI, CPP, OAS and

tax). Today, employers provide information many times and in multiple formats and frequencies to meet the requirements of the siloed programs across all levels of government. Extensive cooperation between HRSD, SD and CRA in Year Two of MSC resulted in an agreement to take forward the E-payroll concept to business plan. This has the potential to transform the delivery of services to employers. In Year Three, MSC worked with CRA to build the business plan and identify the implementation activities that will allow the Government of Canada to make a significant impact in the $4.5 billion cost to employers of complying with government reporting requirements."

[7] Formal announcement of Service Canada was included in the 2005 federal budgetary package (as part of an allotment for service improvement initiatives). Cabinet approval for the concept was given in 2005, although a number of machinery and governance issues remained unresolved at that time, notably whether the entity is to have separate departmental status and relative powers to work in concert with other departments and agencies. Whatever form it eventually takes, it will likely begin as an evolution of MSC, working primarily as a regrouping of service functions from both HRSDC and SDC. An initial notification of Service Canada was sent to employees of both departments in late May 2005, and more formal public announcements re mandates and restructuring are expected in the fall of this year.

[8] Source: http://www.pwgsc.gc.ca/text/factsheets/secure_channel-e.html.

[9] For a review of the 'shared services' concept, see Chapter 1.

[10] The intergovernmental perspective on security matters is the focus of Chapter 7. However, it is noteworthy here that, in regard to the secure channel, the federal government envisions a national infrastructure that can and will eventually be adopted by provincial governments for their own e-government needs. However, the channel was built largely for federal specifications by federal actors, with no formal consultative mechanism involving provincial authorities, so progress toward any intergovernmental deployment has been slow, and there are doubts in many provinces about whether such a path is better for them than devising their own solutions (a theme returned to in the next chapter).

[11] Background documents to the 2005 federal budget speech included a reference to and brief description of the (among others) three key initiatives referred to here: Service Canada, a secure technology infrastructure (i.e., the secure channel), and shared administrative services. Each area received a two-paragraph overview of the intent, but no specific strategies or planning documents were or have been released despite considerable discussion and effort within government on both and the manner in which they are interdependent. Announcements on formal plans for all three areas are

expected in the fall of 2005, and the future of Service Canada is addressed at length in Chapter 7. For the budget background details, please see http://www.fin.gc.ca/budget05/booklets/bkmgte.htm.

12 These areas, however, are tied to procurement—another function of PWGSC and one with important implications for both the ongoing management of the secure channel and most aspects of government technology relying on private sector involvement in some manner (as discussed in the preceding section of this chapter).

13 A division of PWGSC focuses on common IT infrastructure and services for the government as a whole (coordinating with the CIO office of TBS responsible for more high-level policy and direction-setting issues). Discussions are under way to create a partially autonomous subagency (likely within PWGSC) to augment the authority of this group—enabling it to act as a shared service provider of IT services for all federal departments. Similar plans are under way for other nontechnological administrative services (e.g., human resources and payroll, travel services, etc.), not unlike several provinces that have opted for similar models.

14 Given that the creation of Service Canada in 2005 denotes the transition between what has been undertaken to date (at the time of writing) and what is to come, further discussion on these matters is deferred to the more forward-looking commentary of Part Three.

15 Source: http://www.solutions.gc.ca/pki-icp/gocpki/e-transactions/e-transactions_e.asp.

16 The Canada Revenue Agency became the first unit to make use of the channel in providing a service offering to citizens (specifically an online change of address function). Subsequently, the first e-pass-based offering for businesses became the record of employment (ROE) on the web application, offered by then HRDC.

17 In 2002-03, Denis Coderre, minister at the time, was the lead federal proponent for exploring a new national card—an expression of interest that generated much debate and resistance among privacy advocates, who had expressed some interest in the late 1990s in seeking a form of smart card for use in all provincial programs such as health, transportation, and social assistance (with fraud control and waste reduction perhaps more prevalent as motivators than online service delivery for the Conservative government at the time).

18 Various threats and their widening magnitude are reviewed in Chapter 2. Two incidents in Canada reported during June 2005 reflect a growing trend likely to reinforce cautiousness among governments in seeking ways to minimize risk within their operations. In one incident involving a US-based third-party company managing credit card files, a security breach put at risk

up to 240,000 Canadian Visa cardholders, and during the same week it was announced that a Canadian credit-rating agency, Equifax Canada, had also suffered a breach several months prior that had resulted in the theft of data from more than 600 consumer files.

[19] "This role includes overseeing and enforcing two federal privacy statutes; the *Privacy Act* that applies to all federal government institutions, and the new *Personal Information Protection and Electronic Documents Act (PIPEDA)* which extends personal data protection rights to the federally regulated private sector. The OPC is responsible for ensuring that the gathering and handling of personal information, in the public and private sectors, does not violate the privacy rights of Canadians" (Bloomfield 2004).

[20] In the hours following the terrorist attacks, the town of Gander, Newfoundland (with a population of roughly 11,000) welcomed some 6,000 unexpected travellers from diverted aircraft, mostly Americans (two years later many Americans would return to participate in an organized gathering of goodwill to mark the occasion). One week later nearly 100,000 Canadians gathered on Parliament Hill in Ottawa (along with the American ambassador to Canada) to pay homage to the human loss of September 11th.

[21] Estimates peg bilateral commercial exchanges across the border in excess of $2 billion per day, with approximately 200 million border crossings each year (including business and leisure travellers).

[22] The smart border agreement generally speaks to the secure flow of people and goods, a secure infrastructure, and coordination and information sharing in the pursuit of these objectives. The first action commits the two countries to jointly develop on an urgent basis common biometric identifiers in documentation such as permanent resident cards, NEXUS (a pilot initiative of pre-screening frequent border crossers), and other travel documents to ensure greater security. The second action calls for the installation of biometric security measures on permanent residency cards.

[23] Specifically, in the 2001 federal budget, the government allocated $7.7 billion in new funds over five years on a range of initiatives and reforms centred on public security and safety and anti-terrorism. Following the auditor general's report, one public opinion poll conducted in April 2004 showed rising support among Canadians for higher spending on anti-terrorism (fifty-five percent of those surveyed) and military defence (fifty-four percent) (Fife 2004).

[24] Bill C-36 adds a definition of 'terrorist activity' to the Criminal Code. The definition will cover an action that is "taken or threatened for political, religious or ideological purposes and threatens the public or national security by killing, seriously harming or endangering a person, causing substantial property damage that is likely to seriously harm people, or interfering with

or disruption of an essential service, facility or system." The definition also makes it clear that disrupting an essential service is not terrorism if it occurs during a lawful protest or a work strike and is not intended to cause serious harm. The new bill gives police the power to detain a suspected terrorist for seventy-two hours without charge, compel Canadians to testify during an investigation, and intercept a wider range of private conversations for a longer period of time. The bill affects other legislation, such as the Income Tax Act. Organizations supporting terrorist groups that claim to be charities can now be stripped of their charitable status. The bill also allows the government to store the DNA of suspected terrorists, to compile lists of terrorists and their organizations, and to freeze and take away their assets (http://www.cbc.ca/fifth/featurestories/protest/laws.html).

25 Source: http://www.oag-bvg.gc.ca/domino/reports.nsf/html/20050201ce.html. The focus of this audit included five key areas: cooperation and information-sharing among lead organizations on IT security; development and implementation of IT security standards to support policy; effectiveness of the Government Security Policy and existing security measures; contingency planning; and risk management.

26 "The latter four organizations (Foreign Affairs, Citizenship and Immigration, Solicitor General and Privy Council Office) have not yet provided a representative. Foreign Affairs said that its resources should more properly address the threat to its personnel and assets abroad and that increasingly scarce resources from a 'foreign ministry' should not be devoted to matters that are better left to domestic agencies. Immigration told us it supports the concept and attributes its absence to the lack of permanent funding available for that purpose. Solicitor General Canada said that although it has not assigned a specific representative, its officials are fully engaged in all functions and work initiated by the Centre. The Privy Council Office told us that it has no intelligence collection mandate but is actively involved on a daily basis in the processing of information produced by INSAC" (Auditor General of Canada 2004, 24).

27 Indeed, the Senate committee report went further in underscoring the absence of an intergovernmental architecture for cooperation and the resulting dearth of resources and capacities on the front line (i.e., local-level governments and emergency service providers).

28 Information on the various players and initiatives is available at www.safecanada.ca. Within the realm of cybersecurity, one new initiative created in February 2005 is the Canadian Cyber-Incident Response Centre (http://www.ocipep.gc.ca/ccirc/index_e.asp).

29 The minister is also responsible for a portfolio of six agencies: Canada Border Services Agency, Canada Firearms Centre, Canadian Security Intelligence

Service, Correctional Service of Canada, the National Parole Board, and the Royal Canadian Mounted Police.

30 Source: http://www.cbsa-asfc.gc.ca/newsroom/factsheets/2004/0124passenger-e.html.

31 The privacy commissioner of British Columbia has voiced his concern about surveillance and data-mining efforts, underlining 'function creep' as a serious threat (Loukidelis 2004). He also underscores problems of secrecy and complexity that impede public accountability and raise the prospect of unintended consequences, the latter a prevailing theme of O'Harrow's (2004) documentation of American instances of faulty electronic systems.

32 This measure was largely a reaction to the scandal involving the previous federal privacy commissioner, who was found to be in abuse of expense-reporting guidelines — an episode that triggered a rippling effect across other areas of government. Another example — once again arguably driven by public scandal — is the extension of the auditor general's mandate to include most aspects of federal Crown corporations.

33 To illustrate this point, the first media coverage about Service Canada occurred in early 2005, prior to the budget, when leaked documents were interpreted by the media as a plan to decentralize a significant number of administrative jobs from Ottawa to regional offices. Although some relocation may occur, the significance of the service transformation agenda and its objectives for modernizing government operations was completely missed.

34 Such improvements are the result of the more recent agency status conferred upon what had formerly been the Department of Revenue Canada, a move that, while preserving ministerial accountability for overall activity and reporting to Parliament, accorded higher levels of managerial and operational autonomy to senior managers formerly empowered with direct responsibility for the agency's management. The significance of this shift in the accountability regime is returned to in Chapter 7 in terms of discussions pertaining to the formation of a new Service Canada entity.

35 From an internal memo issued in mid-May 2005 to all HRSDC and SDC employees from the offices of the deputy ministers responsible for both departments.

36 Interviews with several sources close to Service Canada confirm the delays in not only endorsing Service Canada in principle at the cabinet level but also, importantly, sorting out critical structural issues pertaining to the new entity that will shape its authority, mandate, and capacity. The Treasury Board president acknowledged in his address to the May 2005 Lac Carling Congress on E-Government and Service Transformation that focusing cabinet members on service renewal and public sector reform issues is extremely difficult in the best of circumstances (and clearly the precarious standing of

the Liberal minority government in seeking passage of its 2005 budget may be regarded as less than optimal in this regard). With her defection to the Liberals, Belinda Stronach thus became one of two ministers most directly affected by, and responsible for, Service Canada (along with Ken Dryden).

[37] The federal government CIO position has been formally vacant (filled with a person 'acting' in the post) for much of 2004 and 2005. In late 2005, the president of the Treasury Board announced plans for a strategic review of the function and the subbranch within the central agency.

[38] Although it is easy to frame the federal Liberal government difficulties in 2004-05 in the context of the Sponsorship Scandal, much of the research reviewed in Chapter 4 certainly applies to the Canadian context, both provincially and federally, suggesting broader systemic troubles. Moreover, provincial experimentations with democratic reform are growing, a theme examined in the next chapter.

[39] During the first week of July 2005 alone, the Government of Canada's main portal provided more than 200 'what's new' announcements.

[40] The 2005 GOL report offers the following evidence of citizen input: "According to a 2004 on-line survey with the Government of Canada Internet Research Panel, 65% of those surveyed agree GOL will be good value for tax dollars, 68% agree GOL will result in faster service and 70% agree GOL will increase the ability of Canadians to contact government. These very encouraging numbers indicate that GOL is on the right track and responds to citizens' expectations and needs."

[41] The portal—www.consultingcanadians.gc.ca—was created to serve as an online gateway to all federal government consultation initiatives in a manner modelled after a similar initiative in the United Kingdom.

[42] The government has announced the creation of a consultative body, the Cross-Cultural Dialogue, to better engage ethnic communities in policy discussions. As well, a national advisory board is to be appointed, presumably comprised more of experts than of average citizens.

[43] In 2004-05, the House of Commons spent just under $40 million on its Information Services Directorate and nearly $23 million on corporate services, collectively encompassing a budget of roughly $63 million, within which a small portion would be devoted to ICT investments and upgrades, including website management (House of Commons Report to Canadians 2005). Such amounts pale in comparison to the estimated $4 billion in annual ICT spending by the executive branch of the federal government, an estimate that does not include the additional $800 million (multiyear) allocation for GOL and the secure channel.

[44] For these passages and a more detailed discussion of the consultation process, please see the parliamentary subcommittee's reporting of its consultation

activities, available online at http://www.parl.gc.ca/Infocomdoc/37/2/sper/studies/reports/humarp05/08-ch1-e.htm#TOCLink_08_1 (or www.parl.gc.ca/disability to follow more updated links).

Notes to Chapter 6

1. One example is the City of Vancouver (www.vancouver.ca), with three prominent service streams for residents, businesses, and visitors. The City of Toronto's main portal (www.toronto.ca) is organized similarly through four main themes: living, doing business, visiting, and accessing city hall.
2. All of the municipalities surveyed allowed for the completion of one or more of these functions online, although in some cases an additional offline step may be required (e.g., residents wishing to register for recreational classes may first be required to visit or call the recreation centre in order to receive an identification number (PIN) that can subsequently be used to complete selection and confirmation online.
3. An online review of twenty-five of Canada's largest municipal governments revealed that nearly four-fifths allowed for some form of payment online, whereas a similar review of twenty-five smaller municipalities (serving populations of fewer than 10,000) found just one in five doing so.
4. Various research and consultancy commentaries have underlined that in the future many of the present government-run service delivery channels may prove to be redundant or less efficient and effective than delivering services via intermediaries in the private sector or the nonprofit sector. Currently, as discussed in Chapter 1, the contours of choices in this regard remain more centred on government-built capacities or partially outsourced capacities via private sector partnerships that nonetheless remain part of the overall public sector apparatus (particularly in terms of presentation externally, where the visibility of government delivering benefits is a key consideration in this regard).
5. This logic may, at times, be contradictory since geographically large but remote communities with small population bases may stand to benefit from using digital channels of transacting. Yet realizing this benefit requires a reliable broadband infrastructure for the community at large, coupled with municipal capacities to deliver services in such a fashion, and the evidence in North America suggests that in both respects a significant urban-rural gap remains (Hudson 2001; Gerster and Haag 2003).
6. Source: http://www.nlc.org/Newsroom/Nation_s_Cities_Weekly/Weekly_NCW/2005/03/07/2529.cfm.

7   For instance, in Victoria, British Columbia, a citizen can pay a parking ticket only during regular business hours since the telephone agent essentially uses the same online system that is widely available over the Internet (twenty-four hours a day).
8   A good summary of the portal project is available for downloading via the search function of the main City of Calgary portal (www.calgary.ca).
9   Text of the address (delivered on February 8, 2005), retrieved online via the mayor's office via the city's portal: www.calgary.ca.
10 There are at least fifteen active 311 systems in the United States serving nearly one-quarter of the American population.
11 The 311 application outlines three types of activities that can be covered by such a system: (1) service response — road conditions, traffic lights, water main breaks, garbage services, sewer systems, building permits, animal control, water management, noise complaints, transit inquiries, abandoned vehicles, and nonemergency police and fire services; (2) transactions — property taxes, business licensing, ticket payments, recreation facilities; and (3) general information — mayor's office and city council referrals, general service complaints and compliments.
12 Motorola's Customer Service Request system is based on a municipal government-centric model that focuses on capturing citizen service requests; responding to citizen information requests and inquiries; identifying the proper agency and jurisdiction to respond; identifying duplicate and related problems with city infrastructure, urban blight, or needed human services; tracking the resolution and accountability of agencies and departments to provide service delivery within desired service-level goals; and integrating with legacy systems usually required for service request resolution (Motorola briefing information to and provided by the City of Calgary).
13 Further background information on both the initiative and the launch is available via the city's portal: www.calgary.ca.
14 As of June 2005, most of the call centre functions dispersed at one time across business units were consolidated within a central 311 venue, representing approximately sixty percent of total municipal calls. Perhaps the most notable function that remains separate at present is transit as well as the more seasonally sensitive taxation support service. The mayor of Calgary has been clear about the eventual objective of the city: the replacement of blue pages that in the past have comprised over 500 listings and more than 300 unique numbers with two telephone numbers, 911 (for emergency services) and 311 (for everything else).
15 In the case of Calgary, based on its positive experiences with developing a portal (a project realized on time and under budget according to publicly available and council-approved reports), city officials are confident in

their control and review systems that feature ongoing involvement and scrutiny by councillors (not all of whom are likely to be entirely and equally supportive of the project). Similarly, the City of Toronto is currently engaged in an exhaustive planning exercise with key stakeholders both inside and outside the municipality, partially delaying its own 311 implementation to ensure openness and preparedness.

[16] In 2002, the federal government spent an estimated $4 billion on its IT infrastructure (excluding GOL-related projects and new capital projects), whereas the City of Winnipeg's corporate IT budget for the same year was approximately $15 million (once again new capital spending).

[17] Many municipalities have been much quicker and more comfortable seeking outsourced security solutions for online payments and transactions (in comparison to the federal government's building of its own secure channel). The City of Vancouver, for example, partners with Soltrus Technologies for its own direct payment needs (www.soltrus.com — a consortium of Telus, CIBC, and Verisign Inc.). Clearly, however, the scope of service and corresponding risks are far less for a local government than for the federal government.

[18] The fact that a coalition was formed to seek CRTC approval for 311 has spawned a strong intermunicipal emphasis on knowledge sharing and joint promotion. One City of Calgary employee closely involved in the 311 initiative there has been granted a year's leave, with private sector sponsorship, to work with other local governments across the country.

[19] The councils bring together senior public servants in a largely informal manner as intergovernmental relations involving formal agreements remain the domain of central agencies working closely with the executive branches of provincial and federal governments (whereas the representation of municipalities remains a quandary because of their constitutional status as 'creatures of the provinces').

[20] Closing remarks made by a federal government official at the May 2005 Lac Carling congress.

[21] Source: http://www.parl.gc.ca/37/3/parlbus/commbus/senate/com-e/defe-e/rep-e/rep03vol1-e.htm#D.%20Identifying%20the%20Need%20for%20Improved%20National%20Coordination

[22] Source: http://www.cse-cst.gc.ca/en/documents/cpf/hassard_pres.pdf.

[23] The 2005 Lac Carling e-government summit included a well-attended session on Service Canada (reflecting the interest and anticipation across the senior managerial ranks of both the public and the private sectors). It was rather telling that the sharpest questions, bordering on criticism, for Service Canada representatives came from provincial officials engaged in like-minded reform processes within their own jurisdictions who were clearly unaware

ENDNOTES 317

of federal plans and deeply concerned about the lack of alignment and dialogue between both levels of government.

24 This sentiment has been conveyed repeatedly and publicly by Deputy Prime Minister Anne MacLellan and Deputy Minister Margaret Bloodworth. Other senior government officials involved in security matters confirm this intent, insisting that informal dialogues and information exchanges are expanding.

25 Source: http://www.psepc-sppcc.gc.ca/publications/news/2005/20050124_e.asp.

26 Source: http://www.psepc.gc.ca/publications/speeches/20040528_e.asp.

27 Two useful sources provide a detailed examination of these issues: the first a federal task force on local support for homeland security (http://www.homelandsecurity.mo.gov/6-17_TASK-FORCE-REPORT-FINAL.pdf), the second a report prepared by the US mayors' association (http://www.usmayors.org/72ndAnnualMeeting/homelandreport_062504.pdf).

28 Source: http://www.homelandsecurity.state.pa.us/homelandsecurity/cwp/view.asp?a=378&q=127249&homelandsecurityNav=|.

29 Much of this contrast between Canada and the United States is owed to the more direct and extensive links between state and federal levels (notwithstanding debates surrounding jurisdictional boundaries and intrusive actions). State equality within the Senate and the greater activism and collective clout of the fifty states in Washington mean that, paradoxically, there is often less outright resistance to (and more energy dispensed on influencing) the more regular federal government efforts to pass laws and programs contingent on or seeking to shape state action in some manner.

30 Details are available online at http://vancouver.ca/corpsvcs/financial/pdf/COV2004BudgetFinal-web.pdf.

31 Source: http://www.toronto.ca/budget2005/budgetworkbook.htm#.

32 A review of twenty-five of Canada's largest municipalities (generally sophisticated in terms of online presence and services, as reviewed in the previous section) revealed little systemic pursuit of e-democracy (i.e., more direct forms of public involvement via online channels). A small number of municipalities maintain public chat forums (which do not appear to have extensive use or clear links to committee and council mechanisms driving municipal policies and decision-making). One exception to this trend is the City of Toronto's launching of its first-ever e-consultation during the winter and spring of 2005, a formally adopted, multichannel engagement effort tied to attempts to harmonize planning bylaws across all segments of the city (from previously autonomous sections).

33 The emergence of citizen response systems such as 311 has caused some angst among elected officials at the local level who fear that such forms of

direct ties could circumvent their own visibility and utility in the eyes of their electorate.

34 The City of Ottawa is a case in point. Since amalgamation, a council of twenty-one members serves a population base of just over 850,000 citizens (compared with a mix of eighty-four full-time and part-time elected officials across the previous two-tiered system). During the first council term under the city, there was much debate about a decision by councillors to pass a law expanding their office budgets (a move deemed necessary in response to the dramatically higher constituency workloads facing members in their respective wards, many of which dwarf the size of many smaller municipalities across the country.

35 Whereas communication is one way in orientation, focused on crafting a message and informing, consultation is about seeking input and engaging. Each approach requires a different mentality, unique skill sets, and varying uses of technology.

36 Whereas approximately forty percent of local government revenues come from transfers from the central government (including conditional and unconditional transfers), just over fifty percent of revenue comes from direct income taxes levied locally (the remainder comprised of nontax revenue). Accordingly, the largest shares of taxation accrue first to local governments and second to national authorities (McMillan 2004).

37 The second phase of the e-government program is expected to consolidate the shift toward federalism in Italy by bringing local administrations closer to citizens and enterprises, by stimulating local self-government capabilities, and by providing a common strategic vision to all the actors involved in the process. Program investments will focus on building up capabilities at regional and local levels and will be structured around five core policy priorities that will receive central government funding: development of local infrastructure (EUR $61 million); territorial spreading of online services for citizens and business (EUR $86 million); inclusion of small towns and provinces in the e-government project (EUR $25 million); development of e-democracy (EUR $10 million); and promotion of new services for citizens and enterprises (EUR $9 million). The complete strategy is available (in Italian only) online at http://www.cnipa.gov.it/site/_files/e-gov%20Fase%202%2004-11-031.pdf (source: http://europa.eu.int/idabc/en/document/1841/339).

38 Source: http://www.cwf.ca/abcalcwf/doc.nsf/doc/oped_gibbins_032405.cm.

39 This $105 million (multiyear) program is an extremely limited initiative on a national scale (reflecting budgetary pressures from an economic slowdown and a post-September 2001 focus on security; prior estimates

and hopes were axed on a multi-billion dollar initiative to bring broadband to every community in the country). Results of the first round of funding were announced in January 2003, with eighty-nine successful applicants representing roughly 1,149 communities (many applicants covering multiple communities). Successful applicants use the funding for the development of business plans to be submitted to then compete for implementation funding. Details of the program are available online at http://broadband.gc.ca.

[40] The Government of Canada's internal flagship strategy to deliver services online has received nearly $900 million in multiyear funding. Between 1999 and 2003, the federal government spent nearly $800 million in direct advertising and communications. The total funding allocation for broadband initiatives to potentially several thousand rural and remote communities across the country is just over $100 million over several years (unclear in public presentations of the initiative how many years).

[41] In 2005, Belgium formally launched its Belgian Government Interoperability Framework designed to foster more open and shared standards and a digital basis for information sharing and cooperation across all levels of government (http://europa.eu.int/idabc/en/document/4285/194).

[42] The Canadian Policy Research Network (www.cprn.ca) is one such example.

[43] As part of a comparative survey project polling Americans, Mexicans, and Canadians on federalism and different levels and styles of government (in June 2004), only thirty-six percent of Canadians trusted the federal government to do a good job in carrying out its responsibilities (a decline of twelve percent since 2002). In contrast, sixty-nine percent reported trusting their local governments, the gap between federal and local levels growing by thirty-two points since 2002 (www.cric.ca).

[44] This characterization applies more to central Canada than elsewhere since Toronto, Montreal, and Ottawa have all undergone recent amalgamations (whereas Vancouver has not). Elsewhere, many midsized cities, such as Halifax, Winnipeg, and Calgary, have either been amalgamated from previous structures to current unified city models, or this latter model has been in place for some time.

[45] The provincially appointed transition boards in Ontario sought to create municipal governance models that vested high degrees of authority and control in the offices of the mayor and the chief administrative officer respectively. Yet, despite parallels to the control exerted by prime ministers and premiers, differences remain by virtue of the absence of formal parties and the need for strong coalition-building and persuasion to win council approval.

[46] For more information on SSH, please see www.ssha.on.ca.

47 The Province of Ontario stands alone in Canada as the only jurisdiction without a formalized set of subprovincial or regional authorities to govern health care operations and delivery mechanisms (notwithstanding the present changes being discussed, the LHIN model that, as will be discussed, is a response of sorts to modify present arrangements). For a useful discussion of regionalization issues across Canadian provinces, please see www.regionalization.org.

48 This period began in 1995 when a Conservative (right-wing) majority government was elected after ten years of centrist and social democratic rule: emerging from a crippling recession in the early 1990s, the province faced rising debt and deficit levels, and the population proved open to a message of tax cuts and government cutbacks to spur growth and innovation. Ironically, the present Liberal government also inherited a burgeoning fiscal deficit from the Conservatives in 1993 (leading to a tax increase in contravention of its electoral pledge not to do so and ongoing calls to the federal government to address what Ontario and other provinces regard as a structural imbalance in the taxation capacities and spending obligations of different government levels—a theme explored more fully below).

49 As part of a comparative survey project polling Americans, Mexicans, and Canadians on federalism and different levels and styles of government (in June 2004), just thirty-seven percent of Ontario respondents 'trusted' their provincial government to do a good job in carrying out its responsibilities, a decline of fifteen percent since 2002 (www.cric.ca).

50 Selection of the local network CEOs and chairpersons, for example, has been tightly controlled by the province with limited local input (and certainly no democratic mechanism called for to elect subsequent members). The tone of the plan at present is more focused on interstakeholder links and technological interoperability than community dialogue and engagement (although the latter remains an objective to be pursued by the local networks once they are established).

51 This analysis (and the corresponding prescriptions reviewed earlier in the paper) by Abelson and Eyles was made in the context of the most recent national royal commission on health care, and its indictment of existing structures and approaches applies in equal terms to both provincial and federal levels.

52 Source: online correspondence with an FCM official in February 2005.

53 As just one dimension of this challenge, cities will vary greatly in terms of the pressures for linguistic diversity in online operations and channels. Indeed, it is rather surprising to find that Toronto, the world's most ethnically diverse city, functions online exclusively in English, a limitation unlikely to be sustainable if serving the entire population is the goal of the municipal authority (www.toronto.ca).

Notes to Chapter 8

1. However, in early June 2005, Prime Minister Martin addressed the annual meeting of the FCM in St. John's, Newfoundland, and promised municipal leaders 'a seat at the table' in making future decisions impacting local governments. No specific mechanism or time frame was announced, undoubtedly due in part to varying attitudes among provinces about the appropriateness of any such direction.
2. The results of the foreign policy review released in April 2005 are a good example; the issue is discussed more fully in Chapter 10.
3. In the short-term, this problem is only partially alleviated by the fact that Service Canada will essentially begin with a fusion of subentities of two departments (HRSDC and MSC) that were at one time unified within the HRDC. The interrelationships between both departments and their respective ministers and Service Canada will be an important test case for the latter-mentioned entity's capacity to orchestrate change and integrated delivery channels with other units.
4. Savoie puts forth the view that ministerial accountability is often interpreted in an overly encompassing and rigid manner, which he seeks to rectify by invoking a differentiation between answerability and responsibility and underscoring that ministers are responsible only for their direct actions while being answerable for all actions under their authoritative domains.
5. Many of these new directions are transnational, a theme explored fully in the subsequent chapter.
6. Sweden has wrestled with whether such an approach can coexist with e-government's emphasis on government-wide architectures and interoperability. The country undertook an independent study of the Spanish state of Catalonia's e-government approach (viewed as highly centralist) and concluded that it could not be imported into Sweden. While various mechanisms have been introduced to facilitate better cooperative links and knowledge-sharing across the Swedish public sector, the networked, contractual model is viewed as the foundation on which future reforms will be based.
7. In 2003, more than forty percent of all returns were filed online, and CRA is a key partner in federal horizontal processes aimed at both service integration and domestic security by virtue of its information holdings on individuals and organizations.
8. Details of the new Service Canada model are expected by late 2005, but the timing of a pending federal election could provoke a delay. Two major issues—and sources of uncertainty and contention leading up to such announcements—are (1) the degree to which Service Canada will exist as a

stand-alone body from its two parent units, HRSDC and SDC (and if separate what sort of accountability mechanisms will be used), and (2) the manner in which Service Canada will interact with other departments and agencies in pursuing integrative service delivery objectives.

9 Source: http://www.apsc.gov.au/media/briggs120505.htm.

10 There remains much disagreement and complexity in terms of how senior managers and deputy ministers in particular should be held to account. The Aucoin and Jarvis report provides a thoughtful and comprehensive review of both the current Canadian context and comparative experiences from other Westminster countries, and their report is careful to distinguish between traditional line departments (for which deputy ministers should be held publicly to account via Parliament, according to the authors, but only on the strict basis of those duties conferred to them by the Treasury Board and the Public Service Commission) and more autonomous and arm's-length agencies. In the latter case, the authors state that "holding government agencies accountable, however, may require that they be given more independence" (47). My view is that Service Canada requires special status as an autonomous government agency with an executive head (i.e., DM equivalent) directly and publicly accountable for results, not unlike the CRA model with indirect ministerial oversight. However, unlike CRA, such political oversight should be channelled through a single minister rather than a subset of ministers (perhaps a new model of a cabinet committee) that would openly and collectively overview Service Canada and report politically on its collaborative results in achieving new integrative service arrangements.

11 The federal government's GOL External Advisory Panel, for example, released a report in 2004 calling on the prime minister to assume direct leadership for GOL and its subsequent phases of service transformation — arguing that doing so was the only means to ensure the requisite degree of change to overcome systemic barriers and resistance.

12 This point is explored further in the next chapter since it pertains to continental interoperability and the management of bilateral and trilateral governance relations.

13 Indeed, recent lessons from the federal government's secure channel initiative are relevant here since the absence of such action initially has made provinces skeptical about the suitability of the federal initiative in terms of both cost and performance. Rather than collaborating to foster a new intergovernmental platform, the federal government now finds itself 'selling' its product and, in the process, competing against other in-house and market-driven alternatives.

14 E-procurement denotes the use of online channels for issuing tenders and receiving bids: the widening scope of an online marketplace offers more

potential for the purchaser to benefit from competitive cost pressures as well as faster and more effective coordination in managing government-wide supplies (and this logic can extend among several governments, notably at the local level, where individually small municipalities can benefit from such centralized purchasing power).

15 This type of approach is being deployed in an internal and highly secretive fashion between groups of public servants and proposing companies. The logics of openness and citizen engagement embraced throughout this book suggest potential benefits in a more public component to such processes, thereby reducing cynicism and suspicion, building support, and strengthening the prospects for a form of shared accountability to take hold as the companies commit publicly to achieving specific outcomes. At the same time, some process restrictions would be required to respect proprietary knowledge of companies (in increasingly rare instances, however, as the open source movement attests to a world where such restrictions are more the exception than the norm).

16 Ultimately, the choice is between more bodies, smaller and more focused on niche responsibilities, versus fewer bodies with more integrated functions. In choosing the former (as a stronger basis for developing new competencies in a more collaborative and flexible manner), the new partnership entity should likely be separate from CIOB (itself housed within the Treasury Board), and any new shared services entity with internal IT responsibilities across government should likewise be hived away from PWGSC. All of these changes are predominantly incremental insofar as the existing CIO architecture remains in place. As discussed further below, however, an evolution in the CIO function for government may well require its own separation from TBS—into a newly constituted central agency led by a CIO with joint accountability to both the executive and the legislative branches.

17 A more focused PWGSC could then be left primarily with responsibilities for the procurement of all goods and services of a nondigital variety, such as real estate, supplies, services, and so on, as well as ongoing contracting responsibilities that would be shared in some measure with the new IT partnership network working in close association with the CIOB.

18 "Facilities can receive anywhere from one to five stars depending on how they rank compared to other nursing homes. Facilities that fail to meet, or correct upon minimal standards at the time of inspections are placed on a special nursing home guide watch list" (Eggers 2005, 246 note 8).

19 If such a politically neutral and publicly accountable body were created, it could warrant inclusion of what is currently the federal commissioner of information body (a single body at the provincial level encompasses both

information and privacy issues). A key issue for such a new body (as it is for the Office of the Information Commissioner) is a mechanism for financing its operations involving multistakeholder oversight and input rather than direct government control (i.e., TBS currently approves the information commissioner's budget).

[20] The executive (i.e., the government) could well maintain its own CIO position to denote the senior manager in charge of the technological and informational apparatus for departments and agencies: regardless of the name, the function itself would remain essential, and it is not uncommon to have multiple CIOs at different levels in any organization; alternatively, the name of the position at the head of the new authority could be altered.

[21] On this point, there is broad agreement that the legislature requires strengthening to exert greater oversight and contribute better to policy and legislative agendas. Yet the devil, of course, remains in the detail, a point that applies more broadly to much of the discussion of a reformed information infrastructure. This point is returned to in the conclusion, but suffice to say that as important as any reform idea itself is the design process for moving in new directions (a process that must transcend partisan control of the government of the day and comprise a direct role for the citizenry).

[22] For example, the welcome page for the public sector (either federally or provincially) would comprise a politically neutral site with three selections: the governing executive, the legislative branch, and a neutral information venue designed in a manner to facilitate political dialogue on and public understanding of key matters of interest.

Notes to Chapter 9

[1] The Crossing Boundaries initiative has established a national council of elected officials that denotes at least an initial forum for discussing the nexus between digital technologies and democracy (www.crossingboundaries.ca).

[2] Upon arrival at the main Government of Canada webpage (www.gc.ca), users are greeted with a variety of options to link them to the executive branch (primarily to complete services): accordingly, the prime minister is featured prominently. The only links to the executive branch are indirect via 'about government' functions that lead within two to three clicks to the main parliamentary page (www.parl.gc.ca). The prominence of the executive branch (in terms of promotion and coverage as the centrepiece of the federal apparatus online) in cyberspace seems to reflect the views put forth in public administration more generally about executive dominance

over the legislative function. Provinces are similarly organized, and while some provinces do have a direct link from their main splash pages to the legislature across both levels, the much higher degree of resources and sophistication in the executive pages over those of the legislature is evident from even a cursory review.

3   Source: www.eurocities.org.
4   The emphasis within Parliament should be on deliberation and extended debate since even without question period there would be no shortage of opportunities for soundbite statements by politicians to the television media. An online (and renamed) version of question period could feature the submission of written requests, inquiries, and viewpoints (e.g., as privacy commissioners have on key matters), with a corresponding reporting mechanism for the government to respond.
5   See Chapter 4 for a review of the appropriate literature and examples.
6   Such is perhaps the design challenge of digital democracy — since tools such as blogs, while presented as interactive, often begin as a forum for self-expression and then evolve into a venue for limited viewpoints on select issues by individuals or groups more keen to advocate or promote a position than to engage in compromise. Creating a public space for learning is thus the key requirement.
7   In 2004 and 2005, a parliamentary subcommittee began an examination of electoral reform: however, by late 2005, no meaningful progress or discussion had ensued.
8   Countries with the most collaborative styles of decision-making and governing offer important lessons in this regard, including the smaller countries of middle and northern Europe, but this point also applies to the functioning of democratic governance at the European level, where coalitions of like-minded political movements are the norm of parliamentary process and deliberation.
9   Comparisons of public affairs coverage across private and public networks are revealing since current affairs shows offered by the former tend to be more sensationalist and less deliberative than similar offerings on public television: the creation of specialty political channels (e.g., CPAC) denotes an acknowledgement of this dilemma, with the private sector contributing resources in partnership with government to promote civic affairs in a more exclusive venue. Creative solutions and investments are warranted in cyberspace if a space for the public interest is to coexist meaningfully with marketable services and commercial channels. Such is yet another reason why online engagement opportunities such as blogs, chat forums, and the like cannot remain outside the domain of the formal public sector but must be adapted and promoted as a key and legitimate element of

democratic activity, a hugely important issue for younger generations that will determine democracy's future.

10. This point is not to imply that it is wrong to be critical of e-democracy but that, relative to even five years ago, it is extremely difficult to mount a case that formal democratic processes can or should remain disengaged from online life. Even the most casual review of governments around the world reveals a steadily rising set of experiments in online democratic practices and processes such as voting, consulting, and results reporting.

11. Background information on the initiative is available online at http://www.victorianedemocracy.info. However, the inquiry's final report is available via the state's parliamentary website at http://www.parliament.vic.gov.au/sarc/E-Democracy/Final_Report/Final_Report.pdf.

12. Source: http://www.crossingboundaries.ca/.

13. Clearly, however, a forum such as Crossing Boundaries may also benefit from more degrees of freedom than a formalized inquiry or body.

14. The Government of Denmark was one of the first national governments to undertake a broad study of the implications of open source systems, concluding that they should be viewed as an increasingly strategic element of the government's digital infrastructure in moving forward.

15. Source: www.parliament.uk. A notable subportal from this site is the multimedia site Explore Parliament (www.exploreparliament.uk), an initiative of the parliamentary education unit focused on outreach to schools and students.

16. For instance, Stephen Coleman, a leading UK researcher in e-democracy, has been highly critical of the UK Parliament online (in presentations to house committees reviewing such capacities), arguing for a much stronger focus on creating a portal that can serve as a 'gateway' into sites, portals, and blogs of particular interest to young people. He has also been a leading proponent of more advanced and interactive portals for members themselves. Similarly, a volunteer group in the United Kingdom (www.theyworkforyou.com) aims to increase political awareness and understanding online and provide citizens with opportunities to both know more about, and engage with, elected officials.

17. The foundation reports that in 2004 the US Congress received more than 200 million communications, a fourfold increase in less than a decade, attributable mainly to the Internet (www.congressonlineproject.org).

18. This pilot, which has since been disbanded, was created under the auspices of Heritage Canada and Crossing Boundaries, and a report detailing the concept of a digital commons is available via the latter body (www.crossingboundaries.ca).

19. Here the insight of Roger Gibbons, professor, president of the Calgary-based Canada West Foundation, and long-time proponent of western Canadian

interests and devolution, is of interest. He has argued that federalism is out of step with a digital world and that provinces may well lose out in visibility and relative importance to a more activist and national-federal government (2004). In a more recent commentary, in July 2005, he argued that, while Alberta could thrive as an independent state, it is better off abandoning traditional federalist fights and focusing on creating a model of governance success and prosperity within its own borders as much as possible, thereby leading by example. Such sentiments are of relevance not only for Quebec but also for many subnational jurisdictions (e.g., Scotland, Catalonia, the Flemish and Walloon regions of Belgium, etc.) that have traditionally sought either more political autonomy or independence. It may well be that a more virtually connected world will weaken the case for outright separation in such cases, due to both the need for interoperability across many governance levels and the potential for such jurisdictions to simultaneously distinguish themselves online and through their own application of digital technologies. Such federalist trajectories are dependent, of course, not only on the local dynamics of identity and power but also on the responses and choices of more senior-order governments and the relational governance mechanisms developed across all levels.

Notes to Chapter 10

[1] Arar's deportation and torture in Syria are not disputed. However, the reasons for his deportation remain mired in mystery in large part, as discussed in this section, due to national security laws limiting the divulging of government documents in public. Arar's camp claims that the basis for his ordeal was groundless — perhaps involving misinformation gathered within public authorities in Canada and then shared with US officials. The Canadian government appointed the Commission of Inquiry to independently examine the events and actions of the case involving Canadian officials and authorities.

[2] Specifically, by agreeing to the government's wishes, the government, in turn, withdrew its legal challenge from the Federal Court of Canada to keep the information in question secret (the information pertains to testimony of various government officials made in camera: the commission maintained its view that the information should be released and emphasized that it would seek public disclosure at a time and in a manner that would not interfere with the inquiry. Details of the agreement, along with all proceedings of the inquiry, may be viewed online at www.ararcommission.ca).

[3] The issue was triggered by the proposal of the BC government to contract out the administration of the provincial public health insurance program.

In the summer of 2003, the BC Ministry of Health put out a request for proposals seeking a private partner to take over the administration of the BC Medical Services Plan (MSP) and Pharmacare. The province selected Maximus, a private American company with a Canadian subsidiary. The British Columbia Government Employees' Union (BCGEU) then mounted a court challenge to this contracting out. The challenge is a judicial review of the province's decision to contract out based on two grounds: (1) contracting out contravenes the 'public administration' requirement of the Canada Health Act; (2) contracting out violates the BC Freedom of Information and Protection of Privacy Act (FOIPPA). The second ground served as the entry way for the BC privacy commissioner to examine the case.

4   Canadian media coverage of US government action and debate is extensive, particularly in light of the sort of issues examined in this section. Moreover, many Canadian viewers regularly watch cable news channels and public television programming from American broadcasters that often feature substantial coverage of American politics and policy.

5   The figures are results of a study undertaken by InfoAmericas, a market intelligence, research, and consultancy firm, and reported by the Government of Canada online at http://www.dfait-maeci.gc.ca/can-am/docs/active/img001398_1.pdf.

6   Countries exempt from this new policy include Australia, Brunei, Ireland, New Zealand, Singapore, and the United Kingdom (as well as its territories).

7   There appeared to be some confusion over the precise specifications of the new policy, since 'passport' was not specified (and the president acknowledged the potential for some flexibility in other options provided that security considerations are met). Importantly, in Canada, no other options present themselves, although there are widening discussions of an exploratory nature across both countries about a new form of interoperable continental identification (although one presumes a Canadian passport would be a likely prerequisite for qualification). Accordingly, the Passport Office in Canada is under growing strain to not only keep up with rising demand but also shift its focus from a near-exclusive service orientation to that of security as well (Auditor General of Canada 2005).

8   In 2000, many Mexicans—led by President Fox—hailed the arrival of President Bush as a major turning point in their bilateral relationship (indeed, the American president would break with the tradition of making Canada his first official foreign visit, opting for Mexico instead). Hopes were high for a much more open relationship, particularly with respect to immigration controls. Obviously, 9/11 dramatically altered this dynamic, reinforcing a similar focus on separate bilateral security agendas aimed north and south

(thus, a smart border declaration similar to the Canadian model was also forged with Mexico, although concerns about illegal border crossings have not diminished as a result).

9. Canadian representative John Manley was formerly deputy prime minister and finance minister and the person who negotiated the smart border accord with then-US Secretary Tom Ridge in the aftermath of 9/11. The trilateral commission made six key recommendations covering new institutions, a unified border action plan, a common external tariff, an economic stimulus focus for Mexico, a continental energy and national resource strategy, and deepened educational ties.

10. This view was put forth by former Canadian ambassador to the United States, Allan Gotleib, in his critique of the North American partnership (in the *Globe and Mail* of April 13, 2005). He questioned the new initiative's seriousness in light of numerous generalities and shortcomings, notably an absence of a central authority in each country assigned with responsibility for moving forward and the refusal of the three leaders to regularize their annual meeting (as a basis for monitoring performance and updating action).

11. In 2005, a prominent citizens' organization, the Council of Canadians, organized a cross-country citizens' panel on Canada-US relations, a set of public consultation meetings designed to 'raise awareness of the dangers of the push from Canadian corporate lobby groups for more economic and social integration with the United States.'

12. Within Canada, the auditor general brought to light this danger in her 2005 audit of national security, lamenting her lack of authority over information pertaining to new passenger screening systems installed in Canadian airports (the results of the testing of this new equipment were withheld under national security protecting such information as sensitive and therefore not privy to disclosure).

13. The mandate of the National Security Committee of Parliamentarians (as proposed in March 2005, subject to legislative adoption) would be to review the security and intelligence apparatus of departments and agencies engaged in security and intelligence activities to fulfill their responsibilities. The committee would submit reports to the prime minister, who in turn would table them in Parliament (the prerogative of the prime minister to censor or modify these reports is unclear).

14. Along with the parliamentary committee are three existing review bodies: the Security Intelligence Review Committee (an independent body reporting to Parliament on the Canadian Security Intelligence Service); the Communications Security Establishment (CSE) Commissioner (reviewing the CSE); and the Commission for Public Complaints against the RCMP. The last office in particular has been criticized for lacking authority — since it operates

within the RCMP (much of the criticism has come from the commissioner herself), and this position is subject to review by the Arar Commission (due to RCMP involvement in domestic anti-terrorism activity).

[15] American congressional committees have oversight duties over federal law enforcement and intelligence services (i.e., authority to investigate action, subpoena witnesses, set budgets and structures, etc., albeit often in a shared manner with many bodies). Conversely, in Canada, the only political 'oversight' is the minister responsible (who in turn must also remain at arm's length from direct involvement) and the new parliamentary committee is explicitly a 'review' mechanism. Such distinctions reflect both differences between Canadian and US government structures (parliamentary versus presidential and congressional) and the complexities of balancing political accountability with the independence of law enforcement officials.

[16] The only security-related agency not under the purview of this minister is the Communications Security Establishment (CSE), the national cryptologic agency (providing two key services: foreign signals intelligence in support of defence and foreign policy, and protection of electronic information and communication). The minister of national defence is accountable to cabinet and to Parliament for all of CSE's activities. The minister also provides direction to CSE concerning the performance of its functions. The minister of national defence is supported by two deputy ministers. The national security advisor is accountable for CSE's policy and operations, while the deputy minister of national defence is accountable for administrative matters pertaining to CSE.

[17] Reporting Economic Crime Online (RECOL) "is an initiative that involves an integrated partnership between International, Federal and Provincial Law Enforcement agencies, as well as, with regulators and private commercial organizations that have a legitimate investigative interest in receiving a copy of complaints of economic crime" (www.recol.ca).

[18] Despite being billed as a policy of selective resources and stronger focus, the breadth of the review paper across four main segments—diplomacy, defence, development, and commerce—seems to leave little unattended. Based upon the overriding commitment to address both continental and global agendas, the following countries and regions are mentioned as strategic targets for assistance or partnerships: South Africa, Mexico, South Korea, India, Brazil, China, Japan, the Middle East, and a variety of regional and global organizations. It is also notable that the Internet and ICTs generally are almost without mention in the entire strategic document (a point returned to below), save a pledge to create a new portal for Canadians to access international volunteer opportunities.

References

Aart Scholte, J. 2002. "Civil Society and Governance." In *Towards a Global Polity*, ed. M. Ougaard and R. Higgott, 145-65. London: Routledge.
Abelson, J., and J. Eyles. 2002. "Public Participation and Citizen Governance in the Canadian Health System." Discussion Paper 7, Commission on the Future of Health Care in Canada. www.hc-sc.gc.ca/english/pdf/romanow/pdfs/Abelson_E.pdf.
Accenture Consulting. 2004. "E-Government Leadership: Engaging the Customer." www.accenture.com.
Agranoff, R., and M. McGuire. 2003. *Collaborative Public Management: New Strategies for Local Governments*. Washington: Georgetown University Press.
Allen, B.A., and J. Roy. 2002. "E-Governance and the Partnership Imperative." *Optimum Online* 32 (4): 7-12.
Allen, B.A., L. Juillet, G. Paquet, and J. Roy. 2001. "E-Government in Canada: People, Partnerships, and Prospects." *Government Information Quarterly* 18 (2): 93-104.
Allen, B.A., G. Paquet, L. Juillet, and J. Roy. 2005a. "E-Government as Collaborative Governance: Structural, Accountability, and Cultural Reform." In *Practising E-Government: A Global Perspective*, ed. M. Khosrow-Pour, 1-15. Hershey: Idea Group Publishing.
—. 2005b. "E-Government and Private-Public Partnerships: Relational Challenges and Strategic Directions." In *Practising E-Government: A Global Perspective*, ed. M. Khosrow-Pour, 364-82. Hershey: Idea Group Publishing.
Allman, W., and D. Barrette. 2004. *Opening Submission of the International Civil Liberties Monitoring Group*. Ottawa: Commission of Inquiry into the Actions of Canadian Officials in Relation to Maher Arar.
Andal-Ancion, A., P. Cartwright, and G.S. Yip. 2003. "The Digital Transformation of Traditional Business." *MIT Sloan Management Review* 44 (4): 34-41.
Andison, S. 2004. "IT Procurement Chapter: E-BC Strategic Plan." http://www.cio.gov.bc.ca/ebc/discussion/SRmodel_ver7_Final.pdf.
Andrew, C. 2002. *What Is the Municipal Potential?* Regina: Saskatchewan Institute of Public Policy.

Andrews, R., and R. Cowell. 2005. *Civic Education and Local Government: A Literature Review*. Report prepared by the Centre for Local and Regional Government Research, Cardiff University, for the Office of the Deputy Prime Minister. London: Government of Great Britain.

Aucoin, P., and M.D. Jarvis. 2005. *Modernizing Government Accountability: A Framework for Reform*. Ottawa: Canada School of Public Service.

Aucoin, P., J. Smith, and G. Dinsdale. 2004. *Responsible Government: Clarifying Essentials, Dispelling Myths, and Exploring Change*. Ottawa: Canada School of Public Service.

Auditor General of Canada. 2003. *Information Technology: Government Online*. Ottawa: Government of Canada. www.oag-bvg.gc.ca.

———. 2004. *National Security in Canada: The 2001 Anti-Terrorism Initiative*. Ottawa: Government of Canada. www.oag-bvg.gc.ca.

———. 2005a. *Information Technology Security*. Ottawa: Government of Canada. www.oag-bvg.gc.ca.

———. 2005b. *Passport Services*. Ottawa: Government of Canada. www.oag-bvg.gc.ca.

Bailey, D. 2003. "Globalisation, Regions, and Cluster Policies: The Case of the Rover Task Force." *Policy Studies* 24 (2-3): 67-83.

Bakvis, H., and L. Juillet. 2004. *The Horizontal Challenge: Line Departments, Central Agencies, and Leadership*. Ottawa: Canada School of Public Service.

Barber, J. 1991. *The Prime Minister since 1945*. Oxford: Basil Blackwell.

Barnet, R. 1997. "Subsidiarity, Enabling Government, and Local Governance." In *Urban Governance and Finance: A Question of Who Does What*, ed. H.R. Hobson and F. St-Hilaire, 62-79. Montreal: Institute of Research on Public Policy.

Barney, D. 2000. *Prometheus Wired: The Hope for Democracy in the Age of Network Technology*. Vancouver: UBC Press.

Barry, D. 2004. "Managing Canada-US Relations in the Post-9/11 Era: Do We Need a Big Idea?" Policy Paper on the Americas V XIV 11, Center for Strategic and International Studies.

Batini, C., E. Cappadozzim, M. Mecella, and M. Talamo. 2002. "Cooperative Architectures." In *Advances in Digital Government: Technology, Human Factors, and Policy*, ed. W.J. McIver and A.K. Elmagarmid, 53-68. Boston: Kluwer Academic Publishers.

Bellamy, C., 6 Perri, and C. Raab. 2005. "Joined Up Government and Privacy in the United Kingdom: Managing Tensions between Data Protection and Social Policy. Part II." *Public Administration* 83 (2): 395-415.

Bennett, C.J., and C. Raab. 2003. *The Governance of Privacy*. Burlington: Ashgate.

Bloomfield, S. 2004. "The Role of the Privacy Impact Assessment." Office of the Privacy Commissioner of Canada, Ottawa. http://www.privcom.gc.ca/speech/2004/sp-d_040310_e.asp.

Borins, S. 2004. "A Holistic View of Public Sector Information Technology." *Journal of E-Government* 1 (2): 3-29.

Bots, P.W.G. 2003. "Estimating the Added Value of Data Mining: A Study of the Dutch Internal Revenue Service." *International Journal of Technology, Policy, and Management* 3 (3-4): 380-95.

Bradford, N. 2004. "Place Matters and Multi-Level Governance: Perspectives on a New Urban Policy Paradigm." *Policy Options* 25 (2): 39-44.

Brown, D. 2005. *Vendor Engagement Strategy Consultation: Final Report.* Ottawa: Public Policy Forum.

Brown, M., ed. 2003. *Grave New World: Security Challenges in the 21st Century.* Washington, DC: Georgetown University Press.

Bryant, A., and B. Colledge. 2002. "Trust in Electronic Commerce Business Relationships." *Journal of Electronic Commerce Research* 32: 32-39.

Burnham, D. 1980. *The Rise of the Computer State.* New York: Random House.

Cairncross, F. 2002. *The Company of the Future.* Cambridge, MA: Harvard Business School Press.

Cameron, D. 2005. "Koreans Cybertrip to a Tailor Made World." *The Age* [Melbourne], May 9. http://theage.com.au/articles/2005/05/06/1115092684512.html?oneclick=true.

Camp, J. 2003. *Identity in Digital Government.* Research workshop report, sponsored by the National Science Foundation and Kennedy School of Government.

Canadian Policy Research Network. 2004. "Citizens' Dialogue on the Ontario Budget Strategy 2004-2008." Ottawa. www.cprn.com.

Castells, M. 1996. *The Rise of the Network Society.* Oxford: Blackwell.

Center for Digital Government. 2004. "Open Source – Open Government: An Executive Guide to Making Strategic Decisions about Open Source Software in Public Sector Service Delivery." www.centerdigitalgov.com.

Charih, M., and J. Robert. 2004. "Government On-Line in the Federal Government of Canada: The Organizational Issues." *International Review of Administrative Sciences* 70: 373-84.

Chen, W., and B. Wellman. 2003. "Charting and Bridging Digital Divides: Comparing Socio-Economic, Gender, Life Stage, and Rural–Urban Internet Access in Eight Countries." AMD Global Consumer Advisory Board. www.amdgcab.org.

Chen, Y.C., and J. Gant. 2001. "Transforming Local E-Government Services: The Use of Application Service Providers." *Government Information Quarterly* 18 (4): 343-55.

Cherny, A. 2000. *The Next Deal: The Future of Public Life in the Information Age.* New York: Basic Books.

Clarke, R. 2004. "The Internet and Democracy." In *Future Challenges for E-Government,* ed. J. Halligan and T. Moore, 47-63. Canberra: Government of Australia.

Clifford, M. 2004. *Identifying and Exploring Security Essentials.* Upper Saddle River, NJ: Pearson Prentice Hall.

Coe, A. 2004. *Government Online in Canada: Innovation and Accountability in 21st Century Government.* Cambridge, MA: Kennedy School of Government.

Coe, A., G. Paquet, and J. Roy. 2001. "E-Governance and Smart Communities: A Social Learning Challenge." *Social Science Computer Review* 19 (1): 80-93.

Coglianese, C. 2000. "The Design of International Institutions." In *Governance in a Globalizing World,* ed. J.S. Nye and J.D. Donahue. Cambridge, MA: Brookings Institution Press.

Coleman, S. 2003. "The Future of the Internet and Democracy beyond Metaphors, towards Policy." In *Promise and Problems of E-Democracy: Challenges on Online Citizen Engagement,* ed. OECD, 143-60. Paris: E-Government Project.

Coleman, S., and D. Norris. 2005. "A New Agenda for E-Democracy." *International Journal of Electronic Government Research* 1 (3): 69-82.

Commission on Legislative Democracy. 2004. *New Directions: Public Involvement and Citizen Engagement.* Fredericton: Province of New Brunswick.

Corbett, M.A., and J. Roy. 2003. "E-Government and Strategic Outsourcing: Opportunities and Challenges for Public Sector Leaders." *CIO Government's Review,* July: 8-13.

Courchene, T.J. 2005. "'E-the-People': Reflections on Citizen Power in the Information Age." *Policy Options* 26 (3): 43-50.

Courtois, B. 2005. "The US Patriot Act and the Privacy of Canadians." Text of paper presented to the conference Privacy and Security—Synergies in an E-Society, Victoria, BC, February 11.

Culbertson, S. 2004. "Building E-Government: Organizational and Cultural Change in Public Administrations." In *E-Government Reconsidered: Renewal of Governance for the Knowledge Age,* ed. L. Oliver and L. Sanders, 59-78. Regina: Canadian Plains Research Center.

———. 2005. "E-Government and Organizational Change." In *Practising E-Government: A Global Perspective,* ed. M. Khosrow-Pour. Hershey: Idea Group Publishing.

Curtin, G., M.H. Sommer, and V. Vis-Sommer, eds. 2003. *The World of E-Government.* New York: Haworth Press.

Dawes, S. 2002. *The Future of E-Government.* Albany: Center for Technology in Government.

De Rosa, M. 2003. "Privacy in the Age of Terror." *Washington Quarterly* 26 (3): 27-41.

Denning, D. 2003. "Information Technology and Security." In *Grave New World: Security Challenges in the 21st Century*, ed. M. Brown, 47-61. Washington, DC: Georgetown University Press.

Drake, W.J. 2004. "ICT Global Governance and the Public Interest: Infrastructure Issues." Memo 3 for the Social Science Research Council's Research Network on IT and Governance.

Drezner, D. 2004. "The Global Governance of the Internet: Bringing the State Back In." *Political Science Quarterly* 119: 477-98.

Dunleavy, P., H. Margetts, S. Bastow, and J. Tinkler. 2003. "E-Government and Policy Innovation in Seven Liberal Democracies." Paper presented at the Political Studies Association Annual Conference, Leicester University, April 15-17.

Dutil, P., J. Langford, and J. Roy. 2005. *E-Government and Service Transformation Relationships between Government and Industry: Developing Best Practices*. New Directions Series. Toronto: Institute of Public Administration in Canada.

Dutta, A., and K. McCrohan. 2002. "Management's Role in Information Security in a Cyber Economy." *California Management Review* 45 (1): 67-87.

Dwyer, P. 2004. "The Rise of Transparency Networks: A New Dynamic for Inclusive Government." In *Future Challenges for E-Government*, ed. J. Halligan and T. Moore, 114-27. Canberra: Government of Australia.

Edelman Corporation. 2005. *Edelman Annual Trust Barometer*. www.edelman.com.

Edwards, A.R. 2004. "The Moderator in Government-Initiated Internet Discussions: Facilitator or Source of Bias?" In *eTransformation in Governance: New Directions in Government and Politics*, ed. M. Malkia, A. Anttiroiko, and R. Savolainen, 150-68. London: Idea Group Publishing.

Eger, J. 1997. "Cyberspace and Cyberplace: Building Smart Communities of Tomorrow." *San Diego Union-Tribune*, October 26.

Eggers, W. 2005. *Government 2.0: Using Technology to Improve Education, Cut Red Tape, Reduce Gridlock, and Enhance Democracy*. New York: Rowman and Littlefield Publishers.

E-Government Policy Network, Government of Canada. 2004. "Transforming Government and Governance for the 21st Century: A Conceptual Framework." In *E-Government Reconsidered: Renewal of Governance for the Knowledge Age*, ed. L. Oliver and L. Sanders, 3-32. Regina: Canadian Plains Research Center.

English, J., and E. Lindquist. 1998. "Performance Management: Linking Results to Public Debate." In *New Directions*. Toronto: IPAC New Directions Series. http://www.ipac.ca/files/newdirect2.pdf.

Entwistle, T., and S. Martin, 2005. "From Competition to Collaboration in Public Service Delivery: A New Agenda for Research." *Public Administration* 83 (1): 233-42.

Essex, L., and M. Kusy. 1999. *Fast Forward Leadership*. London: Prentice Hall.
Evans, K.G. 2002. "Virtual Dialogue and Democratic Community." *Transformative Power of Dialogue* 12: 157-77.
Ferry, S. 2003. "Jane Fountain: Examining the Flow." *Government Technology* August. www.govtech.net.
Fletcher, P. 2004. "Portals and Policy: Implications of Electronic Access to U.S. Federal Government Information and Services." In *Digital Government: Principles and Best Practises*, ed. A. Pavlichev and G.D. Garson, 52-62. Hershey: Idea Group Publishing.
Fountain, J.E. 2001. *Building the Virtual State: Information Technology and Institutional Change*. Washington, DC: Brookings Institution Press.
———. 2002. "Electronic Government and Electronic Civics." Forthcoming chapter in *Encyclopaedia of Community*, ed. B. Wellman. Thousand Oaks, CA: Sage Publications.
———. 2004. "Digital Government and Public Health." *Public Health Research, Practice, and Policy* 1 (4): 1-5.
Fukuyama, F. 2004. *State-Building: Governance and World Order in the 21st Century*. Ithaca: Cornell University Press.
Galindo, F. 2002. "E-Government Trust Providers." In *E-Government: Design, Applications, and Management*, ed. A. Gronlund, 121-50. Hershey: Idea Group Publishing.
Garson, D., ed. 2004. *Digital Government: Principles and Best Practices*. Hershey: Idea Group Publishing.
Gasco, M. 2003. "New Technologies and Institutional Change in Public Administration." *Social Science Computer Review* 21 (1): 6-14.
Gath, S. 2004. "Electronics Health Records for Australia: Some Legal and Policy Issues." In *Future Challenges for E-Government*, ed. J. Halligan and T. Moore, 6-17. Canberra: Government of Australia.
Gattinger, M. 1998. "Local Governments On-Line: How Are They Doing It and What Does It Mean?" In *Citizen Engagement: Lessons in Participation from Local Government*, ed. Katherine A. Graham and Susan D. Phillips, 200-22. Monograph of Canadian Public Administration 22. Toronto: Institute of Public Administration of Canada.
Geiselhart, K. 2004. "Digital Government and Citizen Participation Internationally." In *Digital Government: Principles and Best Practices*, ed. A. Pavlichev and G.D. Garson, 320-43. Hershey: Idea Group Publishing.
Gibbons, R. 2004. "Federalism and the Challenge of Electronic Portals." In *E-Government Reconsidered: Renewal of Governance for the Knowledge Age*, ed. L. Oliver and L. Sanders, 33-42. Regina: Canadian Plains Research Center.
Gibson, R. 2002. "Elections Online: Assessing Internet Voting in Light of the Arizona Democratic Primary." *Political Science Quarterly* 116 (4): 561-83.

Goldsmith, S., and W.D. Eggers. 2004. *Governing by Networks: The New Shape of the Public Sector.* Washington: Brookings Institution Press.

Good, D. 2003. *The Politics of Public Management.* Toronto: University of Toronto Press.

Government of British Columbia. 2004a. *The Evolution of the CIO: From Technician to Executive Strategist.* Victoria: Office of the Chief Information Officer.

———. 2004b. *E-Government Plan 2004-2007.* Victoria: Office of the Chief Information Officer.

Government of Canada. 2005. "A Role of Pride and Influence in the World — Overview: Canada's Foreign Policy Review." www.dfait.gc.ca.

Government of Ontario. 2005. "E-Government." Office of the Corporate Chief Information Officer. www.cio.gov.on.ca.

Grabbe, H. 2005. "Conclusion: The Politics of Freedom, Security, and Justice in the Enlarging EU." In *The Area of Freedom, Security, and Justice in the Enlarged Europe,* ed. K. Henderson, 161-67. New York: Palgrave Macmillan.

Graham, K.A., and S.D. Phillips. 1998. *Citizen Engagement: Lessons in Participation from Local Government.* Monograph 22. Toronto: IPAC.

Gronlund, A. 2003. "Emerging Electronic Infrastructures: Exploring Democratic Components." *Social Science Computer Review* 21 (1): 55-72.

Hale, C. 2002. "Cybercrime: Facts and Figures Concerning This Global Dilemma." *Crime and Justice International* 18 (5-6): 24-26.

Halligan, J., and T. Moore, eds. 2004. *Future Challenges for E-Government.* Canberra: Government of Australia.

Hampton, K., and B. Wellman. 2003. "Neighboring in Netville: How the Internet Supports Community and Social Capital in a Wired Suburb." *City and Community* 2 (4): 277-98.

Hansard Society. 2004. "Political Blogs: Craze or Convention?" http://www.hansardsociety.org.uk/assets/Final_Blog_Report_.pdf.

Hansen, H.K., and D.S. Salskov-Iversen. 2003. "Remodelling the Transnational Political Realm: Partnerships, Benchmarking Schemes, and the Digitalization of Governance." Paper presented to the European Group of Public Administration Annual Conference, forthcoming in *Journal of International Studies.*

Hart-Teeter. 2003. *The New E-Government Equation: Ease, Engagement, Privacy, and Protection.* Washington, DC: Council for Excellence in Government.

———. 2004. *From the Home Front to the Front Lines: America Speaks Out about Homeland Security.* Washington, DC: Council for Excellence in Government.

Hayden, P. 2005. *Cosmopolitan Global Politics.* Burlington: Ashgate.

Health Care Network of Southeastern Ontario. 2005. "Southeastern Ontario Information Technology and Communications Strategy, 2005-09." www.seohealthnet.com.

Heeks, R., ed. 1999. *Reinventing Government in the Information Age: International Practice in IT-Enabled Public Sector Reform.* London: Routledge.

Heeks, R., and A. Davies. 1999. "Different Approaches to Information Age Reform." In *Reinventing Government in the Information Age: International Practice in IT-Enabled Public Sector Reform,* ed. R. Heeks, 22-48. London: Routledge.

Henrich, V.C., and A.N. Link. 2003. "Deploying Homeland Security Technology." *Journal of Technology Transfer* 28: 363-68.

Hermida, A. 2005. "The US Has Got an Image Problem When It Comes to the Internet." *BBC News Website,* October 11. http://news.bbc.co.uk/2/hi/technology/4327928.stm.

Heymann, P.B. 2001-02. "Dealing with Terrorism: An Overview." *International Security* 26 (3): 24-38.

Ho, A.T. 2002. "Reinventing Local Governments and the E-Government Initiative." *Public Administration Review* 62 (4): 434-44.

Hodges, S., and D. McFarlane. 2004. "RFID: The Concept and the Impact." In *The Security Economy,* ed. OECD. Paris: OECD.

Holden, S. 2004. *Understanding Electronic Signatures: The Keys to E-Government.* Washington, DC: IBM Center for the Business of Government.

Hoops, J. 2004. "The De-Humanized Employee." *CIO,* December, http://www.cio.com/archive/120104/keynote.html.

Howe, P., R. Johnston, and A. Blais, eds. 2005. *Strengthening Canadian Democracy.* Montreal: IRPP.

Hozler, M., L. Hu, and S. Song. 2004. "Digital Government and Citizen Participation in the United States." In *Digital Government: Principles and Best Practices,* ed. A. Pavlichev and G.D. Garson, 306-19. Hershey: Idea Group Publishing.

Hubbard, R., and G. Paquet. 2005. "The Quail Enigma." *Optimum Online* 35 (3): 12-22.

Hudson, H. 2001. "Access to the Digital Economy: Issues for Rural and Developing Regions." Working paper, Telecommunications Management and Policy Program, University of San Francisco.

Hunold, C. 2001. "Corporatism, Pluralism, and Democracy: Toward A Deliberative Theory of Bureaucratic Accountability." *Governance: An International Journal of Policy and Administration* 14 (2): 151-67.

Huysman, M., and V. Wulf. 2005. "The Role of Information Technology in Building and Sustaining the Relational Base of Communities." *Information Society* 21: 81-89.

ICCS. 2003. "Integrated Service Delivery: A Critical Analysis Report." Sponsored by the Public Sector Service Delivery Council. www.iccs-isac.org.

ITAC. 2004. "Task Force on Large IT Projects." Presentation to the Government of Ontario Sponsored Review Panel, Ottawa. www.itac.ca.

Jaeger, P.T. 2002. "Constitutional Principles and E-Government: An Opinion about Possible Effects of Federalism and the Separation of Powers on E-Government Policies." *Government Information Quarterly* 19: 357-68.

Jelich, H., R. Poupart, R. Austin, and J. Roy. 2000. "Partnership-Based Governance: Lessons from IT Management." *Optimum* 30 (1): 49-54.

Jensen, J.L. 2003. "Public Spheres on the Internet: Anarchic or Government Sponsored — A Comparison." *Scandinavian Political Studies* 26 (4): 349-74.

Jordan, M. 1999. "Ontario's Integrated Justice Project: Profile of a Complex Partnership Agreement." *Canadian Public Administration/Administration publique du Canada* 42 (1): 26-41.

Joshi, J.B.D., A. Ghafoor, and W.G. Aref. 2002. "Security and Privacy Challenges of a Digital Government." In *Advances in Digital Government: Technology, Human Factors, and Policy*, ed. W.J. McIver and A.K. Elmagarmid, 121-36. Boston: Kluwer Academic Publishers.

Juillet, L., and G. Paquet. 2002. "The Neurotic State." In *How Ottawa Spends 2002-2003: The Security After-Math and National Priorities*, ed. G.B. Doern, 69-87. Don Mills, ON: Oxford University Press.

Kamarck, E.C. 2004. "Applying 21st-Century Government to the Challenge of Homeland Security." In *Collaboration: Using Networks and Partnerships*, ed. J.M. Kamensky and T. Burlin, 75-93. Lanham, MD: Rowman and Littlefield Publishers.

Karakaya, R. 2003. "The Use of the Internet for Citizen Participation: Enhancing Democratic Local Governance?" Paper presented to the Political Studies Association Annual Conference, University of Leicester, April 15-17.

Kearns, I. 2004. "Public Value and Electronic Service Delivery: The UK Experience." In *E-Government Reconsidered: Renewal of Governance for the Knowledge Age*, ed. L. Oliver and L. Sanders. Regina: Canadian Plains Research Center.

Kernaghan, K. 2005. "Moving toward the Virtual State: Integrating Services and Service Channels for Citizen-Centred Service Delivery." *International Review of Administrative Sciences* 71 (1): forthcoming.

Kernaghan, K., and J. Gunraj. 2004. "Integrating Information Technology into Public Administration: Concepts and Practical Considerations." *Canadian Public Administration* 47 (4): 525-546.

Kieley, B., G. Lane, G. Paquet, and J. Roy. 2002. "E-Government in Canada: Services Online or Public Service Renewal?" In *E-Government: Design, Applications, and Management*, ed. A. Gronlund, 340-55. Burlington: Idea Group Publishing.

Kim, S., and H. Lee. 2004. "Organizational Factors Affecting Knowledge Sharing Capabilities in E-Government: An Empirical Study." In *KMGov 2004, LNAI 3035*, ed. M.A. Wimmer, 281-93. Laxenburg: International Federation for Information Processing.

Koch, C. 2003. "Your Open Source Plan." *CIO*, March 15. www.cio.com.
———. 2005. "A New Blueprint for the Enterprise." *CIO*, March 1. www.cio.com.
Kossick, R. 2004. *The Role of Information and Communication Technology in Strengthening Citizen Participation and Shaping Democracy: An Analysis of Mexico's Initial Experience and Pending Challenges*. New York: United Nations Telecommunications Research Program.
Kotkin, J. 2000. *The New Geography: How the Digital Revolution Is Reshaping the American Landscape*. New York: Random House.
Kraemer, K., and J.L. King. 2003. *Information Technology and Administrative Reform: Will the Time after E-Government Be Different?* Irvine: Center for Research on Information Technology and Organizations.
Kruger, E., M. Mulder, and B. Korenic. 2004. "Canada after 11 September: Measures and 'Preferred' Immigrants." *Mediterranean Quarterly* 15 (4): 72-87.
Langford, J. 2002. "The Management of Public-Private Partnerships." In *New Players, Partners, and Processes: A Public Sector without Boundaries?*, ed. M. Edwards and J. Langford. Canberra: National Institute for Governance.
Langford, J., and Y. Harrison. 2001. "Partnering for E-Government: Challenges for Public Administrators." *Canadian Public Administration* 44 (4): 393-416.
Langford, J., and J. Roy. 2005. "E-Government and Public-Private Partnerships in Canada: When Failure Is No Longer an Option." *International Journal of Electronic Business*, forthcoming.
———. 2006. "E-Government, Service Transformation, and Procurement Reform: The Evolution of Industry–Government Relations in Canada." In *The Encyclopedia of Digital Government*, ed. A. Anttiroiko, forthcoming.
Lawther, W. 2002. *Contracting for the 21st Century: A Partnership Model*. Washington, DC: PriceWaterhouseCoopers Endowment for the Business of Government.
Lee, M. 2004. *E-Reporting: Strengthening Democratic Accountability*. Washington, DC: IBM Center for the Business of Government.
Leitner, C. 2004. "eGovernment in Europe: The State of Affairs." *Eipascope* 1. www.eipa.nl.
Lenihan, D. 2002. *E-Government: The Message to Politicians*. Ottawa: Centre for Collaborative Government.
Lenihan, D., T. Valeri, and D. Hume. 2002. *Information as a Public Resource: Leading Canadians into the Information Age*. Ottawa: Centre for Collaborative Government.
Lenihan, D., and A. Hanna. 2002. *E-Government: The Municipal Experience*. Ottawa: Centre for Collaborative Government.

Lightman, A. 2002. "The World Is Too Much with Me: Finding Private Space in the Wired World." The Hart House Lectures, University of Toronto, March.

Lindquist, E. 2005. "Strategy, Capacity, and Horizontal Governance." *Optimum Online* 34 (4).

Lodge, J. 2003. "Toward an E-Commonwealth? A Tool for Peace and Democracy?" *Round Table* 372: 609-21.

Loukidelis, D. 2004. "Identity, Privacy, Security: Can Technology Really Reconcile Them?" Address by Privacy Commissioner of British Columbia, Victoria. www.oipc.bc.ca.

Lukensmeyer, C.J., and L.H. Torres. 2003. "Common Ground Development: Redefining Participatory, Democratic, Economic Development." *Northeast Journal of Economic Development* Autumn: 5-23.

Lyon, D. 2004. "Surveillance Technologies: Trends and Social Implications." In *The Security Economy*, ed. OECD. Paris: OECD.

Lyon, D. 2004. "Surveillance Technologies: Trends and Social Implications." In *The Security Economy*, ed. OECD. Paris: OECD.

MacIntosh, A. 2003. "Using Information and Communication Technologies to Enhance Citizen Engagement in the Policy Process." In *Promise and Problems of E-Democracy: Challenges of Online Citizen Engagement*, ed. OECD, 19-140. Paris: E-Government Project, OECD.

MacIntosh, A., A. Malina, and S. Farrell. 2002. "Digital Democracy through Electronic Petitioning." In *Advances in Digital Government: Technology, Human Factors, and Policy*, ed. W.J. McIver and A.K. Elmagarmid, 137-48. Boston: Kluwer Academic Publishers.

MacIntosh, A., E. Robson, E. Smith, and A. Whyte. 2003. "Electronic Democracy and Young People." *Social Science Computer Review* 21 (1): 43-52.

Mackay, G. 2004. "Getting Payments at Centrelink." *Australian Social Work* 57 (4): 354-64.

Mahrer, J. 2005. "Politicians as Patrons for E-Democracy? Closing the Gap between Ideals and Realities." *International Journal of Electronic Government Research* 1 (3): 1-14.

Malecki, E.J. 2003. "Digital Development in Rural Areas: Potentials and Pitfalls." *Journal of Rural Studies* 19: 201-214.

Malkia, M., A. Anttiroiko, and R. Savolainen, eds. 2004. *eTransformation in Governance: New Directions in Government and Politics*. London: Idea Group Publishing.

Malloy, J. 2003. "To Better Serve Canadians: How Technology Is Changing the Relationship between Members of Parliament and Public Servants." http://www.ipac.ca/files/newdirect9.pdf.

Manz, M., and A.H. Trechsel. 2004. "Multi-Level E-Governance: The Impact of ICTs on Social Security Implementation within a Federal State." e-Working Paper 02, E-Democracy Centre, University of Geneva.

Marche, S., and J.D. McNiven. 2003. "E-Government and E-Governance: The Future Isn't What It Used to Be." *Canadian Journal of Administrative Sciences* 20 (1): 74-86.

Marshall, S., W. Taylor, and X. Yu. 2004. *Using Community Informatics to Transform Regions.* Melbourne: Idea Group Publishing.

Mattessich, P.W., M. Murray-Close, and B.R. Monsey. 2001. *Collaboration: What Makes It Work?* 2nd ed. Amherst: H. Wilder Foundation.

McDavid, J., and I. Huse. 2003. *Public Performance Reporting: Legislator Perceptions of Performance Reporting Principles and Assurance of Credibility.* Victoria, BC: School of Public Administration, University of Victoria.

McIver, W.J., and A.K. Elmagarmid, eds. 2002. *Advances in Digital Government: Technology, Human Factors, and Policy.* Boston: Kluwer Academic Publishers.

McMillan, M.L. 2004. *Financial Relationships between Regional and Municipal Authorities: Insights from the Examination of Five OECD Countries.* IIGR Working Paper 3. Kingston: Queen's University.

Melitski, J., et al. 2005. "Digital Government Worldwide: An E-Government Assessment of Municipal Web-Sites." *International Journal of E-Government Research* 1 (1): 1-19.

Meyers, D.W. 2003. "Does 'Smarter' Lead to Safer? An Assessment of the US Border Accords with Mexico and Canada." *International Migration* 41 (1): 5-44.

Mitchinson, T., and M. Ratner. 2004. "Promoting Transparency through the Electronic Dissemination of Information." In *E-Government Reconsidered: Renewal of Governance for the Knowledge Age,* ed. L. Oliver and L. Sanders, 89-106. Regina: Canadian Plains Research Center.

Moon, M.J. 2002. "The Evolution of E-Government among Municipalities: Rhetoric or Reality?" *Public Administration Review* 62 (4): 424-33.

Moon, J., and D. Norris. 2005. "Does Managerial Orientation Matter? The Adoption of Reinventing Government and E-Government at the Municipal Level." *Information Systems Journal* 15: 43-60.

Moritz, R., and J. Roy. 2000. "Federal IT Workforce: Demography, Community Renewal, and Leadership." *Canadian Government Executive* 4: 12-15.

Mornan, R.G. 1998. "Benefits-Driven Procurement: A Model for Public and Private Sector Collaboration." *Optimum* 28 (1): 38-43.

Mullen, P. 2004. "Digital Government and Individual Privacy." In *Digital Government: Principles and Best Practices,* ed. A. Pavlichev and G.D. Garson. Hershey: Idea Group Publishing.

Nadeau, R., and T. Giasson. 2003. "Canada's Democratic Malaise: Are the Media to Blame?" *Choices*.

Nelson, M.R. 1998. "Government and Governance in the Networked World." In *Blueprint to the Digital Economy: Creating Wealth in the Era of E-Business*, ed. D. Tapscott, with A. Lowy and D. Ticoll, 274-98. New York: McGraw-Hill.

Norris, D. 2005. "Electronic Democracy at the American Grassroots." *International Journal of Electronic Government Research* 1 (3): 1-14.

Norris, P. 2000. "Global Governance and Cosmopolitan Citizens." In *Governance in a Globalizing World*, ed. J.S. Nye and J.D. Donahue, 155-77. Cambridge, MA: Brookings Institution Press.

—. 2003. "Will New Technology Boost Turnout? Experiments in e-Voting and All-Postal Voting in British Local Elections." Paper prepared for the British Study Group Seminar, Minda de Gunzberg Center for European Studies, Harvard University.

—. 2005. "The Impact of the Internet on Political Activism: Evidence from Europe." *International Journal of Electronic Government Research* 1 (1): 20-39.

Nugent, J.H., and M.S. Raisinghani. 2002. "The Information Technology and Telecommunications Security Imperative: Important Issues and Drivers." *Journal of Electronic Commerce Research* 3 (1): 1-14.

Oates, B.J. 2003. "The Potential Contribution of ICT's to the Political Process." *Electronic Journal of E-Government* 1 (1): 33-42.

Obi, T. 2004. "E-Government in Korea." Presentation to APEC Telecommunications and Information Working Group, 29th Meeting, Hong Kong. http://unpan1.un.org/intradoc/groups/public/documents/APCITY/UNPAN016387.pdf.

O'Donnell, O., R. Boyle, and V. Timonen. 2005. "Transformational Aspects of E-Government in Ireland: Issues to Be Addressed." *Journal of E-Government* 1 (1): 23-32.

OECD 1999. "Performance Contracting: Lessons from Performance Contracting Case Studies—A Framework for Public Sector Performance Contracting." Policy brief.

—. 2001. "The Hidden Threat to E-Government: Avoiding Large Government IT Failures." PUMA policy brief, March 8.

—. 2002. *Territorial Review of Canada*. Paris: Territorial Reviews and Governance Division.

—. 2003a. "The E-Government Imperative." Policy brief. www.oecd.org/dataoecd/60/60/2502539.pdf.

—. 2003b. "Engaging Citizens Online for Better Policy-Making." Policy brief. http://www.oecd.org/dataoecd/62/23/2501856.pdf.

—. 2003c. "E-Government in Finland: An Assessment." Policy brief. http://www.oecd.org/dataoecd/20/50/13314420.pdf.

——. 2004. *The Security Economy*. Paris: OECD.
O'Hara, K. 2004. *Trust: From Socrates to Spin*. Cambridge, UK: Icon Books.
O'Harrow, R. 2004. *No Place to Hide*. New York: Free Press.
Oliver, L., and L. Sanders, eds. 2004. *E-Government Reconsidered: Renewal of Governance for the Knowledge Age*. Regina: Canadian Plains Research Center.
Ontario Hospital Association. 2005. *Transformation Agenda Risks and Opportunities Report: e-Health as the Strategic Enabler*. Toronto: Ontario Hospital Association. www.oha.com.
Ostroff, F. 1999. *The Horizontal Organization: What the Organization of the Future Looks like and How It Delivers Value to Customers*. New York: Oxford University Press.
Ougaard, M., and R. Higgott, eds. 2002. *Towards a Global Polity*. London: Routledge.
Pacific Council on International Policy. 2002. "Road-Map for E-Government in the Developing World." www.pacificcouncil.org.
Palfrey, J.G. 2004. "Submission to the Workshop on Internet Governance." International Telecommunications Union, Berkman Center for Internet and Society, Harvard Law School.
Paquet, G. 1997. "States, Communities, and Markets: The Distributed Governance Scenario." In *The Nation-State in a Global Information Era: Policy Challenges*, ed. T.J. Courchene, 25-46. The Bell Canada Papers in Economics and Public Policy. Kingston: John Deutsch Institute for the Study of Economic Policy.
——. 2000. "The New Governance: Subsidiarity and the Strategic State." Paper prepared for the OECD Forum for the Future Conference on 21st Century Governance: Power in the Global Knowledge Economy and Society, Hannover.
——. 2004. "There Is More to Governance than Public Candelabras: E-Governance and Canada's Public Service." In *E-Government Reconsidered: Renewal of Governance for the Knowledge Age*, ed. L. Oliver and L. Sanders, 181-204. Regina: Canadian Plains Research Center.
——. 2005. *The New Geo-Governance: A Baroque Approach*. Ottawa: University of Ottawa Press.
Paquet, G., and J. Roy. 2000. "Information Technology, Public Policy, and Canadian Governance: Partnerships and Predicaments." In *Handbook of Public Information Systems*, ed. G.D. Garson, 53-70. New York: Marcel Dekker.
——. 2004. "Smarter Cities in Canada." *Optimum Online* 33 (1): 2-20.
Parent, M., C.A. Vandebeek, and A.C. Gemino. 2004. "Building Citizen Trust through E-Government." In *Proceedings of 37th Hawaii International Conference on System Sciences*.

Parry, K. 2004. *e-Democracy.* SN/PC/2600. London: Parliament and Constitution Centre.

Pastor, R. 2001. *Toward a North American Community.* Washington, DC: Institute for International Economics.

Pavlichev, A., and G.D. Garson, eds. 2004. *Digital Government: Principles and Best Practices.* Hershey: Idea Group Publishing.

Peterson, S. 2005. "Picking Up the Tab." *Government Technology.* www.govtech.net.

Polese, M., and R. Shearmur. 2002. *The Periphery in the Knowledge Economy.* Moncton: Canadian Institute for Research on Regional Development.

Preyer, G., and M. Bos, eds. 2002. *Borderlines in a Globalized World.* Dordrecht: Kluwer Academic Publishers.

Prins, J.E.J., ed. 2001. *Designing E-Government: On the Crossroads of Technological Innovation and Institutional Change.* The Hague: Kluwer Law International.

Provincial Auditor of Ontario. 2004. *Electronic Service Delivery.* Toronto: Government of Ontario. http://www.auditor.on.ca/english/reports/en04/en04t.htm.

Public Policy Forum. 2003. *Clusters and Gateways Survey: Preliminary Results.* Ottawa: Public Policy Forum.

PWGSC. 2004. *Parliamentary Secretary Task Force: Government Wide Review of Procurement – Concepts for Discussion.* Ottawa: Government of Canada.

Radl, A., and Y. Chen. 2005. "Computer Security in Electronic Government: A State-Local Education Information System." *International Journal of E-Government Research* 1 (1): 78-99.

Reed, B. 2004. "Accountability in a Shared Services World." In *Future Challenges for E-Government,* ed. J. Halligan and T. Moore, 139-58. Canberra: Government of Australia.

Reid, J. 2004. "Holding Governments Accountable by Strengthening Access to Information Laws and Information Management Practices." In *E-Government Reconsidered: Renewal of Governance for the Knowledge Age,* ed. L. Oliver and L. Sanders, 79-88. Regina: Canadian Plains Research Center.

Remmen, A. 2004. *Images of E-Government: Experiences from the Digital North Denmark.* Aaolborg: Department of Development and Planning, Aalborg University.

Rheingold, H. 2002. *SmartMobs: The Next Social Revolution.* New York: Perseus Publishing.

Richman, R. 2004. "Metropolitan Governance and Telecommunications Policy: Changing Perceptions of Place and Local Governance in the Information Society." In *eTransformation in Governance: New Directions in Government and Politics,* ed. M. Malkia, A. Anttiroiko, and R. Savolainen, 169-96. London: Idea Group Publishing.

Ridell, S. 2001. "ICTs and the Communicative Conditions for Democracy: A Local Experiment with Web-Mediated Civic Publicness." In *Designing E-Government: On the Crossroads of Technological Innovation and Institutional Change*, ed. J.E.J. Prins, 85-109. The Hague: Kluwer Law International.

———. 2004. "ICTs and the Communicative Conditions for Democracy." In *eTransformation in Governance: New Directions in Government and Politics*, ed. M. Malkia, A.-V. Anttiroiko & R. Savolainen, and R. Savolainen, 85-108. Hershey: Idea Group Publishing.

Riley, T.B. 2003. *E-Government vs. E-Governance: Examining the Differences in a Changing Public Sector Climate.* Ottawa: Commonwealth Centre for E-Governance.

Roberts, A.S. 2002. "Administrative Discretion and the Access to Information Act: An 'Internal Law' on Open Government?" *Canadian Public Administration* 45 (2): 175-94.

———. 2003. "NATO's Security of Information Policy and the Right to Information." In *National Security and Open Government: Striking the Right Balance*, 149-70. Syracuse: Maxwell School of Citizenship and Public Affairs, Syracuse University.

———. 2005. "Spin Control and Freedom of Information: Lessons from the United Kingdom and Canada." *Public Administration* 83 (1): 1-23.

Ronchi, S. 2003. *The Internet and the Customer-Supplier Relationship.* Aldershot: Ashgate.

Rosenau, J.N. 2002. "NGOs and Fragmented Authority in Globalizing Space." In *Political Space: Frontiers of Change and Governance in a Globalizing World*, ed. Y.H. Ferguson and R.J. Barry Jones. Albany: State University of New York Press.

Rosenberg, D.K. 2000. *Open Source: The Unauthorized White Papers.* New York: IDG Books Worldwide.

Roy, J. 2003. "The Relational Dynamics of E-Governance: A Case Study of the City of Ottawa." *Public Performance and Management Review* 26: 1-13.

———. 2004. "The Four Challenges of E-Government." *Optimum Online* 34 (4): 13-17.

———. 2005a. "Services, Security, Transparency, and Trust: Government Online or Governance Renewal in Canada?" *International Journal of E-Government Research* 1 (1): 48-58.

———. 2005b. "E-Governance and International Relations: A Consideration of Newly Emerging Capacities in a Multi-Level World." *Journal of Electronic Commerce* 6 (1): 44-55.

———. 2005c. "Security, Sovereignty, and Continental Interoperability: Canada's Elusive Balance." *Social Science Computer Review* 22 (2): 1-17.

———. 2006. "Differentiating and Linking E-Government in Developed and Developing Nations: A Search for National Reforms and Transnational Alignment." In *Global E-Government: Theory, Applications, and Benchmarking*, ed. L. Al-Hakim and K. Soliman, forthcoming.

Safai-Amini, M. 2000. "Information Technologies: Challenges and Opportunities for Local Governments." *Journal of Governance Information* 27 (4): 471-79.

Salter, M. 2004. "Passports, Mobility, and Security: How Smart Can the Border Be?" *International Studies Perspective* 5: 71-91.

Sassen, S. 2002. "A New Cross Border Field for Public and Private Actors." In *Political Space: Frontiers of Change and Governance in a Globalizing World*, ed. Y.H. Ferguson and R.J. Barry Jones. Albany: State University of New York Press.

Savoie, D.J. 1999. *Governing from the Centre: The Concentration of Power in Canadian Politics*. Toronto: University of Toronto Press.

———. 2003. *Breaking the Bargain: Public Servants, Ministers, and Parliament*. Toronto: University of Toronto Press.

———. 2005. "The Public Service: The Glue Is Coming Unstuck." *Policy Options* 26 (3): 51-55.

Saxenian, A. 2002. "Transnational Communities and the Evolution of Global Production Networks: Taiwan, China, and India." *Industry and Innovation* 9 (3): 183-202.

Schelin, S.H. 2004. "Training for Digital Government." In *Digital Government: Principles and Best Practices*, ed. A. Pavlichev and G.D. Garson, 263-75. Hershey: Idea Group Publishing.

Scholl, H. 2005. "Motives, Strategic Approach, Objectives, and Focal Points in E-Government-Induced Change." *International Journal of E-Government Research* 1 (1): 59-78.

Science Council of Canada. 1984. *A Workshop on Information Technologies and Personal Privacy in Canada*. Ottawa: Government of Canada.

Scott, M. 2004. "Building Institutional Capacity in Rural Northern Ireland: The Role of Partnership Governance in the LEADER II Programme." *Journal of Rural Studies* 20: 49-59.

Segal, H. 2005. "Politics since 1980: A Little Humility Would Have Gone a Long Way." *Policy Options* 26 (3): 13-18.

Selian, A. 2004. "The World Summit on the Information Society and Civil Society Participation." *Information Society* 20 (3): 201-15.

Shaw, R.B. 1997. *Trust in the Balance: Building Organizations on Results, Integrity, and Concern*. San Francisco: Jossey Bass Publishers.

Shearman, P., and M. Sussex. 2004. *European Security after 9/11*. Aldershot: Ashgate.

Sims, H. 2001. *Public Confidence in Government, and Government Service Delivery*. Ottawa: Canadian Centre for Management Development.

Sirmakessis, S. 2004. *Text Mining and Its Applications*. Heidelberg: Springer.
6, P. 2001. "E-Governance: Do Digital Aids Make a Difference in Policy Making?" In *Designing E-Government: On the Crossroads of Technological Innovation and Institutional Change*, ed. J.E.J. Prins, 7-20. The Hague: Kluwer Law International.
———. 2002. *Towards Holistic Governance*. New York: Palgrave MacMillan.
———. 2004. *E-Governance: Styles of Political Judgment in the Information Age Polity*. New York: Palgrave Macmillan.
Slaton, C.D., and J.L. Arthur. 2001. "Public Administration for a Democratic Society: Instilling Public Trust through Greater Collaboration with Citizens." In *Designing E-Government: On the Crossroads of Technological Innovation and Institutional Change*, ed. J.E.J. Prins, 110-30. The Hague: Kluwer Law International.
Slaughter, A., C. Bildt, and K. Ogura. 2004. *The New Challenges to International, National, and Human Security Policy*. Washington: Trilateral Commission.
Smith, R. 2004. "Centralisation and Flexibility in Delivering E-Services: Tensions and Complements." In *Future Challenges for E-Government*, ed. J. Halligan and T. Moore, 126-35. Canberra: Government of Australia.
Standing Senate Committee on National Security and Defence. 2004. *National Emergencies: Canada's Fragile Front Lines*. Ottawa: Parliament of Canada.
Stevenson, H. 1998. *Do Lunch or Be Lunch*. Cambridge, MA: Harvard Business School Press.
Stowers, G.N.L. 2004. *Measuring the Performance of E-Government*. Washington, DC: IBM Center for the Business of Government.
Strickland, L.S., and L. Hunt. 2005. "Technology, Privacy, and Homeland Security: New Tools, New Threats, New Public Perception." *Intelligence and Security Informatics*. Special issue of *Journal of American Society for Information Science and Technology* 56 (3): 220-35.
Su, S., et al. 2005. "Transnational Information Sharing, Event Notification, Rule Enforcement, and Process Coordination." *Journal of E-Government Research* 1 (2): 1-26.
Surowiecki, J. 2004. *The Wisdom of Crowds: Why the Many Are Smarter than the Few and How Collective Wisdom Shapes Business, Economics, Societies, and Nations*. New York: Doubleday.
Swedish Agency for Public Management. 2004. *Public Administration in the E-Society, Short Version*. Stockholm: Government of Sweden.
Tapscott, D., and D. Ticoll. 2003. *The Naked Corporation: How the Age of Transparency Will Revolutionize Business*. Toronto: Viking Canada.
Torrisi, A., and L. Mezzanotte. 2004. "Security Products: Inside the Italian Electronic Identity Card." In *The Security Economy*, ed. OECD. Paris: OECD.

Turner, T. 2004. "Accountability in Cross-Tier E-Government Integration." In *Future Challenges for E-Government*, ed. J. Halligan and T. Moore, 128-38. Canberra: Government of Australia.

Vander Ploeg, C.G. 2002. *Big City Revenue Sources: A Canada-U.S. Comparison of Tax Tools and Revenue Levers.* Calgary: Canada West Foundation.

Vivian, R. 2004. "Elements of Good Government Community Collaboration." In *Future Challenges for E-Government*, ed. J. Halligan and T. Moore, 27-46. Canberra: Government of Australia.

Weber, L., A. Loumakis, and J. Bergman. 2003. "Who Participates and Why? An Analysis of Citizens on the Internet and the Mass Public." *Social Science Computer Review* 21 (1): 26-42.

Weil, P., and M. Broadbent. 1998. *Leveraging the New Infrastructure: How Market Leaders Capitalize on Information Technology.* Cambridge, MA: Harvard Business School Press.

West, C. 2001. *Techno-Human Mesh: The Growing Power of Information Technologies.* Westport, CT: Quorum Books.

Whyte, A., and A. MacIntosh. 2004. *Summary of D6.2 Final Tool Evaluation and E-Democracy Evaluation Report.* www.edentool.org.

Wilhelm, A.G. 2000. *Democracy in the Digital Age.* London: Routledge.

Wilson, T.D. 1997. "Information Management." In *International Encyclopedia of Information and Library Science*, ed. J. Feather and P. Sturges, 187-98. London: Routledge.

Wilson, W., and E. Welch. 2004. "Does E-Government Promote Accountability? A Comparative Analysis of Website Openness and Government Accountability." *Governance: An International Journal of Policy, Administration, and Institutions* 17 (2): 275-97.

Wong, D. 2002. *Cities at the Crossroads: Addressing Intergovernmental Structures for Western Canada's Cities.* Calgary: Canada West Foundation.

Woodward, V. 2003. "Participation the Community Work Way." *International Journal of Healthcare Technology and Management* 5 (1-2): 3-19.

Yankelovich, D. 1999. *The Magic of Dialogue: Transforming Conflict into Cooperation.* New York: Simon and Schuster.

Zinnbauer, D. 2004. "E-Government As Driver for More Institutional Transparency? A Closer Look at Interests, Policy Frames, and Advocacy Efforts." Research Memo II, Social Science Research Council. www.ssrc.org.

Zussman, D. 1996. "Do Citizens Trust Their Governments?" *Canadian Public Administration* 40 (2): 234-54.

INDEX

Accenture Consulting, 22, 25, 26, 112, 296n5
access to information, xxiii, 58–60, 65, 130–31
accountability, 198, 229–30
    complexity and, 286
    information access and, 68–69, 117
    for learning, 210–14, 222–23
    ministerial. *See* ministerial accountability
    in Modernizing Services for Canadians, 117
    networked, 206–18, 215, 222–23
    in provincial e-government, 161–62
    shared, 69–70, 113, 131
    three kinds of, 210–11
    trust and, 98
added customer value, 90, 91
Advance Passenger Information/ Passenger Name Record (API/PNR), 125
age
    civic engagement and, 247–48, 279
    cyberculture and, 289
    national identity and, 278–79
agencies, 89, 100–01, 210
Alberta, 146
Alcock, Reg, 128
Anti-Terrorism Act (Bill C-36), 124, 310n24

anti-terrorism measures, xiii, xxi, 2, 32, 39, 44, 100, 124–25, 153, 200
    border-related, xxix, 123–26, 328n7
    limits to e-governance from, 67
    trust and, 98
    public service and, 87
    secrecy and, 65–66
    by United States, 40–43, 258–59. *See also* Patriot Act
Arar, Maher, 200, 260–62, 327n1
Arar Commission, 260–62, 263, 269, 327n2
attack ads, 287
auditor general, 53, 231, 303n4, 312n32
Australia, 16, 25, 71–72, 212, 243, 245
authentication, 36, 38–39, 116, 123

banking, 33, 68
Belgium, 184, 319n41
Big Brother state, xxiv
Bill C-36 (Anti-Terrorism Act), 124, 310n24
biometric passports, 38–39, 43, 45, 300n8, 300n9, 302n18
Blair, Tony, 62–63
blogs. *See* weblogs
border security, xxix, 123–26, 263–64, 328n7
British Columbia, 156, 219, 280
    consultation in, 159
    e-government in, 144–49, 164
    electoral reform in, xxv, 159–60

outsourcing/partnerships in,
146–48, 262, 327n3
response to Patriot Act in,
150–51
technology procurement in, 220
transparency and trust in, 154–55
broadband access, xv, xix, 11–12,
63, 97, 146, 169, 182, 195, 314n5,
318n39
Broadband for Rural and Northern
Development, 182
Bronconnier, Dave, 170
budgets, 155–57, 177
Budget Transparency and
Accountability Act, 155
bureaucracy, 71–72. *See also* complexity
trust, power and, 51–52, 87
Weberian, 290
power in, 51–52
Bush, George W., 258

cabinet. *See also* ministerial
accountability
e-government and, 132
reforms to, 215
secrecy and, 52, 59
sharing of accountabilities and,
285
Calgary, 169–71, 186, 315n15
Canada. *See also* federal government;
municipal government; provincial
governments
accountability reforms in,
210. See also accountability;
reforms
ballistic missile defence
initiative and, 265–66
continental governance and, 45,
259–64, 269–71, 278
e-democracy in, 178–80, 243–44.
See also e-democracy

e-government in, xix–xxvi, 25,
26. See also e-government
identity management in, 39. See
also identity
local emergency responders in,
175, 176
Canada Border Services Agency
(CBSA), 125
Canada Health Infoway, 35, 152
Canada Revenue Agency, 115, 130,
210, 309n16
Cappe, Mel, 127
centralization, 16–17
complexity and, 284–86
entrenchment of, 89–90
innovation vs, 131
risks from, 93–94, 285–86
security and, 70–71
Centre for Research and Information
on Canada, 185
Centrelink, 212
CEO Charter for Digital
Development, 277
chief information officers (CIO), xx,
17, 19
centralization and, 17, 89
challenges facing, 17–18, 70
clusters of, 144, 145
government information
agency as, 226
multinational coordination and,
44
public sector, 18, 141, 142–43,
145, 226
China, 277
choice revolution, 234
CIA model, 46
CIO Council, xxvi, 148, 173
cities, 180–84, 195, 202, 281, 318n36.
See also municipal government
citizen-centric governance, 7–13, 46
global trend toward, 27

integrating online services and, 113–14
in Modernizing Services for Canadians, 114, 117
in Ontario public service, 144
shared services and, 20
citizen engagement, xvi–xvii, 81–85, 94–97, 140, 158, 199
accountability and, 212–13
customer relations vs, 74
in intragovernmental coordination, 185
in Ontario, 156–57, 192–93
resistance to, 83
responsibilities of, 231–41
trust and, 81–85
young voters and, 247
citizens
serving vs mobilizing, 242
as spectators, 53–54
citizenship, xxviii, 231–35, 287
See also citizen engagement; democracy
Citizens Initiated Performance Assessment (CIPA), 73
Citizen's Request Management System, 62
Clark, Glen, 154
co-accountability, 207
collaboration. See also horizontal governance; intergovernmental coordination
barriers to, 291
procurement vs, 218
public-private, 220. See also partnerships
in representational government, 239
transformative, 290–93
collaborative authority, 222
collective engagement, 94–97

communication, 63, 213, 226, 246–47, 250
community, deliberation and, 286–89
competencies, in-house vs external, 20–22
competition, 242–43
competitive advantage, 90
complexity, 21, 67–72
centralization and, 284–86
proportional representation and, 239
reform vs, 286
transparency and, 67–74, 82
compliance, 90
computer viruses, 30, 41
confidentiality, 35, 46. See also privacy
Congressional Management Foundation, 249–50
Congress Online, 249–50
Connecting Canadians, 112
consultation, 93
on disability programs, 134–36
in Ontario, 158–59, 191
principles of, 135–36
transparency and, 93, 153, 156–57
continental governance, 45, 259–66, 269–71, 278
contracts, 20–21, 221. See also partnerships
contractual governance, xxvii–xxviii, 209–10, 223
control, coordinated and shared, 290–91. See also power
convenience fee, 10
conversation, 287
corruption, 50–51
costs
of access to information, 59–60
of e-government, 9–10, 27, 182, 297n4
of information services, 194–95, 221, 296n7, 313n43

of procurement and
  partnership, 219
of public sector, 202
of security surveillance, 41–42
of service delivery, 1–2, 6–7
of 311 systems, 171–72
Council of Europe, 45
Council on Foreign Relations, 264, 265, 271
Cross-Cultural Roundtable, 268, 313n43
Crossing Boundaries, 128, 243, 324n1, 326n13, 326n18
customer service mentality, 202, 212
Customs Act, 125
cybercrime, 30
Cybercrime Convention, 45
cybersecurity. *See* security (online)
Cyworld, 289
Czechoslovakia, 184

data-mining, 41
decentralization, 16–17, 89–90. *See also* centralization
Declaration on Protection of Privacy on Global Networks, 37
democracy
  citizen engagement and, 81–85, 232–35, 239. *See also* citizen engagement
  cross-border, 256
  digital/online, xvii, 231–32. *See also* e-democracy
  information access and, 59
  media influence on, 239–40
  reforms to. *See* democratic reform
  secrecy and, 51–52, 57
  trust and, xvi, 79
Democratic Renewal Secretariat, xxv
demographics, 94–95. *See also* age
Denmark, xvii, 62, 181, 326n14

departmental model, 88
Department of Public Safety and Emergency Preparedness Canada (PSEPC), xxi
developing nations, 50–51
Digital Cities Survey, 169
digital divide, 11, 84, 95, 146, 195, 233
diversity, 195
downloading music, 234, 295n2, 304n17

e-charter, 96–97
e-commerce, 6, 273
e-democracy, 82, 95, 242
  debate over, 83–84
  development of, 93, 241–52
  education and, 287. *See also* education
  intergovernmental, 252–54
  in municipal governments, 176–80
  template for, 245–52
  variables for, 245–47
education
  about government process, 68–70, 246–47, 250
  democracy and, 50–51, 62, 235, 246–47
  expectation gap and, 79
  about identity protection, 38
  Internet use and, 82
efficiency, 7
e-government, x–xi, xix–xxvi, 132, 198, 292. *See also* Government Online (GOL); Service Canada
  challenges of, xi–xix
  costs of, 9–10, 27, 297n4
  e-democracy and, 95
  future of, 95, 99–103
  global trends in, 26–27
  history of, in Canada, xix–xx, 8
  obstacles to, xvii–xviii, 74–76

provincial, 144–49, 164
ranking of countries for, 25–26
traditional public services vs,
   10–11
transparency and, 69–70. See
   also transparency and trust
in United States, 9, 11, 18,
   25–26, 164
e-health, 34–35, 151, 186–93. *See also*
   health care
E-Health Council, 151
electoral reform, 146, 155, 159–60,
   163, 232, 239, 244, 305n24
Electronic Health Record (EHR), 35
electronic service delivery (ESD), xii–
   xiv, 140. *See also* service delivery
emergencies, 174–76
employee engagement, 85–92
employment postings, 169
encryption, 56, 121
engagement. *See also* citizen
   engagement
      collective, 94–97
      public employee, 85–86
      trust and, 98
e-pass, 120–21
e-payments, 169
E-Payroll, 115
e-procurement, 219, 322n14
e-reporting, 73–74
e-rights, 233
Estonia, 62
European Union, 44–45, 164, 266–67,
   276
Eves, Ernie, 155
executive branch. *See* cabinet
expectations gap, 79

federal government. *See also*
   Government Online (GOL);
   Service Canada

centralization of functions
   in, 202, 222. See also
   centralization
e-government in, 112–18. See
   also e-government
information arm of, 225–26
online presence of legislature
   of, 134–36
security and, 118–26
transparency, trust and, 127–34
federalism, xvii, xxviii–xxix, 180–83,
   195
Federal/Provincial/Territorial
   (FTP) Council on Identity, 121–22
federated architecture, xxviii, 12–20,
   120, 142, 195, 254, 281, 286
Federation of Canadian
   Municipalities, 195
file-sharing, 234
Finland, 243, 245
firewalls, 56
Florida, 225
foreign policy review, 270, 279, 281
front line security gap, 174–76, 194
function creep, 126, 312n31

Germany, 59
Global Digital Divide Initiative
   (GDDI), 277
global economy, 277–78
global governance, 272–82. *See
   also* continental governance;
   intergovernmental coordination
globalization, 256–82
   governance challenges in, 272–82
   interoperability in, 264–270
   security and, 276–77
   transnational coordination and,
      256–59
global-local connectedness, 280–81
Global Readiness Index on E-
   Government, 26

Global Security Survey, 31
Gomery Inquiry, xxi–xxii
Google, 291–92, 302n17
government. *See* federal government; municipal government; provincial governments
Government of Canada. *See* federal government; Government Online; Service Canada
Government Online (GOL), xx, xxii, xxvi, 111
   history of, 112–18
   secure channel of, 118–21
   shared accountability in, 131
Grove, Andy, 57

Hansard Society, xv–xvi, 64
health care, 34–35, 225
   e-government systems for, 34–35, 151–53, 186–93
   federal input into, 202
Homeland Security, 40–43
   centralized leadership and, 70–71
   costs of, 66
   Internet and, 47
   risks to Canada from, 259–64
   trust issues and, 42–43, 81
Hong Kong, 39
horizontal governance, xxi, 13, 99–102. *See also* integrated service delivery
   among ministers, 214
   border security and, 124–25
   global trend toward, 27
   in provincial public service, 140, 145–46
   in public service, xx, 127–30, 206–08
   secure channel and, 120
   transparency in, 69
hospital wait times, 225

House of Commons Information Committee (UK), 249
HRDC grant scandal, 210
Human Resources and Skills Development Canada (HRSDC), xx, 114–15

IBM, 22
identification cards, 38–39, 43, 98, 121, 264, 302n18
identity, 34, 36–40
   in e-democracy culture, 250
   homeland security and, 42–43
   in Modernizing Services for Canadians, 116
   secure channel and, 121
   theft, 36–37
incrementalism, 180, 191, 197, 241–42, 268
inertia, 75, 127–30, 182, 193–95, 287
information, 224–28. *See also* communication; education
   complexity of, 161–62
   control of, xxiii–xxviii, 51–52, 54, 58, 75, 132–33. See also secrecy
   management. See information management
   mishandling and theft of, 34, 122, 126, 200
   performance, 73
   security and, 67–70
information and communication technologies (ICTs), ix, 4, 76, 137, 147. *See also* technology
   negative side of, 86, 147
   global governance and, 257–59, 273–74, 277–78
   in new public management, 16
   in Ontario e-government, 142–43
   outsourcing of, 16

centralized and decentralized, 16–17
reforming and upgrading, 23–24, 124
in UK e-democracy, 249
Information and Information Technology Strategy, 142
information broker role, 224
information control, xxiii–xxviii, 51–52, 54, 58, 75, 132–33. *See also* secrecy
information management, 58–65
   in other countries, 62–63
   in provinces, 162–63
   in public service, 129, 130
   seven levels of, 90–91
   system requirements for, 61
information technologies. *See* information and communication technologies (ICTs)
Information Technology Association of Canada (ITAC), 147
infrastructure architecture, 244
insourcing, 24–25
Institute for Citizen-Centric Service Delivery, 148–49
Integrated National Security Assessment Centre, 125
integrated service delivery, 13, 100, 296n8
   barriers to, 13–14, 20, 113
   four variations of, 8
   identity issues and, 36
   in Ontario, 143–44
   in 311 systems, 170–71
integration
   of ministries, 100. *See also* intergovernmental coordination
   with United States, xxix–xxx. *See also* continental governance; security (domestic)

Intel, 57
intergovernmental coordination, 173-76, 195, 256–59
   in e-democracy, 252–54
   front line security gap and, 174–76
   of leadership and accountability, 217
   need for, 199
   obstacles to, 176
   in Ontario e-health, 187–89
International Telecommunication Union (ITU), 275
Internet. *See also* information and communication technologies (ICT)
   access to, xv, xix, 11–12, 63, 97, 146, 169, 182, 314n5, 318n39
   domestic security and, xxiv, 66, 274–75, 276, 281
   emergence of, ix, xii, xix, 5–6, 10–12, 36–37
   in globalization, 257, 259
   impact of, 51, 83, 88
   imperative of, 102–03
   inquisitive culture of, 129
   legal parameters of, 200
   nation-state identity and, 184
   open source movement and, 55
   public sector use of, 10–12
   security, 29–32. *See also* security (online)
Internet Corporation for Assigned Names and Numbers (ICANN), 274–75, 281
interoperability, xxix, xxx, 14, 90
   in global context, 264–70
   in North American security, 40, 43, 124, 194, 200, 264–68
   privacy and, 34
   in provincial government, 148, 152–53, 192
   in public service, 113

sovereignty vs, 43–45, 265
of technology, 245–46
Italy, 39, 181, 318n37

Japan, 25
Joint Emergency Preparedness
Program, 175
Joint Solutions Procurement
Process, 148

knowledge net, 91, 92
Korea, 88, 289
Kyoto Accord, 109

Lac Carling summit, 149, 316n23
laws
anti-terrorism, 124–25. See also
Patriot Act
access to information, 65
identity protection, 38
Internet, 200
privacy, 122–23, 310n19
leadership, 290
learning. See education
learning organization models, 87
legislature, 134–36, 164, 244–45. See
also Parliament
library clause, 42
Linux systems, 56–57
Local Government in Scotland Act,
181
Local Health Integration Networks
(LHIN), 189, 191, 192
London transit bombings, xxiii–
xxiv, 98

management, 19, 102, 208–09, 213,
288. See also chief information
officer (CIO)
accountability of, 209, 322n10
by stress, 86

information. See information
management
networked and coordinated
101, 213, 291
open source and, 57
reform to, 92
theory y and theory x, 87
Manley, John, xix, 132
Martin, Paul, xxi–xxii, 128
McGuinty, Dalton, 155
Meaningless but Unique Number
(MBUN), 121
media, 239–40
Metcalfe's Law, 30
Mexico, xxix, 265–68, 328n8
Microsoft, 26, 57, 63, 65, 299n22
ministerial accountability, 13, 71,
100, 215, 321n4, 322n10. See also
accountability
Canada Revenue Agency and,
210
empowered managers vs, 213
traditional model of, 206–07
ministers and ministries
accountability for, 100,
215. See also ministerial
accountability
cooperation among, 214–17,
284–85
domestic security and, 330n15
Modernizing Services for Canadians
(MSC), 114–17, 121, 212
Motorola, 171–72, 315n12
Multilateral Agreement on
Investment (MAI), 258
multinational corporations, 256
municipal government, xxv–xxvi,
183–86, 317n32
deficiencies/ needs of, 180–81,
194, 195
federal payments to, 180–84,
195, 202, 318n36

front line security gap and, 174–76
impetus for change from, 253
service delivery and, 168–74
transparency and trust in, 176–80

NAFTA, 200
National Emergencies: Canada's Fragile Front Lines, 174
nationalism, 184
National Security Policy, xxi, 125, 174–75
nation-state, 184, 256, 258
Netherlands, 181
NetWork BC, 146
networked accountability, 206–18, 215, 222–23
networked administration, 209–10
networked governance, 102
networked management, 101
networking, xi, xxiv, 30, 85, 88, 258–59. *See also* integrated service delivery; intergovernmental coordination
New Brunswick, 141, 143
new public management, xxv, 15–17, 87, 89, 206, 207
New Zealand, 16, 25, 209
nongovernmental organizations (NGOs), 257
North America, 45, 71, 264–69, 271. *See also* continental governance
North American Leaders Summit, 265
North Jutland county, 62
Nova Scotia, 161
NYCServ Epayment Project, 9–10

OECD Ministerial Conference on Electronic Commerce, 37

Office of the Privacy Commissioner (OPC), 122–23
online services, xv, xix, 35, 63, 97, 146, 169, 182, 195, 314n5, 318n39. *See also* e-government
Ontario, 140–144, 149, 280, 298n16, 320n47
   accountability in, 161
   consultation in, 158–59, 191
   democratic renewal in, xxv, 157–58, 244
   e-government in, 140, 164
   e-health in, 151, 186–93
   online service delivery in, 141–43
   private sector partnerships in, 146–47
   technology procurement in, 220
   transparency and trust in, 155–59
Ontario e-Health Council, 187–88
Ontario Health Information Standards Committee (OHISC), 187
Ontario Office of E-Health, 187
openness, 54, 66, 98, 286, 323n15. *See also* secrecy; transparency and trust
open source software, 54–58, 246
operational support, 90, 91
organization, 198
   of public sector, 198–99
   stove pipe or specialized, 290
organizational complexity, 67–72
Ottawa, 186, 318n34
outcome orientation, 66, 72
outreach, 92–94
outsourcing, 16, 20–24, 150, 261–63, 297n9, 327n3. *See also* partnerships

Parliament. *See also* federal government; provincial governments
   adversarial nature of, 236

citizen engagement in, 237–38
power of, 52, 134–36, 229–32
reforms to, 236–37
traditions of, 199, 206, 236–37
Parliamentary Committee on National Security, xxx, 133–34, 217, 268, 271–72
parliamentary officers, 53
Parliamentary Sub-Committee on the Status of Persons with Disabilities, 134, 135, 248
partnerships, 27, 218–24
    between agencies, 222–23
    Calgary–Motorola, 171–72
    contracts vs, 20–21, 21
    outsourcing vs, 21. See also outsourcing
    Patriot Act and, 150–51
    in provincial e-government, 150
    shared services and, 20–23
passports, 38–39, 43, 45, 264
Patriot Act, 42, 65–66, 124, 150–51, 200, 261–63, 267–68, 301n15
Pennsylvania, 176
Pentagon, 71
PentaSafe, 31
performance frameworks, 113–14
    performance reporting on, 62, 72–75, 130–31, 161, 235
personal information. *See* privacy
political parties, 7, 229–30, 238
power
    customer service mentality and, 202–03
    information and. *See* information control
    open source movement and, 57–58
Prime Minister's Office, 52–53, 216, 270
privacy, 32–36, 43
    border security and, 126
    as challenge of e-government, 114
    laws, 122–23, 310n19
    Patriot Act and, 150–51, 200, 261–63
    public willingness to suspend, 66
    secure channel and, 121–22
    storing/sharing information and, 34, 200
    surveillance activities and, 39–40, 200
Privacy Act, 260
privacy commissioner, 53
Privacy Impact Assessment (PIA), 122–23
private sector. *See also* outsourcing
    in globalization movement, 277
    partnerships with, 20–23, 20. *See also* partnerships
    in provincial e-government, 146–47
    Patriot Act and, 150–51
    procurement with, 218–24
    public sector vs, 68, 219, 292
procurement, 218–24. *See also* contracts; outsourcing; private sector
property taxes, 168
provincial governments, xxv, xxix
    British Columbia. See British Columbia
    e-democracy initiatives in, 244
    e-government choices of, xxv
    e-health and security issues of, 149–53, 161–62, 186–93
    lessons from, 162–65, 254
    loss of confidence in, 190–91
    New Brunswick, xxv, 141, 143
    Nova Scotia, 161
    online services of, 140–49, 164
    Ontario. See Ontario
    transparency and trust issues of, 153–62

public engagement, 81–85, 199, 212–13. *See also* citizen engagement
Public Inquiry on Electronic Democracy, 243
Public Safety and Emergency Preparedness Canada (PSEPC), 125
public sector/public service. *See also* Government Online (GOL); Service Canada
  accountability in, 206–07, 213
  change and, xxx–xxxi, 99, 197–98
  contracting authority in, 221–22
  culture of, 212–13
  e-government initiatives by, 132, 248–49
  employee engagement in, 84–92
  leadership issues of, 208–09, 226
  horizontal governance in, 127–30
  Internet security and, 33–34
  organization issues of, 198–99
  paralysis of, 214. See also inertia
  partnering and procurement in, 223
  participative democracy ideals of, 127, 128
  reform, 14–15, 88, 193–94. See also reforms
  seamless, 252
  tradition and, ix, 206–07
  transparency of, 209
Public Works and Government Services Canada (PWGSC), xx, 120, 204, 309n13

Question Period, 236, 240, 325n4

radio frequency identification devices (RFID), 39
record management, 116

reforms, xxviii, xxxi, 92, 283
  democratic, 75, 85, 101–02, 153, 165, 178–79, 195, 197, 217
  electoral, 146, 155, 159–60, 163, 232, 239, 244, 305n24
  information management, 50–51
  interoperability and, 14–15, 35
  parliamentary, 215, 236–37
  service delivery, 23–24, 85, 101, 117, 126, 128. See also Service Canada
regional governance, 186–92. *See also* municipal government
regionalism, 280–81
Reid, John, xxiii
rent control, 158–59
reporting, 72–75, 224. *See also* accountability; performance reporting
Reporting Economic Crime Online (RECOL), 274, 330n17
rights, insufficiency of, 232–35
Roberts, Alasdair, xxiii

San Diego County, 22–23, 298n15
scandals, xxi, 118, 197, 210, 222, 240, 312
Scandinavia, 25, 191
Scotland, 181, 243
secrecy, xv, xxiii–xxiv. *See also* information control
  in Arar inquiry, 260–62, 327n2
  border security and, 126
  in cabinet, 52, 215–16
  culture of, xvi, 42, 54, 59, 130, 268
  Internet culture and, 130
  intolerance of, 51–52
  national security and, xxix–xxx, 65–67, 272
  in public service, 129, 207, 214

security and, xxiii–xxiv, 65–67,
    91–92, 119, 268–70
simplification and, 203
secure channel, 118–21, 149, 322n13
security (domestic), 2, 125–26
    in Arar inquiry, 260–62
    border, xxix, 123–26, 328n7
    continental, 264–69, 271
    municipal government and,
        xxvi, 174–76
    openness in, 133–34
    parliamentary review of, xxx,
        133–34, 217, 268, 271–72
    secrecy in, xxiii–xxiv, 65–67,
        91–92, 119, 268–70. See also
        secrecy
    trust and transparency issues
        in, 127
    in United States, 40, 43. See also
        Patriot Act
security (online), xii–xiv, xxi, 2,
    29–32, 124–25, 329n13, 329n14
    access to information and, 101
    anti-terrorism measures and,
        xxxi, 29–32. See also privacy
    behaviour and, 31
    in Canadian e-government, 99,
        114, 118–23
    centralization and, 71
    CIA model of, 35, 46
    identity and, 36–40. See also
        privacy
    limitations to, 42
    Patriot Act and, 150–51. See
        also Patriot Act
    privacy and, 32–35. See also
        privacy
    in provincial e-government,
        149–53
    reframing of, 98
    service integration and, 46
    surveillance activities and,
        39–40
Security and Prosperity Partnership
    for North America, 265
self-governance, xxix
Senate Standing Committee on
    National Security and Defence,
    xxi, 125
separatism, 326n19
September 11 aftermath, xxiv, 2, 65.
    See also anti-terrorism measures
    impacts of, 46, 123–24, 204
    cross-border travel after, 263–64
    identity management since, 39
    interoperability since, 111
    privacy concerns since, 38, 40
    secure channel and, 121
    security since, 41, 42, 200. See
        also Patriot Act; security
        (domestic)
Service Canada, xx, xxii, xxvii, 117–
    18, 308n7, 312n36
    accountability in, 198, 211–13, 216
    ministerial control of, 222
    paralysis of, 205–06, 214, 222
    private-sector partnerships of,
        221
    reforms to, 204, 221
    secure channel and, 119–21
    shared accountability in, 131–32
    transparency of, 127, 130–33, 221
service delivery, xx, 1–2, 5–28, 99,
    283. See also Government Online
    (GOL); Service Canada
    complexity and, 68
    electronic, xii–xiv, 140
    integrated. See integrated
        service delivery
    intergovernmental cooperation
        and, 285–86
    mentality, 133, 232–35

in Modernizing Services for
Canadians, 116–17
in municipalities, 168–69
Service Delivery Council, 173
service mentality, 186
Service New Brunswick (SNB), xxv, 141, 143
ServiceOntario, 143–44
shared services, 20–25, 119, 189
simplification, 71, 72, 203, 214
Singapore, 8, 25–26
Single Transferable Vote (STV) system, 159–60
smart border, 124, 310n22, 329n9
smart cards, 121, 309n17
smart community, 182
smartmobs, 289
smart networks, 281
Smart Systems for Health (SSH), 187
social capital, 87–88, 89
Social Development Canada (SDC), xx
social insurance numbers, 121
social insurance registry (SIR), 116
sovereignty, 43–45, 265, 269
spin, xxiv, xxviii, 62, 129, 203
sponsorship scandal, xxi, 118
strategic insight, 90
Stronach, Belinda, xxii
surveillance activities, 39–43
Sweden, xxvii, 83, 209–10, 223, 321n6
Switzerland, 181
symbolism, 237

taxation, 195
tax filing, 12, 112–13
technocracy, xxiv
technology, ix, 20, 28, 88, 245–47. *See also* information and communication technologies (ICTs)
for access to information, 60–61
accountability and, 212
democratic change and, xviii, 3–4, 288
federal spending on, 183
identity management and, 38–39
reforms to, 23–24, 85
security and, 272
smart communities and, 182
supportive vs central role of, 90–91
surveillance, 86–87
trust in, 3–4, 80–81
website, 7–8, 9
television, 298
terrorism, 258–59. *See also* anti-terrorism measures; September 11 aftermath
terrorist watch lists, 42
theory y and x management, 87
311 systems, 169–71, 173–74, 233, 315n11, 315n14, 317n33
Toronto, 172, 177, 186, 280, 292, 317n32
Torvalds, Linus, 56
tradition, 199, 203, 205, 206
transactional services, 10, 112–13
transfer payments, 180–84, 195, 202, 318n36
transformation, 91
transformative collaboration, 290–93
transparency and trust, xiv–xix, xxiii, 2–4, 50–54, 68–80, 97–99, 102, 224
citizen engagement and, 81–85, 94–98, 235
culture of, 197
employee engagement and, 85–92
external outreach and, 92–94
in federal e-government, 127–34
information management and, 58–65

in municipal government, 176–80
open source software and, 54–58
organizational complexity and,
  65–74, 82. See also complexity
performance management and,
  72–75
in provincial e-government,
  153–62, 163–62, 165, 190
in public service, 207, 209, 213
in security sector, 66, 269–70
simplicity and, 71, 203
technology and, 80–81
transparency networks, 51
Treasury Board, xx

unions, 7
United Kingdom, 15–16
  access to information in, 62–63
  accountability in, 209
  blogging in, 64
  e-democracy in, 247, 248–49
  e-government in, 326n16
  identity management in, 39
  insourcing/outsourcing in, 25, 220
United Nations, 25, 257
United States, 16
  in Arar inquiry, 260–62
  continental security and, xxix,
    40–45, 258–66, 271. See also
    Patriot Act
  Canadian relationship with,
    xxix–xxx, 123–24, 263
  control of e-commerce by, 274–76
  cynicism regarding, 269

e-democracy in, 239–40, 249–50
global governance and, 273
identity management in, 39
information control in, 65–66
municipalities in, 169, 175, 176, 178, 181
online programs, 9, 11, 18, 25–26, 164
secrecy in, 42
unilateral actions of, 258–59, 275

Vancouver, 168, 177, 314n1
vertical hierarchies, ix, xvii, 13, 87–89, 98, 113, 206, 290
Victoria state, 243, 250
Vienna, 62
visas, biometric, 43
vloggers, 63

Wales, 96–97
weblogs, xv–xvi, xvii, 63–64, 240, 289, 295n1
websites, 7–8, 9
Westminster governance, 63, 64, 83, 177, 270
  disenchantment with, 154
  resistance to openness in, 137
  secrecy in, 47, 52, 130
Winnipeg, 186
wiretapping, 42
World Summit on the Information Society, 276
World Trade Organization (WTO), 257, 258, 275

young people. *See* age